Fighting for Life

American Military Medicine
in World War II

ALBERT E. COWDREY

THE FREE PRESS
A Division of Macmillan, Inc.
NEW YORK

Maxwell Macmillan Canada
TORONTO

Maxwell Macmillan International
NEW YORK   OXFORD   SINGAPORE   SYDNEY

The Free Press
A Division of Macmillan, Inc.
866 Third Avenue, New York, N.Y. 10022

Maxwell Macmillan Canada, Inc.
1200 Eglinton Avenue East
Suite 200
Don Mills, Ontario M3C 3N1

Macmillan, Inc. is part of the Maxwell Communication Group of Companies.

Printed in the United States of America

printing number

1 2 3 4 5 6 7 8 9 10

Library of Congress Cataloging-in-Publication Data

Cowdrey, Albert E.
    Fighting for life: American military medicine in World War II /
    Albert E. Cowdrey
        p. cm.
        ISBN 0–02–906835–5
        1. World War. 1939–1945—Medical care—United States.
    Medicine, Military—United States—History—20th century.
    I. Title.
    D807.U6C685 1994
940.54'7573—dc20   94–8280
                                                                CIP

To

TOM WHAYNE, SR., M.D.

Colonel, U.S. Army Medical Corps, Retired,

Who Lived It

Contents

Acknowledgments

F ew authors can claim to have written a book alone, and this is especially the case with a historian who undertakes to write about the medical side of war without having been either a medic or a combat veteran. I was born seven years too late to be swept up in the great World War II draft, and my personal medical history has been entirely as a patient in military and civilian hospitals. As a historian, on the other hand, I have had the privilege not only of working in the records of the Army surgeon general but of dealing with many people who know military medicine intimately.

Chief among my teachers has been Robert J. T. Joy, MD, for thirty years a medical officer and now a recognized authority on the history of his specialty. Several officers of the Army Nurse Corps, including Colonels Rosemary McCarthy, Mary Frank, and Patricia Wise, helped to make me aware of the large and still mostly unwritten history of nurses at war. Colonel Richard V. N. Ginn did me the same favor in regard to the Medical Specialist Corps. Joseph Kralich was an excellent source of information on enlisted medics. I owe a special debt to the veterans who consented to be interviewed and/or to criticize early drafts of my work; this book is dedicated to one of them, Tom F. Whayne, MD, who has been my kind and exacting mentor for a number of years. I also owe special thanks to Harry L. Behrman, MD; Benjamin M. Baker, MD; Robert C. Bornmann, MD; Allan D. Callow, MD; William Jordan, MD; Currier McEwen, MD; Robert C. Muehrcke, MD; and Robert P. Phillips.

Indeed, I can say honestly that I have never listened to a veteran talk about the war without learning something that I needed to know. Fortunately, many have written their own accounts of their experiences, and references to both published and unpublished accounts will be found in this volume's notes. Gratitude is also due to the organizers of many World War II symposia, especially those held in Texas and Honolulu by the Admiral Nimitz Foundation, where I collected names, did interviews, and spent happy hours listening to the interplay of veterans' recollections of their own experiences with historians' papers drawn from the written records of wartime.

Among the scholars to whom I owe a special debt, Dale C. Smith of the Uniformed Services University of the Health Sciences has been generous with his insights, as have my friends and co-workers at the Army's Center of Military History, especially Mary C. Gillett—the Medical Department's biographer—and Graham A. Cosmas and Mary Ellen Condon-Rall, my co-authors of the operational histories of Army medicine in the European Theater and the Pacific War. Jan Kenneth Herman of the Navy's Bureau of Medicine and Surgery has done his considerable best to increase my knowledge of his service's long and insufficiently celebrated medical history. For awakening and sustaining my interest in medical history I have many people to thank, but perhaps John Duffy, James Cassedy, and James Harvey Young more than any others.

Finally, I wish to acknowledge that *Fighting for Life* owes much to my editor at The Free Press, Joyce Seltzer, to whom I first proposed this topic, and to Cherie Weitzner, who provided me with many an insightful suggestion. Any errors that remain in the text, however, are mine alone; *mea culpa* to those who may remember things differently.

Introduction:
War and Healing

During the Battle of the Huertgen Forest in November 1944, Major Lew Giffin of the Army Medical Corps recalls that he lived for a time with his surgical team in an abandoned monastery and operated in a tent outside. One day a dark-haired young six-footer was brought in with a hole in his belly just above the pubis. He was lying under a woolly GI blanket with his bare feet sticking out at the end of the stretcher. Asked how he felt, he said, "Lousy, Doc. I hurt like hell!"

The feet were alarming. Giffin noted that the man's toenails were white as cotton. Eight transfusions had failed even to color them blue. A quick examination showed why. The man's belly was distended, tense and drumlike. He was, as another doctor remarked, "bleeding inside from a real gusher!" In the surgical tent a nurse administered anesthetic and Giffin made a 6-inch incision, exposing the peritoneum, the translucent sac that covers the inter-

1

nal organs. "Instantly," he later recalled, "the thin membrane ballooned with a bluish-red liquid."

He nicked the peritoneum and a 12-foot jet of blood shot up and splattered against the canvas overhead. Giffin grabbed a sterile towel and threw it over the wound in case the now contaminated blood dripping from the tent roof fell back on the patient. Doctors and nurse heaved the operating table with its occupant a yard to the right, and work resumed.

Blood welled from the incision, overflowed the table, spattered and spread on the canvas tarp that covered the ground—"a regular bloodfall." With a gloved hand Giffin spooned clotted blood from the abdomen. With "loud snuffling noises" the metal suction tube drew out more, filling a gallon jug, then a second and a third. Transfusions went on continuously, pumping the blood through rather than into the apparently dying man. The only thing that mattered now was finding the bleeder. The aorta and the iliac arteries were undamaged. A deep cut into the pelvic floor brought up a huge new mass of clotted blood from below. The soldier's systolic blood pressure sank to 30 and his pulse rate rose to 180. Giffin's own pulse probably matched the patient's, while his blood pressure was at the opposite extreme.

Then he spotted the bleeder—a mere glimpse before the blood submerged it again, but enough. A clamp was in his hand and he closed off the middle sacral artery. Miraculously the bleeding ceased. The crisis was over. Gradually the patient's skin warmed, his pulse quieted to 80, his blood pressure rose to 110 over 65. He had absorbed 31 pints of blood, had a perforated small intestine and two holes in his bladder. But he was alive and he was going to recover.

Shortly afterward, Giffin saw the man again in the postoperative ward. Looking cheerful and full of life, he asked what had happened to him.

"Oh, nothing much," replied Giffin. "Just a little hole in the belly." Then the surgeon turned his back, so that his patient "could not see me while I shuddered."[1]

That was military medicine as it was known to the public through news stories that customarily emphasized the dramatic surgical intervention. Within limits it was a truthful picture:

Surgery was so basic to wartime medicine that all military doctors, regardless of specialty, were officially termed surgeons. Many a wounded man owed his life to a surgeon's actions in just such a moment of crisis.

But surgery was not the whole story. Military medicine had wider, more impersonal aims. Its ultimate purpose was to conserve the fighting strength of the armed forces. Such a goal demanded a kind of medicine that practiced most of the specialties found in the civilian profession, plus public health, plus a system for extracting, treating, and moving the injured under fire that had no precise equivalent anywhere else. Military medicine meant curing disease and, since wars are won by physically and mentally functional people, preventing disease as well.

The microbes that cause disease and infect wounds had always been the secret foe of armies, an enemy within that historically caused more devastation than the human enemy outside. The very gathering of an army provoked outbreaks of disease. Young men assembled in crowded camps amid masses of strangers, under stress and far from home. Even in the twentieth century, many a young soldier went no farther in his journey toward war, dying (sometimes even before he donned the uniform) of some common disease to which his sheltered civilian life had never exposed him.

In field service the hard living and dirt, the misery and filth of sieges, and the lice, flies, and mosquitoes that preyed upon soldiers and sailors increased the toll. Much of the early history of military medicine consisted of the efforts of surgeons and commanders to ward off disease, a foe whose agents they could not see and whose methods of warfare they did not understand. Because they were so often unsuccessful, their record was largely tragic.

Homer opened his *Iliad* with a memorable description of an epidemic devastating the Greek camps before Troy that was halted only by submission to an angry Apollo. In the three thousand years that followed, medicine made progress, but not enough to prevent similar disasters. When, in the late spring of 1776, American revolutionary forces invaded Canada, six of every ten men came down with smallpox. Little could be done for the victims, whose suffering was "almost Sufficient to excite the pity of Brutes, Large barns [being] filled with men at the very heighth of smallpox and not the least things, to make them comfortable." John Adams lamented that the smallpox was ten times more terrible than the enemy; certainly it was so for men who were lying in filthy shelters, tormented by clouds of mosquitoes and flies. Some of the sick, a witness wrote, "could not See, Speak, or walk. In one day two had large maggots, an inch long, Crawl out of their ears."[2]

The epidemic was a principal cause of the invasion's failure, and the experience convinced George Washington that his Continentals must all be inoculated against smallpox. He issued the necessary order, and in so doing joined a long line of distinguished commanders and surgeons who had sought to prevent disease in their armies. The Book of Deuteronomy had spoken with the voice of God when it ordered soldiers to defecate outside their camp; King Louis XIV of France had condescended to act as a surgeon general for his armies when he ordered the burial of filth (*interrement des ordures*); eighteenth-century doctors, knowing nothing of the microscopic parasite that carries malaria or the role of the mosquito in spreading it, had tried to keep armies from camping in the vicinity of marshes, firmly believing that fever was caused by the bad air (*mal aria*) that gave the illness its name.[3]

Yet three millennia of religious exhortations, medical urging, and commands by kings and generals brought only limited success as long as the nature of contagious disease remained unknown. The same problem blocked surgeons' efforts to prevent or combat wound infections. Wounds caused by the thrust of sword or spear, and deep penetrations by arrow and bullet, breached the body's natural defenses and let the enemy in. Shards of metal carried dirt and bits of filthy clothing inside, along with any germs that might be riding on them. Abdominal wounds released microbes normally confined to the intestinal tract to spread ruin through the rest of the body. The surgeon then put his probe, knife and fingers into the wound, compounding the infection.

Deep wounds became islands within the body, isolated from the bloodstream by the destruction of nearby arteries and veins. Filled with serum and anoxic, dying tissue, wounds were natural petri dishes for culturing whatever bacteria the body might harbor or the wound might have introduced. The effects of hospital gan-

grene during the Civil War underlined the horrors of the prean-
tiseptic age. Probably caused by *Streptococcus pyogenes*, the infection advanced like the hour hand of a clock, too slow to follow
with continuous observation but fast enough to be evident over
short periods of time. "The skin around . . . the wound sloughed
off, revealing flesh that slowly turned 'reddish, greenish, purplish,
or black,' while the gray edges of the opening grew wider at the
rate of half an inch an hour. Arteries and even bones were rapidly
exposed and the stench of rotten meat filled the air. . . . The patient's breath became sickly sweet, his body alternated between
chills and sweats, and his pulse grew ever faster, ever feebler."[4]

Out of the Civil War, with its hundreds of thousands of dead,
came no great new advance in medical science. American doctors
and surgeons put aside their uniforms vastly experienced but un-
enlightened about the causes of infection and disease. Still, the
war had brought a revolution to the way American armies organized their medical services. The Army of the Potomac set up an
ambulance service and a systematic chain of evacuation to remove
the wounded man from the battlefield. Both the Union and the
Confederacy built elaborate systems of military hospitals where
volunteer nurses gave patients care. Doctors *triaged*—sorted—the
wounded according to the severity of their injuries. Holding military rank for the first time in war, doctors took charge of the
wounded to a greater extent than ever before, giving a model and
standard to other nations. Surgeon General William Hammond
and the innovative medical director of the Army of the Potomac,
Jonathan Letterman, laid the foundations of the modern American military medical system, and their ideas later went around the
world.

Improved organization came first to the battlefield. Then within a few years a new surgery followed, and then a new science of
medicine, and suddenly everything became different.

Hardly was the Civil War over when surgeons in England, led
by Joseph Lister, began to deliver their patients from infection by
scouring implements, hands, and the patient himself with carbolic
acid solution. The discovery that specific microbes caused various
diseases followed, transforming medicine by suggesting new
means of prevention. Doctors learned to immunize against dis-

eases other than smallpox. Aseptic surgery sharply reduced the danger that operations would add to the infection of the wound, and by the 1890s the operating room was rapidly becoming modern in appearance and ritual. *Debridement*, the surgical cleaning of wounds by cutting out dying tissue, reduced the danger of infection further.

The Russo-Japanese War of 1904–5 announced the advent of the new era on the battlefield, with the Japanese giving the West eagerly studied lessons in wartime preventive medicine and—remarkably, in view of the Imperial Army's later record—the humane treatment of prisoners. A decade later, World War I brought the armies of Western Europe and North America their first experience of both industrial war and modern military medicine. Machine guns, high-powered rifles, massed artillery, aerial bombs, and poison gas killed some 14 million men. But among the legions of the wounded a very large number survived by virtue of the new medical science.

Americans came to the struggle late but determined to follow the best models. The Army Medical Department was transformed. Doctors who had been enrolled by the medical reserve corps in time of peace strengthened the small cadre of regulars. A variety of specialists worked in the hospitals. The department signed up not only women nurses (the army nurse corps had been set up in 1901, after the Spanish–American War) but administrators, technicians, and ambulance drivers. The army, too, was transformed. Rigorous medical examinations for draftees weeded out many who were unfit; vaccinations protected recruits against some diseases; better rations fed them. Special quartermaster units provided baths and steamed their clothing to kill lice. Unit surgeons performed the tedious rituals needed to keep masses of men alive and healthy in a septic environment, checking their food and latrines, inspecting them for venereal disease, and keeping their immunizations current. Unbelievable as it might have seemed to American soldiers in the trenches—scratching their "cooties," wading through liquid stews of mud and excrement, and living in foul holes with rats and flies—they were the beneficiaries of the insights of modern public health. The ironic proof was that Amercan soldiers now were as likely to die by shells, bullets or poison gas as by disease, which as recently as the Civil War had killed two soldiers for every one struck down by the enemy.[5]

A remarkable aspect of World War I was the fact that the immobile lines of the Western Front suffered only one major epidemic, the worldwide outbreak of influenza in 1918–19. For almost four years the war in France and Belgium was an immense and interminable siege—always the sickliest of military operations, when armies hunker down amid their own wastes, polluting the water they drink and exchanging vermin and disease. Two decades before, typhoid had ravaged Americans gathering to fight the Spanish–American War, but now there was a useful vaccine that all soldiers received. Louse-borne epidemic typhus devastated the Eastern Front, ultimately killing millions, but the Germans by rigorous discipline kept their armies in good health. In 1918 hundreds of thousands of German soldiers shifted from the Eastern Front to the louse-infested Western trenches without bringing typhus with them.[6]

As impressive as the new science of prevention was the care given to the wounded. Every army set up a chain of evacuation that was far more elaborate than in the past. A system of dedicated medical units supported the fighters, and an ambulance service removed the sick and wounded from the line. A sequence of hospitals provided them a gradation of treatment, elementary near the front, complex and sophisticated farther to the rear. A basic problem of the chain was that those who were worst hit had to travel the farthest. What to do with those who could not be moved without killing them? The French devised a system for bringing emergency stabilizing treatment to the forward hospitals that was soon copied by other armies. In 1914 a Paris crowd that included the French Nobel Prize winner Alexis Carrel and the American brain surgeon Harvey Cushing watched the first motorized hospital (*auto-chir*), a progenitor of the auxiliary surgical teams of World War II and the MASH surgeons of later wars, demonstrate its mobile operating room.[7]

There were other important advances in the special art of bringing the new medicine to the men who fought. Americans learned from the British a rational system for handling so-called shell shock, the emotional crisis sometimes brought on by exhaustion and stress. A very different kind of shock—wound shock, brought on by loss of blood—also received care in specialized units set up to receive the badly wounded. Neurosurgeons removed steel from living brains; plastic surgeons restored men disfigured by wounds; and the injured recovered health and vigor in centers set aside for their rehabilitation.

Governments and armies continued to explain the purpose of all the care as support for the war effort. Soldiers were kept healthy to fight, and the wounded were saved to conserve manpower and support the morale of their comrades. But of course, many of the wounded never returned to the front, even if they recovered. Men who were too badly injured ever to serve again often received treatment more elaborate than those who could be salvaged for military ends. The postwar medical systems that treated veterans reflected their political influence and the compassion or bad conscience of civilians, not the needs of armies present or future. The medical systems did more than support the fighting strength; through them, the demands of humanity overlaid and mingled with the destructive impulses of war.

Paradoxes of many sorts pervaded the new military medicine. Organizationally, the medics formed part of the logistical system—the complex apparatus of supply, replacement, and repair that supported the fighting units. Yet saving lives and healing bodies could not actually be equated with repairing trucks or shipping rations. The industrialized nations spent lavishly for their wounded for a multitude of reasons—military, humanitarian, and political. To advance the healing science and elaborate the military organization that made it effective had become as much an imperative as keeping up with the latest wrinkles in the technology of destruction. In the era of the Great War, no nation could be considered civilized and progressive unless it did both.

After three thousand years of development, military medicine, borne upward by the modernization of armies and navies and the creation of medical science, had reached heights never imagined in earlier times. Unfortunately, the military forces also wielded constantly improving implements of destruction, and the course of events after 1918 soon demonstrated that the weapons were all too likely to be used.

With its fourteen million dead, its aftermath of revolutions, and its devastating epidemics, World War I shook the existing world order to its foundations. After a brief period of stabilization in 1925–29, a worldwide economic depression struck a new blow, and a decade later the possibility of a second and worse twentieth-century war looked all too real.

The medical implications were more than sobering. The struggle of 1914–18 had not really been a world war. Fighting took place in a few African and Asian colonies of Germany, and some bitter warfare involved limited forces in the Middle East. Otherwise the war was almost entirely confined to Europe, including European Russia. On the Western Front, the trenchlines were fixed and the apparatus of civilization, with its railroads and hospitals, lay only a few miles behind the fighting. The achievements of military medicine had rested at least in part on that base. Yet a continuing transport revolution created the possibility of a genuinely planetary conflict, which, from the medical viewpoint, meant confronting all sorts of weather and every type of disease under the harsh and uncompromising conditions of combat.

A new war might be not only wider but worse. World War I had introduced airplanes, tanks, and poison gas to the battlefield, and far-ranging submarines to naval warfare. Research and development during the interwar years made all those weapons more sophisticated. The airplane completed its evolution from a fragile net of wood and cloth into an enclosed metal capsule powered by improved engines and able to carry large loads—of passengers, freight, or bombs—for hundreds of miles. The number of possible victims of war grew steadily. During the Spanish Civil War of the 1930s, fascist bombs demonstrated that civilians as well as soldiers now lived on the front lines. Military thinkers elaborated new theories of armored and amphibious fighting. Theoretical physicists were at work on ideas about the structure of matter that in time would produce weapons of terminal power.

Total war was an old notion, never quite realized in reality. Technical advances ensured that the definition of totality was changing rapidly, although its new dimensions could be discerned only dimly during the interwar years. The medical professionals of the American armed forces kept abreast of their two paradoxical professionals as fighters and healers, but they saw the future no more clearly than anyone else during the sleepy years that followed the armistice of 1918. The new emergency, when it came, would be a shock more jarring and violent than any in the past.

1

Before the Battle

Ultimately it would come with an exploding bomb on Ford Island in Pearl Harbor on a Sunday morning that for Americans—still sleeping, groggily awake, or eating breakfast at five minutes before eight o'clock—changed the world forever. To many of the men and women who would have to fight the war, the years between 1919 and 1941 seemed in retrospect a time of drowsy irrelevance and missed opportunities either to avert the calamity or to prepare the nation to meet it. Yet, until a few years before Pearl Harbor, few Americans had seemed to feel any great sense of urgency about the possibility of war.

Despite the immense changes under way in the armies and navies of Europe and Japan, American armed forces and their medical components remained small during the interwar years, and in fact—with some exceptions in the later 1930s—became smaller. Military medicine attracted only a small minority of American physicians, in part because the civilian profession grew increasingly prosperous after World War I. The doctors who joined the Army or the Navy Medical Department during the 1920s simply liked the military life or hoped to intern at military hospitals, or—when the Depression came in 1929—put on the uniform because they needed a government paycheck. Many civilian doctors joined the medical reserve corps, serving part time in return for their yearly active-duty pay.

Doctors who were members of the regular army and navy lived lives that their civilian colleagues, usually rooted to their practices and patients, would have found strange indeed. One army medical officer, Crawford Sams, remembered mainly the journeys that carried him, his family, and his horses—polo was a theme of his life in the peacetime army—from coast to coast, and south to the Panama Canal Zone. Home meant a succession of military posts: San Francisco, where his house at Land's End overlooked the misty magic of the Golden Gate; Washington, D.C., where he taught military science and tactics to fledgling doctors; Carlisle Barracks, Pennsylvania, where the medical field service school trained the new doctors to be military officers. He studied the art of war in the Infantry School at Fort Benning, Georgia, and at the Command and General Staff College in Leavenworth, Kansas, surrendered his civilian ways—including a longtime hope of specializing in neurosurgery—and instead learned to take "quiet satisfaction with a career in trying to keep people well."[1]

The memoirs of a navy doctor who later became surgeon general of his service recorded even wider travels. Born a Virginia hillbilly, Lamont Pugh first saw the navy when he was twelve and Theodore Roosevelt's Great White Fleet—"those beautiful white ships with their glistening brass ventilating louvers and other trimmings of brass"—dropped anchor in Hampton Roads. In time the future surgeon left the mountains, learned medicine, and saw a great part of his country's Pacific empire. He spent much of his time practicing a jack-of-all-trades medicine whose principal aim was keeping healthy people well—examining his men on shipboard, diagnosing and dosing them, patching up sailors who were injured in accidents (even in peacetime shipboard was a dangerous place) and doing general surgery afloat and ashore. He participated in the ceremonies of military life, often with considerable fuss and feathers, attending the captain's weekly inspection in frock coat with belt and sword; on special occasions he wore a cocked hat with his full-dress uniform. That was the navy way.[2]

Overseas posts were much sought after. Subject to the needs of their patients, medical officers like others kept "tropical hours"— half a day for work and half for sport. Pugh relished the quiet years he spent with his family on tropical Guam. Army doctors and nurses who served in the Philippines just before World War II stored up warm recollections of a pleasant, drowsy outpost of empire, comfortable yet exotic. Madeline Ullom, an army nurse who volunteered for a tour in the islands, thought it a choice assignment where "all posts were considered desirable." In Manila she lived in airy quarters with bamboo furniture, attended by house-boys in white jackets. Interesting work on the wards of Sternberg General Hospital, visits from Chinese merchants displaying linens and silks, and sports—tennis, bowling and swimming—filled her days. Social life revolved around the Army–Navy Club, the Mani-la Hotel, the Jai-Alai, and Tom Dixie's Kitchen. The great social event of the year came when the military and their dependents gathered around radios at the club to hear the overseas broadcast of the Army–Navy game.[3]

So regular was the life, and so orderly, it might have seemed likely to go on forever. The structure of authority in military med-icine encouraged the sense of stability, for it was firm and tradi-tion-minded. The army's Medical Department and the navy's Bu-reau of Medicine and Surgery formed typical military pyramids. Each had a surgeon general at the top, a major general in the army

The Regular Medical Departments in 1939[4]

	ARMY	NAVY
Doctors	1,098	841
Nurses	652	439
Medical Administrative Corps	64	—
Dentists	221	255
Veterinarians	126	—
Hospital Corps	—	4,267

and a rear admiral in the navy. Each department segregated its health-care professionals into corps—doctors, nurses, dentists, and veterinarians. In the navy, enlisted men and warrant officer specialists in fields allied to medicine formed the Hospital Corps. Both departments were very small, in line with the needs of the nation's armed forces, though the army had a substantial backup force of 23,339 reserve officers of all types.

The different corps were separate but unequal, and the names they bore did not necessarily describe all their military functions. Military dentists, for example, did much more than take care of soldiers' and sailors' teeth. On the day of battle they were the utility infielders, whose professional training made them second choice when no physicians were available to run battalion aid stations, do emergency surgery, and manage the movement of casualties. Veterinarians cared for the animals—an especially important function in the army, where horses and mules still provided much of the motive power. But veterinarians also checked food to ensure that it was wholesome and free of disease, a function they had first developed by inspecting slaughterhouses.[5]

Army professionals in fields allied to medicine—from physiologists to sanitary engineers—received only reserve commissions in the Sanitary Corps; they could not become regular officers. Their equivalents in the navy received warrants in the Hospital Corps. Nurses after 1921 held what was called relative rank, meaning that they received the insignia of lieutenants and captains but not the pay or command authority. A progressive surgeon general secured the creation of the army's Medical Administrative Corps (MAC), to open officer rank to able sergeants and to relieve doctors of some administrative jobs in the hospitals and elsewhere. But, with budgets shrinking during the Depression, later surgeon generals monopolized almost all the available officer slots for the doctors. When World War II began, hospital administration was a recognized profession in civilian life, but there were only a few dozen medical administrative officers in the entire army.

Doctors dominated the departments, outnumbering and outranking all the other officers combined. They practiced a kind of medicine unlike any in civilian life. By its nature, military medicine was impersonal; the doctor–patient relationship seldom had time to form.[6] The basic concern was health, not sickness (though even the healthy young men the medical officer primarily served had a propensity for catching infections, especially the venereal ones). Sometimes the medical officer commanded a unit, with all the responsibilities that faced the commander. But whether he was commander or staff officer, he took orders from nondoctors and accepted responsibility for the health of men and women he would never know as individuals.

Not all the men who joined the armed services, M.D. in hand, could adapt to the life. Not all wanted to. Some tried the military for a while and then got out. After facing a typically rigorous selection board, new doctors in uniform studied military medicine at the Army or Navy Medical School and sometimes received postgraduate clinical training in general hospitals. Army officers went to the Medical Field Service School for military training and exercises. But many "thoroughly disliked the place," precisely because it demanded soldiering rather than doctoring. In the class of one future leader of the Medical Department, so many decided to resign after a course featuring field maneuvers and daily 26-mile horseback rides that the surgeon general had to come up from Washington to try to "convince [them] of the importance of field training."[7]

Yet many reached a personal compromise between the profession of medicine and the profession of arms. Those who kept their commissions embarked on a life of considerable variety and promise. Some of the ablest found their way into general hospitals and laboratories maintained by the armed services, where they might win distinction by treating patients, doing research, or learning to administer elaborate medical organizations. Such men were often marked out for high rank, especially during peacetime. Normally, the President selected the Surgeon General of the Army from among the commanders of the five general hospitals in the continental United States—Walter Reed, Army and Navy, Fitzsimmons, Letterman, and William Beaumont. Colonel Norman T. Kirk personified the military clinician. An excellent orthopedic surgeon, he spent twenty years in major hospitals, including Walter Reed, Sternberg, and Letterman, before receiving command of a new general hospital in 1942. He was a diplomate of the Ameri-

can Board of Surgery, a fellow of the American College of Physicians, and member of an array of medical associations.[8] In short, a
thoroughgoing professional whose ties to civilian medicine would
help to make him Army Surgeon General during World War II.

At the opposite pole, some doctors took to the military life with
such enthusiasm that they ceased to be doctors except in name.
(Before World War I, one such enthusiast—General Leonard
Wood—had gone on to become Army Chief of Staff and a conservative candidate for President.) Most of those who stayed in the
armed services struck a balance that permitted them to find satisfaction in a world where they could be good doctors only by
being good soldiers, and vice versa. There were some basic simi-
larities between the profession of medicine and the profession of
arms. Neither doctor nor officer worked nine-to-five; both were
constantly on call. Both professions dealt at the most basic level
with human capability, and the conservation of physical strength
and emotional stability that was the business of medicine contributed essentially to the survival of an armed force in war.

The navy doctor had some special adaptations to make. There
were differences both obvious and subtle between the medical services of the army (which included the Army Air Corps) and the
navy (which also served the Marine Corps). The navy, said a per-
ceptive civilian physician who considered joining both, was smaller and more centrally directed. The doctor entered an organization that was clannish, almost intuitively linked, whose members
seemed to move together like "a school of fish or a flock of birds
[that] will suddenly turn and take off in a different direction."
While army medical units "traipsed along like gypsies" behind
forces on the move, the navy doctor had his precisely assigned
space aboard ship and traveled as an integral part of the complement. Unlike his army counterpart, he commanded no separate
medical unit yet was viewed by his fellow officers as a full-fledged
member of the captain's staff, as expert in his own technical field
as, say, the communications officer was in his.[9]

Navy surgeons directed the enlisted corpsmen, who were a special breed. Many men remained in the medical department
throughout their careers, the fortunate and able rising to the rank
of chief petty officer. On the smaller ships an independent duty

corpsman might be the only medically trained man aboard, normally treating minor injuries and ailments but in combat bearing an extraordinary responsibility for managing serious cases as well. Navy corpsmen who served with the marines tended to adopt the view that they supported an elite organization and acted accordingly, winning a remarkable number of battlefield decorations. United in their own corps, with their own journal to record their experiences, navy enlisted medics had a sense of corporate identity denied to the army's looser formations, who were, however, as capable and brave.[10]

Regular naval medical officers also led lives that were more varied in some respects than those of their army counterparts. Because they cared for the marines—and because the marines were the nation's service of choice for foreign interventions between the wars—many more navy than army regulars saw life in the field in foreign posts from Panama to China. Socially, the naval medical officer at home enjoyed the advantages of his service. Assignment to port cities made him more a part of urban society than the army officer, who was frequently assigned to posts in small towns or the country. Most doctoring and all research were done ashore in naval hospitals and laboratories.

Its smallness and its technological bent made the navy more attuned to its scientific officers, including the medics. Yet many army medical officers were highly integrated into their service, attending its schools, learning the tactics and strategy of war, and forming friendships among rising line officers that would mean much during the crisis to come. As one graduate said, after attending Command and General Staff, "I knew how a division staff was supposed to run," a crucial matter for the regular officer whose future job during the war would be to fit a medical system then largely staffed by citizen soldiers into the army machine."[11]

Enticed by security, the respect accorded the uniform, and the opportunity to treat strong young people who usually recovered, many doctors adopted the life of the officer corps with enthusiasm. They liked the formal socializing, the feeling of membership in an extended if unequal family, and the clubby sense of comradeship whenever two officers met anywhere in the world. Most achieved a personal balance between their two diverse professions, acquiring the habit of command and at the same time honing their medical skills as general practitioners and surgeons to the community of uniformed men, their wives, and their children.

For the specialists and the researchers, life closely resembled the civilian norm in great hospitals and laboratories. Because there were so few administrative officers, doctors also performed a variety of jobs—running medical supply depots, for example— and tasks in military administration and command that had no precise civilian equivalent. Those who served on posts had what amounted to practices among officers and men, families, and retirees. Their lives followed the rhythms of the officer corps, meaning that they were on call twenty-four hours a day, but with much time available for sports. They enjoyed some amenities; in the peacetime army camps, or on the navy's ships and bases ashore, life offered a kind of spare comfort. Often drawn from hardworking backgrounds among the nation's plain folk, the officers of the medical services led middle-class lives in the United States and enjoyed modest affluence overseas.

For those who could accept the discipline, it was a good life, useful and honorable, touched with adventure and spiced with the exotic flavors of strange lands. But during the 1930s war broke out again, first in Asia and then in Europe, as Japan, Italy, and finally Germany embarked on programs of aggressive expansion.

The decisive break came in the late summer of 1939. On September 1, twenty-five years and one month after the opening of the last war, Germany invaded Poland. A week later, President Franklin D. Roosevelt declared a limited national emergency. Suddenly everything had to be made ready, and there was no longer any time.

American military medicine faced the crisis in an unpromising state—two small bureaucratic agencies serving the peacetime needs of the least impressive armed forces of all the major powers on earth. On paper the Army Medical Department possessed an array of field medical units, which together formed the chain of evacuation along which a wounded man moved from warfront to home front. At the company level, aidmen would go into battle along with the fighters, give the wounded man first aid, drag him out of the line of fire, and summon litterbearers to carry him back to an ambulance pickup point. A doctor would see his injury at a battalion aid station and, if his condition were serious enough, order him to be carried to a collecting or clearing station. The clearing station, a forward unit resembling a mobile clinic, would give more sophisticated emergency treatment and send the patient, if his wound so warranted, to a field or surgical hospital. Ultimately an evacuation hospital would ship him out of the combat area if he needed long, complex treatment to recover. In the communications zone and the zone of the interior, general hospitals would stand ready to apply the most modern techniques to save his life and restore him to health.

Unfortunately, short peacetime budgets meant that not much of this apparatus existed in reality. The backbone of the medical department on the eve of war was a system of five general hospitals in the United States plus one in Hawaii and one in the Philippines, and 104 smaller station hospitals that served major posts. The department had the sum total of five field units—four medical regiments, designed to support one division each, and a medical squadron for the air corps. There were no mobile hospitals to accompany the troops to the field; the surgeon general hoped to staff such units by reviving a World War I policy, under which civil hospitals and medical schools sponsored "affiliated" reserve units. In August 1939 the War Department approved the idea, and affiliated units later brought much of the nation's best medical talent into the service.[12]

Many reservists were summoned to serve on extended active duty—a source of strength, new ideas, and challenge to customary ways of thinking. The call of patriotism brought in new volunteers as well, both young and established doctors, the former becoming lieutenants and captains, the latter field-grade officers. The surgeon generals had long had a policy of appointing consultants, senior physicians whose tasks included visiting hospitals to give instruction in their specialties and to ensure the maintenance of high clinical standards. Other consultants served the field armies, carrying high-quality supervision to the units in their army area. Consultants in every specialty now had to be chosen, offered suitable rank, and acquainted with their duties.

New hospitals had to be constructed for the training camps and staffed and equipped. Enlisted men had to be turned into litter-bearers, ambulance drivers, and technicians in four medical replacement training centers that combined traditional basic training with instruction in anatomy, pharmacy, and nursing. Through the Red Cross, skilled women volunteered in increasing numbers for the Army Nurse Corps, and increasing numbers of experts in the other health-care professions had to be found and woven into the military fabric. Rife with future trouble was the area of medical supply. The only reserve of medical equipment on hand was left over from the last war, and medical supplies of every sort soon grew tight. Germany was shut off as a source of supply, and American efforts to provide war materiel for England and France increased the strain on the nation's undeveloped drug and surgical equipment industries. Yet the new American units had to be equipped somehow.[13]

Despite a tangle of difficulties, the two military medical departments grew rapidly. They had to. Even though the first hostile shot had yet to be fired, medical assistance was needed to build the new forces and to keep them healthy once they were in uniform. The navy got bigger without essentially changing its charac-

The Medical Departments in 1941[14]
(Regulars plus Reservists on Extended Active Duty)

	ARMY	NAVY
Doctors	9,235	1,957
Nurses	5,433	524
Medical Administrative Corps	833	—
Dentists	2,357	511
Veterinarians	530	—
Hospital Corps Officers	—	195
Enlisted	—	10,547

ter, but the new army was a force altogether different from the small volunteer force of professionals that had guarded the nation and its Pacific empire during the interwar years. In 1940 Congress declared a partial mobilization and enacted the first peacetime draft. Throngs of men poured into the army, and lesser throngs volunteered for the navy, marines, and air corps. Deciding who was to be taken became a fundamental medical task.

Because the army took all draftees until 1943, its doctors played a key role in writing standards and selecting the nation's soldiers from the millions of young men who registered with the Selective Service System. The draft began as a process of careful selection, but after Pearl Harbor it became a sweep of almost any male who lacked an exemption, was of proper age, was physically functional, was not demented, and fell within certain height and weight guidelines. Overwhelmingly, the system worked by compulsion, for many male volunteers to all the services were inspired by the pressure of the draft. Women—later to play an important role in the war, especially in the wartime medical services—were the only volunteers who faced no compulsion at all.

Formal physical and mental standards set by the army determined whether a man was drafted or not. When the draft began in 1940, army policy set the standards high. The service expected to take in only about 800,000 men and wanted, understandably, the best it could get. (By late 1942, by way of comparison, Selective Service was processing about 600,000 men a *month*.) Not only were physical standards comparatively rigorous, but Selective Service had only three main categories. A young man was either rejected, judged fit for all duty, or marked for limited duty. Since the army could meet its needs from those who were fit for all duty, even the limited-duty men were not drafted. Army standards were adopted by the Selective Service to guide its 30,000 volunteer medical examiners, civilian doctors who served without pay.[15]

Once again, as in World War I and the later phases of the Civil War, the army became the nation in arms. As it did, political pressures invaded the process of selection. More than 40 percent of the registrants were rejected as physically or mentally unfit, setting the stage for a round of public lamentation over the degeneracy of the American male. In part the outcry reflected the national love of breast-beating, in part the sharp political fights that had taken place over national health insurance during the 1930s. Draft rejections gave supporters of the defeated program a welcome stick to beat the American Medical Association (AMA) for failing to protect the national health. Within broad limits, however, health is what you define it to be, and many men were rejected simply because the army, like the nation at large, had not yet accommodated its thinking to a war in which quantity was to mean a great deal more than quality. Others failed the physical and mental examinations for reasons that did no credit to American society. For example, the poor schools, poverty, and excessive disease rates that plagued African Americans caused young blacks to be rejected at almost twice the rate of whites.[16]

The most acute public displeasure regarding the draft, however, developed over differences between the civilian doctors who served Selective Service and the mostly military doctors who worked at the army induction stations. Too often a young man was accepted by his local board physician, quit his job, sold his car, staged a last drunk, bade a tearful farewell to friends and family, and went off to camp—only to be rejected when he arrived. There were many reasons why rejections of men who had been accepted by local boards ran 10–15 percent on average. Civilian examiners tended to think their first duty was to build up the army, while military doctors believed that their duty was to give it the best human material obtainable. Honest differences of opinion, unfamiliarity with standards, haste, and boredom may also have affected the examiners. Draft examining easily bred a perfunctory attitude. When Bill Mauldin was examined as a young National Guard volunteer, he encountered a notable lack of rigor.

"They didn't really test our eyes," he complained, "they sort of counted them. I never saw so much as a stethoscope that day." One doctor "seemed to be interested in nothing but hemorrhoids." A young man, one of whose testicles had "strained its moorings and left its colleague hanging some four or five inches higher," was accepted for service with the note "left varicocele" on his medical record.[17] At this stage of the war, in short, too many were called for the number chosen.

Yet for millions of Americans the "physical" was their first point of contact or collision with military medicine, and the place where their own war began. It was not much as a human experience. Before the war started, many men got their preliminary checkups in a doctor's office. But greater speed and standardization were needed. In mass examinations, men were supposed to be processed by a group of doctors at the rate of twenty-five an hour, which at two minutes a man left the doctors ten minutes out of every sixty to confer on difficult cases. The examination was supposed to include the Wassermann test for syphilis, X-ray of the lungs, and urinalysis, with other laboratory tests for specific cases—for example, checking a genital discharge for gonorrhea. Attire was specified—men were to be fully clothed during the eye, ear, nose, and throat and the dental exams, and completely nude for the rest. However, a good deal of variation existed in the early days; some men went before the doctors dressed rather absurdly in bathrobe and shoes, and some may never have removed their clothing at all. At any rate, the Selective Service later made nakedness mandatory after induction stations discovered that a few men had passed their preliminary examinations despite the fact that they had only one leg! And so most men spent hours shuffling from one examining station to another in their bare skin, among a sweating or shivering throng; at one mass physical, later in the war, three thousand were examined at one time.[18]

The question of what was to be done with rejectees appeared early on. Too many men were not up to the standards of the early draft, and too many who were healthy and literate hurriedly volunteered for other services to escape it. Lewis B. Hershey, the director of Selective Service, was driven to poetry by the results:

Ten little registrants standing in a line,
One joined the Navy, and then there were nine.

Nine little registrants, sitting on a gate,
One broke a vertebra, and then there were eight.

Eight little registrants, talking 'bout heaven,
One went conscientious, then there were seven.

Seven little registrants, what a strange mix!
One became a pilot, and then there were six.

Six little registrants, very much alive,
One went and drowned, and then there were five.

Five little registrants full of canny lore,
One stole a pig and then there were four.

Four little registrants, spry as they can be.
One became twenty-eight, then there were three.

Three little registrants, all alone and blue,
One fed his relatives, then there were two.

Two little registrants, what can be done!
One went to a psychiatrist, then there was one.

One little registrant, classified 1-A,
Physically, mentally, morally okay.

One little registrant to tote a big gun,
He got married and then there were NONE![19]

The bottom of the manpower barrel began to show almost at once, leading to calls for "rehabilitation" of the rejected and "rehabilitation" of young men in anticipation of service. President Roosevelt got behind the movement, finding money to be used by Selective Service in providing simple medical and dental care for those who were easily salvageable. Lowering the standards and treating the men after induction would have been simpler still, but the army did not have enough doctors, dentists, or hospital beds.

The coming of the war in December 1941 changed the game entirely; standards dropped precipitously, and the medical service expanded enormously. Now the army hired psychologists to test illiterate men with symbols and pantomime. Almost toothless men got their uniforms and their dentures in that order. Men with correctable vision problems received glasses and went to the firing range. Of course the motivation was the needs of the mass army. But the result was a whole generation of young men who received simple but crucial rehabilitation through the military that they might not have gotten under the treatment-for-pay system prevailing in the civilian world.[20]

From the army's view, it was a good bargain. Nobody doubted then or now that the physical examination was crucial to the war effort. Standards were determined to some extent by policy, for the nation had to decide what kind of army it wanted before examiners could give it the kind of men it needed. Truly serious physical conditions were always grounds for rejection, and excluding the unfit—and, at the same time, rehabilitating the marginal—was absolutely fundamental to building armed services that could win the war.[21]

However, there was another side to the selection process that caused many problems: the effort to select men who were sound of mind as well as body. Psychiatry differed from other medical specialties, for the great advances in surgery and the discoveries of the late nineteenth century that had transformed internal medicine had meant little to the study of mental disorders. In the 1940s the study of the mind remained in much the same state that all medicine had been in during the 1860s. Psychiatry featured a variety of sects, a multitude of insights, much hard information, and a number of genuine healers and pioneers exploring the most varied avenues of treatment. But it had no core of tested theory that was accepted by all its practitioners, and as a result different psychiatrists thought in terms that were varied and sometimes contradictory.

In civilian medicine a rough division had grown up between psychiatrists who worked with chronic mental patients in asylums, most of whom relied upon physical methods of treatment, and psychoanalysts who treated neurotics. Among the latter, Freud's influence was great, and many brought the master's views into military practice when they donned the uniform. They tended to see the fighting man as a product of his personal history and to believe that his future behavior under stress ought to be predictable to some degree. Hence they believed that they could exclude the unfit from the ranks by detecting psychological flaws ranging from florid psychoses to ambiguous states that included "psychopathic personalities." This catchall category included alcoholics, homosexuals, the emotionally unstable, pathological liars, petty offenders, kleptomaniacs, pyromaniacs, and "those highly irritable and arrogant individuals, so-called 'guardhouse lawyers,' who are forever critical of organized authority," as well as dreamy types who "do not have personality traits which enable

them to make a satisfactory adjustment owing to introversion, eccentricity, impracticalness [sic], or vagrancy." Had all such people
actually been excluded, it would have been a much smaller army.[22]

Eager to save the government money, time, and trouble, the
Adjutant General accepted the claim. The war years then provided
a long and embarrassing demonstration that the claim could not
be made good. Described by one psychiatrist as "a cursory neuro-
logic evaluation and a simultaneous psychiatric 'impression,'" psychiatric examinations of draftees combined an extremely basic
oral intelligence test, standard tests for balance and coordination,
and questions such as, "Were you ever arrested for being drunk?"
and "How do you get along with the girls?" The time allotted for
determining a man's mental stability was absurdly short; one psychiatrist recalled a day when he saw 512 men. Another summed
up the result: "Most NP [neuropsychiatric] rejections were, and
are, 'by guess and by God'!"[23]

As psychiatric rejections mounted alarmingly, a stream of paper
aimed to correct the situation issued from the surgeon general and
the War Department. A technical bulletin ordered the induction
of anybody with a "reasonable chance" of adapting to military life
and sought to prevent examiners from giving an adverse diagnosis
on flimsy evidence. But standards for judging mental and emotional problems, compared with those for physical conditions, remained distressingly vague. What actually constituted a neurosis?
"I think," a psychiatrist said, "the concept . . . varied according to
the number of psychiatrists involved, in the ratio of about one different concept per psychiatrist."[24]

Tending to confirm this judgment were studies by the National
Research Council that raised serious doubts as to whether breakdowns in military service could be predicted. Investigators traced
young men from Yale and Harvard who had received adverse
evaluations from campus psychiatrists during their college years.
Many turned in good wartime records. Apparently the inherent
tendency to mature and learn by experience could not be assessed
easily, if at all. A study by the Selective Service looked into men
who had been rejected for psychiatric reasons but afterward accepted into the army under the more relaxed standards introduced later in the war. More than 79 percent had given satisfacto-

ry service. In a similar group of navy enlisted men, discharged for psychiatric reasons but later readmitted, 88.5 percent served competently.

The total numbers rejected for service on psychiatric grounds were staggering—1,992,950 men in all, comprising 30 percent of all rejections. Meanwhile, 379,486 men who were originally passed by psychiatrists and accepted for the service had to be separated for psychiatric reasons, and roughly 356,000 more for marginal reasons that included inadaptability and bed-wetting. Psychiatric disability was the largest single cause of medical separations from the army, constituting 45 percent of all discharges for disability. Rejecting many who were fit and accepting many who were not, the science of the mind began World War II by demonstrating its own immaturity. Its failure, in the context of the national emergency, was a serious one.[25]

Despite all the problems of the selection process, the new army took form. Even in 1940 its strength rose from 210,000 to 1.7 million, and the huge maneuvers held that year in Louisiana, Tennessee, and North Carolina gave many an officer his first experience with a plausible imitation of modern war. New medical officers presumably met the military side of their profession with the same shock felt by their predecessors in earlier days, all the more so because many of the new men considered themselves civilians in uniform, citizen soldiers with only a temporary commitment to military service.

In fact, the civilian influence on military medicine was growing rapidly, not only because the majority of medical officers were reservists and volunteers but because the whole medical profession was being swept up into a growing frenzy of national preparedness. Throughout the country, "medical preparedness" became a watchword and very quickly a cliché. Month by month, the AMA's *Journal* published reports from England under the blitz, news of developments on the medical policy front, and lists of American doctors who had volunteered or whose reserve units had been called into service. Even for those who did no more than give some time to the Selective Service, assist as part-time volunteers at a local military post, or care for the patients of a departed colleague, the tempo of life was different.

While the excitement struck the most unlikely spots—the secure Middle West as well as the East and West coasts—there were
places where war seemed especially close. One was the nation's
westernmost city, the capital of the Territory of Hawaii. A keystone of the Pacific empire the United States had built up over the
preceding half-century, the islands for decades had been central to
American military planning for the eventuality of war with the region's other expanding empire, Japan. Sensitive to the islands' exposed position, physicians in Honolulu launched a remarkable experiment in cooperative effort. The chief surgeon of the army's
Hawaiian Department was Colonel Edgar King, by most accounts
a difficult, domineering, able man whose chief weakness was his
inability to delegate responsibility. Despite his personality and the
habits born of thirty-four years of service in the United States, the
Canal Zone, the Philippines, and China, King labored to bring the
military and civilian medical professions together.

"In wartime think of everything—take nothing for granted," he
warned, and under his sharp eye and at the urging of the Honolulu Medical Society local doctors made ready in every way they
could. The society worked closely with the army and navy surgeons at Schofield Barracks and Pearl Harbor to staff emergency
hospitals. (King even put a civilian in charge of the program.)
Hospitals prepared to evacuate their convalescents and to receive
new casualties in a crisis; fireproof schools were converted into
hospitals; an ambulance corps of women volunteers borrowed
civilian trucks, which workmen modified for use as ambulances.
Civilian aid stations were set up, attendants assigned, and supplies
stockpiled.[26]

Meanwhile, the army and navy expanded their own medical establishments. The Army Air Corps got a new hospital at Hickam
Field; Schofield Station Hospital and Tripler General Hospital
both expanded; the old medical regiment assigned to the "square"
(four-regiment) Hawaiian Division was reorganized to support
the "triangular" (three-regiment) divisions formed out of it. The
navy's hospital at Pearl Harbor—standing on Hospital Point, just
south of Ford Island with its proud array of battleships anchored
offshore—was already one of the best in the service. A mobile

base hospital arrived in November 1941, and construction crews began making it ready for use.[27]

Local doctors studied up on the needs of wartime medicine. Important changes in therapeutics were under way, arriving with theatrical precision just before the war did. In the mid-thirties, chemicals derived from aniline dyes—the sulfa drugs—were marketed in Europe. For reasons that no one understood as yet, sulfanilamide and related compounds stopped bacteria from multiplying, allowing the body time to assemble its defenses and attack the invaders. Physicians looked on with amazement as hitherto unconquerable infections cleared up under treatment.[28] Meanwhile, experiments with a recently discovered antibiotic—penicillin—were going on in laboratories. In 1941 British researchers arrived in the United States, urging Americans to attempt to do what they had so far failed to do themselves: mass-produce the new agent. Medicine was entering an era when it would be able to kill infections deep inside the body and defeat diseases that up to now had been almost invincible. That alone would make World War II different from any that had been fought before.

Eager to hear the latest word on the innovations that were beginning to remake the treatment of wounds, the medical society in Hawaii invited Dr. John J. Moorhead to take the long journey from New York and to address its membership. One of the nation's most distinguished practitioners of traumatic surgery, Moorhead had learned his craft in World War I, winning the Croix de Guerre, the Cross of the Legion of Honor, and the Distinguished Service Cross during nineteen months on the Western Front. He had gone on to become a founder of the American Board of Surgery, a fellow of the College of Surgeons, and a colonel in the Medical Reserve Corps. Moorhead embodied to a remarkable degree the mixed military and civilian experience of many twentieth-century American doctors.

Moorhead flew to San Francisco, then took the *Lurline*—"newest, largest and most swanky" of the Matson Line ships that voyaged to the islands—with his course of lectures mapped out. He opened with a talk called, "Treatment of Wounds, Civilian and Military." In the audience of three hundred were both civilian and military doctors, a microcosm of the alliance that now character-ized the island and that would soon typify the whole medical mili-tary establishment as well. The lecture apparently featured solid information on debridement, delayed closure, and the use of sul-fanilamide to prevent infection. Pleased at the large turnout and the enthusiastic reception, he decided to give his next talk to the city's surgeons at downtown Queen's Hospital on Sunday morn-ing, December 7, 1941.[29]

2

Awakening to War

It was a typical Hawaiian winter day, the north shore of Oahu steeped in broken clouds that hung upon the mountain tops but left leeward Honolulu clear. The sun was long up, and the ships along Battleship Row beside Ford Island were splendidly visible. A nurse on the USS *Solace*, a navy hospital ship newly arrived in the harbor, was admiring "an unusually vivid rainbow." Then bombers came flashing down from the green Waianae Mountains to the west and torpedo planes began wheeling in from the sea.[1]

Explosions racked the ships; bombs hit Hickam and Wheeler airfields and the Naval Air Station at Kaneohe on Oahu's north shore. Under the ruins or the sea some 2,300 Americans died and 1,100 more were wounded. The navy took the heaviest hits and counted the greatest number of dead and wounded, for the object of the attack was primarily the Pacific Fleet. The *Oklahoma* capsized, and a single armor-piercing bomb exploding in a magazine sank the battleship *Arizona*, entombing 1,177 men after one of the mightiest blasts of the war.

Even while the attack went on, small boats darted into the burning oil slick that surrounded the *Arizona* to pull survivors from the water. Longboats and smart flag officers' gigs hauled oil-soaked, scorched, and wounded men to treatment and returned for more. Only the crew's quarters of the mobile base hospital had been put up, but every major ship had its own sickbay, and the presence of the *Solace*—gleaming white, encircled by a broad green stripe and marked with red crosses—was providential.[2] Most casualties wound up either in its wards or at Dock C, the closest to the naval hospital. Seventy percent were burn cases; some were unrecognizable. Those who were conscious tried to mumble their names.[3]

Medical corpsmen broke out morphine to dull pain, tannic acid jelly for burns, plasma and saline solution to replace lost blood volume and body fluids, and sulfa drugs to fight infection. On the warships, main battle dressing stations were filled with the men who had been injured or burned; on the *Nevada*, a first-aid station was set up under the overhang of No. 4 turret on the main deck aft. Ashore, the marine barracks and the officer's club in the Navy Yard became impromptu receiving wards. Medical officers arrived on the run from their homes; corpsmen from sunk or damaged ships made their way ashore; and Red Cross nurses hastened to the hospitals. Civilians drove the wounded to treatment in their cars, braving strafing Zeros, and stories were later told of prostitutes from the Hotel Street red-light district who volunteered to nurse the men they had served in other ways in the past.

At the unfinished base hospital, corpsmen pried open crates to get at supplies, moved the wounded into the crew's quarters, and soon were treating 110 patients. At Ewa, west of Pearl Harbor, the hospital tents of Marine Aircraft Group 21 were burning, and the dozen or so wounded received treatment in the open, exposed, along with like the corpsmen who bent over them, to enemy machine guns. At the Pearl Harbor Naval Hospital patients were thrust into any available bed as they arrived. Burn cases filled the medical wards. Among those who were conscious, some were hysterical, some depressed, all deeply anxious. But many men arrived unconscious, and some died without waking. More than three hundred corpses accumulated, many of them nameless, some with fingers too charred and mangled for the pathologist and his technician to take prints. By midnight the hospital had a jam-packed morgue and 960 living patients crowding the space intended for 250; doctors, nurses, and corpsmen worked in relays for forty-eight hours straight.

Living or dead, the casualties were a visible prophecy of the coming war at sea. Fractures were everywhere—simple bone breaks, compound fractures with surface wounds, crushed and scattered comminuted fractures. Most patients had been burned, either deeply by fuel oil or widely and superficially by the flash of exploding ordnance. How badly a man was burned depended largely on the clothing he wore, and early on a Sunday morning in the tropics most had been wearing very little. Even tee shirts or cotton drawers had provided some protection from flash burns, and men who had been fully dressed usually had been burned only on their faces and hands. Lying stripped on hospital bunks, patients had the look of photographic negatives, their absent clothing printed on their bodies in white.

Nearly all the men who had been in the water were coated with oil, whose removal from burned flesh the Pacific Fleet Medical Officer inadequately described as "tedious, at times painful." In the naval hospital, corpsmen used ordinary flit guns to spray tannic acid solution over the endless burned bodies. Doctors mixed sulfa drugs with the oils and jellies then used to protect and soothe burns. Late at night medical officers still labored by the blue flashlights allowed under blackout regulations, probing constricted or collapsed veins with hollow needles to inject saline, glucose, and plasma. The days that followed saw the initial chaos resolve into grim order: the daily change of dressings, the removal of sloughed skin, the debridement of dead and dying flesh by the surgical knife.[4]

Army wounded were fewer and, though flash burns were common, the soldiers had not been roasted by burning fuel oil. At the first news of the attack Doctor Moorhead hastened from his aborted lecture to Tripler General Hospital, then a complex of wooden buildings in Fort Shafter near the awninged bungalows that housed the army's leadership in Hawaii. Without undue formality he was restored to active duty, and as Colonel Moorhead he took charge of the three operating rooms and the nine surgical teams that assembled to work in them. He briefly gave his staff of military and civilian surgeons technical instructions on the methods he wanted used, and all got to work with a "fine spirit of co-operation."[5]

But almost everyone was new to mass-casualty situations, and the confusion in the hospital showed it. The second-floor operating rooms opened off a single passageway that quickly became cluttered with the wounded. A civilian surgeon told a reporter that some patients were carried into surgery without having their clothes removed and without any preliminary cleaning. Surgeons had to wear the same gloves all day, washing them between patients, and one doctor worked bare-chested in pajama bottoms for lack of proper attire. When blood and plasma ran short, one surgeon, J. E. Strode, phoned Dr. Eric Fennel, who had helped to set up Hawaii's first blood bank less than a year before. "Fennel dashed to Tripler bearing a large clothes basket filled with plasma and the tools for treating shock" and spent the rest of the day giving transfusions.[6]

Despite everything, however, the surviving casualties were relatively fortunate people. Some injuries were appalling, but many patients seemed unaware of their pain as the doctors fought shock, cleaned wounds, and sprinkled them with sulfanilamide crystals to fight infection. When local bloodbanks were depleted, a call for blood and plasma went out by radio. It brought in five hundred volunteers during the first hour, and hundreds more came during the days that followed in answer to renewed radio and newspaper appeals. The wounded fought for life surrounded by friends, cared for in ample hospitals, and supported by the resources of an American city where damage, outside the military reservations, was minimal. They were young and healthy, well-fed and rested, and their wounds were comparatively clean.[7]

No more atypical situation could be imagined. Though the American–Japanese war began with an air attack on one city and ended with the destruction of two others, most of its battles were to be fought in the most primitive regions of the earth, and most of its casualties were to be weary men with contaminated wounds. The true face of the war and its medical crises appeared not on

Oahu but two thousand miles to the west, in the Commonwealth of the Philippines, where an army died, cut off and abandoned.

———————

The Philippines had fallen into American hands after the war with Spain in 1898—the pearl of a short-lived American empire in the Caribbean and the Pacific. While fighting both Spaniards and native guerrillas, American soldiers and governors had called upon the newborn medical science of their time to combat the horrendous diseases of the tropics. In so doing they imitated the European colonialists already at work in many tropical lands. A British Indian Army surgeon discovered the role of the mosquito in spreading malaria. The American Army introduced modern public health as part of its military takeover—a way of protecting its own troops while demonstrating to reluctant natives the benefits of American rule.

Half-consciously, colonialists were beginning to learn how to wage a new kind of war. Yet their jungle wars were limited affairs—low-intensity conflicts, in the terminology of a later era. Theoretically at least, the great powers understood that at some time in the future they might have to fight one another in the jungle. By 1920 plans had already existed in the locked cabinets of the American General Staff that envisioned a defense of the Philippines against Japan, pinpointing the islands of Manila Bay and the jungle-covered peninsula of Bataan as the last bastions of defense. Bataan was one of the most heavily malarial regions in the world, and no practical means of controlling the disease existed there except to use quinine, an old remedy of limited effectiveness.

By 1940 growing tension with Japan had awakened the Philippines to a time of hasty preparation. A former chief of staff, General Douglas MacArthur, was summoned out of retirement to head the Philippine Department. His forces were sizable but not uniformly useful. The Philippine Division provided the defenders with a small force of high quality, while the militia units of the Philippine Army offered them quantity alone. MacArthur's surgeon, Colonel Wibb E. Cooper, was an able regular who relied on a unit formed of Americans and Filipinos, the 12th Medical Regiment of the Philippine Division. Cooper tried to supply the inexperienced and ill-trained militia with some senior surgeons and training in the elements of field medicine. Like Edgar King in Hawaii, he drew upon the civilian resources of the islands, commissioning doctors and nurses in the Philippine Army and arranging with the Red Cross to evacuate civilian casualties in time of need.

His principal military hospital was Sternberg General in the noisy, crowded heart of Manila near the muddy Pasig River and the old walled city called Intramuros. He had half a dozen station hospitals scattered from Baguio, a cool post in the northeastern hills of Luzon, to primitive, jungled Mindanao in the far south of the archipelago. In 1941 Cooper began to organize a hospital center in Manila, enlarging the stuccoed buildings that dated from the time of the Spaniards and converting nearby structures for medical use. Most medical supplies were stored in the city, and a scheme advocated by General MacArthur and accepted by the War Department to meet the invader on the beaches came too late to scatter them through subdepots. Plans were advanced to use Malinta Tunnel on the fortified island of Corregidor as a hospital. Because the old war plans envisioned a fighting defense of Bataan Peninsula, across Manila Bay, Cooper shipped equipment for a thousand-bed hospital there in the autumn of 1941, storing it in a warehouse in the tiny village of Limay.[8]

In 1940–41 some of the glow went off the once comfortable life of the garrison. The number of nurses at Sternberg almost doubled, but field exercises increased and social life declined. Alerts became more frequent. Though white-jacketed Filipino houseboys still went through the rituals of service, the pleasant lifestyle of the Americans was changing, its imperial assurance sapped by warlike preparations and a growing sense of unease. People even failed to make reservations at the club to listen to the broadcast of the Army–Navy game from the States. Army nurse Madeline Ullom, noting the changes, felt "regret . . . that the recently assigned personnel could not view and enjoy the opportunities that had once been ours."[9]

While clouds of smoke still hung over Pearl Harbor, the Japanese launched an equally devastating assault against the Philippines. Aircraft that hopeful army planners had counted upon to halt an enemy invasion were smashed at Clarke Field, north of

Manila, and other installations. Two days later, the navy yard at Cavite was destroyed, with heavy casualties. As on Oahu, burned and battered bodies poured into military and civilian hospitals. The center of the action was at Sternberg, where casualties lay about the well-tended lawn among the blossoming hibiscus, and doctors worked sometimes for two days running. In the station hospital at Fort McKinley, south of the capital, surgeons cut, swabbed, and stitched in the stifling operating room. In the strange silence induced by morphine and shock, fresh cases awaited the "steady-handed anesthetists [who] drove long, glistening needles" into their spines.[10]

The first enemy landings came on December 10. Numerous, brave, and ruthless, the Japanese easily defeated the American and Filipino defenders. Medical personnel from outlying posts began to withdraw with their patients to the medical center in Manila. Then, two days before Christmas, General MacArthur's headquarters declared the capital an open city and ordered evacuation across the bay to Bataan. Under intermittent air attack, medics crossed and recrossed Manila Bay through the last week of 1941, bringing patients and supplies. Some reached Bataan by water; others joined the caravans that circled Manila Bay, heading to the same destination. Ahead lay the worst of all worlds, from the viewpoint of military medicine: a siege in a jungle, with too many people to care for and inadequate medicine and food.

Meanwhile, the Asiatic Fleet, the defenders' lifeline to the rest of the world, sailed away for lack of air cover, joining in efforts by Dutch, British, and Australian forces to slow the Japanese invasion of the East Indies. Misfortune dogged the allies from the first. As ships were sunk, the Japanese pulled some survivors from the water, so that a growing number of naval prisoners began to trickle into the enemy's prison camps—among them, some doctors and corpsmen on whom many lives would depend in the years to come. Others narrowly escaped death or capture.

In the fighting near Java, the seaplane tender *Langley* went down, and her 450 survivors were picked up by American destroyers. A few days later the men were shifted, in predawn darkness and a heavy sea, to the oiler *Pecos* to be returned to Australia. The ship's young medical officer, Lieutenant Joseph L. Yon, found himself with more than a full load of patients. The men of the *Langley* suffered from shock, exposure, and exhaustion; many were burned, and many were fracture cases. Yon was at work on an operating table when the ship's siren warned of a new attack. Japanese planes swept down, bombs rocked the *Pecos*, and the tiles that lined the operating room began to fly. Yon and his chief pharmacist's mate lifted their patient to the floor and continued work on their knees.

> When I heard the machine guns and the anti-aircraft guns begin to rattle, I knew that we had about thirty seconds before we either had another hit or a near-miss. We would give them about ten seconds and then drop down alongside the patient, the chief on one side and I on the other, and wait for the ship to jump. . . . As soon as the ship ceased shuddering, we got onto our knees and began to work on the injured [man] until the next bomb was due.[11]

Hit five times, the *Pecos* began to settle at the bow. Orders came to abandon ship. Crewmen wrestled the wounded up onto the main deck, now awash, where Yon tied the worst cases to kapok mattresses taken from the officers' berths and gave each a drink from the captain's scuttlebutt—his cask of fresh water. Every patient was then assigned to an able-bodied crewman, who went into the sea with him. It was dusk before a ship appeared on the horizon. Somebody fired a flare. Out of the gathering darkness emerged one of the destroyers that had saved the men when the *Langley* went down. The survivors of the oiler's crew were hauled aboard again, the crew shared out their clothes, and Yon became medical officer of the destroyer, which lacked one of its own.

Home to hundreds of extra men, some of whom had lived through two sinkings, the slender ship set out at high speed for Australia, bucking and pitching through a choppy sea. Yon worked over his patients on a table in the officers' wardroom, saw them bedded down, and checked a last time to see that all were sleeping. Then he picked his way through the passageways of the dark, incredibly crowded ship to the main deck, found a place by one of the warm stacks, and curled up in a clutter of sleeping bodies. It was, he said later, "the closest to heaven I had ever been."[12] In time all arrived safe at Australia's western port of Perth.

They were the lucky ones. The sea and the air were already proving to be the decisive elements of the Pacific war. In the Philippines the Americans had lost control of both, and that meant hunger, disease, and ultimate annihilation for the forces still resisting on land. They were a mixed bag of men and women, units and services. As the navy withdrew from the Philippines, some of its doctors and many corpsmen remained behind, either serving with the 4th Marine Regiment or joining up with army units, like one young naval surgeon who began his study of ground warfare by performing an amputation in a ditch during an air raid.[13]

Colonel Cooper set up his new headquarters on the fortress island of Corregidor with the rest of MacArthur's staff, while two rough hospitals took shape on Bataan, Number One at Limay, a hamlet of bamboo houses on stilts, and Number Two in the jungle and bamboo thickets to the south at Cabcaben. Commanding Number One was the former executive officer of Sternberg, Colonel James W. Duckworth. Memorable for his height and massive physique, Duckworth was a long-service regular whose "cool nature . . . never perceptibly ruffled in any crisis" would stand his patients in good stead during the fighting and for years afterward in Japanese prison camps. Commander at Number Two was Colonel James O. Gillespie, another regular medical officer who became the historian of malaria on Bataan.[14]

Jungled and mountainous, the 450-square-mile peninsula was well suited to a defensive battle, but its harsh and tangled landscape prevented speedy evacuation of the wounded, and its lush forests offered little food for the more than 100,000 soldiers and civilians crowded into it. Bataan was plagued by malaria, the mosquitoes that spread the disease multiplying primarily in the foothills, where they bred in the shadow of jungle foliage in cool streams running down from the slopes of the mountains. One of the oldest and most widespread of human afflictions, malaria is caused by microscopic parasites that invade and destroy the red blood cells, in the process causing spasms of chills and fever that rack the sufferer every one, two, or three days. The most dangerous form of the disease, malignant (or cerebral) malaria, can kill its victims; all forms weaken and exhaust.

Even before the war Bataan had defeated efforts by the Commonwealth Government to suppress the disease. The army put its faith in quinine, a drug that did not cure malaria but halted the spasms. Despite its shortcomings, quinine was urgently needed and, almost from the beginning, in short supply. The men and women who fought on Bataan endured both benign and malignant malaria, and some unlucky victims suffered from both at the same time. In January 1942 the prophylactic dosage of 10 grains a day had to be cut in half, and a few months later all effort at prevention was abandoned and the remaining drug saved for those who were sick in hospital. The death rate from malaria was low, but the depletion of strength caused by the seizures weakened both the Japanese attacking Bataan, who could obtain replacements, and the defenders, who could not.[15]

Pervasive disease interacted with wounds and hunger. Men who could ill afford to lose strength contracted both bacillary and amoebic dysentery; lack of vitamins in an increasingly restricted diet affected the mucous lining of the bowels and caused inflammation and diarrhea. The soldier's daily ration was halved in the first week of January, and caloric intake steadily decreased, from about 2,000 a day to 1,500 in February and about 1,000 in March. (Four thousand might better have met the needs of young men in combat.) Quality declined with quantity. Milled rice lacked thiamin (Vitamin B1), and the deficiency caused beriberi with its typical neuritis, swollen limbs, and cardiac damage. Deficiencies of vitamin C produced scurvy, with its symptoms of anemia and spongy gums, while lack of niacin caused pellagra, with its attendant "three D's"—dermatitis, diarrhea, and dementia.

The men suffered from muscle weakness and night blindness— a symptom of vitamin A deficiency—and vitamin deficiencies impaired healing in the wounded. The quartermasters slaughtered all the available water buffalo, and the soldiers ate polo ponies, pack mules, and even cavalry horses. For hospital patients MacArthur ordered full rations, but little could be done about quality even when quantity was sufficient. "When a water buffalo was roasted," a nurse later recalled, "it was not so bad . . . but when it was stewed, Heaven was not too high for the odor."[16]

One boatload of hospital patients, with a few nurses and surgeons led by the Medical Corps's Colonel Percy Carroll, escaped the trap. An old interisland steamer, the *Mactan*, was fitted up as a hospital ship, painted with the markings prescribed by the Geneva accords, and sent south to Australia. Despite their reputation for ruthlessness, the Japanese, alerted to the mission through the good offices of Switzerland, respected the ship (as they did most hospitals during the Philippine campaign). Yet the voyage was no pleasure cruise. The old ship was infested with ants, which worked their way under bandages to feed on the wounds. Beyond the Celebes the ancient engine overheated, and smoke billowed up from below; in the Macassar Straits a storm struck. After stopping at recently bombed Darwin, Australia's northernmost port, Carroll reached Sydney at the end of an unforgettable twenty-seven-day voyage only to have a port commissioner come aboard and pronounce the *Mactan* "entirely unseaworthy."[17]

For the great majority of the men and women remaining on Bataan there was no escape. It was the medics' daily task to treat a growing load of sick and wounded with ever diminishing supplies. Filipino workmen built double- and triple-deck bunks in the hospital wards. Shortages were erratic; enough sulfanilamide was on hand to prevent infection in open wounds, but gas-gangrene antitoxin was not. This lethal infection got its name from the bubbles produced by anaerobic bacteria infecting deep muscle wounds. Gas gangrene forced surgeons (as hospital gangrene had forced their forebears in the Civil War era) to amputate limbs that otherwise could have been saved. The infection consigned to the makeshift morgues young men who in other circumstances might have lived.[18]

By March 1942 front-line forces were scarecrow outfits with malaria rates nearing 80 percent. Since many vehicles were also breaking down and the hospitals were packed, line units increasingly retained their sick. Even battalion aid stations, which normally held no patients at all, were attempting to provide care for hundreds. For the time being, this was all very well; there was little to give the patients at the rear even if they could have been carried there, and along the fighting line the dense jungle canopy hid them from enemy planes. The month was relatively quiet as the Japanese, bloodied in combat and decimated by malaria and dysentery, drew back. But tactical units might have to move at any time. Then what would become of patients immobilized in the forward areas?

The allies, if they had known of it, might have taken some comfort from the sickness that afflicted the Japanese soldiers. Japanese disease rates reflected failings in their supply system and ways of thinking among their leaders that were later to cost them dear. The imperial high command had launched its great push for empire with no realistic attempt to calculate the supply requirements of its forces or the amount of shipping that would be needed to nourish and sustain them. Japanese leaders had opened the campaign in the Philippines with supply allocations tied to a rigid timetable. Although Japan was conquering the Dutch East Indies, center of the world's quinine supply, Japanese troops on Bataan apparently had enough of the drug for only one month—the officially predetermined length of the campaign. After the lapse of two months, only three thousand effectives remained in the attacking army. The surgeon of their 14th Army estimated in February that ten thousand to twelve thousand of his men were sick with malaria, dysentery, and beriberi. A Japanese interpreter later told American prisoners that the ineffective rate in some units of the 14th Army had reached 90 percent, with a substantial death rate, and that Sternberg General Hospital in Manila was packed with sick Japanese soldiers from Bataan.[19]

There may have been other reasons for the enemy's failure to protect the health of their men. In 1941–42 Japan was waging war in the tropics for the first time. Its military experience to date had been mostly in cold regions (Siberia, Manchuria) and temperate ones (China). As yet, perhaps the empire's military leaders simply did not understand how the tropics could disable an army. Much anecdotal evidence from later campaigns suggests that Japanese troops showed poor malaria discipline. And the prevailing ideology of the Imperial Army—with its self-conscious medievalism, its emphasis on blind obedience, and its romantic notions of the nobility of endurance, honor, and death—did not encourage rational thinking about the physical limitations of flesh and blood.

In any case, Japan's soldiers paid the price. At the time, the war was going splendidly for the empire. Its navy controlled the western Pacific, and its merchant fleet faced few dangers from American submarines, whose torpedoes rarely hit their target and still more rarely exploded. Yet even in Japan's moment of triumph, its army proved seriously deficient in the preventive medicine that was to be a key to the successful prosecution of war in the jungle.

Yet the Japanese who fell ill could be replaced by troops fresh from the conquest of Malaya, a campaign that had kept to its timetable and had overwhelmed the British in about two months. Meanwhile the Americans and Filipinos had grown hungrier and sicker. Colonel Cooper estimated that malnutrition, malaria, and intestinal infections had reduced the combat efficiency of Bataan's defenders by more than 75 percent—physical debility that would contribute directly to an appalling mortality in prison camps after the fall.[20] Upon those forces renewed assaults began in April.

As the defenders buckled under the pressure, chaotic evacuation of the wounded began in the jungle darkness. Blacked-out rattletrap buses and trucks inched over the rutted dirt roads, drivers seeking their way by the blue glow of dimmed headlights. Bizarre traffic jams developed amid the dense jungle foliage and on the narrow coastal roads. For a time one convoy of wounded was caught between friendly and enemy fire. Some seven thousand patients reached the rear areas in the first week of April, but little could be done for them. In the hospital at Cabcaben, thousands of bed patients demanded attention, and walking wounded continued to stagger into both hospitals. Viewing the crowd of patients, who could not be moved and now lay in the enemy's direct line of fire, the commander on Bataan, General Edward P. King, decided that "we have no further means of organized resistance." Entering the Japanese lines to surrender, King looked with amazement at the soldiers, "surprised by the alert expressions on their faces and the vigor of their actions. I had grown so accustomed to lack-lustre eyes and lackadaisical movements."[21]

Bataan fell on April 9, 1942. Medical factors had played a complex role in the campaign. Disease had decimated the Japanese even as it deprived many defenders of the physical capacity to fight, forcing them to surrender even though weapons remained in their hands and ammunition in their pockets. Overall, disease had not been a decisive factor, although General MacArthur and his successor, General Jonathan Wainwright, both claimed that it had been. In reality, the outcome of the battle had been decided on the first day of the war by the destruction of the Pacific Fleet and MacArthur's ground-based aircraft. All the rest had been heroism and pain, a matter of delaying the enemy and weakening his forces, until the defenders were overcome by their own weakness and the enemy assault.

Yet the impact of disease on both armies had provided an accurate image of what the war would become on the jungled islands of the Pacific. A third combatant had taken part in the fighting, striking at both sides but ultimately dealing the harshest blows to the army that could not replenish itself. General Disease would as surely be a factor in the Pacific war as General Winter and General Mud in the battles then raging on the plains of Russia. The control of disease would shape the fighting on the jungled islands— never the sole factor in the outcome of the battles, sometimes an insignificant one, but in a few instances a truly critical element in deciding victory or defeat.

There were many epilogues to the tragedy of Bataan as the fortified islands of Manila Bay fell and the American and Filipino forces elsewhere either surrendered or disappeared into the forests and mountains to become guerrillas. In comparison with the miserable life ashore during the last days, the island fortress of Corregidor was almost luxurious. The tadpole-shaped island had no jungles, no local sources of malaria, deep tunnels for protection, and stocks of canned goods for food. Bombs and shells came screaming in, but treatment for the wounded was close at hand. Colonel Cooper divided the island into zones and assigned medical officers and enlisted men to each. Litter-bearers retrieved the wounded from the surface gun emplacements—usually at night—and carried them into the underground complex called Malinta Tunnel.

Here stood the headquarters, the civilian government of the Philippines, a thousand-bed hospital, the main storehouses, and the power plant. The hospital had its own entrance to Malinta, and the wards filled laterals off the main tunnel. An army nurse who had been evacuated from Bataan marveled at the luxury of beds and white enameled tables, electric lights, running water, and flush toilets. Medical treatment for the wounded was relatively sophisticated. Gas gangrene seldom had time to develop, for most casualties reached the surgeon within an hour of wounding, and the opening of the wound to air, debridement, and the use of sulfanilamide halted infection.[22]

Nothing could mask the thunder of the guns, the dust and heat, or the smell of wounds and bodies. Here as on Bataan the hospital wards had to be double- or triple-bunked as the number of casualties increased. The defenders lost heart as time went on, and even optimists began to admit that no help was coming from the United States, which had a two-front war to fight and a shattered Pacific Fleet. A nurse saw the connection between the rising number of wounded and the plummeting morale when she wrote that "the grimy unwashed bodies would come in on their stained stretchers, carried on a wave of silence and spreading fear."[23]

Yet the defenders by and large remained healthy. Their diet was monotonous and small, but the enemy was still a few miles distant, and the nature of the battle confined the defenders and limited their expenditure of energy. To the surprise of some medics, there were few psychiatric cases in the tunnels of Corregidor; combat exhaustion was not yet a factor, and bizarre behavior offered no hope of escape from the besieged island. Rested, fairly well nourished, and lacking any option but to fight on, the defenders offered stout resistance to the end.

On May 5 the Japanese landed on Corregidor, and the death agony began. American soldiers, marines, coast artillerymen, and anti-aircraft gunners fought together as infantry, inflicting and taking heavy losses. The ferocity of the combat gave another foretaste of the merciless war that lay ahead, as litterbearers were gunned down by accident or intent, and many wounded lay helpless in the front lines. On May 6, recognizing a hard reality, General Wainwright surrendered Corregidor. The end had come by enemy assault, not by attrition, and the defenders who had not been wounded passed into captivity in relatively good health.

Their fate in prison and that of the Battling Bastards of Bataan who had preceded them wrote a final and most tragic postscript to the Philippine disaster. The loss of the Philippines marked the last mass surrenders by American forces to the Japanese. Most of the captives had more than three years of imprisonment to endure, often in conditions as extreme and harsh as any faced by the much-abused POWs of World War II.

At one time, in the war of 1904–5, the Japanese Army had provided the West with a model through its humane treatment of Russian captives. Japan's leaders had been different then, Confucian gentlemen who hoped to release their nation from unequal treaties with the West by demonstrating that their nation was civilized according to contemporary European definitions. The generation that followed had brought in a different type of army officer operating in a national context of resentment against the West and increasing ruthlessness toward fellow Asians.[24]

With surrender a court-martial offense for its own soldiers, Japan proved indifferent to the sole sanction that impelled nations to treat captured enemies decently—the threat of retaliation. Japan had declined to ratify the Geneva accords of 1929 on the revealing grounds that it might be obligated to treat prisoners better than its own brutalized soldiers. In fact, systematic physical abuse aimed supposedly at toughening the men characterized Imperial Army training, and many guards passed on the same treatment to the POWs under their power.[25]

In the Philippines the brutality was especially hard to bear, because so many prisoners were in poor physical shape. Many survivors of Bataan entered captivity already suffering from hunger and malaria, only to undergo the 110-mile Death March, which cost hundreds of Americans and five thousand to ten thousand Filipinos their lives. Their destination, Camp O'Donnell, was the first and in some respects the worst of the prisons the POWs would inhabit for more than three years, a half-finished enclosure that epidemic dysentery quickly turned into "a vast sewer, foul and stinking." At Cabanatuan, another large camp on Luzon, prisoners from Corregidor experienced hunger and epidemics of malaria, diphtheria, and dysentery that crammed the camp hospital with more than 2,500 patients and the cemetery with corpses. Under the gaze of helpless medical officers, who lacked everything that was necessary for their care, men with diphtheria lay beside others dying of the disease and heard them gasping for breath; men dulled by hunger ate their rice beside the dead and dying "apparently indifferent to the filth, flies, foul odors and the utter horror of the situation." The dying were dragged to Zero Ward to be laid on what looked like the "floor in a slaughterhouse . . . with bloody liquid stools all over the place."[26]

If such conditions had lasted, few prisoners would have survived the war. But O'Donnell was closed, and late in 1942 the Japanese brought in more food and allowed Red Cross packages into Cabanatuan. Recovery was dramatic; the death rate plunged, and on December 5, 1942, an American medical officer noted a milestone—the day passed without a single death in the camp hospital. Moreover, after the first great wave of deaths, doctors noted that survivors were adapting physically to hunger and stress. Apparently the body could learn to extract whatever nutrients were available; some symptoms of malnutrition began to clear up before the rations were increased. But subsequent cuts in the ration, and the stress and violence that accompanied movement to new camps, apparently upset the fragile balance and caused new losses.[27]

As the war went on, there were many moves in the lives of most prisoners. They were shuffled about in the Philippines and sent by sea to camps in Formosa, Korea, Manchuria, and Japan itself. The lucky ones went early in the war, when the seaways were comparatively safe for Japanese ships. Those who went later faced great peril from American submarines and planes. No voyage was more terrible than that of the *Oryoku Maru* in December 1944. As usual, it sailed without markings to indicate that it held prisoners. Many American medical and dental officers were aboard, as well as other senior officers and a number of chaplains. Conditions were appalling; the prisoners were jammed into stifling holds and denied water; some suffocated, while others "raved and fought in the claustrophobic darkness." Bombed and strafed by American planes, the ship foundered off Subic Bay, and the prisoners were transferred to the *Enoura Maru*, which in turn was bombed and sunk in the harbor of Takao, Formosa. Here more than three hundred dead POWs were interred in a sandspit, while the remainder continued on the *Brazil Maru* to Japan, arriving in bitter cold on January 31, 1945. Of more than 1,600 men who embarked, between five hundred and six hundred apparently survived the trip. Among the dead were about half the army doctors who had served at Sternberg Hospital in Manila and Hospital Number Two on Bataan, and many navy medical personnel from Bilibid prison in Manila.[28]

Conditions in Japan varied from camp to camp. Not all the prisons were vile, and not all the Japanese were cruel. In one camp a large hospital was constructed by a mining corporation for the prisoners' benefit, and some Japanese physicians were both able and concerned. Kindness by civilians was recorded, too, and at least one camp was a relative showplace, with athletic equipment and prisoner theatricals for amusement. The steady increase of starvation in all the camps reflected the fact that Japan was losing the war; its cities were devastated, and prisoners of war simply stood last in line for food in a nation filled with hungry people.[29] When all allowances have been made, however, Imperial Japan's treatment of its prisoners was largely a mixture of indifference and brutality, and the camp conditions ranged downward from spartan to intolerable.

Enlisted men were the worst off, compelled to labor at war production in factories and mines, often under dangerous conditions. Their hunger was extreme; a sailor originally captured on Guam recalled seeing his fellow prisoners eat "beetles, snakes, silkworms, rancid copra, fodder stolen from the horses' feed buckets." For those who were injured or became sick, medical care was usually poor. American doctors had little to work with; they improvised their own equipment, making bone saws from scraps of metal and crude microscopes from field-glass lenses. One surgeon used cocaine as an anesthetic in an operation and, "lacking sutures, sealed off the wound with branding irons."[30]

Yet in many camps care would probably have been better if the prisoners had simply been let alone. They were not. American doctors were subject to interference not only by Japanese doctors but by medical noncoms. At the Shinagawa camp the chief doctor was accused of using prisoners in bizarre experiments and narrowly escaped execution as a war criminal when a postwar court found that he was insane. There were even worse happenings: a Japanese biological warfare establishment in Manchuria, where

Chinese and Russian prisoners were used as human guinea pigs; a number of cases in Japan itself where captive American airmen were drugged and dissected alive for the instruction of medical students and observers, both military and civilian.[31]

The conditions of the prison camps and the stories that soon emerged about them underlined a lasting reality about the Pacific war: that it would be fought with very little mercy.[32] As it progressed, the Japanese discarded the rules that prescribed protection for the wounded and those who cared for them. As a result, the medic would go armed and in as much peril as any soldier of the line; the red cross would be treated as a bullseye, and the wounded would be spared nothing. Americans responded in their own way, shooting down individual Japanese who tried to surrender and waging a strategic bombing campaign that was, even for World War II, uniquely awful. For those whose business was healing, a jungle war against a ruthless foe would present extraordinary challenges, as the battles of 1942–43 quickly made clear.

3

Medics Afloat and Ashore

Before the land forces were through fighting in the Philippines, the fleets were in combat at sea. Until the enemy could be halted there, the Allies had no future in the Pacific. The navy medics, with their long experience afloat and ashore, soon were in action again as fighting spread in the south and central Pacific.

Like other sailors, navy doctors, nurses, and corpsmen spent more time ashore than afloat. Their hospitals, their laboratories, their recruiting, and most of their training activities were carried out on land. Many served with the Marine Corps, doing their most important duty on the beaches and beyond. When the war began, about one-fourth of all navy medical personnel were assigned to twenty-one fixed hospitals, two of which—in the Philippines and on Guam—fell to the Japanese early in the war. Movable hospitals included both hospital ships and mobile base hospitals. The ships were one of the wonders of the war. Everything about them was deliberately contrived to mark them off as noncombat vessels; shining white amid camouflaged vessels, they

51

traveled brilliantly lighted at night, except when in convoy. By international agreement, nothing of a military nature could be brought aboard. For a long time their nurses were the only American women who reached islands where combat was still going on. Hospital ships could either hold and treat patients or, as floating ambulances, carry them to rear-area general hospitals for treatment. As Lieutenant (j.g.) Hilda Combes of the Navy Nurse Corps said, "We were, to tell the truth, the luxury ship of the battle fleet—the soda fountain, the lending library, the movie theater, the church."[1]

By contrast, mobile base hospitals were typically spartan units, made in prefabricated sections for use at remote outposts. Perhaps they were not as mobile as advertised; a future surgeon general of the navy complained that they were portable in the same sense that the Empire State Building was portable—if you cut it into enough pieces, it too could be carried around. In mid-1942 the navy created advanced base units to expand its overseas network. Each base had its own hospital, and—as in the army—the hospitals were generally constructed by the doctors and corpsmen, because the construction battalions (Seabees) that were supposed to build them were taken up with the higher-priority needs of combat. One medical officer reported that construction jobs were assigned on the basis of medical specialties: "The brain surgeon put on the roof, the dental officer installed the ventilators, the psychiatrist put up the side walls, the eye man put in the windows, one surgeon laid the decks, and another surgeon and the skin man put in the floor beams while the obstetrician dug the holes and put in the footings for the foundations."[2]

Despite the hard work, navy medics, like other sailors, generally lived well in comparison with their counterparts in khaki. As one medical officer recalled, he signed up with the navy in his fourth year of medical school because it seemed "a more gentlemanly service . . . cleaner, gentler, no foxholes."[3] The army liked to complain that the navy got the gravy, and there was some truth to the saying. Except on the older submarines—where crowding, heat, and dampness made for very poor living, quite apart from the enemy's depth charges—life aboard ship was almost invariably cleaner than the animal-like existence of men in the field. But good living was not the invariable rule. Some navy doctors underwent isolation and acute boredom in isolated stations. One, later to have a distinguished career in the National Institutes of Health, recalled wartime service that took him from a refueling depot on Iceland to a cargo ship in the Pacific, where, like Thomas Heggen's fictional Mister Roberts, he spent the rest of the war sailing from Tedium to Apathy and back. Doctors who treated crewman in tropical waters saw many of the same ills that bedeviled the soldiers and marines ashore. "Some of the men have their whole body covered with rash and sores," wrote a seaman on the U.S.S. *Montpelier*, serving in the waters off the Solomon Islands. "The rash gives you no rest, it itches and it is impossible to sleep because of the heat."[4]

Interrupting the tedium were times of acute peril. Combat on shipboard created terrible hazards that were unknown ashore, except to tank crews. A ship was home and fortress when whole, but a steel coffin packed with explosives and fuel oil when enemy fire tore its skin. Then it became a hellish place. Lighting systems failed, the dark compartments were shut off from one another, fires burned, and the injured lay in pools of oily water among mangled corpses and fragments of jagged steel. Medics worked in gas masks as the passages filled with poisonous fumes. "This type of warfare tops them all for horror," said a seaman. "There is no safe place to hide, and if you land in the water the huge sharks that are longer than a good-sized room are always close by."[5]

Even in fleets, ships were comparatively self-contained, and no army-style chain of evacuation could exist. Evacuation at sea might mean the transfer of individual wounded by lines from ship to ship, over which patients were passed in bo'sun's chairs or basketlike Stokes litters. Even that had to be delayed until the fighting was over, for vessels maneuvering against the enemy could not pause to offload or receive casualties. At worst, evacuation might mean a mass exodus like that on the *Langley*, when the crew abandoned a doomed ship.

In order to save lives during naval battles, medical personnel quickly learned to build up supplies of the basics—sulfa drugs, morphine syrettes, wound dressings, plasma, and plaster-of-paris for casts—despite the frustrations of requisitioning from far-off depots in the United States. Early in the war, blood plasma was in short supply; a cruiser was lucky to receive a dozen pints, only enough for one or two burn patients, and large ships soon began to set up blood banks aboard. When they prepared for battle, medical officers learned to disperse their supplies over their ship in GI garbage cans, recognizing that any central supply might be inaccessible to those who needed it. But the same bomb or shell that caused casualties might also burn out the lockers where dressings were stored, and so every corpsmen carried forty or fifty with him in case of need. He also carried tourniquets for shutting off the blood flow to an injured limb—just pieces of white line and sticks, for the rubber tubing provided by navy supply became slippery with blood and loosened, allowing some of the wounded to bleed to death.[6]

Medical care in naval combat was not the job of doctors and corpsmen alone. Every officer had to know first aid, for he might have to care for his own wounded in some isolated part of the ship until help arrived. Every crewman might have to be a medic, for "it became apparent that if lives of the men were to be saved during time of battle, they had to be saved by their own shipmates." To accustom enlisted men to the sight of blood, a navy doctor recommended encouraging them to witness surgical operations at every opportunity. They had to learn how to drag a wounded man away from his gun without adding to his injuries; what to do for a fracture without making it worse; how to use a morphine syrette; how to recognize shock and treat it.[7] The ship was medically prepared when all its complement had become apprentice medics, and not before.

In turn, real medical enlisted men sometimes had to be apprentice doctors, especially on smaller ships that sailed without a medical officer aboard. Here the independent duty corpsman formed a one-man divison, reporting directly to the captain. During World War II, the submarine was not so much an undersea ship as it was a surface vessel with the power to attack and hide from attack underwater. But its long voyages into enemy waters and its periods under the waves left its crews as isolated as those of bombers, and for much longer periods. Lengthy tedium was interrupted by episodes of desperate peril. "At 330 feet, fire in the maneuvering room, all power lost," a report of one submarine action read. "Thick toxic smoke filled the maneuvering room and the after-torpedo rooms." Heat was intense; the men stripped to their shorts but still passed out. Mental strain interacted with the physical; under intolerable tension, crewmen sometimes vomited and defecated while enduring depth-charge attacks.[8]

On a submarine, a naval medical officer wrote, the pharmacist's mate "will be the doctor, the dentist, the nurse, and at times, even the chaplain, all rolled into one." On the *Silversides*, three days before Christmas 1942, Pharmacist's Mate T. A. Moore took out an appendix 20 fathoms down. The normally routine operation took four hours; three men held the patient on the wardroom table, while Moore searched for the appendix. Ultimately he found and removed it, although he and others in the group inhaled too much ether and almost passed out. The patient's convalescence was almost as tense as the surgery. An hour after the operation, the *Silversides* "tangled with a destroyer," and the patient began his recovery "to the tune of torpedo firing, two depth charge attacks, two 'crash dives,' and an aerial bombing which knocked him out of his bunk."[9]

In the long run the submarines would destroy not only Japan's warships but the merchant fleet on which its empire depended. Navy fliers would destroy their enemy counterparts and would deal crushing blows to the enemy's surface fleet. Battleships would become the floating artillery for dozens of landings on hostile shores. But the allied counterattack at sea began with a couple of shoestring victories and an invasion that almost failed.

At the Battle of the Coral Sea in May 1942, allied forces fought a Japanese fleet to a tactical draw that proved, in the longer perspective, to be a strategic victory. This was naval warfare in a new style, with fleets based on aircraft carriers exchanging blows without ever coming in sight of one another.

Part of the price that Americans paid was the loss of the *Lexington*, bombed, torpedoed, and ultimately sent to the bottom. As the carrier burned, the order to abandon ship was given, and destroyers moved in to pick up the crew. Uninjured men slid 60 feet

down lines from the towering flight deck; others dived into the
sea, to be retrieved and sometimes treated for injuries caused by
landing on floating debris. Wounded were taken off by line or by
small boats. The destroyers, loaded to bursting, moved away before a climactic explosion destroyed the *Lexington*. Beset by submarine alerts, they transferred most of their patients to larger
ships by small boats after dark. All care had to be given on warships. On one cruiser the medical officer sorted the incoming
wounded and segregated cases by type and severity: burns together, men needing operations, men in shock. The dental office became the ship's morgue. Only the most serious cases went to the
sick bay; many wounded lay in cots on the weather deck under
the sky. Corpsmen gave plasma, intravenous saline, and glucose,
while the junior medical officer supervised blood-typing and
transfusions of whole blood drawn from the ship's crew. As usual
in the early days of the war, two-thirds of the patients were
burned more or less severely, for men had not yet learned the
value of going into combat fully clothed against the flash of exploding ordnance. After the wounded had spent five days aboard,
a hospital ship arrived to take off all who still required treatment,
and the cruiser that had served as clearing station and field hospital returned to its usual duties.[10]

The critical role of the carriers meant a new role for naval aviation medicine. The specialty had developed late, as the carrier itself had. Carrying airplanes around on an odd-looking, flat-
topped ship had long seemed a peculiar idea to battleship
admirals, and the navy, as a small and clannish service, could be
even more resistant to change than the army. In 1938 the navy's
division of aviation medicine had exactly one medical officer and
one clerk, and the navy as a whole had forty-eight flight surgeons,
whose main duty was giving physical examinations to the three
thousand men then serving in various aviation units. For decades
the navy had no school for its flight surgeons—the army trained
them—and did no research in the field.

Then Pearl Harbor forced the navy to center its planning not
on the sunken battleship fleet, but on the carriers that were still
afloat. At sea victory through airpower turned out to be much
more than a slogan. Soon many naval medical officers were flying

regularly, and some took flight training and became naval aviators. They learned their new trade at first hand, won the respect of the aircrews, and joined the staffs of aviation fleet commands. At the end of 1939, a school for flight surgeons had opened at the Pensacola Naval Air Station; after the war began, research facilities were added, and the establishment grew into the School of Aviation Medicine and Research. Naval air medicine concentrated mainly on the Pacific theaters, on the special stresses endured by carrier pilots, and on the problems of divebombing that led navy researchers to develop a pressure suit to prevent blackouts. The importance of air evacuation, established in the first year of combat, continued to grow and led to the establishment in 1944 of the navy's school for flight nurses at the Naval Air Station in Alameda, California. Navy aviation burgeoned, and aviation medicine grew with it, ultimately staffing an aircraft carrier fleet that numbered more than a hundred ships, plus all the Marine Corps air units. It grew to include 1,200 medical officers, suffered 2.5 times the combat death rate of the Navy Medical Corps as whole, and became essential to fighting the war in the Pacific.[11]

Future glories, however, were not yet foreseeable in June 1942, when a major Japanese fleet was detected, heading for Midway Island at the north end of the Hawaiian chain. An American force moved to intercept it, and one of the decisive naval battles of history followed, fought by land-based and carrier-based aircraft. The Japanese were beaten, but again the Americans paid a price. With the carrier *Yorktown* on fire, the scenes of the *Lexington's* sinking were repeated. Again stretcher cases were lowered from the flight deck, while small boats from destroyers and cruisers plied the waters, recovering sailors and aviators who had parachuted or ditched their craft after failing to land on the burning flight deck. However, medical officers tending the wounded noted at once that they had many fewer burns to treat than in the Coral Sea a month earlier. Knowing the effect of bomb flashes (the *Yorktown* had fought in the Coral Sea) men had worn full clothing, tying the ends of their trousers, wearing gloves, and keeping the hoods of their jumpers over their heads. As before, the wounded were sorted and bedded down; some ships held three times their complement, "packed with human bodies in all states of dishevelment and fatigue, but hungry nevertheless." Cooks performed mightily; crewman gave up their bunks to survivors of the *Yorktown* and slept topside in the warm tropic nights; men who had come "aboard with nothing on but a coat of oil" received new issue from the supply officers and the crews.[12]

Lose, draw and win, navy medical personnel had undergone catastrophe and triumph within the first six months of the Pacific fighting. Doctors and corpsmen had learned crucial lessons, had saved many lives, and had changed their thinking from the habits of peacetime to the exigencies of war. Yet navy medics were soon to find the greatest number of their patients ashore. The outcome of the battles in the Coral Sea and off Midway gave the marines their opportunity to take vengeance on the Japanese by striking back at Guadalcanal.

As the enemy began to move south again, aiming at Australia and the shipping lanes, the navy-run South Pacific Area command launched the first American counterstroke. In the Solomon Islands, the U.S. Marines formed the cutting edge of the attack, and navy doctors and corpsmen followed them ashore.

The navy traditionally provided medical care for the marines; dispensaries and naval hospitals treated them in camp, and field hospitals and evacuation hospitals followed them to war. Medical officers and corpsmen served in the fighting units of the Fleet Marine Force, the corps's striking force, and the medical system kept pace as the organization of the Fleet Marines grew from brigade to divisional units. Medical field service schools retrained hospital corpsmen as field medics, and indoctrination courses acquainted newly called up naval reservists with their duties as marines. A medical battalion supported each marine division, and each marine regiment and battalion had a medical section. Once ashore, the marines, functioning in their roles as light infantry and shock troops, endured all the discomforts and miseries of ground combat. They suffered with the weather, slept on the ground, were harassed by mosquitoes and flies, and caught whatever diseases the local vectors carried. Nowhere in the war were conditions much worse than on the island chain that was the marines' first objective.

"Guadalcanal," an official history remarks, "was not a pic- turesque South Pacific island paradise." Hot and wet, its coastal lowlands and mountain valleys covered with coconut plantations or tangled jungle, it was loathed by all who fought there. Into "that fucking island" went young Americans in a patched-together campaign whose main hope of success lay in its sheer improbabili- ty.[13] Japanese hard at work on an airstrip scattered before the un- expected attack, leaving behind cooked but uneaten meals and hot but undrunk tea. Clothing was left scattered as if by a storm as owners hastily chose the items they would need to live in the jun- gle and fled. Though snipers' bullets whined out of the thickets, the Americans found themselves in possession of an airstrip on which their lives would soon depend. Around the renamed Hen- derson Field they set up a perimeter they would defend for the early months of a long and difficult campaign.

One of the first things they noticed was the heat. A few miles' march left men "staggering, gasping from sheer airlessness, and al- most senseless from exhaustion." On the grassy, waterless hilltops thirst assailed them, despite the tropical rains and the pervasive wet of the lowlands. Hunger and sickness followed. Confusion and inadequacy plagued the supply system; some marines arrived hungry at Guadalcanal because their transport had run out of all food except soup. They might not have had enough food to fight on, except that large supplies of enemy rice fell into their hands. "Captured enemy supplies," the 1st Marine Division surgeon re- called, "were the difference between a starvation diet and one well above that point" during the early phases of the battle.[14]

Other shortages abounded. Too few salt tablets were on hand for men who sweated continuously in the smothering heat. Short of sulfanilamide, the marines had bought 60 pounds from a New Zealand drug company with which to fight the battle. Inept load- ing of the ships compounded the problem. Some reserve medical supplies were put at the bottom of the ships' holds and remained inaccessible; some were never unloaded. Refrigerators never got ashore, and as a result biologicals spoiled in the heat. But the Japanese had abandoned medical supplies as well as food, and the marines gratefully used whatever they found.[15]

Unfortunately, they failed to take much care of themselves. In the first months malaria control was farcical. Amazingly, "insect repellents were not used and were not available." No specialized navy antimalaria units existed as yet, and precautions as basic as oiling standing water were taken, if at all, by individual officers on their own initiative. Mosquito nets had been issued to the troops, but most had contrived to lose them during the voyage. The man on patrol hated such gear, for he had "neither the time nor the strength to bother about mosquito bars and head nets and gloves." He was concerned with killing and being killed, and so, a fatalistic Marine Corps history said, "perforce he caught malaria, and in many cases became as surely a casualty as though he had been wounded."[16]

Soon the marines faced the possibility of being cut off as well. After their initial surprise, the Japanese recovered their spirit and began spasmodic efforts to drive the Americans off Guadalcanal. Day after day the "spine-tingling, hushed murmur of distant planes" announced a new bombardment to the men ashore, while enemy planes and ships battered the fleet at sea. Then, after a crushing defeat off nearby Savo Island, the American navy sailed away. For a time the marines were truly alone on their wretched spot of real estate in the vast Pacific, assailed by the enemy and at the mercy of the environment.[17]

Meals came twice a day, messes of rice and canned and dehydrated foods. Potable water ran short, because too many men were crowded into a perimeter that lacked large streams. Water drawn from the little Lunga River had to be supplemented with wells, springs, and rainwater caught as it ran off roofs. As they dug in, worked on the airstrip, and patrolled the jungle, all in exhausting heat, the troops' physical condition steadily deteriorated. Jungle wet and fungus infections laid siege to the infantryman's prime movers, his feet; in a single battalion during August, 159 men were put out of commission by foot ailments.[18]

Care for the sick and wounded was provided by a division field hospital, two smaller hospitals under tents, a medical battalion with its aid stations, and three hospital corpsmen to each line company. Medical personnel shared the danger to the fullest. Even within the marine perimeter nobody was safe, for the area was a mere patch on the island, and the service troops camped close to the airfield, the bullseye for enemy bombardiers and gunners. But the medics did not stay inside the perimeter. A corpsman went out with every patrol, and a medical officer accompanied any action that involved more than two companies. Forward aid stations were scratch affairs; the journalist and novelist John Hersey described one as merely a jumble of equipment and supplies under a lean-to of four upended stretchers, covered with a poncho. Marine bandsmen, playing a role that dated back centuries, became combat medics in battle and went on patrol and into firefights carrying first-aid supplies, stretchers, and rifles into "the places where the enemy is doing our side most hurt, in order to rescue the wounded."[19]

The evacuation system was elementary. Casualties were carried or walked to the rear, "young fellows with bandages wrapped scarflike around their necks or with arms in slings, or with shirts off and a huge red and white patch on the chest." Hersey saw a party of them, most with cigarettes dangling from their lips and eyes "varnished over with pain."[20] At the aid stations they were loaded into the first available vehicle—jeep, ammunition truck, or prime mover—and taken to ambulance points or directly to the hospital. One advantage of the small perimeter was that hospitals were close enough to food and ammunition dumps for supply vehicles returning from the front to drop off casualties on the way. Normally a regimental collecting station would have stood between the aid station and the field hospital to gather, sort, and forward the wounded. On Guadalcanal the short distances made the collecting station unnecessary, releasing its personnel for stretcherbearing. That was important, because in the heat the usual four-man bearer squad was not big enough to carry a wounded man very far. Short distances and extra manpower meant that the average interval between wounding and treatment was only one to two hours, and that, in turn, was the best guarantee against infection or death by internal bleeding or shock.[21]

A feature of military medical administration is the evacuation policy. Doctors estimate their patients' time of recovery, and any who seem likely to spend more than a specified time in the hospital are sent to the rear. The length of the evacuation policy indicates the state of development in the local medical system. Com-

manders prefer to hold onto as many patients as they as can, because a man once lost to the chain of evacuation may never return—and his replacement may never arrive. For most of the
fighting on Guadalcanal, the evacuation policy was only ten days
to two weeks, meaning that almost any serious case had to be
taken away by sea or air. Evacuating the wounded was immensely
eased by the return of the fleet, after a more combative admiral,
William Halsey, took command of the South Pacific Area. Chances
improved further with the growth of air supply. Braving enemy
fire, transport planes began to fly into the island early in September, and many left with a load of eighteen patients on stretchers or
thirty-six sitting up. The pilots were lucky as well as courageous.
By December, almost 2,900 patients had been taken off Guadalcanal by air—almost three times as many as by sea—without a single lost life. Marine Corps Transport Squadrons were joined in the
work by planes of the navy and the Army Air Forces; an air force
flight nurse apparently was the first American woman to set foot
on the island during the war.

Considering the 500 miles that separated Guadalcanal from its
rear bases, this was an impressive record. The flights saved lives
not only by their speed but because a wounded man unavoidably
endured much rough handling when he had to be moved from an
ambulance to a small boat and from the boat to a ship. On a plane
he was loaded only once, and the ride was smooth and easy. Both
medics and patients owed much to the pilots; many a wounded or
desperately ill man owed them his life.

Rightly or wrongly, many of the men who stayed on Guadalcanal envied the wounded who escaped, for the enemy and the
jungle were unrelenting. Japanese efforts to drive Americans out
began in late August. Savage and uncoordinated, their piecemeal
attacks in the end assured their defeat. But there was no sense of
inevitability on the Tenaru River, where the first attack hit; the
Japanese penetrated the marine lines, only to be stopped by reinforcements and butchered by a counterattack. A second assault by
stronger forces in late September was narrowly turned back.[22] Disease proved an abler enemy. The first signs of a malaria epidemic
appeared during the opening weeks, and nobody was prepared to
deal with it. Some medical officers were as inexperienced in fight-

ing tropical diseases as the men, and many unit commanders viewed preventive medicine as a diversion from the war rather than a precondition for winning it. Paradoxically, medical officers had the responsibility for preventing disease but lacked the power to order the necessary countermeasures; commanders had the power, but lacked the responsibility. The results were tragic.

Malaria broke out in the third week of August, and its progress in the 1st Marine Division was classic: 900 cases that month, 1,724 the next, 2,630 in October. By mid-December the division had counted more than 8,500 hospital admissions for malaria alone. Ninety percent of its men caught the disease, and many had multiple attacks. When army units arrived to stand beside the marines, they shared the same disease rates. An army medical officer remarked that eight of every nine men in his hospital were there to be treated for disease, not wounds.[23] In September a campaign of prevention began, using a synthetic drug invented by a German researcher before the war and sold under the name Atabrine. At once medical officers noted that "it was impossible to get cooperation from officers and men . . . even under bivouac conditions," to say nothing of patrol.

Complaints against the yellow pills were legion. Atabrine was bitter, like "yellow gall," and appeared to impart its own sickly hue to the skin. Worse, it was falsely rumored to make men impotent. In fact, it sometimes caused headaches, nausea, and vomiting, and in a few cases it produced a temporary psychosis. A man would suddenly declare that he was Jesus, became agitated and violent—or sometimes stuporous and catatonic—and when the drug was withdrawn would return quickly to normal.[24] Yet Atabrine was effective, if only the men could be made to take it. A great part of the problem was simply that the proper dosage had not yet been worked out; the old malaria remedy of quinine was actually more toxic, but after more than a century of use it was better understood. In an effort to ensure that Atabrine tablets went where they were supposed to go, medics or NCOs from the combat units stood at the head of mess lines to watch marines and soldiers take their tablets, and even looked into their mouths.[25]

Despite increasingly rigorous health discipline, the combination of jungle warfare, short supplies, unwilling men, and irresponsible commanders formed a massive obstacle to controlling disease. Between November 1942 and February 1943, army units on Guadalcanal counted malaria hospital admissions equivalent to 420 per thousand men per year—that is, if the rate had continued for a year, four of every ten soldiers would have been hospitalized. Doctors refused to excuse men with temperatures lower than 104° from front-line duty or patrols. Among the marines, a plan to hospitalize malaria cases for ten days had to be abandoned for lack of beds; many of the sick got treatment only while their illness was acute, and then were sent back to their units. Of the estimated 100,000 cases of malaria that Americans suffered in the South Pacific Area, probably 60,000 were contracted on Guadalcanal.[26]

Fortunately, the death rate was low. But fighters can be knocked out of service without dying. Initial attacks and frequent relapses depleted the ranks; a few sufferers had twenty or more bouts with the disease. Malaria caused devastating ineffectiveness that was all the worse because the disease did its damage among relatively small forces fighting in an extreme forward location and supported tenuously by long supply lines that ran through submarine-infested waters.

Toward the end of November the navy set up base malaria control units—the first seen on Guadalcanal. A month later the army's American Division launched an all-out campaign of education for officers and men and established a field hospital devoted to malaria cases alone. The division made the administration of Atabrine in proper doses and at the proper times a command responsibility. But the epidemic was deeply rooted by that time and did not reach its peak until February 1943, when the battle was over. By then the rate was about 4,000 per 1,000 troops per year—on average, every man would have four attacks in the course of a year.[27]

Other afflictions added to the suffering of the troops. Skin diseases caused much misery. Everyone was dirty and wet, and fungus infections picked the most sensitive areas to make raw, invading the armpits and getting between the toes, into the groin and between the buttocks. Dengue broke out, another mosquito-borne disease characterized by high fever and an all-over soreness that gave it the common name of breakbone fever. Especially in the frantic first weeks, the perimeter was filthy, with open latrines left by the Japanese and newer ones dug in haste by the Americans. As a result, flies multiplied and gastroenteritis (the familiar traveler's disease of tropical lands) helped to fill hospital beds. Though many cases were light, symptoms were sometimes disabling, with uncontrollable diarrhea and "dizzying fever and nausea."[28]

The end result of all these afflictions was a force riddled with illness, including many of the men who were supposedly well. Marine Major General Alexander A. Vandegrift, the American commander, estimated that half of his men were "in no condition to undertake protracted operations." Medical sources were more cautious, estimating that when the crisis of the campaign occurred, 20 to 25 percent of the Americans—marines, soldiers, airmen of various services, and Seabees—were out of commission from disease at any one time. When the 1st Marine Division left the island in December, navy doctors made a careful study of one regiment to see what the months of duty on Guadalcanal had done, concluding that one man out of three was unfit for "any duty that might involve combat."[29]

Such losses conceded to the enemy what might have been a decisive advantage. Fortunately for the Americans, their own sufferings were not the whole story of Guadalcanal. For critical months they were on the defensive and could, relatively speaking, conserve their energy. From the beginning they had food, even if rations were short and often unpalatable. They had medical supplies, many provided by the enemy. From forty-eight hours after the first landing, they had hospitals, sheltered either in wooden buildings left by the Japanese or under canvas. Despite every misery, things could be worse—as the Japanese discovered. On Guadalcanal the enemy's poor performance in supplying and maintaining its forces became a decisive element in its ultimate defeat.

The Japanese who fled from the airstrip on Lunga Point on August 7, 1942, were probably the best-supplied forces the enemy ever maintained on Guadalcanal. Their supply line was long and subject to air attack, and a recent comprehensive history of the campaign terms the Imperial Navy "almost criminally negligent in relentlessly forwarding troops without a commensurate increase in supplies." The result was a story of a declining diet and worsening health at the very time when Americans were tardily making up for their initial failures. As food became scarce, the Japanese ate lizards, bamboo sprouts, taro, and coconuts to fill their bellies. The effect of the short food was worse than it might have been because the basic rice-based Japanese army ration was poor in thiamin (vitamin B1). Japanese soldiers were known to show the symptoms of beriberi even in garrison, and any breakdown in supply during combat produced the disease, with its early symptoms of swollen legs and burning feet and its later effects of general debility and damaged hearts. Not surprisingly, the men called Guadalcanal "Starvation Island."

In contrast to the Americans, whose preventive medicine was poor at the beginning but radically improved at the end, the Japanese forces had no effective system of suppressive medication to control malaria; their quinine supplies, as on Bataan, were inadequate and soon depleted. They had no effective mosquito repellents and few mosquito nets. They had left their horses at Rabaul and lacked motor transport, throwing upon sick men the exhausting task of moving heavy loads through the hot, moist jungle on their backs. Wounded and sick Japanese probably suffered a very high death rate for lack of medicines and a scratch evacuation system that depended largely on small boats operating after dark. The Japanese seem to have had no proper field hospital; the sick were kept in the line or, if helpless, were laid on mats under temporary shelters of palm thatch and given such medicines as might be available. A 1944 study of the Guadalcanal records by American medical intelligence officers concluded: "Miserable, without shelter, soaked with rain, underfed, and with little hope of evacuation, the Japanese died in large numbers."[30]

The crisis of the campaign ashore came in October. Defeated in earlier fighting, the Japanese systematically increased their forces to about 15,000 men, of whom probably a third were fresh troops, newly arrived. After some fumbling, they attempted a coordinated offensive, moving toward the lightly held left of the American line through deep jungle and over harsh mountain ridges. The march was wearing, and the soldiers carried their supplies and ammunition while living on "half rations of raw rice."

Despite the fresh troops, most of the men had already been in the Solomons long enough to develop malaria, and "everyone who had been on the island any length of time was debilitated." Infantry units mustered one-fifth to one-third of their authorized complements; one of their commanders later protested that throughout the campaign he "had been so weakened by malaria that he had found it difficult to make decisions."[31]

In this condition the Japanese opened an attack with an advantage of nine to one in numbers at the point of contact. Exhausted by their epic march and confused by the tangled web of jungle in which they struggled, they faced resolute defenders in prepared positions, who were supported by accurate and heavy artillery fire. Defeat condemned the Japanese to another retreat, under conditions even worse than before. A junior officer noted, "I must take a rest every two meters. It is quite disheartening to have only one tiny teaspoon of salt per day and a palmful of porridge."[32] Their situation pretty well summed up the Guadalcanal equation: the determination and martial skill of both sides; the advantages of the defense; the influence of the jungle; and the differential effects of hunger and disease.

While the struggle went on ashore, the American Navy gradually took control of the Solomon waters, though not without heavy losses. When the new carrier *Wasp* was torpedoed, 20 percent of the ship's complement were wounded and 10 percent were declared missing in action. Ninety-nine percent of the injuries were burns, and most of the rest were fractures of the long bones, lacerations, and shrapnel wounds.

When her sister ship the *Hornet* went down in the Battle of the Santa Cruz Islands, five dressing stations were knocked out in the first enemy attack. One, outside the captain's cabin, was hit by a bomb; the second had to be abandoned after a burning plane crashed into the side of the ship; the third, in the Sick Bay on third deck aft, lost its lights when a bomb and a torpedo exploded nearby. The fourth was destroyed by a bomb exploding in the next compartment amidships, killing the chief medical officer; the fifth was demolished when a bomb that had penetrated the deck below it blew up. Wounded were concentrated on the fantail on mattresses salvaged from the crews' quarters, and were transferred (probably tied into Stokes litters) by lines to destroyers, which passed them in turn to the hospital ship *Solace*. Here only 40 percent of the casualties were burn victims, an equal proportion suffered shrapnel wounds, 10 percent were fracture cases, and the rest a miscellany of injuries.[33]

In October, the navy startled the Japanese by beating them after dark—a time they considered their own—in a battle off Cape Esperance, at the north end of Guadalcanal. The two fleets sought each other in the ghostly illumination of a night that was moonless but starry, with a flicker of heat lightning, a soft breeze, and gentle swells that "crinkled the sea."[34] American sailors sweltered in blacked-out compartments under dogged-down hatches, while radar operators searched for the enemy. Shortly before midnight Japanese ships were detected, approaching in column. It was a textbook situation, and for twenty minutes or so the Americans savaged their foes. But at ten minutes after midnight Japanese gunners found a target.

The cruiser *Boise*, illuminated by flashes from her own guns, was hit fore and aft. Lookouts spotted two pale torpedo wakes, and the *Boise* swung to starboard, passing between them. Then two more 8-inch shells hit forward, and a third punctured the hull. The main magazine exploded with a blast of superheated gas that seared almost a hundred men to death. Seawater, pouring in through a truck-sized hole in the bow, doused the fire and probably saved the ship. The surgeon, Commander Edward C. Kenney, had trained the crew in first aid and had dispersed his medical supplies, precautions that now became critical to saving many lives. Already sealed into compartments to fight, the crew had to shore the watertight doors to withstand the furious pounding of the sea. The sickbay was out of commission, 2 feet of oily water slapping at the bulkheads. The captain's cabin, meant to serve for a topside dressing station during battle, had been wrecked. Corpsmen accompanied repair parties into the damaged areas, carrying the wounded out with great difficulty through dark spaces littered with empty shell cases. Sixty-seven bodies were recovered. Some were unmarked—killed by the blast impact transmitted through the ventilating system. Forty more floated out of reach in the blackness of the flooded magazines, whether dead of blast, fire, or drowning, none could tell.

In a makeshift dressing station aft, Kenney spent an hour examining the wounded. All in all, their condition was a tribute to their shipmates; battle dressings had been snugly applied and the corpsmen were able to release tourniquets without starting hemorrhages. Under Kenney's eye they treated burns with gentian violet, a dye used as a mild antiseptic, and covered them with vaseline gauze strips. The medical officer cautiously debrided the worst wounds, well aware that he and his patients might have to abandon ship at any minute. The bad fracture cases could not be tied down in traction, and splints and casts had to be movable through narrow corridors. The poisonous gases of the explosion continued to claim lives. One seaman, apparently well one day, appeared the next cyanotic—literally blue in the face—and gasping for breath. He died soon after of pulmonary edema, despite every effort to save him.

By then the *Boise*'s own wounds had been roughly patched, and she was plowing back through the seas toward the protected harbor at Noumea in New Caledonia. Living together in the confines of a ship always had familial overtones; sometimes the closeness made for intense irritation, but it also produced a deep bonding that paid off in crises. Captain Edward J. Moran, weary from days of combat and struggles to save his ship, found time for hourly inquiries about the progress of the patients. Shipmates visited the injured, and any call for blood of any type was answered within minutes by more donors than Kenney could use. The mutual support had nothing to do with science, but it was an effective part of naval medicine.[35]

———————

As command of the Americans ashore on Guadalcanal passed to the army, the retreating Japanese endured a sort of Bataan in reverse as they fought and retreated along the coasts and amid the steep jungled mountains and matted ravines of the island's interior. The campaign was not a perfect mirror image, for the Japanese bases were comparatively close, and many of their men survived to fight another day. Yet in many respects the similarity was striking.

Japanese preventive medicine, poor at the climax of the campaign, was all but impossible by the end. Virtually every Japanese soldier had malaria, and captured diaries told of a monotonous existence of suffering and gradually escalating deaths from incoming shells, starvation, and "the usual sickness," as one officer called it. "Dec. 26th," reads one such document:

> Asabo Kasuo also died of the illness. Malaria fever affected his mind and he acted peculiarly. This death increased the large number of those killed in action and from disease to 18 men [in one platoon]. This makes approximately the total of casualties we received in occupation of Hong Kong and Java.[36]

Growing American air and seapower made resupply—for a time, even by destroyer and submarine—almost impossible for the Japanese. The same diary recorded that "even in the face of the enemy, the men's minds were entirely occupied with the thought of eating." Richard Frank's history of the Guadalcanal campaign reports one Japanese lieutenant's rule of thumb for determining life expectancy among his men:

> Those who can stand—30 days.
> Those who can sit up—3 weeks.
> Those who cannot sit up—1 week.
> Those who urinate lying down—3 days.
> Those who have stopped speaking—2 days
> Those who have stopped blinking—tomorrow[37]

The Japanese were probably responsible for some of the malaria that afflicted the American troops; as the Japanese retreated, mosquitoes that had been biting them remained to feast on their enemies. The few prisoners taken by the Americans were riddled with not only malaria but nutritional disease, especially beriberi.

Between 10,000 and 11,000 Japanese soldiers were ultimately evacuated from their last stand on Cape Esperance by destroyers that made the run from Bougainville at night, saving many lives. But the evacuation could not undo the attrition of the battle. The reports that reached American medical intelligence of their condition on arrival at a Japanese base were grim: "Ragged, emaciated, dirty, covered with skin infections, and open sores, without arms, exhausted and haggard, hundreds shivering with malaria or prostrated by dysentery, wounds festering, demoralized and shaken, ridden by war-neurosis."[38] The Japanese themselves recorded that almost all the troops evacuated from Guadalcanal were sick, and that 3,500 men had to be hospitalized and 4,000 more treated for lesser illnesses; that all the evacuees were grossly undernourished, shook with fever, suffered uncontrolled diarrhea, and had been so long without food that they could digest only porridge.[39]

From the vantage point of history, it now seems clear that adequate food supplies were *never* available to the Japanese soldier on Guadalcanal.[40] The consequences of disease and hunger showed in the statistics, slippery and disputable as those were. Americans estimated that some 44,000 Japanese were dispatched to Guadalcanal, of whom 4,300 were lost at sea. Only about 1,000 were made prisoners. Army headquarters in the South Pacific Area reported that some 24,000 to 28,000 Japanese died on Guadalcanal, of whom at least 9,000, or roughly 30–40 percent, perished of disease. Even that figure may be too low. In 1944 American medical intelligence analysts estimated that two Japanese died of disease for every one who died of wounds. As for the Japanese's own estimates, a paper prepared for the Imperial General Staff reported that only 33,600 of their men reached Guadalcanal—a figure a quarter lower than the official American estimate. Of those, 65 percent died—a much higher proportion than the Americans supposed. Of the 19,200 dead, only 8,500 were "killed in actual combat," the majority perishing by malnutrition, malaria, diarrhea, and beriberi.[41] Such a proportion was not impossible; Americans during the Civil War took a similar ratio of casualties from disease while fighting among their own people in a temperate climate.

The impact of disease upon an undernourished army devoid of adequate preventive medicine, supplies, and care underlined the achievements of the Americans in a wearing and desperate campaign. They had not only outfought their enemies but outsupplied them; they had salvaged their wounded and begun to deal with the jungle environment and the appalling sick rates that it produced. *Begun*, however, was the operative word. The armed forces in the Pacific had embarked on their education in the meaning of jungle warfare. In no sense were Americans, despite their victory, graduates of that harsh school, as the battles that accompanied and followed Guadalcanal demonstrated all too clearly.[42]

4

The Green Hells

On battlefields stretching from the Solomons to Burma, the medical problems of jungle warfare continued to mount. For a time after General MacArthur reached Australia, it seemed that the next battle might be fought there, perhaps in the island continent's tropical north. But after the Battle of the Coral Sea, the eyes of allied commanders turned instead to the strange land that lay beyond the warm waters of the Torres Strait.

As a battlefield, New Guinea was unique—a huge, primitive island of sometimes stunning beauty, with cloud-capped mountains, tangled jungles, painted headhunters, glorious birdlife, and abominable diseases. It seemed to belong to a younger earth where life was more fecund, its forms more preposterous and splendid. But those who fought there found intolerable labor and death in an endless variety of forms. Men shivered on the towering mountains of the Owen Stanley Range and sweated everywhere else. Fungal infections quickly entered any break in the skin, intestinal ills were pervasive, and malaria was almost universal. Scrub typhus could kill, while lesser diseases made patients appreciate death.

Port Moresby, on the south coast, was a hot, drowsy colonial town—"a few houses, hotels, warehouses and docks squatting on a hill that rises from a curving harbor."[1] In August 1942, a three-thousand-man Japanese force of crack troops was ordered to capture it and began to climb the tangled slopes of the cloud-swathed Owen Stanleys. They carried very little food, expecting to live off the countryside, but the mountains had few native villages to plunder, and the jungle offered no sustenance. Climbing up and down almost vertical slopes in incessant rain, crossing thundering mountain torrents, and hacking through tangled jungle brought the soldiers close to exhaustion. Equal or greater labors befell the Australians who struggled against them, fighting and falling back "through a fetid forest grotesque with moss and glowing phosphorescent fungi." The walking wounded stumbled or crawled before them; stretcher cases were carried by teams of native bearers. There were reports of a man wounded in the spine "walking crabwise" in the retreat, with a friend who helped push him up the slopes, and of a one-legged man who "crawled and hopped vigorously along the track," hoping to escape the enemy.[2]

Facing stiff resistance, the Japanese on orders from Tokyo abandoned their epic march when they stood less than 40 miles from Port Moresby. The return was even worse than the advance. The men ate grass and collapsed from hunger. The Australian units were also devastated. Bronzed veterans of the Middle Eastern fighting emerged from the mountains waxen, bony, and caked with mud. Of more than two thousand casualties suffered in the retreat, 84 percent had fallen victims to the local diseases, especially dysentery. An American advance party trying to flank the Japanese to the east fared as badly, struggling up misty Ghost Mountain under a five-day cloudburst, suffering violent attacks of dysentery and emerging at the village of Jauré exhausted and fever-ridden.[3]

With the enemy diverted by the fighting on Guadalcanal, MacArthur's multinational Southwest Pacific Area command began feeding reinforcements into Port Moresby. By autumn, the troops were turning it into a frontier boomtown. They put up latrines along the coast and dumped garbage into open pits. Soon a plague of flies created an epidemic of diarrhea. Engineer bulldozers, tearing roads and airfields out of the bush, let in sunlight and gouged myriad ruts into the soil, which filled with rainwater. As it happened, the local anophelines—the mosquitoes that carry malaria—bred most rapidly in shallow puddles and in sunlight. There were as yet no malaria control units, and the disease spread rapidly through the army.

But more than local problems endangered the health of the fighting men. Almost everything was against them. The campaign was a shoestring operation. The United States had crushing responsibilities around the world, and national policy was to defeat Germany first. Shipping was in short supply, like all the matériel of war, and medical supplies often lost the competition for space in favor of ammunition and rations. The Australian bases from which the campaign was launched had only begun to assemble forces. There were too few medical units and almost no coherent preventive medicine, and the buildup accompanied the battle instead of preceding it. The haste and improvisation that had marked Guadalcanal were just as evident in New Guinea, and had the same effects.

The Japanese suffered too. As they staged a fighting withdrawal to the north coast, the Australians pressed after them through the mountains, establishing airfields as they went. Planes began to fly in troops and carry the wounded back to Moresby. Linking up, Australian and American forces advanced toward the Japanese positions around Buna Village, Buna Station, Gona, and Sanananda Point, on the shore of the Solomon Sea. Here the Japanese dug in, camouflaging their bunkers of reinforced coconut logs so expertly that many an allied soldier died without seeing the position from which he was slain. Fresh Japanese troops landed in mid-November with supplies, but the coming of allied warplanes brought a new season of want. Virtually all Japanese soldiers had malaria, and hunger pressed them hard. Enemy troops got one-quarter to one-third rations if they were lucky, and "units stationed in the fringe areas . . . faced starvation."[4]

Japanese destroyers, landing barges and submarines attempted to resupply their men, but all the ships were subject to attack, and on return voyages the few wounded who could be extracted from the jungle received no medication and no shelter from the sun and rain. As each side hammered at the other's tenuous supply line, conditions became abominable for both alike, but on the whole worse for the Japanese, who ate coconuts, grass, and leaves. Some apparently resorted to cannibalism, eating the corpses of their enemies. Combat fatigue was extreme, and a postwar study by Japanese veterans concluded that "the death rate of the mentally unstable was extremely high as was the number of mentally unfit."[5] Hunger and exhaustion may explain the death rate among their sick and wounded. The records of the field hospitals of their 21st Independent Mixed Brigade ultimately fell into allied hands and indicated that 45 percent of their malaria cases died, as against less than 1 percent for Americans. So did 55 percent of their wounded, perhaps from infection, and an astonishing 60 percent of their patients with dysentery and enteritis. Such numbers, if accurate, could only have recorded the impact of disease on starving men.[6]

The allies, also riddled with sickness, waded through swamps flooded by the Girua River to attack the invisible bunkers without benefit of tanks or flamethrowers. They were hungry, too. All supplies had to be flown in by cargo planes or floated in by luggers that crept around the coastline. Both airfields and ships were often attacked by Japanese planes from Rabaul. Antimalarials, salt, vitamin pills, and tablets for chlorinating water were in short supply. Malaria increased steadily; dysentery was all but universal. Morale plunged, for it seemed the Japanese bunkers could not be taken. For a time, the destruction of the attacking army by disease seemed more than a mere possibility. The tactical situation reversed Guadalcanal, for the Japanese were able to defend, saving their energy. On the whole, the disadvantages seem to have balanced out. American medical intelligence analysts judged conditions on both sides so poor that "the balance of health factors [was] not decisive."[7]

The allied soldiers, weakened as they were, could be saved only by victory. The Americans were in a perilous position when MacArthur sent his favorite troubleshooter, Lieutenant General Robert L. Eichelberger, to revive the attack. He was not encouraged by the appearance of his men: "No one could remember when he had been dry. The feet, arms, bellies, chests, armpits of my soldiers were hideous with jungle rot." He ordered the medics to take the temperatures of an entire company. "Every member—I repeat, every member—of that company was running a fever."[8]

The nightmarish battle of sick and hungry men resumed early in December. Slowly the remaining enemy were killed off. The Australians took Gona, after suffering heavy losses; the Americans occupied Buna Village, from which the enemy had withdrawn, and seized Buna Station on January 2, 1943. MacArthur's 5th Air Force gradually took control the skies. The situation of the Japanese who still clung to the Papuan coast was desperate. Absolute lack of pity characterized the fighting. Breaking into an enemy hospital at Sanananda, allied soldiers slaughtered the patients; the Japanese routinely bombed allied hospitals and shot medics at work on the wounded. American casualties, knowing that snipers would aim at the flicker of white in the jungle, tore the bandages off their wounds until the medics began to dye bandages green. The few Japanese prisoners, though feverish and starving, reportedly tried to kill themselves and their own weaker fellows in captivity.[9]

By the end of January 1943, the disputed coastline was in allied hands. The cost was heavy, especially to the 32d Infantry Division, which had borne the brunt of the American effort. As soon as the fighting stopped, the division surgeon had the temperatures of a cross-section of the unit taken—675 men in all. More than half were running fevers, whose cause "in order of prevalence . . . is . . . Malaria, Exhaustive States, Gastro-Enteritis, Dengue Fever, Acute Upper-Respiratory Infection, and Typhus (scrub)." Nearly three thousand men were in hospitals because of sickness, and airplanes were carrying 50 to 100 more back across the mountains to Port Moresby every day. Eight of every ten casualties had been caused by disease, and almost half by malaria alone.[10]

Shortly after the Buna campaign, the epidemic of jungle fevers, chiefly malaria, peaked at 6,600 per 1,000 per year—on average, every man could expect to go to the hospital *six* times a year, unless the allies used the breathing space their victory had won them to introduce preventive medicine. For General Douglas

MacArthur, a commander who hoped to stay on the offensive, the losses to disease were unacceptable. But as late as March 1943 he had not made the command decisions that alone could impose the necessary health discipline on officers and men.

There were bright spots in treatment and evacuation. In Australia, MacArthur's chief surgeon, Colonel Percy Carroll, had devised a very small portable surgical hospital—twenty-five beds—staffed by doctors and enlisted men selected for their strength and endurance. The hospital was supposed to be totally self-sufficient. Officers and men carried its gear down jungle trails where no wheeled vehicle could go, and set it up under light cotton tents close to the fighting line. Buna was the first real test of the portable and it was a great success. Typically, the four officers and twenty-five enlisted men of the 3d Portable flew from Moresby to a new airstrip at Dobodura on the north coast. From there they carried 1,250 pounds of equipment in pack frames to the lines in front of Buna, pitching their tents a few hundred yards from the Japanese in the dense shade of a grove of black rubber trees. While bullets clipped leaves from the branches and punched holes in the tents, the surgeons performed sixty-seven major procedures—chest operations, amputations, and resections of the bowel—during their first week under fire.[11]

Then the growing number of malaria cases began to transform the portable's role as a surgical hospital. Not a single standard army hospital appeared north of the mountains, although the 2d platoon, 2d Field Hospital, served as a holding unit at Dobodura Airfield.[12] There was simply no other place to put the sick, and no way for the portables to turn them away. Soon only about 10 percent of their patients were wounded men; the rest had fallen victim to the local diseases. The little hospitals became the medical workhorses of Papua. Instead of serving a narrow purpose—using front-line surgery to stabilize the nontransportable wounded—they became supplementary aid stations, holding wards for malaria cases, and mini-evacuation hospitals. Their medics scrounged tents, got hold of vehicles, and called in the affable, multitalented natives of New Guinea to build huts roofed with grass and palm thatch to shelter their patients.

An American journalist spent a night with the 12th Portable

only 200 yards from the Japanese lines, sleeping in such a hut and waking from time to time when machine guns chattered down the road, or a mortar round burst with "the heavy expansive note of a bass drum." During the hours of darkness a torrential rain poured through the roof, setting his boots afloat. The morning brought hot sunlight, and the enlisted medics appeared, stripping blankets from their bearded patients and spreading bedclothes on the grass to dry in the sun. A corpsman sponged the rubber-covered table that constituted the operating room; another, counting medical stores, flicked away a questing ant as long as his thumb. Others stacked the wire basket litters in which casualties took their jeep rides to the airport. Helmeted drivers waited for the day's work to begin, their jungle-green fatigues already black with sweat. Then the cook called out, "All right, come'n get it," and feverish patients, stumbling out of bed, reached for their messkits.[13]

The variety of duties that they performed was what made the portables so valuable to hard-pressed commanders. The price was that they ceased to be portable except in name, for they had no way to carry their patients and no field hospital to send them to. Playing many roles, all essential, the portables embodied the best that the Pacific medics had to offer at this early point in the war—physical strength, soldierly courage, clinical skill, and the willingness to think anew.

Another success story of the campaign surely was air evacuation. Transports dared the cloud-wrapped, storm-beaten heights of the Owen Stanleys primarily to bring supplies and reinforcements to the fighters on the north coast. But their return flights meant life to the wounded and the sick, many more of whom would have died if the slow luggers plying the coastwise traffic had been the only means of returning them to allied bases. Air evacuation was an idea that had been born in the early years of flying but had only recently come to maturity. Traditionalists had condemned early experiments on the reasonable ground that "the hazard of being severely wounded is sufficient without the additional hazard of transportation by airplane."[14] During World War I, Europeans had used the dead space in the fuselage behind the pilot to hold a stretcher, and American trials dated from 1918. Gradually during the interwar years emergency "mercy flights" had become more common. Transports as well as small planes had been adapted to carry stretchers, and some were equipped with brackets to hold banks of stretchers in case of need.

In the Southwest Pacific, Colonel Carroll was an enthusiastic supporter of air evacuation. He was hoping to persuade the theater to dedicate some transports to medical use alone. Such air ambulances were supposed to be painted with Geneva markings like the hospital ships, and could hope for a similar degree of protection from attack. But planes were not abundant, and the sight of empty transports returning from supply missions caused them to be pressed into service for the wounded, just as troopships, once their human cargo had been discharged, became floating ambulances and crude hospital ships for the return voyage.

In June 1942 the War Department had given the responsibility for air evacuation to the Air Forces, ending a dispute over whether it should belong to airmen or medics. In fact the flight surgeons, flight nurses, and enlisted technicians soon became the key figures in keeping patients alive and comfortable during long-distance flights, and many shorter hops as well. On New Guinea the system was improvised, the flights were brief, and many men crossed the mountains unattended. Planes coming into the airdromes near Port Moresby flew hand-made flags—red for stretcher cases, white for walking wounded—to warn the ambulances of what sort of human cargo they carried.[15]

Crude as such methods were, they signaled the opening of a new chapter in medical transport. Air evacuation came into its own during World War II as a necessary and indeed routine way of moving the sick and wounded. Specifically, it proved itself during 1942 in the waste places of the earth: on Guadalcanal and Papua, and in the North African desert, where American planes helped the British to ferry their wounded away from El Alamein. Despite its dangers, air evacuation revolutionized the traditional chain of evacuation, extending it in space, compressing it in time, and reaching into near-inaccessible locations. The air ambulance saved men who had been too badly wounded to travel in any other way, and by the same token it burdened the hospitals with complex and desperate cases that in any earlier war would not have lived to reach the surgeon. It preserved life, and if used carelessly it depleted the fighting strength of armies by removing the lightly injured or "shell-shocked" hundreds of miles to the rear. For good and ill, but chiefly for good, it was of incalculable significance.

With Bataan, Guadalcanal, and Buna behind them, the Joint Chiefs of Staff toyed with the idea of selecting Admiral Chester Nimitz's Central Pacific Area, with its semitropical islands and malaria-free coral atolls, for the main American effort against Japan. Later, however, they adopted a strategy of advancing on two fronts, south and central. As President Roosevelt said, there were many roads to Tokyo, and he intended to neglect none of them.

This two-fisted approach resulted in campaigns that were equally bloody and bitter, yet as different from one another as the fighting in Italy was from the war in Russia. The southern attack followed what General Eichelberger called the jungle road, and a hard way it proved to be. A navy flight surgeon in the South Pacific wondered at the paradox of beauty and horror that he saw in its islands. From above they seemed like "tiny odd-cut emeralds" floating on a sapphire sea, but at ground level they were places of mud, heat and disease, and now they had been filled by the war with the added "sweat and stench of human rot."[16]

Much of the smell was evident in the South Pacific Area's next battle. The job of conquering the Japanese-held Solomons was begun so poorly, from a logistical and medical standpoint, that Guadalcanal might never have happened at all. New Georgia, a large island halfway up the chain, was a land of mountains and tangled forests closely resembling Guadalcanal. Here, in June 1943, the Army's 43d Infantry Division and the 1st Marine Raider Regiment were committed to the most wearing kind of jungle warfare short of every kind of medical support. The soldiers lacked a third of their medics and two-thirds of their supplies, and had only one small hospital formed from the division's clearing platoon. They had no field hospital until most of the fighting was over, and no portables; most of their surgeons were inexperienced in handling war wounds. Logistically, almost everything was mishandled. The 43d was supposed to provide medical supplies both for itself and the marines, but left huge quantities in disorder on the beaches at Guadalcanal. Less than three days into the campaign the troops were calling for more. There was one small navy malaria control unit to protect the whole force of 3,000 navy personnel—marines and Seabees—and the 25,000 soldiers.[17]

Tactically the situation was worse than Guadalcanal, for the Americans had to attack rather than defend, and every advance brought them closer to the main Japanese base at Rabaul. Enemy air raids smashed supply dumps on the beaches and bloodied the Seabees, who spent three days identifying and burying their dead. The marines landed in the dense heat of mangroves on a jungle river shore, bivouacked under a drenching rain, and started their first full day on New Georgia—July 6, 1943—by discarding their bedrolls and gas masks. Then they began a laborious trek along jungle trails, the men scrambling over "huge fallen logs, branches of trees, roots and vines . . . through swamps and mud, and up and down steep coral hills." They spent ten hours going 8 miles and fell asleep in their ponchos, exhausted, under another downpour. The days that followed repeated the story, as they worked their way through mangrove swamps, over jungle rivers, and through matted forest with coral outcroppings. The heat was intense, the humidity trapped by the tangle of trees and vines. Weary men threw away even containers of rations. They carried no plasma; they had no medical supplies except what corpsmen carried in pouches and individual marines in their first-aid kits.

On the morning of July 10 jungle fighting at its atrocious worst began. "Close quarter combat took place frequently," wrote a Japanese officer, "and casualties were continuously increasing."[18] On both sides, exhaustion complicated efforts to treat the wounded. If an injured marine still able to walk received morphine, he would immediately pass out and have to be carried, putting an intolerable burden on others. Corpsmen had to withhold the drug except in cases of extreme pain. Lack of combat experience further complicated their work; young marines who were only slightly injured, and well able to take themselves out of the fighting, instead shouted for help, and medical corpsmen were shot trying to reach them.[19]

American soldiers were undergoing similar trials. Steep slopes, flooded swamps, and unrelenting moist heat wearied them, and at night they found no rest. Aiming at noises and shadows, they killed one another, firing at random, throwing grenades or knifing comrades in the dark. In one battalion that was closely studied, twelve or more of every hundred casualties were caused by friendly fire. In the roadless jungle, men had to carry their supplies in and their wounded out; long treks with heavy bodies through smothering heat wearied the bearers and the patients alike, and caused wounds to become infected. Medical inexperience complicated the problem. New officers unskilled at battlefield surgery failed to debride wounds sufficiently. Evacuation was unsatisfactory. The only aircraft available to carry out wounded during most of the fighting were seaplanes, PBY "Dumbos" named in honor of Walt Disney's flying elephant. Seven-eighths of the casualties went by sea, most of them in LSTs, whose pace demonstrated only too clearly how they had acquired the ironic nickname "Large Slow Targets." Some men spent eighty-four hours with no treatment except first aid and arrived at Guadalcanal with the bubbles and stench of gas gangrene rising from their wounds.[20]

Lack of progress in the battle brought the XIV Corps commander and his surgeon to New Georgia. Reinforcements followed. The 25th and 37th Infantry Divisions arrived with their medical battalions, and a field hospital set up shop on a nearby island. A new offensive got under way, with heavy artillery support and some armor. The main enemy airfield at Munda Point fell on August 6, 1943, an important trophy but bloodily won in a campaign that had been amateurishly organized and bitterly fought.

In preventive medicine the record was mixed. New Georgia was not as malarious as Guadalcanal. The navy's control unit—a mere two officers and nine enlisted men—had the support of the line units. Surveys quickly showed which bivouac areas were heavy breeding places of *Anopheles*, enabling the troops to abandon them. Commanders told off-line details to oil standing water. The clearing stations, the 17th Field Hospital, and the control unit itself all had laboratories and tested blood smears taken from the sick. As far as combat allowed, the men who were not sick swallowed their Atabrine "by the roster," a tablet every day but

Sunday.[21] In other respects disease control was far less successful. Unscreened latrines and a plague of flies spread intestinal ills. The harassed XIV Corps surgeon probably spoke for many medical officers when he declared, "I believe that wire screening offers more protection to the health and well-being of troops than armor plate."[22]

Psychiatric casualties would probably have been heavy anyway, given the exhaustion and heat and stress, but poor leadership increased them. (The 43d Division contributed only 40 percent of the troops but 80 percent of the combat exhaustion cases.) But lack of skilled manpower was also a factor. The division had no psychiatrist, of course—none would be authorized until November. Its medical staff was at two-thirds of its normal strength, and hospitalization on New Georgia was close to nonexistent during most of the battle. A man had only to break down to be shipped out, and if some exaggerated their symptoms, who could blame them for seizing the opportunity to escape the wretched island? Almost two thousand men from the 43d were taken off the island; a psychiatrist in a hospital on Fiji later remembered several hundred patients arriving from New Georgia on a single day. Many were incoherent, weeping or mumbling, jumping at every sound like men "trying to escape impending disaster."[23] Both the 37th and the 25th Division, in contrast, set up rest camps and salvaged thousands who might otherwise have been lost to the battle.

Of the 35,000 Americans who served on New Georgia during the campaign, about 13,500 hospital admissions were recorded for all causes—more than the entire force of Japanese defenders. Only about 27 percent had been wounded, while 62 percent had fallen victim to one disease or another. Americans had every reason to take pride in the courage and endurance of the troops who withstood the terrible conditions and won the battle. But in many respects the commanders had nothing to congratulate themselves upon. The XIV Corps surgeon ticked off the things that would be needed in future operations: mobile surgical units, more convalescent camps to salvage psychiatric casualties, and many more hospital beds much closer to the front. A grim and costly campaign had, however, one major bright spot besides the tactical victory: It compelled the South Pacific Area command—as Guadalcanal apparently had not—to take the medical requirements of jungle warfare seriously.[24]

———————

It was high time someone did. Later that year, thousands of miles to the west, a campaign opened on the mainland of Asia which demonstrated once again that, in a jungle theater, it was possible to beat your enemy and yet lose a key part of your fighting force.

Though obscured by the war in theaters to the east, the fighting in northern Burma was as bad as anything in the Pacific. Comparatively few Americans took part, for the China–Burma–India Theater (CBI) was primarily a British show. But the regiment called Merrill's Marauders contributed long service and much suffering. Victorious over the Japanese, it was destroyed in the end by exhaustion and disease in a theater where command failures and poverty meant that effective preventive medicine did not begin for Americans until 1944—a full year after it came to the Pacific battlegrounds.

The fighting in Burma really opened in 1942, with another of the many allied disasters that marked the year. British, Indian and Chinese forces were scattered and driven out by the Japanese, along with thousands of refugees who left their bones to mark the trails by which they tried to escape. Among those who successfully rode, walked, and paddled through deep jungle by road and river into India was General Joseph W. Stilwell, the tough, acerbic regular who served as chief of staff to Chiang Kai-shek and commander of Chinese and American forces in Burma. Stilwell had been ordered, among other things, to reopen a land route to China in order to keep its forces in the war against Japan.

A long pause followed, enabling Stilwell to train his Chinese troops, build up supplies, and argue with his British superiors, whose enthusiasm for a campaign in north Burma was very small. In late 1943, when he finally received orders to advance, the Japanese were on the move in the opposite direction, invading India far to the south. While British and Indian troops grappled with and held the enemy's main forces during a long siege of the town of Imphal, Stilwell's Chinese armies and his few American engineers marched, fought, and began to build the Ledo Road over densely jungled mountains. In February 1944 a new American regiment joined the fight at the village of Shingbwiyang, where Stilwell surveyed them with satisfaction: "Tough looking lot of babies."

They were a hard-luck outfit, soon to be filled with a touchy resentment of more fortunate men, more famous theaters of war, and especially Stilwell himself. They were known by various names: as the 5307th Composite Unit (Provisional), their uninspiring official tag; as Galahad, their glittering code name; but most widely as Merrill's Marauders. The journalistic coinage was based on the unit commander's name—Major General Frank D. Merrill, "a very bright fellow with a fine New England sense of humor and great dedication to whatever he was about"—and its rough-and-ready style.[25]

The Marauders were drawn from a mélange of other units and committed to fight an experimental form of warfare—deep penetration behind enemy lines—for which their government felt a transient enthusiasm spurred by Winston Churchill, himself a romantic warrior, and by his eccentric protégé, Orde Wingate. Most Marauders had come to Burma from other tropical theaters, and for that reason malaria was sending every man to the hospital on average four times a year when the campaign began. Only Atabrine enabled them to march and fight.[26]

Fate was unkind in other ways. The Burmese jungle—unlike the islands where soldiers and marines fought in the Pacific—was not surrounded by a friendly sea dominated by their country's ships. Because they were the only Americans under Stilwell's mixed command, the Marauders had to demonstrate American resolve and commitment by fighting far past the limit of their physical strength. Yet, because they operated behind enemy lines, medical support usually meant such care as the enlisted unit medics and the regimental and battalion surgeons who walked with them could supply. They were beset by enemies they could not strike back at: nature, international politics, the kind of war they had been assigned to fight. Yet in the teeth of all their enemies they made a 700-mile Long March that proved to be their glory and ruin. The Marauder who became his unit's eloquent historian declared that calling his trek through the Burmese jungles and over mountains to the town of Myitkyina the worst experience of his life would not be enough. "It was so incomparably the worst that at the time I could hardly believe in the rest of my life at all."[27]

The tactics of the campaign ensured exhaustion, promoted disease, and involved the Marauders in four or five major battles. While the Chinese sought and sometimes found the Japanese, the Marauders circled through the jungle, on leech-infested trails that scaled precipices and plunged into deep valleys, to attack the enemy's rear. A few mobile hospitals had arrived in the theater, and the portables were all-important, walking and working in the jungle just as they did on the Pacific islands. But the hospitals followed the main line of the advance, so that the Americans gained less from them than the Chinese. Airdrops replenished supplies, but meagerly; surgeons had to borrow knives and saws from native tribespeople, who, hating the Japanese, also supplied the guides and stretcher bearers without whom the allied forces would have been "absolutely helpless."[28]

When airdrops failed, the Marauders ate their pack animals. They suffered from skin diseases, dysentery, and scrub typhus. Exhaustion was cumulative; the men became dizzy, nauseated, and night blind; lost appetite; and felt increasing muscular weakness. General Merrill had a heart attack. Either through exhaustion or in hope of escaping the jungle, some of his men failed to take their Atabrine and fell out with attacks of malaria. When the Marauders faced the Japanese, they had to fight as line infantry but without artillery to support them. Their medical detachments collected the sick and wounded, who walked if they could and, if not, rode pack animals or were carried in litters until evacuated by small planes landing in meadows or on the sandbars of jungle rivers.

The Marauders were already exhausted and depleted when they crossed a last range of mountains in the valley of the Irrawaddy River and, with their Chinese allies, laid siege to Myitkyina. Here portable hospitals were at hand, as well as a hospital that the American medical missionary, Gordon Seagrave, had volunteered to aid the allies. The surgeons worked outdoors or under shelters rigged from parachutes, in fierce sun or pouring rain, sometimes operating while Burmese nurses held umbrellas over their patients. Some of the wounded, jolting to the hospital in springless oxcarts, suffered as few Americans had since the Civil War.[29]

When the Myitkyina airstrip fell, the allies began to fly their casualties out. But the desperate fight and the politics of the theater intervened again to keep the sick where they were or return them all too quickly. Infantry officers had to hang onto men to fight with, while the medical officers tried to ship at least the worst cases out. In India and along the Ledo Road, where the rear-area hospitals stood, Chinese and American wounded and sick crowded the beds, so that men who did escape Myitkyina were thrown into the replacement system as soon as they healed, with no time for recovering their strength—and found themselves back in Myitkyina again. On the battlefield, sick and well became meaningless terms. Everybody was sick. Scrub typhus was epidemic and almost everyone had dysentery. "Of Galahad's 2d Battalion," the official history notes, "once 564 strong, 12 men were left in action on the 30th" of May 1944.[30]

What could jungle fighting do to a unit? In what was called the Second Burma Campaign (the first had been the allies' ouster by the Japanese) the Marauders suffered only 123 deaths but lost 80 percent of their force to wounds and sickness—399 battle casualties and 2,000 nonbattle. Fevers, known and unknown, knocked out almost 1,500, and most of the rest were accounted for by dysentery. When Myitkyina fell at last on August 2, after seventy-eight days of siege, the Marauders quickly ceased to exist as a unit. More than two-thirds of their successor, the 475th Infantry, were replacements. Effective preventive medicine finally came to the theater in the winter of 1944–45, helping to pave the way for the triumphant British-led campaign that ousted the Japanese from all of Burma.[31]

But that was for the future. The medical problems of jungle warfare embraced not only clinical knowledge—American doctors had to learn to identify and treat exotic diseases—but supply, transport, and above all, command. Until the necessary medicines were available, until treatment could be brought forward and the sick and injured successfully brought out, and until commanders used their full powers to impose health discipline on their troops, long sick lists and partly or wholly disabled forces would continue to be the norm. The prescription was simple to write, though hard to fill under combat conditions. Either the Allies or the Japanese by taking it manfully could win a huge advantage in the jungle war.

5

Gearing Up

Leadership of a different sort was needed in Washington. Here was another warfront, and winning or losing the power struggles that went on in the capital often helped to determine outcomes far from the Potomac.

As they faced the war and its multiplying demands, the surgeon generals of the army and navy needed to reshape their organizations, tap the resources of the civilian research establishment, and find the skilled men and women for whom the ever growing armed forces seemed to have unlimited need. They also faced an influx of civilians and an array of popular and political pressures that in the end transformed the wartime medical departments. In early 1942, Chief of Staff General George C. Marshall pushed through a major reorganization of the War Department. Complaining that the army's general staff had become a "huge, red-tape-ridden operating agency," Marshall was determined to reduce the number of officers with direct access to him by delegating authority.[1]

The creation of three supercommands—the Army Ground Forces, the Army Air Forces, and the Services of Supply (later called the Army Service Forces)—followed. The Army Surgeon General, relegated to the Services of Supply, was denied direct access to the chief of staff. The SOS commander, an elegant but very formidable engineer officer, Lieutenant General Brehon B. Somervell, and his headquarters machinery now had to approve any action that the surgeon general proposed. Few army medical officers were satisfied with the arrangement, which one of them called "an unworkable bureaucracy under some insufferable bureaucrats!"[2]

Understandably, Major General James C. Magee, the surgeon general, disliked the new arrangement and made his feelings known. Marshall, not the most patient of men, grew weary of his complaints against the reorganization and his slowness in adapting to the pace of wartime. Others outside the army were unhappy for other reasons. Florida's powerful Senator Claude Pepper, displeased over the handling of medical manpower, launched a congressional investigation into the policies and organization of both military medical services. Meanwhile charges surfaced of discrimination against women doctors, black doctors (as late as the fall of 1940 the Medical Department had *no* regular black officers, either male or female), and medical sects like the osteopaths.[3]

Whatever the justice of specific complaints, the feeling spread that army medicine was not being run very well. The logical scapegoat was the fifty-nine-year-old native of Ireland who was surgeon general and, in many ways, his own worst enemy. In his time, Magee had survived service against the Moros, Pancho Villa, and the Central Powers, but he was not to survive in office against the combined attack of outside critics and his own superiors.[4]

Lieutenant General Somervell asked for an investigation, and the secretary of war set up a committee headed by a retired medical officer, Sanford H. Wadhams, and composed mostly of civilian doctors connected with leading medical schools. General Magee learned of the investigation only after the committee had been appointed and probably viewed it as a star-chamber proceeding. But that was not entirely true. The majority of members owed little to General Somervell, and their conclusions—reached after lengthy questioning of medical officers and interested civilians— were not always what the chief of staff and the commander of SOS desired to hear.

For one thing, the committee sensibly denounced the whole idea of consigning the surgeon general to the Services of Supply, saying that he belonged back on the army's special staff. (Somervell simply rejected that.) It tried to strengthen the surgeon general's authority over the air force medical service, which was rapidly becoming autonomous. If the investigation was expected to condemn the surgeon general and to bring about his removal, it failed to do so. On the other hand, if Magee had hopes of surviving his season of discontent, he too was disappointed. In fact, General Marshall was "determinedly opposed" to Magee and had already selected his successor.[5]

Brigadier General Albert W. Kenner, then serving in North Africa, was in the great tradition of Marshall selectees: able, even brilliant, probably the best man for the job. His most recent promotion, recommended by Major General George S. Patton, had followed Kenner's masterful handling of four hundred burned and mangled victims of a U-boat attack. Secretary of War Henry L. Stimson also was an enthusiast, repeating to President Roosevelt the argument that he had heard from Marshall: that a wartime surgeon general ought to have experienced "actual service in foreign fields under combat conditions."[6] Roosevelt agreed, and Kenner flew to Washington to begin familiarizing himself with his new job. Everything seemed to be settled.

On April 8, 1943, Roosevelt asked Stimson to reconsider his choice. "As you know," he wrote, "I am in much closer touch with the medical profession in all its ramifications than most people are, and I believe that some other selection could be made which would do more credit to all of us." The ramifications apparently included influential members of the AMA, whose choice for surgeon general was Brigadier General Norman T. Kirk. If Kenner had impressed the soldiers, Kirk had developed excellent ties with the civilians.[7]

As the majority of the Wadhams Committee had demonstrated, civilian doctors did not necessarily see things in the same light as the army leadership. A vast majority of the Medical Corps were now civilians in uniform, and the profession wanted a surgeon general its members knew and trusted. Secretary Stimson had to write a letter to Roosevelt endorsing Kirk's nomination and saying that Marshall agreed, even though, Stimson added, Kenner had the "most outstanding record" in the army. The pill was bitter. Though Kirk accepted Marshall's reorganization (as Magee had not) and proved himself an able administrator, his relations with the chief of staff—a great but not a forgiving man—remained cool.

Marshall appointed Brigadier General Howard M. Snyder, a regular medical officer who was an assistant inspector general, as his liaison with the surgeon general and ordered Kirk to report only through Snyder. Stimson sent a lawyer, Tracy M. Voorhees, into the surgeon general's office to keep an eye on the Medical Department. (In time he became a first-rate troubleshooter for Kirk.) In short, the Medical Department under its new head was to be watched and not fully trusted.[8] Throughout the war, the surgeon general's distance from the general staff was even greater than army organization charts showed.

By and large, the sweeping changes brought by the war were accomplished more smoothly in the navy. Although the two military medical services closely resembled each other in structure and function, they were sharply different in size and style. When World War II began, the Bureau of Medicine and Surgery (BuMed, in naval parlance) was nearing the end of its first century. Under Rear Admiral Ross T. McIntire, the organization controlled all the navy's medical facilities and the training schools of the Medical, Dental, Nurse, and Hospital Corps. The surgeon general had a say in assigning medical personnel, and he took responsibility for everything that affected the health of the navy. Before Pearl Harbor, BuMed included about 5,000 uniformed members and a few hundred civilians; during the war, its size grew to 31,000 military and 13,500 civilians and its internal structure proliferated from 11 to 22 divisions. McIntire, benefiting from his position as physician to President Roosevelt, was promoted in early 1944 from rear admiral to vice admiral.[9]

The surgeon general was, in fact, quite a poor doctor but an excellent politician and administrator. His management of BuMed modernized what in many ways had become an antique. He brought in consultants from civilian life, reorganized the handling of personnel, tightened administration, and set up a professional services division to provide technical guidance for the various medical specialties. He kept his direct access to the Chief of Naval Operations, and his position in the White House certainly did not weaken his voice when, as chief liaison officer for BuMed, he spoke to his fellow admirals about medical needs. In short, while the army weakened and diffused the authority of its surgeon general, the navy moved in the opposite direction.

Statute law fixed the number of people authorized for the Medical, Dental and Hospital Corps as a certain proportion of the total strength of the navy, and legal authority for recruiting additional personnel was automatic. McIntire faced no ongoing struggle with his airmen, as Magee and Kirk had with the Air Forces, nor with the Marine Corps, which failed to discover that a special "marine medicine" existed requiring a separate medical establishment. He selected medical officers for assignments and moved them at will. Running an organization one-tenth the size of the Army Medical Department, he held an unchallenged position and ran a tight ship.[10]

The impact of civilian medicine countinued to mount, exerted partly through the physicians who donned uniforms but in many other ways as well. Some doctors who remained civilians powerfully influenced the military services. In particular, the research establishment continuously provided a rich source of new ideas and discoveries.

For two generations or more, American philanthropists, industry, and—to a lesser extent—government had been finding a new role as patrons of medical research. Researchers, who might be either physicians or nonphysician specialists in one of the life sciences, worked in laboratories and taught in classrooms. Many researchers enjoyed the freedom to follow the path of discovery wherever it led them, subject only to the requirements of whoever funded their work. Foremost among the agencies that organized those free spirits for the war was the Office of Scientific Research and Development (OSRD). Its head, Vannevar Bush, was the nation's supreme technocrat.[11]

Even a sketchy overview of the system that developed requires a brief plunge into a Rooseveltian alphabet soup of agencies. The Committee on Medical Research (CMR), a part of the OSRD from its founding, advised Bush on contracts with universities and hospitals for the conduct of medical research. The committee turned for guidance to the Division of Medical Sciences (DMS) of the National Research Council (NRC), a semipublic body, which had already developed its own relationships with the military medical services. Subgroups of the DMS multiplied rapidly in response to the needs of the military services. By 1943 there were fifty-two committees and subcommittees with almost three hundred civilian experts and uniformed liaison officers sent by the surgeons general.[12]

Despite the flurry of acronyms, not many key people were involved in the effort, and most of them already knew one another. The in-group of professionals who dominated the medical research field was not large and, with occasional bows to other centers of learning and finance, it was tied to the Northeast and its great universities. These men shared similar outlooks on the world and communicated easily among themselves. Together they set up a kind of interlocking directorate: The chairman of the DMS was elected vice chairman of the CMR; the chairmen of the division's eight principal committees became consultants to the committee; and the OSRD undertook to pay the expenses for meetings of the NRC committees. The NRC provided information on what projects needed money and on what researchers were best fitted to handle them; recommendations based on its information were forwarded to Bush, who had access to funds.[13]

Complex relationships also grew up among the services and the scientists. The army, the navy, and the air force conducted intramural research programs, for all had extensive laboratories and able people to staff them. Housed in the service medical schools and special establishments, scientists in uniform developed new treatments for burns and trauma, worked on the blood program, studied survival at sea, and explored the special problems of aviators, submariners, and tankers. But all the services felt the need for some sort of Brain Trust drawn from the rich resources of civilian medicine.

In 1942 General Magee set up what came to be known as the Army Epidemiological Board under the dean of Yale's medical school. (Still later it became the Armed Forces Epidemiological Board and worked for all the services.) Designed to predict and counter epidemic outbreaks among the people in uniform, the board and its subordinate commissions were made up of civilian experts who served for consultants' fees and recommended contracts with researchers for direct funding by the army. There were board members who also belonged to the CMR; others worked simultaneously for the committees and for one or more of the armed services.[14]

The system was frankly elitist and highly functional. It seems unlikely that the whole coordinating effort behind the application of American medical research to wartime needs involved more than five hundred men, some in uniform and some out, and many wearing multiple hats. It included most of the big names of the time in academic medicine, and among the smaller fry were some of the big fish of the future, including Jonas Salk and Albert Sabin, who would later conquer poliomyelitis, and James A. Shannon, a malaria researcher with the Army Epidemiological Board who would later build the National Institutes of Health into a dominating force in American medicine during the postwar era.

The fundamental driving force behind this remarkable aggregation of brainpower was wartime patriotism, which caused medical scientists to serve without pay on the committees and caused universities to provide funds for military research when red tape delayed government payments. The wartime system changed medicine forever, opening the golden coffers of federal support for science wider than ever before and enhancing the public vision of scientific research as a cornucopia of useful knowledge. In fact, wartime science went far toward creating the postwar culture, in which the laboratory was seen as the source both of new terrors and of human hopes for a better and longer life.

By far the most influential voice of civilian medicine, however, did not emerge from the research establishment. The American Medical Association was an organization primarily of practition-

ers led by successful specialists who might or might not have university connections. The organization that had helped to choose a
surgeon general for the army had many other roles to play as well
in wartime medicine.

One critical area was medical education. As medical reformers,
AMA members had fought to upgrade medical schools, incidental-
ly restricting the number of students and the size of the profession.
But the demands of wartime brought quick decisions by many
medical schools to condense the usual four-year course, with vaca-
tions, into three years without time off. To assist the medical
schools, the armed services enrolled students in their reserve programs. They also established the Army Specialized Training Program (ASTP) and the Navy V-12 Program to return qualified
draftees to college campuses, where they lived in quasi-military
conditions while learning critically needed specialties, including
medicine. In wartime medical schools, the army supplied 55 percent of the freshman classes, the navy 25 percent, and the remaining 20 percent were drawn from civilian life. Meanwhile, premed-
ical training was shortened, state licensure laws were amended for
the emergency, and times of internship and residency were reduced. Despite initial misgivings, the AMA either supported or
failed to oppose actively all these changes, properly viewing them
as necessary to the war effort if not always wise.[15]

But the biggest problem was to find practicing doctors for the
military while continuing to meet civilian needs as well. At the
time of Pearl Harbor, the army considered itself to be short 1,500
physicians, and the great expansion of the armed services that followed ensured that the navy, the Public Health Service, and the
Veterans Administration would soon need additional doctors,
too.[16] Acquiring health-care professionals was a problem that differed from all the other military manpower tangles the nation
faced, because most doctors and all nurses had to be obtained by
volunteering instead of compulsion.

Of course, young male physicians and dentists faced the possibility of being drafted if eligible, for their professions gave them
no blanket exemption. On the other hand, there was no specific
doctor draft, like the one that operated after 1951 to supply the
needs of the Korean War and Cold War armies. In World War II a

physician might be drafted because he was male, healthy, and young, but not because he had an M.D. There was plenty of subtle compulsion to serve, moral and otherwise, but civilian health-care professionals were never simply ordered to serve where they were needed, as, for example, they were in wartime Great Britain.

Some sort of central authority was needed to register physicians, judge their qualifications, and try to persuade them to serve where they were most needed. Long before Pearl Harbor, the AMA volunteered its services, taking the view that physically fit doctors ought to serve voluntarily and that the services ought not to demand more doctors than they actually required. The surgeon general of the army agreed and in 1940 proposed that the AMA sponsor a census of physicians to find out how many were ready to serve in a national emergency and in what capacities.[17] When that was successfully accomplished, the AMA proposed that an official Procurement and Assignment Service (P&A) be set up as a clearinghouse to receive requests for doctors, dentists, and veterinarians from the armed forces and other government agencies and match needs to availabilities.[18]

This proved to be a tall order. Wartime had set the population moving, drawing men and women workers to the industries it spawned, breaking old ties, and conjuring whole new communities out of nothing. Some method was needed to persuade physicians to move to areas where local doctors were being overwhelmed by the needs of newly arrived war workers. The President approved the AMA's plan, and in October 1941 an executive order set up P&A under the Office for Emergency Management (later the War Manpower Commission). The service worked closely with the AMA's Chicago headquarters, consulting with its bureau of medical economics and utilizing its *Journal* to urge doctors of appropriate age to join the military, and others to move where they were needed by civilians.[19]

The first wartime appeals were borne on the tidal wave of patriotism that swept the nation from shore to shore after Pearl Harbor, and met with success. Soon afterward, things became more difficult. Just moving doctors around to serve the changing patterns of the civilian population was problematic enough. Doctors who were settled in their practices had plenty to do at home and saw no reason to abandon their patients; young physicians, who were more footloose, were also far more likely to be in uniform. State legislatures were in no hurry to grant out-of-staters temporary licenses to practice. In 1943 Congress offered to pay the moving expenses of physicians and dentists who went into areas of great need, plus a subsidy while they established themselves. But it was the fall of 1944, and the war was approaching its climax both in Europe and in Asia, before the movement of some four thousand doctors had been accomplished and the severer strains in civilian health care had been contained. The lack of an assignment service with coercive power did not deprive war-swollen communities of doctors, but it did allow them to scrape along for years, overworking the few physicians who were present.[20]

The voluntary system also interacted with the nature of conscription as practiced in the United States to excuse some physicians from military service. In 1940–41 many young doctors were not eligible for the draft simply because the age limit was twenty-eight, and medical education, followed by marriage, excused them. In 1942, when the limit was raised to forty-five, the pressure on the reluctant increased, and Selective Service had a stick to wield.[21] Yet for a time in 1942 and again in 1943 the voluntary system seemed likely to fail. The huge increase in the armed forces, the demands for draft examiners, and the needs of civilians ran up against the limitations of volunteering. Paul V. McNutt, who was Roosevelt's key man in manpower questions, berated the medical profession for failing to meet the needs of Americans in and out of uniform.[22]

For their part, local draft boards did not propose to give the military services every single doctor they said they needed. The purpose of Selective Service's network of 6,500 local boards was not simply to provide men for the armed services, but to enable local people, within broad national guidelines, to determine who was needed at home and who was available to fight. A doctor whose local board declared his services to be critical was safe from induction even if he was of military age and in good physical condition. Draft boards were supposed to take P&A's advice on which doctors were needed and which were not, but the power of decision lay with the local boards.

Perfectly genuine local needs excused some eligible doctors, but others took advantage of complaisant boards to stay home and make money in safety. The AMA's *Journal* viewed such behavior as unpatriotic and when a shortage of doctors developed in the armed services bluntly laid the blame on the "failure of young available physicians in the large cities of the country, particularly those of the eastern seaboard, to volunteer." In fact, the states that fell behind their quotas in 1942 were California, Illinois, Pennsylvania, New York, and Massachusetts. All had large cities, and the cities were apparently the problem, for rural areas of the same states did well enough. Country practitioners did not earn much, so that an officer's pay looked better to them, and they were also subject to moral pressure from small, often intensely patriotic communities where everybody knew them. While the big cities did not provide enough doctors to the military, many country districts gave too many and were left stripped of medical care.[23]

Legal evasion angered the military as well as the AMA. Selective Service actually drafted a few hundred doctors who failed to volunteer. But the attitudes of the public remained highly ambivalent. In 1942 the army sent out medical officer recruiting boards to persuade doctors and dentists to sign up and be commissioned on the spot. It had to end the program the same year. Both McNutt, who was now Federal Manpower Commissioner, and P&A protested that the service was depleting civilian communities of doctors, and critics accused the army of hoarding and misusing the doctors it already had.

The real question, however, was a national policy that left individuals such wide latitude to decide whether they would serve and how. Senator Pepper and his colleague, Senator Lister Hill of Alabama, representing states that had oversubscribed P&A's quota for doctors, favored a national service act that would transfer to the government the onus of deciding where and how civilians should serve the war effort. But that would have required a very substantial change in the national culture as well as in the medical profession.[24]

What probably saved the voluntary system was the fact that a great many doctors did volunteer, about 56,000 in the course of the war—probably as many as the armed services really needed.

Voluntarism did not really deny doctors to the military. It did allow the most honorable members of the medical profession to bear the burden of service while permitting some of the least admirable to escape it. And it deprived small and poor communities of their few doctors while allowing larger and richer ones to keep some who probably belonged in uniform.

The record of the military medical services was far from unblemished when it came to obtaining doctors and using them wisely once they had signed up. A leading regular officer who was also a future Army Surgeon General recalled that in World War II he "found an excess of doctors except where they were needed."[25]

In fact, the question of exactly how many doctors the military services needed was never satisfactorily settled. The army claimed to need 50,000 doctors, about 6.7 for every 1,000 of its men and women, and the navy claimed to need 6.5. Both were enormous proportions by civilian standards. (P&A set a goal for wartime civilian care of one doctor for every 1,500 people—one-tenth as many as the services wanted.)

Why did the military need so many doctors? For a multitude of duties, the surgeon generals argued, not all of which involved the treatment of patients; medical officers had to administer, command, and serve on a variety of boards. They had to care for many small posts, separate units, and ships at sea. Above all, the services needed doctors as a firehouse needed firemen: to be there when the alarm rang. None of those explanations cut much ice with bored young MDs in uniform, or with civilians at home who were anxious about their own needs, or with P&A, which accused the army in particular of having too many slots for doctors in its tables of organization.[26]

In short, there is no easy way to assess the realism of the wartime demands that the services made upon the medical profession. Judged by the results, American fighting men got excellent treatment during the war, and the nation's lavish military medical service stirred the envy of its allies and enemies. But whether there were too many doctors or too few in uniform, the evidence seems unassailable that they could have been better used, for their own benefit and for that of the people they served.

One reason lay with the regulars themselves and the habits of mind they had developed during peacetime. The Regular Army Medical Department of the 1930s had been dominated by its doctors almost to the exclusion of other health-care professionals. A Medical Administrative Corps (MAC) had been set up by Congress to relieve doctors of nonclinical duties, but in 1939 the army had only sixty-six medical administrative officers. Some physicians developed an unfortunate habit of claiming that only a man with an MD could run a depot, act as assistant battalion surgeon, or serve as executive officer in a hospital. Civilian doctors coming into the military did not agree; they tended to believe that doctors should be reserved for clinical duties and that "the practice of assigning medical officers, even temporarily, to any type of work that could be performed by non-professional personnel [should] be discontinued promptly."[27]

Such contentions dangerously raised the blood pressure of regulars, who knew perfectly well that a medical officer was an officer as well as a doctor. Some were quite willing to make adjustments to the necessities of wartime; the surgeon general agreed that some lower-ranking posts must change hands, and the Medical Department took the lead in 1941 by authorizing commanders to assign MACs to some nonclinical posts—as adjutants, supply officers, commanders of enlisted medical detachments, and mess officers. (Mess and sanitary inspections were among the duties most disliked by all medical officers, whether regulars or volunteers.) But recommendations for adding more and higher posts to the list were firmly rejected by General Magee, whose mind in this as in other things was set firmly in the habits of the past.

Then reality intruded. Of the 176,000-odd physicians in the United States in 1942, about one-third were available for military service, the others being exempted by age, physical condition, the demands of the civilian population, or simple refusal to volunteer. Of these the army wanted more than 61,000 but made do with about 49,000. The wartime expansion of the army to 89 divisions and about 8 million men and women brought an equivalent growth in the Medical Department. Nine-tenths of the uniformed medical people of World War II served in the army and its autonomous appendage, the Army Air Forces. By the summer of 1944 the medics numbered more than 687,000 men and women, "larger than the Confederate Army in the Civil War, four times the strength of both sides at Gettysburg, and three times the size of the entire Regular Army in 1937." Roughly one soldier in twelve was a medic; the number of Medical Department officers ultimately reached 146,000, including, by mid-1945, some 1,100 blacks, both male and female.[28]

The war, in short, changed the whole makeup of the department's officer corps. The number of Medical Administrative Corps officers rose from 66 in 1939 to almost 20,000 in 1945. As reserve units were absorbed into the army, the number of Sanitary Corps officers increased from 8 in 1940 to 2,500 five years later. And army nurses went from 672 in 1939 to 57,000 by the war's end. Doctors, who had formed two-thirds of the department's officer corps in 1939, made up only a little over one-third in 1945.

Much of this dramatic change reflected the views of the army staff. The army's leaders saw no point in arousing opposition by using the civilian physicians in uniform as company commanders, mess officers, and sanitation officers. In July 1942 the War Department directed commanders to replace medical officers in administrative posts with MAC officers. The invasion of administrative officers, a future surgeon general said, was "frankly repugnant to many [medical] officers steeped in the traditions of the prewar Medical Department," and "some urging" was necessary to make them go along.[29] But necessity, army policy, and the wishes of the civilians in uniform all pointed toward an ampler role for the non-MD.

The Medical Department opened two officer candidate schools for MACs, and their presence increased even in the sacrosanct general hospitals. As registrars, they kept medical records; they became personnel officers, one serving as chief of personnel for the European Theater of Operations; they became medical regulators, managing the movement of patients to hospitals; and they became financial managers, one serving the surgeon general as his chief of finance. Against vigorous resistance from some physicians, they became executive officers of hospitals. But MACs were not only fixtures in the headquarters and the hospitals. Many served the troops as assistant battalion surgeons, and others commanded platoons of litter-bearers under fire, like young Elliott

Richardson, a MAC second lieutenant who landed at Utah Beach on D-Day.[30]

By that time MAC officers had become essential, and they have remained so since. World War II brought about the permanent transformation of the Army Medical Department into a complex health care organization, led by its physicians but comprehending people of many other talents as well. The result was that doctors could spend more time doctoring—and that was to everybody's advantage.[31]

———

Although conservative about their administrative officers, the service medical departments for a generation had been innovators in another respect: through their nurse corps, they were the first parts of the army and navy to accept women members. (Small numbers of women who were physical and occupational therapists also served in the large military hospitals, but only the nurses held "relative rank," meaning that they had the status and insignia of commissioned officers but not the same pay or power of command.)[32]

The female nurse had been a feature of American armies since the Revolutionary War. But it was a slow process to persuade the proverbial man's army and the even more tradition-minded man's navy to accept her, except as a camp follower on the one hand or, on the other, the sort of "lady nurse" who appeared in emergencies to lay cool hands on fevered brows. The Civil War had brought substantial numbers of women into the military hospitals in both North and South, but it took the Spanish–American War to bring about the formation of the Army Nurse Corps and the Navy Nurse Corps. Even then, nurses remained uneasily suspended between civilian and military for nineteen years, neither officers nor enlisted people and frequently disparaged by both. But 1918 brought women's suffrage to the United States, and 1920 saw the nurses awarded relative rank, which they retained through World War II. (Congress granted them equal pay during the war.)

About 75,000 registered nurses served the army and navy during the war—roughly one-third of those in active practice in the

United States. Recruitment for the services was usually through the Red Cross, though there were many exceptions. As with doctors, the armed services constantly demanded more trained nurses, often on obscure grounds. Between early 1943 and early 1945, army requirements rose from 30,000 to 59,000, and as a result the strength of its nurse corps, despite massive volunteering, fell steadily behind the supposed needs from mid-1943 on. The results included relaxed standards, calls for a draft of nurses, and a frantic recruiting program that brought the army more nurses than it needed or knew what to do with after the surrender of Germany in May 1945.[33]

Like doctors, nurses were not all used well. The rhythms of war explained some of the problems. Major Julia Simpson, on a recruiting swing in 1943, warned her listeners that "war is three-quarters waiting and boredom and tiresomeness, and it is one quarter of the hardest work you ever heard of in your life or ever dreamed of."[34] Nevertheless nurses, like doctors, complained frequently about being left idle, and civilians receiving care in depleted hospitals staffed with a few overworked RNs and an abundance of nurses' aids were apt to believe that the armed services had taken too many nurses and were hoarding the ones they had.

In fact, volunteering by skilled women helped to cause a genuine and severe shortage in some communities that had already lost many of their doctors. The result was another program similar to the ASTP and V-12. In June 1943 Congress set up the U.S. Cadet Nurse Corps as a war emergency program. Federal grants were handed out by the Public Health Service to approved schools of nursing, which in turn paid the costs of training cadet nurses—tuition, books, room and board, a special uniform, and a monthly spending allowance. The cadet was not necessarily obligated to join the military, but she had to work as a graduate nurse for at least three years after graduation, either in the armed forces or as a civilian.[35]

Once again the basic problem was the lack of any agency with the power to determine legitimate needs and allocate that scarcest of all resources, trained people. The problem with nurses was even greater than with male doctors, for women could not be drafted at all, and the decision as to whether they would work in or out of uniform was entirely their own. Nevertheless, the War Manpower Commission made an effort. In 1943 Congress assigned the job of allocating nurses by persuasion to the Procurement and Assignment Service. P&A proceeded to put nurses into five categories resembling those of the draft, from Class I, who met the standards of military service and were not needed by the civilian community, to Class V, who were unavailable for reasons of age or health.

Yet it could only invite Class I's to join, not compel them, and the army made its demands without much regard for the categories or anything else except the need it saw ahead.[36] The army wanted about one nurse for every ten military hospital beds; it grounded its estimates on a pyramid of figures predicting future casualty rates that rose steadily as the war spread and intensified. On the other hand, nurse volunteering tended to reflect battles under way or just past, soaring in the aftermath of Pearl Harbor and the major invasions, when the need was clear to all, and then dropping off.

Sexual stereotyping formed another serious obstacle to getting and using nursing talent. Beginning in the 1870s, Florence Nightingale's trained nurse had established herself as essential to the professional care of the sick. But she remained an exploited figure. As a student nurse she was cheap labor for the hospitals, with some duties resembling those of a chambermaid. Even after graduation and lengthy experience, her wages remained low in civilian life. How many women would choose to become nurses when relatively high-paying jobs stood open in wartime industry? Ironically, trained male nurses faced a worse situation than women, for they could be drafted but could not be commissioned in their specialty!

As to why there should be no men in the Army and Navy Nurse Corps, and only a few female doctors in the two Medical Corps, no rational answer could be given. The military, Congress, and probably most Americans of the time agreed that nurses ought to be women, and doctors men, and that was that.

Yet the war brought important changes for women who served in the health care professions. Dieticians and physical therapists were granted relative rank in 1943; women with scientific degrees who were serving in the Women's Army Corps (WAC) received commissions and were later transferred to the Sanitary Corps to work in their specialties. WAC enlisted women were taken into the hospitals as practical nurses and medical technicians; enlisted women even entered the navy's Hospital Corps, to the dismay of many an old salt.[37]

Military nurses became leaders, guiding teams that included male and female enlisted specialists and even prisoners of war. (Some 80,000 prisoners served the military hospitals as everything from laborers to record keepers.) During the 1930s, nurses had spent considerable time in their professional associations debating the question of whether licensed practical nurses enhanced the status of registered nurses or threatened their jobs. The war strengthened the drift toward a system by which patient care was the responsibility of a team working under a registered nurse. Accident and policy combined to make the team larger and more varied than it ever had been in civilian life, and by conferring officer rank and insignia on the nurse gave her an incontestable claim to leadership—at any rate, as long as the war lasted.

In those conditions nurses worked in many more places than the rear-area hospitals that had previously been their bailiwick. Women served in mobile hospitals, on remote Pacific islands, and sometimes in positions of real danger.[38] Yet a mixture of chivalry, prejudice, and confusion continued to limit their opportunities. Because women were usually denied the right to land on hostile shores until the fighting forces had secured the area, nurses were removed from mobile hospitals at just the time when they were most needed, to the detriment of the wounded. Male technicians did the nurses' jobs under fire, including highly skilled tasks in the operating room, although neither officer's rank nor pay could be given them, because they were men. Friction resulted within the medical ranks, for as soon as a newly conquered area was quiet the women nurses reappeared, reclaimed their jobs, and as officers began to give orders to the "techs."

No picture of comfortable, arrogant females should be drawn from this account, however. Nurses constantly pressed for the right to serve at the front or as close to it as possible. Their situation was probably worst in the Southwest Pacific, from a combination of climate, geography, and official chivalry motivated by the atrocious record of the Imperial Japanese Army. Denied the right to practice their profession and take full part in the struggle for which they had volunteered, some nurses in MacArthur's theater suffered from depression in rear-area camps, where poor living conditions were made worse by the fact that their quarters were often surrounded by barbed wire. Armed guards were needed to prevent rape by the hordes of young and not always gentle males who surrounded them, and on some islands officers who dated nurses were instructed to wear side arms to protect them.

In many ways the nurses' condition resembled that of men in idle theaters, like Alaska before the Japanese attack on the Aleutians. Healthy and relatively safe, many men were depressed not because they were in the war but because they were excluded from playing a useful role in it. Fortunately, that was not the customary fate of army or navy nurses. Most of the 76,000 who served with the armed forces were gainfully employed, many were more or less constantly overworked, and a few faced acute danger. Nevertheless, the nation's failure even in emergency to make full use of its women was a striking feature of the time when all Americans were bombarded with daily commands to do their part and be of service.

Women were not the only group to face limits on their opportunities. For American blacks the war was a time of paradox. The fight against Hitler's homicidal racism was one in which they had a special interest. The national crisis also represented opportunity—a time to push their demands and to advance many steps on the long road that led toward equality. It was also a time of disappointments and growing anger, for the nation failed to integrate its armed forces or grant genuine equality to blacks in uniform.[39]

Still, pressure from black leaders and the black press secured them widening opportunities. In 1940 the first black general won his star, and the first black federal judge, William H. Hastie, was appointed Secretary of War Stimson's Civilian Aide on Negro Affairs.[40] Many of the nation's 4,000 to 5,000 black doctors had banded together in the National Medical Association (NMA), for they could join the AMA only through its local chapters, meaning that those who lived in the South—and many other places—were excluded. In 1940 the NMA set up a committee to coordinate health work among blacks in defense industries, and a liaison committee to press for a role for black doctors in the war effort.

The navy was polite but firm; except as mess personnel it had no use for any blacks and consequently none for black doctors. The army was more forthcoming. General Magee promised to use black physicians with all-black units, in all-black hospitals, and "wherever practicable" in wards exclusively devoted to black patients. Similarly, the army gave commissions to about five hundred black nurses in the course of the war, the navy to only four.[41]

In 1942 activation of the all-black 93d Infantry Division at Fort Huachuca, Arizona, led to the creation of a station hospital under a Chicago physician and a chief nurse formerly of Freedmen's Hospital in Washington, D.C. As mobile hospitals were readied for overseas service, black doctors and dentists in the reserves were called into service. The Selective Service used black examiners. Gradually, the list of black medical officers grew, though only in the army; the NMA's liaison committee became a subcommittee of P&A.[42] To the casual observer signs of racial progress were everywhere.

Unfortunately, it turned out that blacks could have either black doctors or integration, but not both. Traditional military segregation had never extended to treatment in hospitals. Before the war, military patients had been highly integrated, largely because of the total absence of black doctors from station and general hospitals—this in spite of the fact that even in the hospitals there were separate tables in mess halls and separate toilets for the two races.[43] Taking in black doctors and nurses meant that segregation could be increased, for the more all-black units there were, the greater the chance that black medical personnel would be needed, that black could serve black, and that the races could be kept completely separate.

As a result, segregation in hospitals increased during the early war years. In addition to Fort Huachuca's station hospital, the war brought all-black wards to hospitals at Fort Bragg and elsewhere. General Magee's explicit aim was to create in the army a system closely resembling the one that existed in the contemporary South. As far as possible, blacks would be treated by blacks; black and white doctors and nurses would not serve together; black patients might be treated by white professionals, but not the reverse. In black units officered by whites, only white medical officers could be used, lest a white officer have to be treated by a black physician.[44] In short, the races were to be as separate as possible and unequal under all circumstances.

Of course, the program failed to work in practice. For one thing, the nation simply lacked enough black physicians to make it feasible. In 1943 the armed services, the National Medical Association, P&A, and the Selective Service agreed that only five hundred would be taken into the army, most from the large cities of the North, which were comparatively well supplied with black doctors.[45] Even if enough black doctors had been available, systematic segregation still would have been impossible, for the chain of evacuation could not be duplicated. The uniform did not fit Jim Crow, despite the best efforts of some official tailors to stretch and alter it. Separate hospitals never proved to be practical, except on a few heavily black posts and in support of all-black units. Elsewhere, black soldiers wound up in army hospital beds according to their diagnoses and medical needs, not their race—very often lying next to white soldiers, as they had before the war. The Fort Huachuca establishment meant expanded opportunities for some black doctors, but it could not become a model for the army.

One loser in the brouhaha over black doctors and nurses was General Magee. The national black press saw the surgeon general as the main obstacle to real integration and hammered him without mercy at a time when his many other critics were also badgering him. Another loser was probably the NMA, which accepted the Fort Huachuca bone and gave up the battle for an integrated medical service. In the conditions of the early 1940s, that fight could not have been won. Nevertheless, there was some truth to the sardonic comment in the *Pittsburgh Courier* that "the National Medical Association won a complete victory for the integration of Negro physicians and nurses on a Jim Crow basis into Jim Crow wards in the United States Army training camp hospitals."[46]

But change was coming. Powerful forces remained unreconciled to the segregation of doctors and nurses. The NAACP, the National Association of Colored Graduate Nurses, and their chief top-level patron, Eleanor Roosevelt, continued the fight, and by the war's end they had begun to win it. In 1945 black nurses were integrated into a number of army hospitals, and the integration of doctors had made at least a gingerly beginning. By then a million or more black veterans were ready to return home, there to press with new urgency for integration across the board.

During World War II, Americans misused substantial portions of their wealth of medical talent through misassignment, racism, sexual stereotyping, and clinging to voluntarism while other nations drafted talent as well as people.[47] Because the nation had much talent available to waste, the failings of the system never reached absolutely critical dimensions. The effect of all the wartime friction was inefficiency, not failure. Enough skilled men and women were found to provide for the needs of all, albeit to a more or less constant chorus of complaint.

If the war had lasted longer, if the United States had become a battleground, like less fortunate nations, then the voluntary system would have been swept away. Even as things were, some of the people who struggled to run the voluntary system were frustrated by their inability to function under it. "If another great war should break out," the doctor who served as P&A's vice chairman said, "I personally think that a body with power over all professional people should be set up."[48]

As matters went, good fortune, genuine patriotism, and the national tradition of holding differences in abeyance to get the job done helped the country to get by, providing somewhat lavishly for the military and somewhat meagerly for many civilians. Misused as they were, medical manpower and womanpower proved to be equal to the task. And the intervention of civilians combined with the imperatives of the war to change military medicine in ways that few could have imagined in the quiet days before the war.

6

School of Battle

As late as the autumn of 1942 Americans had done almost no fighting against Hitler's Germany on land. But that was about to change. Too weak to assault Fortress Europe in 1942, the allies settled on an invasion of northwest Africa, then held only by French forces representing the pro-German Vichy government. The decision meant that the army and navy had to stage a landing by large forces on a hostile shore and to do so with very limited means.[1]

By later standards American medical support was thin at best. As General Kenner said, faced with tonnage limitations the medics realized that "the desirable was also the unattainable" and that "the medical service would have to be run on a shoestring." The plan was complicated, involving both British and American forces and landings on both the Atlantic and the Mediterranean coasts. British hospital ships were available to evacuate wounded from Algiers, but the all-American landings had to make do with sick bays aboard the transports and mobile hospitals ashore. Two

British general hospitals accompanied their troops, but Americans had none until December. Everything about the operation smacked of improvisation and guesswork.[2]

The first shock came when the French refused to surrender as the allies had hoped. The landings on November 8, 1942, met unexpectedly stiff resistance. Near Algiers and at Oran, on the Mediterranean coast, naval gunfire hammered tenacious defenders while French shore batteries took their toll of escort ships and infantry attempting to land. Fighting was also sharp at Casablanca and Mehdia on the Atlantic coast. Americans showed an impressive range of amateurishness and bad luck. Landing craft crews were inexperienced, combat units landed at the wrong places, heavy swells swamped the untried craft, and tanks laboring their way ashore were flooded by seawater or immobilized in deep sand.

Unit medics and elements of the medical battalions suffered from the same confusion as everyone else. Typically, the 48th Surgical Hospital reported that the crews of the landing craft bringing it to shore "were not acquainted with the beach and as a result the personnel were landed over an area of about three miles." The nurses waded ashore under a lowering sky, harassed by sniper fire. Losing track of their equipment, the hospital staff had to borrow everything it needed from a clearing station in the town of Arzew, near Oran. Nurses, doctors, and corpsmen spent their first night ashore with little medicine or food for themselves or their patients. The surgeons had to operate by flashlights.[3]

Other units told similar tales. Collecting and clearing units came ashore too late, carrying the wrong equipment and too little of it. Medics found themselves stranded on the beaches, unable to work for want of supplies and lacking vehicles to catch up with the forces they were supposed to serve. When ambulances arrived, many bogged down in the sand, and their high profile made them excellent targets. Hospital gear had been loaded wrongly, nobody could find it, and when it came to light it was unloaded too slowly. Because so many landing craft were wrecked in the surf, the wounded could not be taken off the beach. Only a few dozen ever reached the transports. Where French resistance was strongest, casualties began to come in before supplies were available to treat them, and hospitals had to be set up hastily in beach casinos, squalid huts, and abandoned barracks.[4]

Yet French resistance, though sharp, was brief, and many defenders quickly changed sides and joined the allies. The medics were lucky that they had comparatively few casualties to care for—any large number would have swamped them. Soon land mines and occasional bombings by German planes were providing the hospitals with most of their patients. Despite the initial shock and confusion, the invasion had succeeded. The green American troops thought that their taste of combat was probably as bad as the war was likely to get. They forgot—as a later historian said— that the French had been "understrength, underequipped, and undermotivated." Few could have guessed how bloody and stressful a learning experience lay ahead in the North African interior and beyond.[5]

With their forces ashore, the allies began to move east toward the Algerian–Tunisian border. Along the Mediterranean coast of Algeria the soldiers saw rich irrigated fields, with vineyards and gray-green olive groves; inland towered the Atlas Mountains, with connected chains that ran north into Tunisia. To young men raised on Hollywood images of Africa, the weather was full of surprises. Especially in the highlands, the wind could be bitterly cold; chill rains fell again and again, sometimes mixed with hail and snow; at night, water froze in canteens. But the afternoons were warm, and some doctors held sick call then so that their patients could strip without turning blue.[6]

In the early days of the campaign, American units were fed piecemeal into the British First Army and received medical support from their allies, whose hospitals, to American eyes, featured both sophisticated clinical skill and spare, understaffed facilities. Some American doctors—including distinguished civilians who had won field-grade commissions on the basis of their standing in the medical profession—found the organization of their own army even more difficult to grasp than the medical system of their allies. General Kenner took aside the portly, balding Colonel Edward D. Churchill, professor of surgery at Harvard before the war, and quietly instructed him in the role the medics played in the military machine. They commanded only their own units;

their chain of command ran not to the theater surgeon but to the commander of the tactical unit they were attached to. Kenner's successor made something else plain: The army did not like end runs, and private correspondence between Churchill and the Surgeon General's office in Washington would not be appreciated. Advice on improving surgery, on the other hand, was badly wanted. Churchill set out for Tunisia to see for himself what was happening. Thus he walked into the aftermath of a disaster.[7]

Late in January the American II Corps assembled in southern Tunisia on the extreme right of the allied line, in a landscape of brown desert scrub and rocky hills. The corps functioned like a task force, doing a field army's job but without its strength and capacity for independent action. Medical units moved up to provide support, including the medical battalions of the three divisions that made up the corps, plus a couple of independent battalions, the 48th Surgical Hospital and the big (and only semimobile) 9th and 77th Evacuation Hospitals to the rear. American ideas of combat surgery were undeveloped, to say the least, especially in the armored units, where a treatment station in a halftrack—a bastard truck with treads in the rear—followed the tanks. There was a prevalent opinion that a combat surgeon could operate on the tailgate of a truck, but, Churchill said, "who was to take care of the patient after the operation [was a question] no one had faced."[8]

Americans were about to try their hand at fighting the Germans independently. Unfortunately for all those who served in it, the II Corps was poorly led. General Kenner noted that its troops were "spread pretty thin, there was no front line as such, combat teams were not mutually supportive, and the sector was held with a prayer."[9] This was an invitation to enemies who needed no encouragement. The Afrika Korps's Field Marshal Erwin Rommel and the commander of the rapidly increasing Axis forces in Tunisia, Generaloberst Juergen von Arnim, plotted a counterattack.

In the predawn darkness of Valentine's Day, 1943, as a cold wind whipped a storm of stinging sand over the dreary Arab hamlet of Sidi Bou Zid, the Germans opened a devastating assault. Outclassed American tanks were quickly smashed, and defended hills engulfed. Medical halftracks gathered up the wounded, and the casualties—including many burned and battered men of the tank crews—began to pour back upon the medical units. The medics fared no better than anyone else in the disaster. Many in forward units were captured, and the normal lines of evacuation were disrupted. Trucks and jeeps became ambulances and hauled suffering bodies to the rear, on long runs made slower and more painful by winding, deeply rutted roads. Aid stations divided into two sections and leapfrogged to the rear, one holding the patients while the other escaped and set up its tents to receive them.

Doctors and nurses tried to continue care as the units fled; corpsmen gave most of the blood that was needed for transfusions. The weather did nothing to make the retreat easier. The Germans punched through Kasserine Pass under overcast and misty skies, with the desert dust turning to winter mud and icy winds howling. The diary of a surgeon from the 2d Auxiliary Surgical Group recorded rough and endless rides through cold nights, sometimes in brilliant moonlight but more often under squalls of freezing rain. "Retreat is a ghastly word," Major Kenneth Lowry wrote. "Only one who has been . . . involved in a retreat can realize the full significance and horror which the word implies."[10]

For all who took part in it the retreat was a revelation of what war could mean to those who were trying to save lives. Major Howard E. Snyder had already had a sharp encounter with war when his unit, the 77th Evacuation Hospital, landed at Mers-el-Kebir, and the staff, after hiking 12 miles to Oran, had taken over civilian and military hospitals filled with hapless patients—"a rather terrifying introduction to combat surgery." They had lived in tents pitched in a vineyard, while receiving boatloads of British casualties. But Kasserine Pass and its aftermath were the big revelations: While more than six hundred wounded flooded in, the hospital had to pack and run during a snowy night.[11] There was simply no equivalent in civilian life for such crises, for the demands they made on the medical personnel and the stress they inflicted upon the patients.

Ultimately the German attack ran out of fuel and supplies in the plains beyond the Kasserine, and the enemy pulled back. American losses exceeded seven thousand men—dead, wounded, missing, or captured. The lines were restored, the American commander was sacked, and II Corps was turned over to Major General George Patton. For a month, while the new commander reorganized, the wounded either recovered or were shipped to the rear. Mobile medical units made ready for a new advance. Whatever else might be said of Patton, he was a fighting commander and intended to resume the battle at the earliest possible date. When he did, the hospitals would fill again.[12]

Patton had his own ideas about managing the wounded. "If you have two wounded soldiers," a medical officer quoted one of his harangues, "one with a gunshot wound of the lung, and other with an arm or a leg blown off, you save the sonofabitch with the lung wound and let the goddamn sonofabitch with an amputated arm or leg go to hell. He is no goddamn use to us any more." The doctor noted rather primly that "as medical men we could not quite agree with some of the principles which [Patton] dictated," adding ruefully, "perhaps it takes this hard-boiled attitude to win battles, but . . ."[13]

Along with the ground troops, the Army Air Forces had arrived in North Africa. The Twelfth Air Force was supposed to provide tactical support, while its transports were to move supplies forward to the fighting line and bring the wounded back. Medical evacuation was assigned third priority, after the moving of troops and supplies; a hundred transports were equipped with metal racks to hold stretchers.

Most of the airmen reached Africa by ship, either with the invasion fleets or shortly afterward. When a toehold had been secured, the planes were flown in. Some pilots were in combat within hours after they landed. Gradually the troop carrier groups, bomber groups, and fighter groups built up, along with their unit medics and dispensaries. American air units soon were dotted over the vast North African theater, defending Casablanca and Oran and pushing their tactical units toward the Tunisian border to fight the Luftwaffe and support the bloodied ground forces.

Americans were still amateur warriors, and life in the African outback was as rough as nature and the enemy could make it.

Some units had no tents, and at airstrips men slept in puptents, in hangars, under the wings of planes, or under the planes themselves.[14] When the enemy bombed and strafed, they dug in around their airfields, sometimes scooping out the dirt with their hands for lack of shovels. Medics slept in water-filled slit trenches, and the wounded received treatment in dugout aid stations. For some luckless units it was an infantryman's life, minus the appropriate field gear and training, and they acquired the same illnesses—mainly dysentery and respiratory infections—as the ground troops. Air force casualties flowed through the dispensaries to American ground force or British hospitals, some them the victims of wounds, some of African diseases, and some of the weather.[15]

Besides enduring their own losses, airmen of the Troop Carrier Command played an increasingly important role in moving ground-force casualties. With its great distances and generally poor roads, North Africa was a perfect theater for air evacuation. Although little needed during the early days, when the allied forces were engaged in occupying settled areas near port cities that had road and rail networks, air evacuation came into its own when the front expanded into Africa's unsettled wastelands. Distances grew to such an extent that even where roads existed, a wounded man could spend a day in a motor ambulance or a day and a night on a train reaching treatment. Formal air evacuation came to the theater in January 1943, only shortly after the emergency system got under way in New Guinea, halfway around the world, and it featured not only the transports but such combat improvisations as installing slings to hold litters in the bomb bays of B-17 Flying Fortresses.

Once started, the system was rapidly elaborated, foreshadowing later developments on the European continent. The ground forces carried their sick and wounded to airfields, provided holding units to care for them, and selected the patients to be flown out. The 51st Troop Carrier Wing supplied the planes, and in March flight surgeons and nurses arrived to tend the wounded while they were in the air. Communications systems were strung together to advise the ground units how many patients they could evacuate and to warn hospitals in the rear how many they must expect to receive. There were endless problems of detail, but by

May more than 17,000 patients had been evacuated by air in the theater, and a model had been created for future campaigns in the Mediterranean region and elsewhere.

The later spread of fighting beyond Africa only increased the need for what was proving to be "the most efficient, reliable and rapid method of evacuation of patients from forward areas" (as the Twelfth Air Force surgeon called it). The theater not only grew larger, it crossed arms of the sea; it spread over Mediterranean islands and portions of Italy. Old fears about the ability of the wounded to endure flight proved to be largely unfounded. In 1944 air evacuation would carry almost 126,000 patients in the Mediterranean Theater, and more than 212,000 by the end of the war. Just as it had on Guadalcanal and Papua, the air ambulance in Africa worked even better than enthusiasts had imagined it could—no longer an experiment, but a normal and crucial contribution to lifesaving in war.[16]

On the ground, allied progress was slow and costly. By mid-March 1943, the II Corps, increased to 90,000 men, was ready to resume the fight. Attacking toward the Mediterranean coast through a rough, barren landscape of eroded earth, dry riverbeds, and brushy mountains, the Americans soon reconquered the region they had lost during the Kasserine battles.

Heavy fighting tested a medical system whose lack of mobility made it more suitable for the static fighting of World War I than the era of mechanized war. Litter-bearers were in short supply, and some wounded men lay twenty hours on hillsides or in stony fields before they were found. Again the hospitals could not keep up, and ambulance hauls were interminable, 50 to a 100 miles to get a man to the evacuation hospitals. Division clearing stations, strengthened by teams from the 2d Auxiliary Surgical Group, had to act as forward hospitals, doing operations that really demanded more time, more equipment, more staff, more everything. Lack of beds to hold the wounded threw another burden on the evacuation system, which responded by shipping out not only men who were seriously hurt, but also the lightly injured, who should have been kept, treated, and returned to their units.[17]

Heading the medical system were, from 1942–45, the army's Major General Norman T. Kirk (top) and, from 1941–45, the navy's Vice Admiral Ross T. McIntire (bottom). Their basic job was to preserve the fighting strength of the armed forces in the face of enemy weapons and epidemic disease. Wars are won by the healthy and strong and their success was a crucial element in American victory. *(National Library of Medicine)*

The aidman was one of the war's unsung heroes. He lived with the troops and was the first to answer a call for help. He gave first aid and helped the wounded out of the line of fire. Often facing the enemy unarmed, he was the foundation of the whole elaborate medical system, with its hundreds of thousands of surgeons, nurses, scientists, and enlisted medics. *(Painting by Lawrence Beall Smith in U.S. Army Art Collection)*

In earlier centuries, disease had caused far more wartime deaths than wounds did. The early days of World War II brought devastating epidemics in disease-ridden jungles of the Pacific and Asia, until preventive medicine brought malaria under control. In New Guinea, prevention began literally with a bitter pill — here, of quinine; later in the war, of the synthetic Atabrine. *(Signal Corps Photo)*

Millions of civilians also survived the war because of military medicine. In World War I, louse-borne typhus fever killed some 3 million people in Europe; in World War II, DDT and the dust-gun enabled the medics to stamp out threatened epidemics in Germany, Italy, and the Balkans. Here, the beneficiary is a Polish DP (displaced person). *(Signal Corps Photo)*

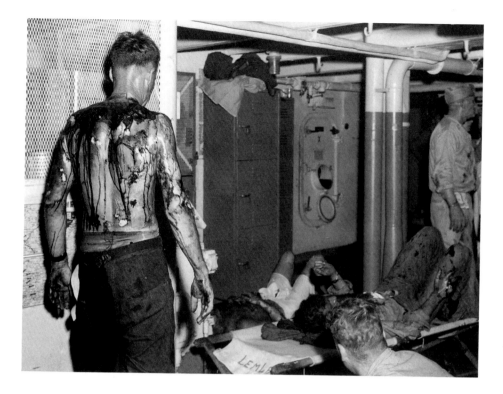

While World War II brought better means of controlling disease, it also brought an array of new and lethal weapons and in consequence a tide of wounded. The first step in treatment took place while the battle raged. Here, a burned and bloody sailor walks to a dressing station after a kamikaze attack off the Philippines *(Navy Photo)*. The war also brought a new understanding of the psychological wounds of the soldier under fire. The army's Colonel Frederick R. Hanson pioneered methods of therapy, with treatment close to the front lines, that ultimately salvaged most victims of what he called combat exhaustion. *(Uniformed Services University of the Health Sciences)*

Blood plasma — the fluid part of the blood, with the red and white corpuscles removed — was a great lifesaver of wounded men because it could be given near the front by enlisted medics. Here, casualties receive plasma in a Sicilian village (above) and on Omaha Beach on D-Day (below). By 1944, Americans had found ways to get refrigerated whole blood to the front as well. *(Signal Corps Photos)*

At the aid station, many willing hands pitched in to help the wounded man. On Okinawa, this marine had to be evacuated from the front line in a Sherman tank because of intense enemy fire. Here, other marines lift him from the tank onto a litter. *(Marine Corps Photo)*

Aid station personnel cluster around a soldier hit in the last battles on the Philippines, giving him plasma, stanching his bleeding, and shading his face from the tropical sun. *(Signal Corps Photo)*

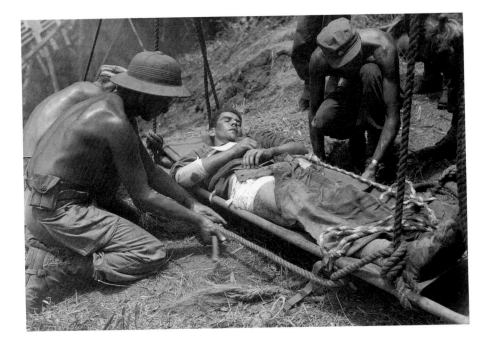

The war was fought in almost every imaginable terrain, and as a result the wounded had to be taken to the rear by a great variety of means. Here, a soldier hit in the Philippines will be swung down a mountainside by ropes, while men wounded in the invasion of southern France prepare to leave the Riviera beaches by landing craft — perhaps the same craft that brought them ashore. *(Signal Corps Photos)*

Most casualties rolled to the rear on wheels. The trip was often a dangerous one. Here, a soldier in the European fighting grimly inspects a bullet-riddled ambulance; survivors of the Battle of Normandy are driven to safety through a mine field. *(Signal Corps Photo; painting by Lawrence Beall Smith)*

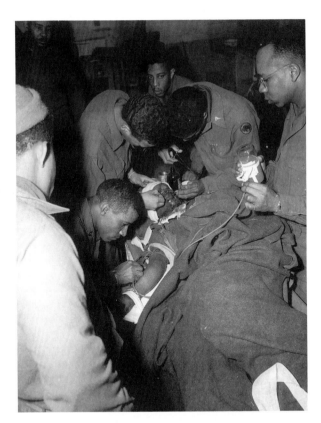

Once the wounded were behind the front lines, treatment continued in the regimental collecting station and the division clearing station. Here, an officer wounded in Italy receives care from medics of the segregated 92d Infantry Division. *(Signal Corps Photo)*

The next step was the field hospital — often a rough-and-ready place, like this navy-staffed facility treating wounded marines and soldiers on Guadalcanal in the early days of the war. *(Navy Photo)*

In the last phase of the campaign, General Omar Bradley took command of the II Corps and marched it across the allied rear to take over the extreme left of the line. Then he wheeled and advanced on Bizerte along the Mediterranean coast. In the Tunisian mountains the terrain was unforgiving, the rocky terraces covered with conifers or prickly shrubs that "tore at men's clothes and flesh with the remorselessness of steel." The Germans sowed the roadsides with mines and fiendishly clever booby-traps that blew off hands and feet and more; they defended reverse slopes masterfully and counterattacked by night. Nature made artillery more deadly, for the explosion of a shell flung out not only its own fragments but shards and splinters of rock that caused many wounds.[18]

Litter carries were long and exhausting, a matter of bearing and keeping level a man's dead weight for half a mile on impossible slopes, and when the bearers reached their destination they could only turn back with quaking muscles to find a new burden and begin again. Bad as it was, however, the fighting was not as pitiless as in the Pacific. Sometimes the enemy shot up ambulances and bombed hospitals, but more frequently the Germans fought by the rules; their artillerymen held fire while the wounded were cleared and carried away, and machine gunners sometimes waved ambulances past their nests unharmed.

After storming fortified hills, the Americans seized the shattered port city on May 7. By then the medical system had matured greatly—six hospitals with more than 3,000 beds supported II Crops—and it was properly disposed, with forward hospitals only 5 to 20 miles behind the fighting line rather than 25 to 100, as in the early days. Evacuation benefited from an increasing fleet of ambulances and a greater understanding and use of air transport. As for the medical personnel, they had become veterans. A medical officer visting a forward hospital watched a small blonde nurse in gray coveralls humming quietly as she worked her way through the wounded newly arrived from the collecting stations. She knelt by a litter to rebandage a shattered foot, lit a cigarette for an officer with a shrapnel wound in his back, called a doctor to give quick attention to a pale young sergeant who had had a grenade explode "almost in his face," and adjusted a dressing on the stump of a German prisoner's arm. The POW watched the first American woman he had ever met with "a glint of admiration" in his eyes. "I wondered how she could do this," the medical officer recalled, "for eight hours—ten hours—fourteen hours—endlessly, so long as they came in the duty ambulances from out yonder where the cannons boomed. But they tell me she did."[19]

When victory came, the medics could look back on a radically compressed learning experience. Only six months had gone by since the first landings on the North African shores. Now Casablanca lay 1,200 miles to the west, almost as far away as the illusions and ignorance they had started with. Not only had medics, comissioned and enlisted, men and women, learned to be soldiers, they were drawing important clinical lessons from their experiences in the field. Almost unnoticed by the troops, medical innovations had begun that would reshape practice in the Mediterranean fighting and ultimately throughout the world.

Some of the innovations developed behind the lines. Africa was famous for its diseases. The troops had escaped malaria largely because of the season, but another and far more lethal disease was at large in North Africa. Marked by a rash on the body, high fever, stupor, dementia, and a variable but often high death rate, typhus was a dangerous and cruel ailment that had acquired a historical dimension through its ability to disable armies.

Winter, war, and famine were the traditional hallmarks of epidemic louse-borne typhus, which had been attacking armies, navies, and embattled civilians at least since the end of the Middle Ages. Its record in the twentieth century, an era of war, was formidable. During and after World War I typhus epidemics had devastated much of Eastern Europe; Serbia had suffered 135,000 deaths, Rumania had lost several hundred thousand, and millions—perhaps 3 million in all—may have died in Poland and Russia.[20]

The approach of another war seemed to threaten a reprise. No known drug, including still-experimental penicillin, killed the microbes that cause typhus in the living human body. Prevention was possible but terribly difficult under wartime conditions. In order to rid themselves of lice, people had to strip and bathe while their clothes were steamed. But steam had no residual action. A soldier entering an infested bunker or a civilian returning to an infested house (or merely rubbing shoulders with an infested person) soon was scratching again. Crowded people caught the disease more easily; cold people protected their lice by failing to change clothes or bathe; hungry people who became ill with typhus died more quickly and in greater numbers than those who were well fed. By its nature epidemic typhus was a classic disease of disorderly times—perhaps *the* classic disease.[21]

A long-lasting effort to develop a workable typhus vaccine matured just as World War II began. Early attempts had entailed infecting individual lice rectally, then dissecting them and grinding up their stomachs. During the war, the Russians developed a grotesque variant on this method. Needing to grow lice in great numbers, Soviet technicians scalded corpses, stripped off the parboiled skin, and stretched it over shallow dishes of blood. Lice lived on the skin and sucked blood through it. Neither of those techniques had answered the need for mass production.

European scientists tried another tack, infecting mice and preparing a vaccine from their lungs. Animal proteins in the serum, however, caused some patients to have serious allergic reactions. Then an American scientist with the Department of Agriculture—Herald R. Cox—devised a method of growing microbes on chick embryos that made the preparation of large quantities of vaccine possible. By 1942 American fighting men bound for the typhus-harried regions of the world, including North Africa, were being routinely inoculated with a Cox-type vaccine.[22]

But it remained unproven in the field. The energetic Colonel James Stevens Simmons of the Army Medical Corps in 1942 launched an imaginative effort to head off typhus. His methods reflected both his own innovative genius—he was a charming man by most accounts, though hot-tempered and impatient with stupidity—and his knowledge, as a regular army officer, of the ways of bureaucratic Washington. In talking the typhus danger over with Captain Charles S. Stephenson of the navy's Bureau of Medicine and Surgery and with Rolla E. Dyer, head of the National Institutes of Health, Simmons became convinced that a commission of experts was needed. He drafted a letter proposing such an organization to Chief of Staff General George C. Marshall and persuaded the surgeon general to sign it.

By the end of the year a mixed group called the United States of America Typhus Commission had been set up, not merely with War Department approval but with the added cachet of an executive order signed by Franklin D. Roosevelt. That was Stephenson's doing. A bureaucratic tactician of rare gifts, he worked through Vice Admiral Ross T. McIntire, who was not only surgeon general of the navy but the official White House physician, to get approval from the President. (Roosevelt never understood precisely what the two doctors in blue were up to; he seems to have had a vague idea that the commission would combat polio.)[23]

With a mixed staff drawn from the army, the navy, the Public Health Service, and the Rockefeller Foundation, the typhus commission set out for Africa in early 1943. Sharp internal squabbles quickly developed among so diverse a group, and Stephenson, who had became its head, went down with a heart attack in Cairo. Since the army surgeon general had been tasked with supporting the commission, Simmons now intervened. He reorganized the group under two brigadier generals of the Army Medical Corps: Stanhope Bayne-Jones in Washington and Leon A. Fox in Egypt. The team was odd but curiously effective. Bayne-Jones, a former dean of Yale Medical School, was a smooth, well-connected academician whose forte was medical administration. Fox was a colorful, usually forthright, and often foul-mouthed regular who relished field work and contrived to get along with everyone from Egyptian *fellahin* to Marshall Tito. (His own colleagues were a frequent exception.)[24]

Meanwhile, the effectiveness of Cox's vaccine had been proved in the field. When American and British forces invaded North Africa in November 1942, one of the most severe epidemics since World War I was raging—more than 77,000 known cases, and perhaps 500,000 more that went unreported. Through this plague American soldiers moved unhurt; they fought battles, slept in native huts, and pursued sex—often with success, to judge by the incidence of venereal disease. Yet, among half a million men, just eleven caught typhus, and none died. Since the disease was almost unknown in the United States, immunity could not have been naturally acquired. The troops' remarkable health record was due to the vaccine, backed up by old-fashioned methods of sanitary discipline imposed by the armed forces.[25]

Those developments helped to define the commission's job. The American armed forces would not need its services, but plenty of other people would. Millions of civilians were already under military control, and millions more—neutral, allied, and enemy— would soon become the military's responsibility. Conquered enemy armies would yield further millions of prisoners, most of them predictably lousy and subject to disease. Supplies of the vaccine were not adequate to protect whole nations, and as a result frantic experimental work went on in Egypt and elsewhere to find new ways to get rid of lice.

Several new insecticides were under development by the Department of Agriculture and the Army; one of them, a Swiss discovery, had been given the acronym DDT. A Simmons protégé, Colonel William S. Stone, served as General Eisenhower's chief of preventive medicine and stood ready to provide both support and supplies. After the North African victories of 1943, a Rockefeller public health expert, Fred L. Soper, began experimenting with louse powders in the prisons of Algeria, where richly infested felons of both sexes made ideal guinea pigs. The Moslem women, however, were reluctant to remove their clothes, until then always a necessary preliminary to killing lice. Soper found another way. Following a suggestion made by a colleague, he bought an ordinary dustgun intended for agricultural use and began to blow DDT under the prisoners' clothing.

The result was a small but magical moment in the history of preventive medicine. The human habit of wearing clothes had always sheltered lice from searching hands and the cold of winter. Now, because clothing held DDT close to the body, adult lice died and new generations died as they hatched out. Soper's technique was painless, required no special training—a public health worker could be taught to operate a dustgun in a few minutes—and brought an immediate reward to the prisoners, who discovered that they could sleep in relative comfort, no longer devoured by their parasites. As news of the discovery spread, DDT appeared on the Algiers black market, a sure sign of popular success.[26]

By the end of the year, a system for combating typhus had taken form, and the chief players were finding their roles. The typhus commission organized the movement of supplies of vaccine, dustguns, and DDT, and provided expert advice to military surgeons and civilian governments. The DDT-loaded dustgun became almost as familiar a sight as the rifle in the transatlantic war zones. Among its chief beneficiaries were refugees, liberated concentration camp inmates, enemy civilians, and Axis prisoners of war, beginning with the vast bag taken after the German collapse in North Africa. But the most impressive demonstration of the newfound ability to control typhus in wartime would come later, after the invasion of Italy.

In the winter of 1943 the population of newly captured Naples was swollen by war, crowded, cold, and hungry. Unruined buildings were jammed to overflowing; thousands of refugees lived a Dantean existence in the *ricoveri*, catacombs whose beginnings dated to the time of the Emperor Nero, amid deep shadows, ghostly lights, and pervasive stench. Cleanliness was impossible for people whose only recourse, in the absence of soap and hot water, was pumice and olive oil. Italian soldiers returning from the Balkans brought typhus to the city with them. As cases began a rapid rise, Stone, Soper, and Fox set up a system of dusting squads, case-finding teams, and isolation hospitals, which snuffed out the epidemic in conditions about as bad as any the war would bring.[27]

Many other tests lay ahead—in Yugoslavia, where typhus ravaged the country during the multisided war among Germans, Serbs, Croats, communists, and monarchists; in Poland, where cases rose steadily among a starving population under a brutal occupation regime; in Greece, as hungry as Poland and soon to be divided by a cruel civil war; and ultimately in conquered Germany and occupied Japan. But the means and organization were now at hand to combat and defeat the disease on the terrain where it had always been most dangerous, in regions devastated by war, and among its favorite victims, the survivors and refugees.

A principal disease of wartime was on the way out—one of the more important achievements of World War II medicine, which has been forgotten precisely because typhus itself has ceased to matter very much. But other and more tenacious ailments were still around for the troops to catch. The end of the Tunisian campaign coincided with the arrival of warm weather, and next step in the Mediterranean campaigns gave warning that breakdowns in prevention were still possible at the critical junction between knowledge and application. Such a breakdown marred the otherwise triumphant campaign for Sicily.

As the new invasion approached, Americans no longer faced the problems associated with greenhorn soldiers or amateurish preparations for combat. They knew how to fight their war, and the medics, like the combat forces, deliberately built on the lessons of North Africa. The Fifth Army Training Center at Arzew put the troops through their paces. Medics learned how to waterproof their gear, enter and leave assault boats, set up on the beaches, and manage evacuation under simulated combat conditions. They wrote a manual for landings that later guided medical troops at Normandy. Unit medics, medical battalions, and field hospital units were selected to land with the assault forces. Regimental medical detachments and volunteers from the 82d Airborne Division's medical battalion prepared to jump into Sicily the night before the seaborne landing.

Materially, the forces that embarked for Sicily were extraordinarily rich in most respects. They sailed in the largest of all allied amphibious expeditions up to that time. The correspondent Ernie Pyle marveled at the fleet of 3,200 ships as it set sail: "On the horizon it resembled a distant city . . . the greatest armada ever assembled up to that moment in the whole history of the world." American forces had new landing craft that included the landing ship tank (LST), the landing craft infantry (LCI), and the amphibious truck (DUKW). The transports and landing craft that carried the troops would also evacuate the sick and wounded from the beaches, and planes would join in as soon as airfields were secured. Evacuation hospitals would be set up in Sicily; in North Africa, now the theater's communications zone, fixed hospitals would receive serious cases and soak up overflows from the battlefront.[28]

The LST was a significant new medical asset. Ungainly, unwieldy, and somewhat unlikely in appearance, with their cavernous tank bays and huge double doors in the bow, the landing ships were turned into troop carriers, because the theater lacked enough transports to haul the eight divisions assigned to the invasion. Once the troops had landed, the LSTs became evacuation ships as well—floating ambulances to return the wounded to North Africa. An army or navy medical officer and four enlisted medics joined each combat-loaded ship when it sailed. Navy beach parties agreed to classify all casualties according to whether they could be carried safely by LSTs or needed the more complex care available only on hospital ships. As matters turned out, the LSTs were just right for the new job given to them. The distance from Sicily to North Africa was not too long, the wounded rested on folding cots in the tank decks, and surgeons performed operations in the sickbays.[29]

Signs everywhere pointed to a more mature medical service supporting a more experienced and confident force. Yet the newfound sophistication had strict limits. Only about five thousand hospital beds were allotted for the sick and wounded on Sicily—perhaps a quarter of what the 200,000-man invasion force needed. Of course, Africa awaited the overflow, but shipping out the not-too-sick and the lightly wounded would weaken the force. Preparations for preventive medicine, especially against malaria, were also poor. Information about the disease environment of Sicily ought to have been easy to come by, but medics and combat arms alike apparently expected the conditions of North Africa in the winter to be repeated on Sicily in the summer. Such holes in its medical armor suggested that the newly formed North African Theater of Operations still had much to learn.[30]

The first recipients of the nasty surprises of war were the men of the 82d Airborne Division. Their jump on the eve of the invasion was marred by bad weather and poor visibility, and the pilots scattered them across southern Sicily. On the beaches in the early hours of July 10, 1943, some units landed in the wrong places, and some craft were lost on the rocks, but for the most part Patton's Seventh Army stormed ashore in fine style against halfhearted Italian resistance and established a deep lodgment.

Medics set up their aid stations and clearing stations under trees or in abandoned stone houses; they assembled their scattered forces and put together the first chains of evacuation. Hospitals began to arrive; nineteen nurses of the 15th Evacuation Hospital came in before their unit was functional and did their first work at the division clearing stations instead. Surgical teams worked with the field hospital platoons and the clearing stations, stabilizing the wounded so they could survive later trips to the rear. Within the first week the medics had many new patients to work on, for German armor staged an attack against the 1st Infantry Division near the coastal town of Gela, and the fighting left the hulks of burned-out tanks scattered over the dusty plain between the mountains and the sea.[31]

Then the Seventh Army struck out into western Sicily, aiming for the provincial capital of Palermo. The war of movement that followed tested the ability of medical units to keep up with the racing combat units, which seized Palermo on July 22. Opposition from Italian forces was spotty; the surgeon of the 2d Armored Division personally captured eight prisoners who "surrendered when intimidated by the colonel's flashlight."[32] But when Patton turned his forces eastward to join the British in a pincer movement against Messina, stubborn fighting quickly developed.

The fall of Palermo roughly coincided with a political crisis in Italy. Dictator Benito Mussolini was ousted and placed under guard, and his successors soon began secret negotiations with the Allies. Uncertain whether to fight for Sicily or abandon it, the Germans mounted a vigorous defense before withdrawing their remaining forces to the Italian mainland. Combat severe and bloody erupted along the precipitous coastal highway that connected Palermo with Messina, and in the mountains that paralleled the coast. Dynamite brought down rockslides to block the roads; medieval towns crowning treeless crags again became fortresses, as they had been in the remote past.

Americans of the 1st and 9th Infantry Divisions fought a savage battle for the rocky fortress town of Troina on Etna's northern slopes. To ease the task of the litter-bearers hauling the wounded through rough country, the aid stations advanced, some to within a quarter mile of the fighting. The 11th Field Hospital and the

11th and 15th Evacs received the serious cases. Meanwhile Americans sought to flank the Germans on the coast by amphibious landings, and the 3d Infantry Division bulldozed its way east through gaps in the mountain roads and the landslides blown by German engineers. Mule trains carried out the wounded, first to aid stations and then to the platoons of the 10th Field Hospital, which "leapfrogged one another from Cefalu to Barcellona."[33]

Despite every effort, the mountains took their toll. Injured men endured stretcher carries that lasted up to seven hours or waited for days in aid stations while bulldozers cleared a way for ambulances to reach them. As they had in North Africa, the Germans generally followed the rules of the Geneva Convention. Their doctors gave treatment to wounded prisoners and avoided having to carry them by leaving them for the advancing Americans to recover. Besides their own army's casualties, American medical units inherited prisoners of war and masses of battered civilians—some of the worst cases at shattered Troina—and gave treatment to all who needed it.[34]

In Sicily a durable association began between the division clearing station and the field hospital platoon. The point of this rather technical development lay in the fact that battlefield surgery had gotten ahead of Army organization. Everyone recognized the need for a small, mobile unit to do emergency lifesaving surgery on the wounded as close to the fighting as possible. Yet the first MASH would not take the field until after World War II was over. In the meantime, theater surgeons had to jury-rig MASH-like combinations out of existing units—or invent their own units. In the Pacific, the portable surgical hospital was beginning to provide one answer. In the war against Germany, surgical teams provided the skilled hands, while the hospital platoons contributed physicians, enlisted medics, and beds. The clearing stations did the triage: treated the lightly wounded and returned them to duty; sent the more serious cases to the rear; and transferred the most seriously injured, who could not travel at all, to the hospital platoons for emergency surgery.

Typical was the setup at San Stefano. Between the coast road and the sea, the 3d Division's medical battalion had pitched tents beside its clearing station and a platoon of the 11th Field Hospital strengthened with surgical teams. Some wounded men arrived on muleback from the mountains. Every one had lived his own adventure. A man with a compound fracture of the left thigh reached the clearing station after a two-hour litter carry and a long ambulance ride down the coast road. He was "perfectly well" on arrival, chatting and smoking a cigarette. Another, with a broken right leg, had been carried down a stream on a litter made from his shirt and two rifles. Then, with two men helping him, he jumped along on his unhurt leg. He came into the clearing station with his leg splinted by a signal-flag stick and a bayonet. He was in good spirits; with a pulse of 90 and blood pressure of 132/70, he had reason to be, though he had had nothing to eat for three days but one K-ration and a little water.

But another man with a fragment wound in the right thigh arrived in shock and much too tightly bandaged. Black blood was oozing from a small wound. Transferred to the 93d Evac, he appeared to develop gas gangrene. The injured leg was purple, the foot cold; he was toxic, disoriented, dehydrated. "At 1200 midthigh guillotine amputation. All great vessels of thigh thrombosed." Had there been a real infection with *clostridia*, the organisms that cause gas gangrene? If so, had the tight bandages enabled the infection to develop? In any case, the leg was gone.[35]

The evacs held, treated, and forwarded the worst cases to North Africa where a hospital center had grown up around Bizerte, with affiliated units staffed by major civilian hospitals and by Tulane, Louisiana State, and Vanderbilt universities. The system was the best and most complete that Americans had seen in the Mediterranean. Its record for lifesaving was superb. About a quarter of the men who were hit by enemy fire died before reaching treatment, but of the others almost 96 percent lived. Of those who lived long enough to arrive at the hospitals, only 1.5 percent died. Such figures testified both to the lethality of the battlefield and the expertness of the medical and surgical care now available to American casualties.

At the same time, the lack of beds on Sicily meant heavy losses through evacuation. Colonel Churchill reflected with some bitterness that the Seventh Army, by refusing to accept responsibility for the care of its own wounded and sick, threw the burden on the zone of communications in Africa, and as a result "the manpower of the Army is now scattered from Palermo to Oran." He compared the work of Patton's staff to a "maniac driving a machine at high speed without pausing to oil or service" it.[36] And neglect of preventive medicine made the situation much worse.

For good and ill, Sicily remained Sicily, even in wartime. In some ways the medical system benefited. Italian prisoners of war provided labor in the hospitals, and lucky patients ate fresh grapes and tomatoes sold by peddlers from painted carts. For all the blood and rubble, and the smell of unburied dead, street urchins sang arias from Verdi when they were not "hijacking GI's" for part of their rations. Arriving from Africa, Colonel Churchill found shattered villages with rooms exposed like doll's houses, all the furniture on view; a column of DUKWs loaded with 3d Division men rolled clumsily through lanes cleared by the engineers, while children ran alongside screaming, "*Caramelli, caramelli!*" and the soldiers threw them chocolate bars.[37]

Unfortunately, gamins and painted carts were not the whole story. Beginning soon after the landings, a wave of sick men crowded into the hospitals, filling first the wards and then extra beds as well, and pushing some units' evacuation policy down to twenty-four hours. Doctors took the temperature of new arrivals, and any whose fever was less than 101°—including many who were passing through their first bouts with malaria—received brief treatment and were sent back to their units. In all, there were about 5,000 American hospital beds on Sicily, but between July 10 and August 20 almost 23,000 patients had to be admitted. Almost 21,000 were Americans, and 13,000 were disease victims. Another 21,000 cases were sent to quarters, and of these almost 15,000 were sick. Since the average U.S. troop strength was 166,000, about a quarter of the American forces was at one time or another laid low by sickness, wounds, or injury. Sickness was the unforeseen element. The disease record of the Seventh Army on Sicily was one of the worst compiled by any American field army during World War II.[38]

The reasons say something about the island battleground and something about the army. In 1943 sanitation was at a primitive level in much of Sicily, and insect carriers of disease—especially flies and mosquitoes—were numerous and lively in the midsummer heat. The troops had been inoculated against typhus, smallpox, typhoid, and paratyphoid, and most had received Atabrine or quinine with their rations since the last week of April. But few medical officers had experience with malaria, and most commanders did not think the disease was important. From Patton down, their attention was fixed on the tactical situation—just like that of Pacific commanders the year before. Only one malaria control unit had landed with the invading forces, and an army moving at top speed simply could not apply the normal control measures. Finally, the troops reacted to Atabrine on Sicily in the same way as their comrades on Guadalcanal. They hated the stuff and avoided taking it whenever they could.[39]

The result was almost 10,000 malaria cases (as against some 8,000 battle casualties) and a great number of "fever of unknown origin" diagnoses that probably concealed both malaria and a local plague, sandfly fever. The overwhelming majority of the huge sick list suffered from either malaria or dysentery or both. The failure to foresee and provide against disease was not only an American problem; the British Eighth Army suffered almost 12,000 malaria cases in one eight-week period, from July 9 to September 10, 1943. For a time the two allied armies lost the equivalent of two divisions to the disease.[40]

Had not the impending collapse of Italy induced the Germans' decision to withdraw, the effect of such widespread ineffectiveness might have been serious indeed. Political instability in Rome compensated for a number of Allied shortcomings, including a lack of seriousness about the impact of malaria. As it was, the troops carried the infections contracted on Sicily with them when they made their leap to the European mainland. Almost a year later, some who were taking part in the Normandy landings would suffer relapses during the battles in northern France.

The Mediterranean campaigns of 1942–43 had been a hard school for Americans, but they had learned a great many things. Brave amateurs had become veterans, wealth had replaced poverty, and early diasters had given way to the triumphs recorded at Bizerte and Messina. New ideas had emerged that were full of promise—not only in preventing typhus but in managing the wounded and treating the stress of combat as well. Insights, how-ever, remained to be applied in practice, and with the invasion of Italy the fighting took a darker turn that soon demanded the ut-most from all practitioners of military medicine.

7

The Stress of Combat

One day toward the end of the Tunisian campaign, Ernie Pyle sat among the clumps of sword-grass on a rocky hillside and watched "the God-damned infantry . . . the mud-rain-frost-and-wind boys" plod along their endless road below him.

"Every line and sag of their bodies," he wrote, "spoke their inhuman exhaustion. . . . They didn't slouch. It was the terrible deliberation of each step that spelled out their appalling tiredness." Young as they were, they appeared middle-aged, and as they approached he saw nothing whatever in their eyes but "the simple expression of being here as though they had been doing this forever, and nothing else."

Too much weariness and fear cast long shadows. From his own experience, Pyle knew the lingering effects of being shelled—the initial rush of delight at escaping a blast alive, but also the later reaction that left him cringing at the sound of artillery. He knew the persistence of battlefield memories that could be evoked by the least thing—"a mere rustling curtain can paralyze a man with memories." He knew how the tense exhilaration of combat gave way to drugged sleep, and the uncanny nights afterward when "the air became sick and there was an unspoken contagion of spiritual dread, and we were little boys again, lost in the dark."[1]

The stress that warfare inflicted on soldiers had been growing steadily. For a century or more the industrial nations had been fielding more and more powerful weapons, integrated to deliver the most lethal possible impact. As armies grew larger, battlefields broadened not only because more fighters were present, but because heavy enemy fire compelled the troop formations to spread out. Small units became separated from the sight of their leaders, and individuals from the shoulder-to-shoulder contact with their comrades that had helped to sustain them during struggles in the past. Battles began to last for days, then for weeks or months, forcing men to spend seemingly endless time under fire. The body's fight-or-flight mechanisms, designed by nature for use in brief emergencies, instead were evoked over long periods by the constantly impending danger of death.

In World War II, the early fighting in the Pacific and Africa brought the effects of fatigue and stress home to Americans. On Guadalcanal and Papua the condition seemed closely linked to the jungle environment, its alienness, its stifling heat, and its tormenting diseases. At night the darkness was profound, and yet obscure movement and strange noises were continuous; on the front lines no man slept well unless he was exhausted. Tension exaggerated small sounds; the fall of raindrops became hostile footsteps, the rubbing of leaves the movement of infiltrators. Behind the illusion lay the reality of sudden and violent death. After the night fears, daylight revealed corpses that seemed to quiver under swarming flies.

In North Africa the landscape was absolutely different, as was the war. But combat was no less wearing. In the hills and arid plains Americans relearned the nature of battle as waged by a warlike industrial state in open country, where the full firepower of its forces could be brought to bear. In early fights preceding the main battles at Kasserine, "psychiatric reactions were responsible for 20 percent of all battlefield evacuations, and for days at a time the proportion ran as high as 34 percent."[2] Such losses were unacceptable; something had to be done.

To understand and control the conditions that resulted from combat stress was a key duty of psychiatrists in uniform. The problem was one of the most complex presented by war. Patients in all theaters showed the same symptoms of intolerable weariness and baseless alarm. Some were stuporous and withdrawn; some tense and violent; some suffered from Parkinson-like tremors or from delusions that mimicked the symptoms of schizophrenia. They were beyond self-control, and orders and threats meant nothing. Weeping, shaking, curling up in the fetal position, or merely numb and unresponsive, they had ceased to be soldiers for a time. No one could depend upon them; they could not depend upon themselves.[3]

In the beginning, many psychiatrists approached the problem from the same angle as the examiners of recruits. Breakdown in combat was not a transient condition but rather the surfacing of an inherent flaw; anyone who was susceptible ought to be excluded from the military, or if inadvertently admitted ought to be shipped out as soon as his unfitness became evident. Many commanders and medical officers gave this perfunctory solution their enthusiastic support. Once a man broke, he was damaged goods and worthless from then on. But the shape-up-or-ship-out philosophy drained away military manpower. There was no way to fight a world war with a small cadre of elite warriors. What was needed was a way of salvaging ordinary men.

Medical officers in the field began feeling their way toward a solution early in the war. On Guadalcanal the marines evacuated their worst psychiatric cases but began to send the others to labor battalions in the rear. An army medical report from the same battle concluded that "the majority of [psychiatric] cases are nothing but a direct result of . . . mental and physical fatigue." Given rest, regular food, and a chance to bathe, "85% to 90% . . . requested to be returned to their respective units."[4] Colonel Martin A. Berezin, a psychiatrist, was for a time surgeon of the Americal Division. Since his commander denounced psychiatric cases as cowards, he diagnosed their problem as blast concussion and gave a prescription of "P&S," meaning pick and shovel. Patients then worked out their fears digging trenches around the hospitals, while receiving nourishment, rest, and the decent and unsentimental kindness they needed to recover. As a result, many returned to combat without relapses, and even those who could fight no more served usefully behind the lines. By sheer good luck, the army had found its first division psychiatrist.

On New Guinea the problem was the same as on Guadalcanal, but the response was less innovative. Those planes taking off from Port Moresby fields and droning south over the Torres Strait toward Queensland proved to be irresistibly attractive to commanders and doctors alike who wished to be rid of their "mental" cases. As a result, salvageable men received a ticket out (and a lasting stigma), while the fighting forces were denied their services at a time of maximum need. And the draining of the theater did not stop there. During 1943, despite efforts at reform, almost 40 percent of the Southwest Pacific Area's evacuations to Hawaii or the United States were loosely classed as mental.[5]

The most famous case exposing the fallacy of the old ways of viewing combat breakdowns occurred not in the Pacific but on Sicily. The Seventh Army commander, Lieutenant General George S. Patton, Jr., held views that were very similar to those enunciated by the Americal Division commander on Guadalcanal. But Patton's way of showing his feelings about psychiatric casualties was unforgettably his own.

On August 3, 1943, Patton paid a visit to the 15th Evacuation Hospital near Nicosia. To declare that Patton's character was contradictory would be an understatement; the same man who had recommended letting an amputee die because "he is no goddamn use to us any more" made a practice of visiting hospitals to inquire about his wounded and often became deeply emotional in their presence. On this day in the admitting tent he happened upon a private who had recently arrived with a diagnosis of "psycho-neuroses [sic] anxiety state—moderate severe." The label meant neither more nor less than other cloudy contemporary phraseology surrounding the condition, and, as a matter of fact, the diagnosis was wrong: The man was later found to be running a high fever, and the hospital's ultimate diagnosis would be chronic dysentery and malaria.[6]

Nevertheless, the man was shaken, possibly by reading the misdiagnosis on his tag as well as by the way he felt. When Patton stopped and asked what was wrong with him, the private replied miserably, "I guess I can't take it."

At this the general lost his own self-control. Patton berated the man, slapped his face with his gloves, seized him, and threw him out of the tent. An enlisted medic picked the patient up and took him to a ward. Back at his headquarters, Patton noted in his diary, "I gave him the devil, slapped his face with my gloves and kicked him out of the hospital. . . . One sometimes slaps a baby to bring it to." He then issued a memorandum to his subordinate commanders, warning them that "a very small number of soldiers are going to the hospital on the pretext that they are nervously incapable of combat. Such men are cowards. . . . Those who are not willing to fight will be tried by Court-Martial for cowardice in the face of the enemy."[7]

A week later Patton visited the 93d Evac on another mission to cheer the wounded. In the receiving ward he found a patient shivering on his bunk with a diagnosis—in this case accurate—of severe shell shock. When Patton questioned him the man began to sob, saying, "It's my nerves, I can hear the shells coming over, but I can't hear them burst."

"What is this man talking about?" Patton demanded. "What's wrong with him, if anything?" Then he called the patient "a goddamned coward, a yellow son of a bitch." He slapped him hard and repeatedly, threatened to have him shot, and waved his pistol in the man's face. The hospital commander, who had entered the tent, had to step between Patton and his victim before the attack ended.[8]

The incidents, which cost Patton dearly, reflected in part traditional prejudices and in part his own strange personality. Yet the problem of how to deal with psychiatric casualties—other than denying they occurred, throwing a tantrum, or shipping them out—was worldwide. In the face of excessive losses caused by the evacuation of combat exhaustion cases, old prejudices began to yield, slowly and reluctantly, to the need to conserve manpower. The army began to make serious efforts to save its psychiatric casualties as functioning soldiers. In 1943 a School of Military Neuropsychiatry opened at Lawson General Hospital in Atlanta, and by the year's end division psychiatrists were listed on the army's tables of organization, even if not many were present as yet in the flesh.[9]

The new approach marked a response to reports coming in from all battlefronts, but especially from the Mediterranean, where "the impetus and success of psychiatry . . . can be traced to the efforts of a single individual, Capt. Frederick R. Hanson, M.C." Born in the United States and trained as a neurologist and neurosurgeon, Hanson had been working in Canada when the war broke out. He joined the Canadian Army and served in its psychiatric hospital in England, where he studied and learned from the experiences of the allies. When the United States entered the war, he transferred to the U.S. Army. But he volunteered to accompany the Canadians on their disastrous raid against Dieppe, and in the process found a first-rate opportunity to study the reactions of men under fire. His experiences in combat helped him to win the confidence of front-line surgeons and commanders alike.[10]

Posted to Africa and attached to II Corps, Hanson soon had many more victims of combat stress to observe. In the aftermath of the Kasserine disaster, a nurse at the 48th Surgical Hospital watched him as he patiently questioned a hundred or so combat fatigue cases in his "low and calm" voice. Hanson found that the psychiatric casualties were indistinguishable in mien from the wounded. "Their faces were expressionless," he wrote, "their eyes blank and unseeing, and they tended to go to sleep wherever they were." He concluded that the most critical factor in causing their condition was simply lack of sleep and instructed the nurses: "Put them to bed. Give huge doses of barbiturates. Awaken them only for meals and elimination. Nothing else. Don't talk to them—let them sleep."[11] Hanson's practical approach, emphasizing sedation and brief therapy, returned about 30 percent of the patients to combat duty in little more than a day, and more than 70 percent after forty-eight hours.

Another key to treating psychiatric casualties was provided by observing the course of those who were evacuated. In line with the view that men with "mental" symptoms should be removed at once—not only for their own benefit but to avoid infecting others with their fears—casualties were hauled hundreds of miles to the Atlantic coast for treatment. By the time they arrived many presented "a changing and . . . bizarre clinical picture" of mutism, amnesia, trembling, battle dreams, and hallucinations.[12] The progress of their illness showed a strong element of purpose. Psychiatric casualties were unlike the wounded in that they became worse, not better, as they moved farther to the rear. Some were simply malingerers, conscious or unconscious, who discovered imaginary ailments, exaggerated the symptoms of real injuries, and developed psychosomatic disorders long before they came within sound of the enemy's guns. But even genuine casualties resulting from the most intense combat might refuse to recover once they entered the chain of evacuation, for they could get farther to the rear and closer to safety only by continuing to be perceived as a bit mad.

Sometimes the whole illness resulted from well-meant efforts at treatment. Often a soldier's first reaction to combat fear and stress was a simple complaint of physical suffering. He appeared before a doctor and related some normal reaction—a stomach that knotted up under shellfire, tension, tachycardia, tremor. But if he were declared sick and evacuated, his original reaction became coupled with his gain in safety and comfort. Remove the battle stress, and the symptoms remained to perpetuate his new and better life in a rear-area hospital. The patient would try to convince not only the doctors that he was sick, but himself as well, in order to suppress his feelings of guilt over abandoning his buddies. His symptoms ceased to be the normal consequences of living in a perverse environment and became self-sustaining as he moved through the chain of evacuation. By its end, the condition of a normal man under stress had become "the hopeless picture [of a neurosis] when it has crystallized at the general hospital."[13]

The rediscovery of these truths (for they had been known to American military medicine in World War I, but since forgotten)[14] did not come in a single moment of revelation. Hanson and his colleagues essentially worked from back to front, first developing ways of handling psychiatric cases in the rear, then moving the work forward until the army's creation of the post of division psychiatrist enabled them to bring treatment to the front lines. By the opening of the battle for Tunisia, Hanson's ideas had matured, and he was able to win a directive from II Corps imposing them on the American forces. Psychiatric casualties were to be held in a hospital close to the front and were to be diagnosed with the term "exhaustion," borrowed from the British Eighth Army. The word was ingenious: It described pretty well the way the patient actually felt, encouraged him to believe that he could recover with rest, and removed the stigma of mental illness. Some psychiatrists complained that the term had nothing to do with the accepted lingo of their specialty, but that was probably one of its advantages.[15]

However, the psychiatrist still had to order evacuation for the most serious cases who resisted front-line treatment. Unavoidably, his judgment of who was "psychotic" rested on his interpretation of symptoms rather than on objective tests. That reflected the current state of the art, in which some of the most serious mental illnesses, such as schizophrenia, were not clinically definable entities. Freudian theory made a virtue of the problem, by treating psychic health and disease as points on a spectrum rather than as real and opposed conditions. In World War II military psychiatry, a psychotic was simply a patient with severe symptoms that persisted despite efforts to relieve them.[16]

As the new method of treatment took form, the combat psychiatrist assumed a practical and limited role. His efforts at therapy did not involve probing deeply into the psyches of his patients. Instead, he conducted sessions in open ward—a kind of "modified group therapy." Patients were encouraged to relive the experiences that had shocked them, and their memories were assisted with injections of pentothal if necessary. Sometimes "dramatic scenes" occurred, with the therapist playing the roles of buddy, squad leader, medic, platoon sergeant, or company commander, while the patient, in a condition resembling chemical hypnosis, recovered memories lost to amnesia. Psychiatrists explained their work to themselves and one another in simplified Freudian terms: the patient's superego, commonly known as his conscience, inclined him to return to duty, and the therapist sided with it in a friendly, supportive way. "Thus many returned, in order to release their super-ego tensions; to feel that they were as good men as their comrades."[17] That was a fairly good definition of why most men fight.

Patients were obliged to conform to ward routine, to wash and shave, and to walk to meals; none was allowed to remain more than three days. On the fourth or fifth, the doctors found, hypochondria set in as the patient attempted to prolong a status he found infinitely more comfortable than combat. For most men, however, removal from the immediate stress of combat did wonders when combined with sleep, a bath, verbalizing their experiences, and receiving comforting words from an authority figure—all in a forward location where air raids still occurred.

It would oversimplify the views of a complex man and physician to say that Hanson argued for the immediate situation as the cause of combat breakdown, while doctors trained in psychoanalytic psychiatry argued for remote events in the patient's past. Yet different military psychiatrists tended to divide roughly along those lines, emphasizing either the situation or some basic weakness in the patient that was activated by stress. Perhaps the importance of Hanson and his colleagues was simply to show that the combat psychiatrist had to act *as if* the situation were the cause, and to respond by adopting whatever method worked in the greatest number of cases, salvaged the greatest number of soldiers, and returned them to useful work either in combat or in noncombat jobs. Theories were neither true nor false but simply irrelevant. Pragmatism was the guide to follow.

The African experience opened the way to a better understanding of those who endured the stress of combat as well as those who broke. In a series of papers first presented at a theater seminar in February 1943, and later collected and published by the surgeon general, Hanson and his colleagues sought to produce a guidebook "unobscured by argumentative theory" for the nonpsychiatrically trained medical officer. In the first place, they warned that normality does not mean the same thing for the civilian and the combat soldier: "To discuss combat neuroses in terms of civil life is to invalidate the inquiry." On the battlefield the abnormal—insomnia, trembling, recurrent nightmares—became normal.[18]

For that reason, psychological health in time of peace was no guarantee against the cataclysmic events of war. Hanson warned that even people of superior emotional stability might become psychiatric casualties. Furthermore, no single factor explained all cases of combat fatigue. In the environment of war, fatigue, terrain, and weather interacted with fear, belief, the quality of leadership, and unit morale. Sickness helped to exhaust a man, and exhaustion could help to make him sick. Under so many pressures, a complete cure of the patient's symptoms might be impossible, but most patients could be returned to duty as effective, functioning soldiers. The psychiatrist had to learn to forgo perfection and to see his work in the context of war.[19]

By the later phases of the African campaign, the proportion of cases who returned to full duty without evacuation from the combat zone was a fairly constant 58–63 percent. The command made division surgeons responsible for the initial treatment of psychiatric casualties, and psychiatrists were attached to all the forward evacuation hospitals. The system's success did not result from any decline in the level of combat. On the contrary, casualties mounted steadily, and the last month's fighting in North Africa brought almost twice as many wounded to the hospitals as the period from New Year's Day to mid-March, which had included the Kasserine debacle. The improvement was real, both in the return rate and in the understanding of psychological stress that had produced it. Hanson's brilliant record caused the Theater Surgeon to appoint him theater consultant in neuropsychiatry and enabled him to secure directives establishing a theaterwide program, which became a model for the army as a whole.[20]

The course of events in the Mediterranean now took a turn that underlined and reemphasized the importance of combat psychiatry. While preparations went forward for the invasion of Italy, the focus of the war shifted to the north. General Eisenhower departed to England to prepare the assault on occupied France. Units and shipping were diverted to England in preparation for Normandy. The North African Theater passed to British control, becoming more than ever subject to Prime Minister Winston

Churchill's long obsession with what he liked to call the soft underbelly of Europe.

All those events tended to make the fighting in Italy less important, yet harder. The purpose of the Mediterranean front slowly was being reduced to holding down German forces that might otherwise deploy to France. Yet, with Italy's surrender, its soldiers abandoned their defensive positions, and when General Mark Clark's Fifth Army staged a combat landing at the west-coast harbor of Salerno, the Germans who had taken the Italians' place put up a stout and bloody resistance from the first day. After the Allies won their foothold, the Germans withdrew to the first of a series of defensive lines, and soon the American Fifth Army and the British Eighth were mired—often in the most literal sense—in a grinding campaign of attrition.

Far from being soft, much of the underbelly of Europe is armored by interlocking mountain chains, none harsher than the Apennines, which form the long spine of Italy. Rivers run east or west from the mountains, segmenting the peninsula and providing natural moats to reinforce the stony mountain walls. The results of attacking in such country were many wounded, many cold injuries in the mountains and mud, and stress induced by profound physical and spiritual exhaustion. For months the Allies confronted the Germans along the Garigliano River and its tributary the Rapido. Beyond the rivers, the ancient abbey of Monte Cassino, crowning one height, gave the enemy unobstructed views of the whole battlefield. Beneath the mountain lay the opening of the Liri Valley, leading to the great prize of Rome, 80 miles to the north.

Incessant winter rains soaked the lowland fields, driving all traffic onto a few narrow roads that were commanded by German artillery. Vainly the Allies battered at these iron gates, for the terrain limited their ability to move elsewhere. Every advance meant fighting up mined slopes against cleverly emplaced machine guns and incessant sniper fire. In mid-November a war correspondent marveled at the ability of the troops holding positions in the bleak mountain ridges to survive and fight amid "that mud, those dark skies, those forbidding ridges and ghostlike clouds that unveiled and then quickly hid the enemy." From the deep, glutinous mud in the valleys to the cold of the rainswept mountains, misery, exhaustion, and danger were the lot of the troops. Frostbite, trenchfoot, and rising rates of combat fatigue resulted. The medics who supported them suffered no less. Litter carries were long and arduous, and danger was everywhere; aid stations huddled in caves, and surgeons in exposed locations worked by flashlight under blankets.[21]

In December a bizarre event on the Adriatic coast brought a new kind of medical emergency. During a night raid, the Luftwaffe found the harbor of Bari choked with allied shipping and sent seventeen vessels to the bottom. Among them was the S.S. *John Harvey*, loaded with 100 tons of mustard gas bombs that had been sent to Italy to be stockpiled for retaliation in case the Germans resorted to gas warfare. Liquid mustard—dichloroethyl sulfide, an irritant chemical that can be lethal if inhaled or swallowed—"began spreading across the harbor, some of it sinking, some burning, some mixing with oil floating on the surface, and some of it evaporating and mingling with the clouds of smoke and flame."

Ship's officers who knew about the gas had been killed. Men struggling in the water were soaked in contaminated oil, and others laboring to put out the fires inhaled the mustard fumes. As victims flooded the local hospitals, British, American, New Zealand, Indian, and Italian doctors at first were baffled by their patients' irritated eyes, chemical burns, and excessive symptoms of shock. Soon many were in agony, severely burned and temporarily blind; some collapsed and died. Official secrecy shrouded the fact that a ship with mustard gas as part of its cargo had been sunk in the harbor. Diagnosis was delayed until Lieutenant Colonel Stewart F. Alexander, a physician who was an expert on chemical injuries, arrived from Eisenhower's headquarters with the crucial information. More than six hundred cases were treated in all, and the death rate was nearly seven times as high as the 2 percent recorded for victims of mustard gas in World War I.[22]

Yet for all its horrors, Bari was just one dreadful accident; the main killer of men was the campaign itself. During that same December an allied assault on the main German lines produced massive casualties. The American 36th Infantry Division alone counted more than two thousand after an attack that left the front immobile and the medical units choked with survivors. Equally desperate were events that followed at the Anzio beachhead. Attempting an end run around the German lines, General Mark Clark landed the American–British VI Corps up the coast at the small resort town that lay only 30 miles south of Rome. Few casualties marred the landing, and Anzio itself fell quickly. But the Germans first contained the invasion and then, in fierce tank assaults, almost destroyed it. Attempts by the Allies to break out failed, and the Germans mounted savage counterattacks, trying to drive the invaders into the sea.[23]

German shells and bombs battered the little enclave, which Hitler called "that abscess." Chivalry went by the board as his forces labored to destroy it. By accident or malicious intent, the Germans bombed three British hospital ships offshore, sinking one of them. Accident heightened the danger. A barrage from German 88s smashed into the 33d Station Hospital. On February 7, a Spitfire fighter attacked a German bomber, which jettisoned its load onto the 95th Evacuation Hospital. No part of the beachhead was safe, and none of the hospitals stood more than 6 miles from the fighting line. Since Anzio and nearby Nettuno drew enemy fire—"marble statues fell in littered patios," an observer wrote, "everywhere there was rubble and mud and broken wire"—the hospitals were set up in open fields, in tents dug into the damp ground and revetted by dirt and sandbags.[24]

Under such conditions, echelons ceased to mean much; rear-area medical units that were normally secure faced the same dangers as battalion aid stations. Among the dead at Anzio were six army nurses, and three others were awarded the Silver Star. To the surgeon general, "the presence of Army Nurses on the beachhead carried a significance which cannot be overestimated." Men on the fighting line felt that if the women could take it, so could they. Officers debated evacuating the nurses but concluded that the move would be unwise, for it would "betray to the combat troops the gravity of their own plight." By staying, taking losses, and winning medals for heroism, the nurses aimed a small but telling missile of their own at the notion that women have no place under fire.[25]

Surely they were needed at Anzio. Even with the arrival of additional hospitals and several medical battalions, the Americans had fewer than four thousand beds for their sick and wounded during the period of heaviest fighting. Through those beds passed 33,000 patients in the course of about four months, while the British hospitals treated almost 15,000 casualties. The two allies shared their work and resources; British casualties who needed neurosurgery often were transferred to American hospitals, while Americans depended for whole blood upon a British field transfusion unit.[26]

The siege brought disease and stress as well as wounds. Malaria was held in check by rigorous control methods and still more by the winter season, but infectious hepatitis spread, probably through fecal contamination of the besieged area with its penned-in thousands. Winter cold and wet discouraged malaria, but the change of seasons brought another affliction in its place. Trench-foot had appeared in the autumn of 1943 and reached something of a climax in the Anzio beachhead. The condition results from failing circulation in the feet—the extremities that carry an infantryman through war. Tight-laced boots and soaking in cold water and mud can both contribute, for cold causes the blood vessels to contract and damages the fine nerve endings, while wetness conducts away body heat. Conditions more likely to cause trench-foot than the Italian fighting of 1943–44 would have been hard to find. The condition was not to be taken lightly; it killed no one, but it sidelined an infantrymen as effectively as a bullet, making its victim a hospital case because he could not walk. Often the pain was agonizing.[27]

As Hanson had warned, all the elements of war interacted to cause combat fatigue. Unfortunately, the psychiatric history of the Italian campaign opened with a general regression to the bad practices of the past in the Fifth Army—apparently because of the views held by the Fifth Army surgeon. Rapid evacuation to North Africa became the rule, producing a flood of casualties, many of whom sported mythical diagnoses of blast injury and similar euphemisms. Soon the abominable conditions of the winter fighting made for an increased load of genuine casualties as well, while the rate of psychiatric losses returned to duty in Italy sank below 20 percent.

On the Anzio beachhead the lack of beds compelled evacuation until mid-February 1944, when an evacuation hospital was designated to handle all psychiatric cases. But the hospital returned less than 10 percent to their units, apparently because it embodied the ideal of forward treatment much too well. Shelled and bombed by the enemy, the hospital was even more perilous than the front lines, providing its patients little rest and no relief from anxiety. Treatment with sedatives only increased their danger, because the hospital had too few attendants to move drugged men to safety when German artillery zeroed in.

In November 1943 the War Department established the position of division psychiatrist, and in the same month the Fifth Army at last allowed Hanson to visit Italy. At his urging, the army surgeon set up a psychiatric treatment center at the 161st Medical Battalion, in a tented hospital where attendants and patients wore battle dress. The location—within the sound of artillery—proved to be excellent; rest and recovery were possible, but escape from the war was not. The unit became a center not only for treating cases but for teaching psychiatrists and doing missionary work among medical and nonmedical officers alike. The concept of the normality of psychiatric symptoms in battlefield conditions became an important guide for doctors who had to distinguish every day between fear and radical discomfort on the one hand and incipient breakdown on the other—no easy task.[28]

In March 1944 an experiment was tried in the 3d Infantry Division at Anzio. Psychiatric casualties were heavy after a winter of siege; the beachhead remained all front and no rear, so that even support troops were subjected to much the same dangers as riflemen and suffered breakdowns under the stress. Captain Joseph Robert Campbell, a "decisive and firm" medical officer with much combat experience, set up a unit staffed by himself, a line officer, and seven enlisted medics to treat psychiatric casualties. The mood was entirely nonhospital; the unit was attached to the division's engineer battalion, and its program featured rest, physical work, and therapy. Campbell returned 66 percent of his psychiatric cases to duty. He also evaluated disciplinary cases from the stockade, returning about one-third of them to duty as well. So promising was the success rate that—in another step forward for combat psychiatry—treatment at division level later became the rule in the Italian campaign.[29]

With his colleagues, Campbell set up the Anzio Beachhead Psychiatric Society to provide mutual support and to discuss interesting cases. In one such session Captain Raymond Sobell, psychiatrist of the 34th Infantry Division, first described a condition that he called the old sergeant syndrome. Sobell's unit was a solid veteran organization, with hundreds of days of fighting behind it in Tunisia and Italy. Its men had increasingly come to believe that they had endured more combat than any other unit in the army and deserved rotation to the United States, if possible, or at least to noncombat duty.

In the relative lull of March and April 1944, with the bitter days of siege just behind and the expected battle to break through the German lines lying just ahead, old hands, usually sergeants or officers, men with long and honorable records, began to show up with anxiety disorders that did not yield to the customary treatments. They were, they said, burned out, all shot, no good. They trembled uncontrollably at shellfire; they froze under danger, unable to think or function; afterward they showed no emotion, only apathy. Such men "sadly admitted that [they were] not sick, but different or changed, and could no longer tolerate combat stress."[30]

The development of combat psychiatry in the theater so far had been fundamentally optimistic, a process of discovering ways to manage the consequences of stress and to help the fighter endure. But the experiences of Sicily and Italy now began to paint a darker and more mechanistic picture of the essentially unavoidable and untreatable consequences of prolonged combat attrition. The studies attracted attention in Washington. In reports to the general staff, the Army Surgeon General speculated about ways to prepare the soldier more adequately to face the stress of battle. Efforts to support morale by propaganda had revealed only the striking insignificance of appeals to the Democratic Way of Life, the Four Freedoms, and other such abstractions. Instead, the relentless grind of combat had begun to produce a type of psychiatric breakdown that seemed to have little to do with childhood repressions, individual weakness, malingering, simple exhaustion, or the initial shock of combat.

Over the course of time, reliable soldiers, well led and adequately supplied, were observed to fail at a fairly predictable rate. Even in Africa, medics had begun to talk about the breaking point—the time when combat service would produce psychiatric breakdown in most fighting men. Italy tended to confirm their observations. Viewing the reports from the theater, the surgeon general in September 1944 concluded that the limit was about two hundred aggregate days. Beyond that point, "the 'worn out' soldier . . . is through." The reason was the cumulative effect produced by the peril of death. "Each moment of [combat]," General Kirk declared, "imposes a strain so great that men will break down in direct relation to the intensity and duration of their exposure. Thus, psychiatric casualties are as inevitable as gunshot or shrapnel wounds in warfare."[31]

Some medical officers denied that any quantitative limit could be set, arguing that the quality of service was the determining factor: A single near miss could use up more of a soldier's limited allowance of days than a long period without traumatic happenings. Others accepted the surgeon general's idea of a time limit but argued over its length. Many officers in the combat arms felt that the limit was only 180 or even 140 days. Some studies suggested that units that fought much beyond 80–90 days were able to endure only because so many men became casualties of wounds or disease before they had time to crack up psychologically. Whatever viewpoint was adopted, the stress of modern war appeared to set limits to human endurance. Those who succumbed to its attrition could not be made effective combat soldiers again.[32]

The only hope was prevention. The British practice of systematic rotation, Kirk claimed, doubled the period of combat effectiveness to about four hundred days. Some form of rotation was essential to keep effective troops on the line in modern war. But American commitments were heavy, and the surgeon general was far down the chain of command. The army recommended the rotation of combat units for periods of rest but left compliance up to theater commanders, who in turn left the matter to field armies, whose commanders might be too pressed to consider it. Attempts by the ground forces to rotate combat troops usually took the form of efforts to relieve individual soldiers with longest service, rather than to establish a definite tour of duty, as the air force did. In general, Americans underrated the importance of unit integrity; they could have learned much from their British allies but failed to do so.[33]

Instead, systematic rotation was left to future wars, and when at last it was introduced it quickly turned out to bring new problems while it solved old ones. Perhaps the only solution was to have shorter wars, if wars there must be. The massive, long-lasting conflict that was World War II took the human system to its limits and beyond.

As the deadlocked armies awaited the spring, the American forces could look back on more than a year of bitter conflict that had matured every aspect of their military machine, though at great cost. The American leaders of the Normandy invasion had emerged from the Mediterranean fighting, and many of the veterans would take part in the battles to come in France. Medically, much had been learned in the same hard school. As the Surgeon General said, "the Fifth Army medical service has in a very real sense served both as an experimental laboratory and as a training ground in preparation for the offensive in Western Europe."[34] That was true in many fields besides psychiatry, in none more than combat surgery and the management of the wounded.

8

Wounded in Action

The journalist Richard Tregaskis, already famous for his
Guadalcanal Diary, had traveled to the other side of the
world to cover the invasion of Italy, drawn by the demands of his
job and an addiction to danger. "The lure of the front is like an
opiate," he wrote. "After abstinence and the tedium of workaday
life, its attraction becomes more and more insistent."[1] He found
what he was looking for in the mountains near Cassino, late in the
autumn of 1943, and almost lost his life in the process.

Wanting to watch the fighting, he followed a blood trail left by
casualties to a hilltop. He had seen what he could of the battle and
was descending the trail again when he heard the "scream of
something coming" and dived to the rocks. A smothering explosion rushed down upon him, and he sensed he had been hit: "A
curtain of fire rose, hesitated, hovered for an infinite second. In
that measureless interval, an orange mist came up quickly over my
horizon, like a tropical sunrise, and set again, leaving me in the
dark."[2]

He woke up lying near his helmet, which had two holes in it. He felt no pain, only a sense that everything was "finished, quiet, as if time had stopped." He saw men running at a half-crouch, but when he tried to shout, the sounds he made were muted and incoherent. He could not talk but after a moment of panic realized that he could still think. In between thought and speech, something in his brain had become disconnected.

Another shell burst with an oddly feeble, tinny sound. A terrified soldier saw him but ran on, saying, "I can't help you, I'm too scared." An aidman dropped down beside Tregaskis, bandaged his head, and gave him a shot of morphine with a needle he did not feel. Then the aidman, too, was gone.

He tried to pick up his glasses, lying near him and miraculously unbroken. It was then he found that one arm wouldn't work. He got up, holding the paralyzed arm like a foreign object, and began to walk. More shells came down; blood covered his glasses like drapery. He met a friend, who helped him to go farther, bearing part of his weight with Tregaskis's good arm across his shoulders. Between shock and morphine, Tregaskis still felt no pain. At a command post in a peasant hut near the edge of some woods, the journalist found an aid station; a doctor looked at his head, and he swallowed sulfa tablets. He found himself a new kind of celebrity, the object of solemn attention from passing soldiers: "me, the Badly Wounded Man."

Tregaskis had entered the chain of evacuation. It was a hard road to travel. An occasional man might ride in comfort away from the battalion aid station, nursing a million-dollar wound that was not life-threatening and promised him a ticket out of danger. But most were not so fortunate. The wounded man pitching about in a litter on a jeep ambulance racing down a rutted road under shellfire was luckier than his Civil War grandfather, because he had morphine in him, springs under him, and sophisticated treatment awaiting him somewhere down the road. In other ways his fate was much the same. Always pain hovered just the other side of the morphine curtain, sometimes poking through like an assailant's blade, and confusion and fear for life and limb rode with him.

Usually his next stop was a collecting station in his regimental area, where his condition was checked again, the lightly injured were separated from the more serious cases, and men with severe wounds received transfusions of whole blood. Then he passed on to the clearing station, whose doctors took any measures that were necessary to halt bleeding, open airways, immobilize fractures, control pain, and discourage infection. At a nearby field hospital the badly injured man went under the surgeon's knife to prepare him to travel further. Then he passed on to the evacuation hospital for complex treatment and, in some cases, preparation for the next journey—this time to a station hospital or numbered general hospital in the communications zone.

In the process, he moved through a succession of commands. As far as the clearing station he remained under the control of his division, and as far as the evacuation hospital under the control of his field army. Organizations called medical groups often managed evacuation to the rear of divisions, or a separate medical battalion might handle the job. Aircraft became ever more important, and for most patients in World War II air evacuation meant a light plane carrying them to some rear airstrip, where medical holding units cared for them and, in time, loaded them on one of the workhorse cargo-carriers, such as the C-47, C-54, or C-54A.

Tregaskis, like most other casualties, passed through the first stages of the system in a daze. He received morphine at the aid station, dozed, and vomited. Consciousness came and went: He was lying in the back of a jeep enjoying the cool air; he was in a tent and heard voices talking about a tetanus shot, but again he did not feel the needle. Stretcher-bearers carried him into another tent, where a bright light glared and gruff voices talked, and then to a third. He was cold and shivered. In a warm tent a doctor questioned him, and he answered in garbled speech. He was X-rayed; a man with a cheerful voice apologized and shaved his head. A surgeon brusquely told him that they were going to operate; then a minister said a prayer.

Tregaskis was sitting propped up on a crude operating table while unseen people moved about his head. Gowned and masked figures gave him a blood transfusion through the veins of one foot. Novocaine had numbed the top of his head. (Like most cranial operations, this one was performed under local anesthesia). In a stupor, he heard occasional voices and "a crunching sound and a snapping of bone as some sort of instrument gouged into my skull." His legs were tied to the table, and they grew stiff as the operation stretched out, hour after hour. The shell had blown fragments of bone into Tregaskis' brain, and pulling them out took time.

After the operation he lay in a peaked ward tent lined with cots. The floor was the hard Italian earth. His days were divided between tormented sleep and nausea, and an enlisted medic called the ward boy held a basin for him when he retched. Since he could keep nothing down, a glucose drip fed him. The right side of his body was numb, the limbs mere objects, and the right side of his face was "as thick and insensible as a layer of felt." Friends and celebrities (and some people who were both) began to visit him. Margaret Bourke-White took his picture, and Ernie Pyle and others of the ink-fingered brotherhood dropped by. But Tregaskis could not talk to any of them. He had women nurses, one of whom patiently tried to make him pronounce her name, and a chaplain who asked him what denomination he belonged to. Tregaskis knew the word was Presbyterian, but he had no idea how to pronounce it.

The neurosurgeon who had done the operation came to see him. Major William Pitts was a young, handsome man, a North Carolinian as all the doctors were, for this was the 38th Evac, an affiliated unit from Charlotte. Pitts explained that Tregaskis had been hit in the left side of the brain, in the region that controlled speech, and in the motor area; he would need six months to recuperate and would wear a metal plate in his skull. Tregaskis learned that Pitts considered three hours of sleep a restful night; he had begun work on Tregaskis, for example, at 4 A.M., after doing three other operations. Perhaps for that reason, Pitts tended to be brusque, but he became less so as the acquaintance ripened.

A friend brought Tregaskis letters from home but, except for random phrases, the words meant nothing to him. Around him the life of the ward moved on. New cases were always arriving. This was an evacuation hospital, and it was a medical turnstile; patients were always being carried in and out. The men who could walk wore red corduroy robes inscribed with "M.D.U.S.A."; of course the letters meant Medical Department,

U.S. Army, but the patients with gallows humor said they stood for Many Die, You Shall Also. When Tregaskis was alone he spent much time brooding over his hard fate, a writer who could not express himself, a correspondent who could not talk or walk or query. He decided to endure patiently until he was on the boat, bound for America, and then, if he had not improved, to jump over the side.

In fact, he began to recover. First the nausea left him. Then, waking from a nap one afternoon, he had the feeling that something was crawling over his hand. Electric tremors crept up into his shoulder and neck. Sensation came back; he could move his hand a bit; he could read a few more words in his waiting letters. The process was slow, halting, erratic still; when he tried to say the name of his home town—Elizabeth, New Jersey—it came out, for some incomprehensible reason, Rooker. All around him patients who were feeling better chattered about their outfits, their homes, and the adventures that had gotten them their wounds, but the man of words remained silent.

He deliberately worked to improve himself, memorizing poems from the *Pocket Book of Verse* and trying to pronounce the words. A lovely night nurse inspired him to try

She walks in beauty, like the night
Of cloudless climes and starry skies,

but the first line was tough and the second defeated him. Finally, he was carried out of the 38th Evac, on his way to a general hospital that had, he noted incredulously, been "set up in a *building*, north of Naples."

He had reached the communications zone. The business of its commands, called base sections, was to gather war matériel and replacements and ship them forward, and to receive smashed equipment for repair and injured men for treatment and disposition. Communications zone hospitals were generally bigger and more permanent—or at any rate, less transient—than those that served the field armies. They had staff and equipment to do complex procedures and facilities to carry out some important research as well.

Despite the obvious advantages of being away from the battle line, not all rear area hospitals were comfortable and safe. The big hospitals existed in every possible condition of safety and danger, rigor and comfort. Those that stood close to the fighting zone shared many of its characteristics, including canvas overhead and seas of mud underfoot. One hospital in Algeria reported that some beds sank to the springs in mud under the weight of the patient; another had to be moved from Tunis because the temperature in the operating room kept going to 135°F. Mass medicine was still the rule; the 6th General Hospital at Casablanca had one vast, 500-bed ward. Depending on the hospital's location, bombs and shells might land altogether too close. On the North African coast, flights of German planes roared over hospitals to drop bombs on the ports where troops and equipment were being loaded for the fighting in Italy.[3]

Italy was blessed with many outsize buildings, usually somewhat damaged. In Naples, a cluster of modern structures originally put up by Mussolini for an exposition celebrating Fascist Italy became a medical center. A big rear-area hospital in the communications zone often was a place of many nations, with its American staff, local civilian hired hands, and prisoner-of-war laborers, as well as guards and hangers-on. All the help did not prevent nurses from having too work much to do, with fifty or so men to a ward. Italian patients started the war as POWs but later became cobelligerents when Italy changed sides; in either case, most were cared for by their own countrymen. Big cities like Naples and Rome tended to become medical centers for all the obvious reasons, especially transport. But hospitals also dotted the countryside, where they were safely remote from the targets favored by enemy bombers.

In the hospital complexes of the communication zone, specialization developed, beginning during the Sicilian campaign. There the North African Theater faced a practical problem: too few surgeons were left in the rear areas, after necessary assignments had been made to the mobile hospitals supporting the troops. The answer was to concentrate the available talent and to assign patients on the basis of their needs. Brain and spinal cord injuries, for example, for a time went to the 78th Station Hospital, eye cases to the 114th Station Hospital, and so forth. The port surgeon at Bizerte sorted the injured at the docks, and the 802d Medical Air Evacuation Transport Squadron did the same at Mateur Airfield. The scheme put a burden on transport, and sometimes beds at the best hospital for a particular patient's type of case were full, so he had to go elsewhere.[4] But the innovation was too sensible not to take root and spread to other theaters. When hospital centers developed, it became possible for different parts of a single complex to specialize, and patients could be moved from one to another without much trouble or loss of time.

Tregaskis found his own general hospital no less wonderful than he had imagined. It had floors! Central heat! In time, amid such luxuries, he improved still further. He learned to walk again, regained in great measure the ability to speak, and, when he reached the next hospital in Africa, was beginning clumsily to type. He was marked for evacuation by plane to the United States. At this point his road diverged from that of the ordinary wounded GI. In all theaters, a special form of hospital developed to handle men whose wounds had healed, but who were not ready to fight again. Convalescence, as everybody knows who has been ill for a long time, is mostly an agreeable experience, with ebbing pains and a warm sense of daily improvement and growing strength. Rear area hospitals could be happy places for men who were getting better, with exercise and physical therapy, amateur sports and theatricals, and Red Cross workers to supply them books and small luxuries, organize games and parties, and listen sympathetically to their troubles and tales of home.

Of course all that was too good to last, and returning health ultimately meant that the patient moved on again. Convalescent hospitals eventually appeared in all the major theaters, for they emptied general hospital beds for the injured men who needed them and put those who were recovering on a course of rehabilitation and physical conditioning aimed at making them fit for service again. At convalescent centers, the men wore uniforms instead of pajamas, stood formations, often slept in tents, and did exercises that were adapted to their abilities. This was the last link in the chain of evacuation. Any soldier in a convalescent hospital could assume that his next stop would be a "repple depple"—a replacement depot, outside the medical system.[5]

———————

Such in outline was the chain of evacuation as it was known to the wounded man. Supporting it was a structure of people and ideas—of skilled men and women, laboratory discoveries and field experience, teaching and commands, bureaucratic organization and individual initiative. Since the system that emerged in the Mediterranean for handling the wounded became a model for other theaters, it is worth examining in some detail.

Among the wounded, the surgeon made the crucial decisions. His was a brusque and bloody trade. "There's only one good way to learn surgery," a medical officer once said, "and that's to get bloody wet."[6] Almost anything that could happen to the human body in peacetime by way of gashing or smashing could occur also in war, and a great deal more besides. The damage that weapons could inflict on the human body was varied and sometimes spectacular. Veterans remembered—sometimes dreamed, years after the war—of bodies literally torn to pieces, of intestines hung on trees like Christmas festoons.

The impact velocity of the missile was a critical factor; superhigh velocities could make even small missiles deadly. Less than a thousandth of a second—the time that the missile was moving inside the victim's body—was needed for a bullet or high-velocity fragment to leave a bleeding track of cut and torn flesh. Surrounding the track was a zone of damage where shock waves of 1,000 pounds to the square inch pulped the soft tissues, broke bones, ruptured blood vessels, and blew the viscera apart. Fragments aside, an explosion by itself could destroy a human body, striking it with a wall of compressed air moving at many times the velocity of a tornado's winds.[7]

The most critical period elapsed between the time a soldier was hit and the time a surgeon went to work on the injury. Crowded into this eventful period, which might range from a few hours to several days, were the trauma of the wound, the victim's escape from the line of fire, first aid given by a medic, initial treatment by a doctor at an aid station, and a trip by ambulance, litter jeep or mule via collecting and clearing stations to a field hospital with its auxiliary surgical unit.[8] The time brought many dangers. A wound was not simply damage to the body, like a crumpled fender on a car. A wound was a process, and if neglected (or, on the other hand, too assiduously examined and reexamined) could easily initiate a downward spiral. Pain prevented the wounded man from resting; bleeding and sweating dehydrated him; and the fear of permanent mutilation or death added to his exhaustion and stress.

Yet most of the men who survived the initial hit and went under the knife in wartime hospitals were not only saved but restored as functional human beings. War surgery was the great lifesaver of those who were injured in combat, and in many ways the Mediterranean Theater became the army's teacher in the managing of the wounded. In staffing its hospitals with surgeons the theater—like the armed forces as a whole—began with good material. The younger men at the forward hospitals were probably the best-trained generation of American surgeons yet to appear, and specialists of the highest quality worked in the big hospitals to the rear.[9]

Experience with war wounds was another matter. Twenty-three years had elapsed between the last battles of World War I and the first of World War II in which American forces took part. Young surgeons entered the military with no personal experience of war to guide them and a tendency to draw the wrong conclusions from their peacetime occupations. "The teaching of wound surgery to a civilian-trained surgeon," Colonel Churchill said, "is not easy. He starts with an underestimation of the severity of war wounds. A surgeon would say, 'But I've worked for years in the Detroit Receiving Accident Hospital. I know how to handle wounds.' But he still would have no conception of the destructive force of high-velocity missiles."[10]

Even older men who had served in 1917–18 faced an entirely new kind of conflict on a scale no one in uniform could remember. The North African–Italian campaigning of 1942–45 marked Americans' lengthiest experience in large-scale conventional warfare since the Civil War. (The Pacific theaters fought longer but with smaller forces, while the European Theater saw larger forces engaged, but for less than a year.) Learning wartime surgery might entail anything from minor adjustments to revolutionary changes in outlook. In the general hospitals military surgery differed from its civilian counterpart mainly in the greater number of wounded and the burden that waves of injuries from major battles imposed on the doctors and nurses. In other respects, one great hospital was much like another, at least as far as treatment went (comfort and safety were another matter). In big military hospitals the sophistication of the surgeons, the equipment, the operating rooms, the preparation of the patient, and the postoperative care were all on the best civilian models.

Matters were different in the mobile hospitals, and every mile closer to the front increased the difference. The division clearing stations, the field hospital platoons, and the auxiliary surgical teams that supported them practiced what the surgeon-author of the novel M*A*S*H later called "meatball surgery . . . a specialty in itself," explaining: "We are not concerned with the ultimate reconstruction of the patient. We are only concerned with getting the kid out of here alive enough for someone else to reconstruct him."[11] That was a hard lesson for some surgeons to learn. As the chief surgical consultant to the British Army in North Africa pointed out, military surgery was part of "the science of warfare," and no operation was complete in itself but rather "a part of a process." It went against the surgeon's grain to do hasty patchwork and then move on to the next patient. But if he performed long, meticulous work of perfect craftsmanship on one man, others who were waiting might die.[12]

Mass casualties demanded a new attitude, for time was of the essence, and forward surgery was in no sense elementary. The technology of destruction had advanced, bringing heavier concentrations of fire, more powerful ammunition, a lethal array of mines and booby-traps, and radical improvements in tanks and airplanes. Bombed, shelled, or blown up by mines, 80 percent of the wounded had injuries that were produced by weapons other than bullets. Hot metal and high explosive did amazing things. Human bodies arrived looking like the work of an incompetent butcher, torn, shattered, and disemboweled, yet still alive. The wounds were ghastly to the eye and complex puzzles to the surgeon, who had to solve them quickly with lives hanging in the balance.[13]

A specialty had to be learned, and in the early days of the war learning military surgery was far from easy. The medical and surgical lessons of World War I were embalmed in huge historical volumes put out by the Army Medical Department, but few surgeons knew of their existence, and almost none had read them. Surgical practice had changed a great deal since 1918, and the advent of new chemicals that slowed or blocked the multiplication of bacteria—the sulfa drugs and, later, penicillin—proved to be both a godsend and a source of confusion to front-line surgeons dealing with the dirty wounds of war. The widely read reports from Pearl Harbor made much of the value of sulfanilamide, without necessarily underlining the context of able wound surgery in which it was used.

The new military surgeon had to learn the value of decisive action. *Debridement*, as Americans used the word, meant cutting out all the dead tissue, but it also meant learning to distinguish and leave what was sound. "One must not mutilate living tissue or destroy functional structures." It meant opening the wound wide to inspection, not performing what Colonel Churchill scornfully called a "vaginal examination" with one or two fingers or a "circumcision" around the place where the missile had entered or exited. It meant delayed closure—leaving the wound open until it was definitely free of infection—but it meant also avoiding the scarring and contractures that might result by cutting along the natural folds and creases of the skin.[14]

As a substitute for proper debridement, rather than a supplement, the new drugs bred a false sense of security in the surgeon. In the patient they permitted something else to breed—thriving colonies of microbes that grew in overlooked corners of wounds where the drugs could not penetrate. Paradoxically, wonder drugs if misused could increase the danger of infection rather than reduce it.[15]

Learning to use the new drugs as adjuncts to sound surgical practice was only one aspect of a broader problem. Both medical science and the technology of war were undergoing swift and revolutionary transformation, and as a result military surgery had to be not only learned but constantly relearned. The teachers of technique and setters of standards were the surgical consultants, senior officers who advised the surgeon general and command chief surgeons down the line. They traveled constantly, observed surgeons at work, and guided them by persuasion and example if possible, with the sanction of military discipline to fall back on if all else failed.

While Colonel Churchill carried out the task for the Allied Force Headquarters, other consultants were assigned to the field armies—an innovation by the North African Theater that was later copied by all others. Serving the Fifth Army was Major Howard F. Snyder, whose account of his own training for a demanding task was representative of many others. A thoracic (chest) surgeon, he began to learn wartime surgery in 1942 at a British hospital in England, working with British surgeons and studying their methods. The first thing he noticed was that the operating rooms were strikingly empty—"no surgical assistants, no nurses, and no attendants of any kind." It appeared that much of the elaborate staffing and ritual that surrounded civilian surgery could be dispensed with (a lesson the portable surgical hospital surgeons of the Southwest Pacific were learning in even more radical form about the same time).

Snyder moved to Africa for his encounter with war. There he worked with British casualties from Algiers and the shocking aftermath of Kasserine. He landed in Sicily on D-Day, served through the campaign, and shortly after its end was appointed to the newly created post of surgical consultant to the Fifth Army. Now his main jobs were to nominate surgeons for open slots, shift able people from overstocked units to strengthen weak ones, make sure that surgical work was done within the general guidelines established by the army surgeon, and ensure that new arrivals learned the essentials of military surgery and that everyone kept up with the progress of the craft. Other consultants did the same. There was also a contrary flow of information from the battlefield to the headquarters. Lessons learned in the school of combat passed via the consultants to the theater surgeon and the commander's staff, to reappear in time as standards and orders that modified the practice of all surgeons. In the process of interchanging experience and thought, basic insights into war surgery and the needs of the wounded emerged.

One of the critical dangers of being wounded was a complex and mysterious condition called shock, which had first been clearly identified (though not explained) during World War I. The symptoms of wound shock were low blood pressure, cold extremities, elevated pulse rate, and a feeling of anxiety that sometimes took strange forms. Colonel Churchill told of a forward dressing station (the British equivalent of a battalion aid station) where a severely wounded British soldier was dying of hemorrhage. Restless and anguished in mind like all victims of wound shock, he could think only of his dysentery, and screamed over and over, "I need to shit! I need to shit!"[16]

Shock made the anesthetist's job especially touchy. A young man in deep shock had the metabolic rate of an old man, and repeated doses of morphine given in the field to kill pain further depressed his respiration. One in every forty to fifty wounded were in shock when they reached the hospital, and the condition seemed to begin a series of destructive changes throughout the body that often ended in death. Indeed, a study done in Italy late in the war identified shock as the primary cause of battle casualty deaths.[17]

Existing medical knowledge of the problem was clouded. Erroneously, World War I researchers had separated shock from hemorrhage, believing that the complicated effects of the condition must have some explanation other than simple loss of blood. After the war, with a much diminished supply of injured bodies to work on, researchers had turned to studying anesthetized animals in the laboratory. Working in conditions that were unrealistically serene, they reached one right and one wrong conclusion. Blood loss was, after all, the basis of wound shock. Then how should it be treated?

Studies by Russian scientists during the mid-1930s had begun to demonstrate the remarkable value of plasma, the fluid part of the blood that remains after the red and white cells have been removed. Researchers studying animals exaggerated the importance of plasma to the wounded, primarily because their laboratory animals were so much more comfortable and better treated than wartime casualties. For a rabbit whose sole trauma was a needle prick, plasma made an adequate blood substitute, as long as the animal rested comfortably in its cage awaiting full recovery. One experimenter, however, noted of his plasma-treated rabbit: "The least exertion would cause the animal to pant heavily."[18]

The reason was that plasma lacked the red cells that carry oxygen to the tissues. Plasma simply filled the veins and arteries, preventing a disastrous fall in blood pressure until the body could regenerate red cells in normal quantities. Of course this was understood, but the practical advantages of plasma encouraged researchers to devise ingenious theories to explain away its inadequacies. To military surgeons on the eve of World War II, the newly revealed wonders of plasma seemed a godsend. Plasma was easy to store for long periods, did not require typing as blood did, could be dried and carried about conveniently. The sheer convenience of plasma may have influenced the misinterpretation of laboratory studies, which seemed to show that loss of red cells in hemorrhage was not as great as had been believed, and that plasma was as effective as whole blood in preventing shock and promoting recovery.

Unfortunately a battlefield was not a laboratory, and the theories of peacetime did not long survive the touch of war. The wounded could not rest quietly. (On the Anzio beachhead—to take an extreme example—active combat raged even around the hospitals.) Their injuries were considerably more severe than a needle prick—often severe, life-threatening damage to major organs that required quick surgical repair if they were to survive. Under such conditions, men who had been brought out of shock with plasma often relapsed and died. They could not tolerate movement, let alone anesthesia and surgery. Deprived of red cells, their tissues underwent a kind of suffocation. And their blood loss often was much greater than anyone had realized, because blood seeped into the wound and the surrounding damaged tissues, rather than out of the body where it could be observed. In short, the condition of the wounded man was worse than anyone suspected, and the value of plasma was less than almost everybody had supposed.

As such observations piled up in the theater, surgeons faced a cruel dilemma. As medical officers had discovered, surgery was part of resuscitation, and the shock team and the surgical team had to cooperate to keep the wounded man alive while the surgeon cut and stitched. The unity of the resuscitative process was one of the most important conceptual advances to emerge during World War II. But of itself it only served to show that quick surgery was necessary, not how it might be made possible without killing patients in shock.[19] Plasma turned out to be wonderfully effective in keeping the wounded alive until they reached medical units, but at that point whole blood was needed to prepare the patient for lifesaving surgery.

As that realization spread, the pathetically small amounts of blood originally used by surgeons in North Africa rapidly increased. When American forces came ashore, some medical units lacked even the basic equipment needed to transfuse blood. In Tunisia, less than one-third of II Corps wounded got any whole blood at all. But the situation changed rapidly in early 1943. Since no program existed to supply the armed forces with whole blood, American units began to imitate the British in setting up their own blood banks, which drew upon the armed forces in the theater. (Probably enlisted medics in the hospitals contributed more than any other single group.) In one hospital the proportion of wounded who got transfusions almost quintupled between March and May. In the first hundred days of the Italian campaign, the ratio rose from about 15 to about 50 percent.

Theater blood banks supported the invasions of Sicily and Italy. The British showed that shipping whole blood for comparatively long distances was "completely practical," as British wounded in Italy were supplied from Egypt until the bank could be moved closer to the fighting line.[20] For a time the Anzio beachhead got most of the whole blood from American banks. An experimental blood transfusion unit was set up to draw Type O (universal donor) blood; medical field laboratories did the processing. A system for moving the blood was developed to tie the individual donor to the collection centers and the centers to the front lines. Mobile blood banks mounted in trucks made the rounds of camps and airfields, a frontline application of the "bloodmobiles" that had been developed in the United States on the eve of the war.

Blood was moved about in refrigerators or insulated boxes and carried into the Anzio beachhead by LSTs, and flown to forward airstrips by the workhorse C-47 cargo plane for distribution by road or sea. Blood flights from Naples to Anzio took half an hour, and the planes also carried penicillin, anesthetics, plasma, and other medical necessities.[21]

Where the Mediterranean led, other theaters soon followed. Under their able chief surgeon, Major General Paul Hawley, medical officers of the European Theater of Operations headquartered in Great Britain studied the Mediterranean experience with care. One of the most important things they learned was that whole blood—which, even though a fluid, was a living body tissue, hard to keep alive, hard to move, and hard to store—nevertheless was "indispensable for controlling shock in severely wounded soldiers."[22] In mid-1943 Hawley decided to set up a blood supply service for the American forces gathering to invade northern Europe. The ETO medical service became the pupil of its British hosts and followed the model of the British Army Transfusion Service as well as the British and American forces in North Africa and Sicily.

Since blood banks were not among the Army's standard units, Hawley designed his own, basing it on a station hospital whose business was to collect Type O blood from volunteers in the Services of Supply. When the armies invaded northern Europe, advance depots using trucks that carried refrigerators would distribute as far forward as the field hospital platoons that accompanied the divisions into battle. Organization of the blood service was complete by the spring of 1944, and the Ninth Air Force guaranteed that space would be available on its aircraft every day for fresh shipments to the continent.

Yet even that late, surgeons were still in the process of discovering just how valuable whole blood was. Battlefield experience kept pushing the point at which whole blood ought to be given farther and farther toward the line of battle. During the breakout from Anzio in that same spring of 1944, whole blood was given in collecting stations, in the regimental areas; by the end of the war, the practice would be routine on all battlefronts.

As estimates of the amount needed per wounded man continued to climb, the theater blood services faced a prospective shortage of donors—the available givers were outnumbered by the potential takers. Even if enough donors could be found, the problem of collecting and processing very large quantities remained to be solved. The answer could only lie in the continental United States, with its huge pool of donors and its elaborate medical establishment, including the Red Cross network that already existed to supply plasma.

And yet more time elapsed before whole blood from the United States began to reach the fighting front. The problem was no longer technical. Setting up an effective system was a practical possibility by 1943, because of technical advances in extending the shelf-life of blood and the increasing speed of air transport. The basic problem appears to have been a logjam of ideas in Washington.

Many officers there lacked battlefield experience and moved only slowly and reluctantly away from the entrenched notions of earlier days. Perhaps Washington was too far from the British— who always seemed to get there first in matters of whole blood therapy—and too close to prestigious groups like the National Research Council, some of whose members had committed themselves to the dogma that plasma was just as good as, if not better than, whole blood. Or perhaps, as one expert later suggested, the minority at the top level who believed that whole blood "was necessary, and had no substitute, in the treatment of severely wounded men" did not speak loudly enough or prove their technical case well enough.

Advocates of whole blood were arguing their point in Washington at least from the early months of 1943, but they were overwhelmed in debate by the fact that the logistics of supplying plasma were so much easier than those of supplying blood. In February 1943 Colonel Churchill asked a friend in the Surgeon General's Office, "Nick, we're totally unprepared to give transfusions overseas, aren't we?"

"Yes," his friend said, "but you must not say anything about it outside of this office. We know we're behind but we can do nothing about it. We meet a stone wall everywhere we go."[23]

Getting whole blood to the field at first seemed an impossible task. "It is . . . out of the question," Captain Douglas B. Kendrick, Jr., had written in 1941, "to supply preserved blood to the combat zone."[24] Instead, collecting and processing plasma had become a major endeavor of the Red Cross and a subject of widespread enthusiasm on the home front. The plasma bottle hanging from a bayoneted rifle stuck in the ground had become an endlessly repeated image of wartime medicine seen in both posters and real photographs from every warfront—a visual plea for donors more powerful than slogans.

The history of the plasma-gathering effort had its own heroes and villains, its own mythology, its own politics, and its own solid achievements. Before Pearl Harbor a black surgeon, Charles R. Drew, had headed the effort. A skilled synthesizer of existing knowledge and a good executive, Drew made the program work and devised the bloodmobile that provided curb service to those who wished to contribute. Ironically, the blood plasma collected for Britain under Drew's leadership was labeled by the race of the donor, presumably so that bleeding bomb victims could refuse, if they so desired, plasma made from "black" blood.

When the United States entered the war, the armed services at first declined to receive donations from blacks at all, creating still another source of deep bitterness among Americans who were already facing discrimination in the armed forces and in wartime industry.[25] The reason alleged was practical. Since black soldiers or sailors could receive plasma made from "white" blood without being degraded, accepting the contributions of black donors only created the duplications and costs inherent in a segregated system. Meanwhile, Drew continued to direct the Red Cross program for the armed services, even though "during the entire time [that he headed it] the policy was not segregation of blood from Negro donors, but rather, exclusion of Negro donors."

Since all scientists understood that blood from a healthy donor was equally good for anybody in need of a transfusion, the Army Medical Department defended the policy on the only possible grounds—"the disinclination on the part of Caucasians to have Negro blood injected into their veins." Politically, the exclusion was an impossibility in wartime; blacks made their resentment felt by politicians, and many whites joined them in protests. The army yielded, and the Red Cross returned to its earlier practice of taking everyone's blood and segregating the plasma. The solution was expensive and complicated and fundamentally made no sense, but it accurately reflected the state of American thinking about blood, race, and patriotism at the time.[26]

Despite the intrusion of racism, the plasma program was a remarkable achievement in health care organization. During the war the Red Cross blood donor service collected more than 13 million pints, processing more than 10 million into dried plasma. (Liquid plasma supplied mainland hospitals, dried plasma went overseas.)[27] Countless lives were saved. But by mid-1943 the realization that other lives were being needlessly lost was beginning to spread. The system originally built to gather, process, and forward plasma had to be modified to provide whole blood as well. "Plasma and albumin work wonders on wounded men," a combat medic wrote, "but whole blood is life itself."[28]

In Washington, Kendrick (now a colonel) had helped to develop the program for collecting plasma, while believing and touting the official dogma about its effectiveness. But he was also in contact with the British and was reading reports from the front. In early 1943 he asked Colonel Churchill to find out whether whole blood was really needed and, if so, how it could be provided. The bitter fighting in the spring brought increased demands from below, as hospital commanders complained to the II Corps surgeon about their lack even of basic equipment to transfuse the blood of their own people into the wounded. Churchill decided "almost as soon as he had arrived in North Africa" that whole blood was needed, and in large quantities.[29]

Change began in the National Research Council's subcommittee on blood substitutes (even though the very name suggested the old dogmas). By mid-1943 the doctors there were recommending the use of whole blood whenever possible, and by the end of the year the same view had taken root in the surgeon general's office. In November the army set up its transfusion service. General Kirk named Kendrick his special representative in the field, and when Kendrick was transferred overseas, a medical officer from the Mediterranean Theater took his place. Until 1944 even military hospitals in the United States were responsible for collecting their own supplies of blood. Then in March the surgeon general agreed that the American Red Cross would supply blood to hospitals in the United States, which had problems collecting enough of their own. The long obsession with plasma, the underestimation of whole blood, and pessimism over the supposed impossibility of transporting it overseas were all beginning to give way.

The need for refrigeration and special processing of blood was met by the Red Cross blood centers, and the need for speedy delivery by the growth of air transport. Shipping blood to the Pacific was a particular problem because of the great distances involved. Navy Captain Lloyd R. Newhouser, who emerged as his service's specialist in the blood program, worked with Kendrick and the Red Cross. A navy surgeon, Lieutenant Henry S. Blake, after becoming disillusioned with plasma on Guadalcanal, devised a box for carrying whole blood containers under refrigeration, only to find that Admiral McIntire, the surgeon general of the navy, was not interested. Blake took his invention to the army, and General Kirk adopted it with enthusiasm. Not to be outdone, the navy then quickly followed suit.

Supplies of whole blood from the United States began to reach forward blood banks in time for the great battles in northern Europe and the final struggles of the Pacific war. The system had its problems. People tended to give blood in surges, depending on the state of the war, with the peak coming during the first six months of 1944 and the biggest single week coming after D-Day. But many adopted the habit of giving regularly, and while most blood continued to be made into plasma, the quantities of whole blood going overseas steadily increased. During the week of March 19–24, 1945, the Red Cross's Blood Donor Service made its biggest shipment of O blood overseas, some 15,000 pints, mainly for the battle of Iwo Jima then raging in the Pacific. The navy blood center on Guam was the main source for the combat zone, and Blake estimated that whole blood saved eight thousand to ten thousand lives.[30]

In all, about 388,000 pints of blood were shipped overseas, 206,000 to Europe via the Army Air Transport Command and 182,000 to the Pacific via the Naval Air Transport Service. Priority went to overseas shipments, with the hospitals of the zone of interior taking surpluses that developed over and above the demands of the fighting fronts. It had taken a long time and much effort to build the system—and to abandon or revise ideas that had once seemed scientific, reasonable, and wise. The end result was something more than a technical achievement. Not only was the wounded fighter more likely to survive, but the people at home were linked to him in a new and intimate way, their blood in his veins, his life extended by their gift.[31]

In military medicine, discoveries mean nothing until translated into systems and commands. With its experience of battle, a maturing field medical service, and increasing supplies of whole blood and penicillin, the Mediterranean Theater was able to write regulations that essentially set the pattern for front-line medical practice in the war against Germany and affected practice in all theaters, including the Pacific.

A significant advance was Colonel Churchill's system of phased evacuation. Of course, the whole basis of the chain of evacuation was echeloning—dividing it by levels, doing emergency repair work on the wounded at the front and more complicated work later at the rear. Churchill's basic idea was to have the process of treatment and evacuation follow the natural healing process as far as possible, making appropriate interventions at every step along the way.

At forward hospitals, this meant *initial surgery*, aimed simply at saving life and halting wound infection. Bleeding was stopped, broken limbs were straightened and protected by plaster casts, wounds were cleaned, explored, and dressed without sutures. In the big hospitals of the Communications Zone it meant *reparative surgery* to shorten the time needed for healing, restore function, and minimize disability. Compound fractures were cleaned and reduced, foreign bodies cleaned out of injured joints, and both penicillin and whole blood used generously; chest injuries were repaired to preserve lung function. Immediate skin grafts were applied to restore losses caused by "the missile, the overenthusiastic surgeon, or infection." Reparative work was best performed between the fourth and tenth day after wounding. It was often followed by a long period of rest and recovery, extending to eight or ten weeks for some fractures. Finally, in the zone of interior *reconstructive surgery* aimed to correct primary defects, eliminate deformities, and begin the process of rehabilitation.

When orders were issued specifying the actions to be taken by surgeons at specific times in specific hospitals, a system emerged that was both regimented and highly effective. Ideally, the wounded man received continuous, integrated care from the time he was hit until he was dispatched home. All earlier notions of treatment, Churchill recalled, "were but faltering steps" toward the system that emerged in the Mediterranean during 1944.[32]

Regulations published by the Seventh Army that year, on the eve of its invasion of southern France, showed the system fully developed. In addition to a blood bank set up by the army, every hospital was ordered to establish one of its own to make possible a "vigorous transfusion-resuscitation program." Blood was to be "used in all places from the battlefield itself to the ZI" (Zone of Interior). Penicillin treatment was to be continuous, from the field hospital to the rear-area base. Treatment of the patients was to be "considered as a continuous unified effort with utmost cooperation and clarity of treatment and records by each echelon concerned."[33]

The dressing first applied by the aidman or in the aid station was, except in case of hemorrhage, to be cut off only in the field hospital, for "innumerable sufferers in every war have been bandaged into their graves at the hands of overenthusiastic dressers." Debridement—the surgical cleaning and trimming away of dead flesh—was to be full and meticulous, with the surgeon warned not to trust even to wonder drugs. Amputations were to be handled conservatively, with every effort made to save the injured limb. No suturing was to be done in field hospitals—that was a matter for the Communications Zone. In fact, there was to be "*No primary suture, except of cranial wounds and some wounds of the face.*"[34] Instead, the wound was left open—not packed with gauze,

as Churchill explained, but with fine mesh gauze inserted "as between the pages of a book" under a snug bandage or light plaster.
When the danger of infection was over, the wound was to be
closed, usually in a week to ten days.

The orders went from one part of the body to the next, and
one possible injury to another, prescribing the general rules within
which each surgeon was expected to exercise his own professional
judgment. The final adjuration could well be posted on the walls
of any hospital, military or civilian: "From start to finish . . . all
those having care of and contact with the wounded, injured, or ill,
must constantly bear in mind that he is one of themselves—a
human being. Carelessness, neglect, and rough or harsh treatment
will never be tolerated. . . . Thus, kindness and consideration go
hand in hand with therapy."[35]

The end result of such methods, multiplied and spread over the
world and refined for the special conditions of many theaters, was
a hospital death rate for the wounded of about 3 percent—or, to
put it another way, a hospital life rate of 97 percent. Transport,
blood, antibiotics, and surgical skill all went into the making of
that remarkable record, perhaps the key achievement of American
military medicine in World War II. Paradoxically, the war was not
a time of revolutionary progress in surgical techniques, although
specialists—perhaps thoracic and plastic surgeons more than any
others—could point to important technical advances in their
fields. Most surgeons agreed that the war's triumphs over death
and disability were a tribute not to their craft alone but to the
total system, and they were generous in assessing the contributions of all the people who made it work.

"There seems to be wide agreement," the *Military Surgeon* reflected shortly after the war, "that the general operative surgery of
our Second World War has not been materially more advanced or
more skillful than that of our previous war. The more brilliant results have been accomplished by bringing that surgery closer to
the casualty both in time and distance. And new factors have
aided in these results, the routine transfusion of plasma, albumen
and whole blood, the use of sulfonamides and penicillin and air
evacuation of casualties." Popular adulation and endless stories of
medical miracles made some surgeons uneasy, for they understood

only too well the limitations of their art. One objected to being "placed upon the uncomfortable pedestal of being 'miracle-makers'; 'miracle-makers' who, unfortunately, cannot perform all the miracles demanded of us."[36]

But, for lay observers, "miracle" seemed a reasonable sort of description for what they had observed or personally undergone. For the wounded, the experience of suffering and helplessness, treatment and recovery was not a nine-days' wonder but a profound and incommunicable experience. What was it like to lose bodily function, or mind, or human semblance and then regain it once more? To anyone who was at all sensitive, the experience brought not only long pain and a brush with death but also an intimate contact with the mystery of things, and a personal revelation of the resources with which flesh and spirit fight against dissolution.

On his last evening in Africa, Richard Tregaskis walked through the hospital with a neurosurgeon to see some of the other head cases. "I saw them," he wrote, "the man with the deep hole in the front of the skull, his nose gone, whose mind would eventually come back to normal, whose face would be restored by plastic surgery; the man who could neither talk nor register words, whose brain was now . . . at the mental level of a rabbit. He, too, with neurological care, should be able to climb back to normal, although he would have to progress through all the steps of evolution—from rabbit to horse to dog to ape, and so on."

Wondering at such things, he ended his account with the hope that the mutilated world might similarly be restored in time. But some injuries take longer to heal than others.[37]

9

Jungle Victories

Nineteen forty-three—the turnaround year in so many respects for the allied war effort—had been marked by steadily growing competence (as well as some continuing failures) in managing threats to the health of the fighting forces. Improvements in prevention, treatment, and evacuation were as sharply marked in the Pacific theaters as in the Near East and were, if possible, even more important for the troops who were moving north toward the Equator on the disease-ridden Jungle Road. A good case can be made that malaria was *the* disease faced by American forces in World War II, and the American research establishment set out in full cry to find better methods of prevention and control.[1]

The Office of Scientific Research and Development's committee on medical research contracted with the National Research Council to guide the effort, and the two in cooperation with the army, navy, and Public Health Service set up the Board for Coordination of Malaria Studies. Thousands of conscientious objectors offered themselves as guinea pigs. Studies of Atabrine established a proper dosage and gave medical officers a way to control the recurrent spasms of chills and fever that racked the malaria victim. Another promising approach was to kill the mosquitoes that carried the disease, and here a kind of nuclear weapon for the war against insects had emerged in DDT, which proved to have almost awesome powers against mosquitoes as well as against lice and flies. Other experimenters, military and civilian, came up with repellents (including 612, later widely used in civilian life), the freon-powered aerosol bomb, and a variety of other advances. But no technical advance could knock out malaria by itself.[2]

Old-fashioned public health discipline was the need, and for that reason the key to success was command responsibility. "When for the first time in history," Sir Neil Cantlie, director general of medical services for the British Army, remarked, "a combatant officer was considered unfit to command a unit on the grounds that he had allowed his men to become ineffective through disease, a new day in military medicine dawned."[3] That day came to American forces in the Pacific theaters during 1943.

Early in the war the indifference of some commanders to malaria had baffled and infuriated physicians. One officer informed a malariologist in the Pacific that combat soldiers had come to "fight Japs," not swat mosquitoes. Yet command responsibility was crucial, for the troops had to be forced to do a number of tiresome things in order to defeat malaria. Swamps had to be drained, pools covered with oil, encampments sprayed. At evening in infested areas personnel had to wear long shirts and trousers, despite the tropical heat; they had to swallow Atabrine, not roll it under the tongue and spit it out; they had to carry mosquito nets and take shelter at sundown whenever possible.

Above all, they had to be persuaded or forced not to catch malaria deliberately in order to get out of further fighting. Malingering was so easy; a man on the front lines need only fail to take an unpleasant-tasting pill to win—perhaps—a ticket away from danger in the form of a disease that probably would not kill him. On the other hand, a death or two in his unit from cerebral malaria caused many a man to see Atabrine in a new light.[4]

In the fall of 1942, the Army Surgeon General, reacting to warnings from the American malariologist Colonel Paul F. Russell and the Australian expert Brigadier N. Hamilton Fairlie, urged theater commanders in malarious regions to set up special control organizations, with a theater malariologist and a variety of small, specially trained units to do the fieldwork: survey units under entomologists, control units under sanitary engineers, plus labor gangs to do the necessary ditching and draining. The first command to request help was the navy-led South Pacific Area. In December MacArthur's Southwest Pacific submitted its request, and commanders in Central Africa, China–Burma–India, the Middle East, North Africa, and the Caribbean Defense Command followed.[5]

By March 1943 units were being activated in the United States and committed to the overseas theaters. The army brought in malariologists by giving them direct commissions and trained its units in the southern United States and along the route of the Pan-American Highway, which was then under construction. General Simmons, who headed the army's preventive medicine division, prodded commanders and won top priorities for the production of DDT.[6] If the Pacific saw a fundamentally logistical war, the small spaces allotted to antimalaria supplies were surely among the best-used in the cargo holds.

While the armies fought, the special units began to conduct a holding action against the disease, first to conserve allied manpower and ultimately to convert the disease from a potent enemy to an unwilling ally. The Japanese ability to protect their own troops, which had been poor even at the beginning of the war, soon went into precipitous decline. Where the disease had hit both sides hard in the first year of the war, it became overwhelmingly more destructive to the Japanese in the second, especially in the forward areas, where the fighting was going on.

The South Pacific command first applied systematic preventive methods under combat conditions on Bougainville. A large, complex island, a tempting target with its six airfields and staging points for Japanese supply ships, Bougainville featured volcanic mountains, areas of dense rain forest, plains checkered with thriving coconut plantations, and a substantial native population—usually a guaranteed reservoir of tropical diseases.

Growing allied mastery of the sea and air had already begun to

isolate the island, when a force of soldiers and marines commanded by the veteran Major General Alexander A. Vandegrift landed
through pounding surf on the marshy shore of Empress Augusta
Bay. Both marines and soldiers brought along ample medical support; the navy sent in three field hospitals to care for the marines,
while the army had turned its clearing companies into divisional
hospitals and followed the invasion with two field hospitals.

Preventive medicine, however, had a tough task ahead. The
landing site had been chosen for sound tactical reasons—it was far
from the main Japanese forces—but offered a poor anchorage for
vessels and only swamps for the troops to live in. The Americans
set up a perimeter in a reprise of Guadalcanal. But they had
learned a great deal about managing disease in a jungle enclave
since then.

The South Pacific now had its own malaria control commission,
which had provided supplies and expert support. The Seabees
drained swamps. The marines had become malaria conscious, and
their troops slept in mosquito-proof jungle hammocks, used
aerosol bombs to discourage mosquitoes, and systematically oiled
breeding sites. The army followed a similar program. The result
was that fewer than 1 percent of the approximately 40,000 men
on the island had to be hospitalized with malaria. None of this
changed Bougainville into a garden spot. The large native population suffered from dengue, scrub typhus, intestinal parasites, and
filariasis, along with the usual tormenting skin ailments. The
troops paid disease an inescapable toll. Deep patrols took marines
and soldiers as much as 4 miles into enemy territory, and those
who were wounded in skirmishes had to be carried back by their
comrades through the steaming jungle. Such wearying treks resulted in wound infections, while the unremitting tension of jungle warfare brought on combat exhaustion.

Yet here, too, progress was being made. For the wounded, surgically equipped LSTs stood offshore. Evacuation went by air and
sea, and instead of each service trying to evacuate its own casualties the navy took sole responsibility. Very few sick or shaken men
left the island; only about seven hundred in all were evacuated
from the island for combat fatigue, and only about a hundred because of malaria. The figures reflected many things—the largely

defensive nature of the fighting; the landing of an adequate number of hospitals to retain patients on the island; and the preventive discipline that controlled disease in a crowded perimeter on a tropical island where it might easily have run rampant.

This was to be the South Pacific Area's last major fight, and the combat units showed the skills of veterans in conducting it, although high casualty rates to friendly fire continued to reflect the realities of jungle warfare. For the Japanese, on the other hand, tragedy loomed once more. Their fortress at Rabaul was slowly being pounded into impotence. They were losing the sea and the air, and hence the possibility of resupply. Even their battle plan sounded like a confession of logistical defeat: "The matter of life or death will be eliminated by high morale. . . . The battle plan is to resist the enemy's strength with perseverance, while at the same time displaying our spiritual strength."[7] Tactically, they were compelled to attack, as on Guadalcanal, adding to the many burdens borne by their diseased and hungry troops.

The fighting was often vicious. At one of the navy field hospitals on Torokina Cape, surgeons were operating on a wounded marine when bullets tore through their tent. The hospital commander, Lieutenant Commander Gordon Bruce, ran to the beach with a few corpsmen and unscrewed three machine guns from boats that had been destroyed during the landing. Drafting a few marines, he set up a defense line against Japanese attackers. While the firing went on, heavy rain began to fall, and the dugout operating rooms under the canvas began to fill with water. With patients on hand needing brain surgery, evacuation was impossible. Work went on late into the night under battery-powered lights. As word of the hospital's danger spread, more marines arrived and set up a perimeter. In the end, 50 patients were evacuated; not one died.[8]

The enemy's main attack on the perimeter came in the early months of 1944 and met a crushing defeat. When the Americans first landed on Bougainville, Japanese forces had numbered about 35,000; by the end of serious fighting in March 1944, about 22,000 were left. Army and navy sources agreed that the fighting accounted for no more than three thousand enemy deaths and that ten thousand others, weakened by hunger, had perished of disease unleashed by the allied logistical victory. The same story was being told at almost the same time in a greater battle to the west.

———————

While the fight for the Solomons went on, General MacArthur's Southwest Pacific command embarked on an epic campaign to drive the Japanese from New Guinea. But first the pervasive, debilitating malaria of the great island's hyperendemic lowlands had to be controlled even if it could not be mastered. MacArthur met the problem in his own unique way.

Surely the time was ripe. Between October 1942 and April 1943 the Southwest Pacific filled six to ten times as many of its hospital beds with malaria patients as with battle casualties, leading a medical inspector to warn that "the enemy's influence upon our noneffective rate is negligible compared to the effect of malaria." In the aftermath of Buna, MacArthur called in Colonel Russell and said, "Doctor, this will be a long war if for every division I have facing the enemy I must count on a second division in hospital with malaria and a third division convalescing from this debilitating disease!"[9]

On March 2, General MacArthur set up the Combined Advisory Committee on Tropical Medicine, Hygiene, and Sanitation to advise him on a broad range of medical issues, malaria included. To head the committee, he selected Brigadier Fairlie, whose recommendations became the theater's standing orders for the control of malaria.[10] Soon the Supreme Commander found other work for the combined committee, using it to plug a gap in his headquarters. MacArthur had selected as chief surgeon of the American forces Colonel Percy Carroll, the regular medical officer who had served with him in the Philippines and had escaped with a shipload of casualties on the *Mactan*, and assured him that he would have the support he needed to do his job. In fact, Carroll saw the great man perhaps a dozen times in two years. Soon the chief surgeon was exiled to the Services of Supply, on an organizational level with the ground force surgeon and the air surgeon. Who was to make medical policy for the theater remained unclear. Then, on September 26, 1942, SWPA issued a delphic general order that read in its entirety, "Colonel GEORGE W. RICE, Medical Corps, United States Army, is hereby announced as surgeon."[11]

What did it mean? Nobody knew precisely. Rice received an office and a secretary but no other subordinates and no clear authority. As surgeon of the multinational headquarters, he played an important role in winning MacArthur's support for the Combined Committee. But in most respects the divided authority he represented caused endless problems. Neither he nor Carroll could tell the land forces what to do with any assurance of being obeyed, nor the task force commanders, nor the airmen. Headquarters, SWPA, had no medical section on the special staff, and as a result American army forces in the theater had no general medical policy; neither did the American forces as a whole; neither did the combined allied forces. Yet all had to work together to combat disease.

MacArthur now ordered the combined committee to advise him on the medical problems of present and future battlegrounds and "any other health measure that might have a major effect upon the operations of the Allied Forces."[12] In short, it became a sort of preventive medicine section, and in some respects a substitute theater surgeon, with the direct access to MacArthur that was denied to both Carroll and Rice. With this backing, the committee ventured to propose new priorities for all classes of supplies, engineer and quartermaster as well as medical, that it needed to fight malaria.

Such supplies had been deficient in SWPA throughout the bitter Papuan fighting. In September 1942 the Australians had dispatched a military mission to the United States and Britain in an attempt to secure a larger supply of Atabrine. Malaria experts and the first units arrived from the United States in February 1943, and a Public Health Service physician was appointed theater malariologist. But priorities continued to block the movement of supplies until midyear. Medical cargo piled up in West Coast ports, and most of what got through piled up again in Australia. At the committee's urging the theater awarded antimalarials top priority—a critical step in a war where every item had to be carried across thousands of miles of water, and every cubic foot of space for goods or people was the object of competing demands. After MacArthur's intervention, Russell recalled, "no serious shortages occurred."[13]

By August a special malaria organization had been set up inside the theater Services of Supply and headquartered in New Guinea. The malaria control organization (later called Headquarters, Malaria Control), which included a growing number of survey and control units, developed a sense of corporate identity and eventually began publishing a mimeographed newspaper (*SWPA Malaria!*) that conveyed new technical wrinkles and gossip about malaria fighters to its farflung membership. Officers and enlisted men from other branches began to seek assignment as malaria fighters, not to escape danger (control and survey units were soon going into beachheads along with the combat forces) but to be part of an organization with prestige borrowed from MacArthur. "The bandwagon is going down the broad highway," the theater malariologist wrote somewhat complacently in September 1943. "[T]he C. in C. [Commander in Chief] is the band master, so all the smart musicians are clambering aboard."[14]

With supplies, manpower, and blessings from above, the job of fighting malaria got seriously under way in the fall. Like most preventive medicine, it was a repetitive and wearying task—training the antimalaria units (many at a malaria school the Australians set up in Port Moresby), then sending them forward, establishing systematic control in conquered areas, and extending it quickly when new landings followed along New Guinea's north coast. The region from Dobodura to Oro Bay was divided into sections, and malariologists and survey units were assigned to each. Native villages were put off limits, and experts located and mapped breeding areas. Above all, unit commanders were made responsible for carrying out control measures.

The results showed in the statistics. In the first six months of the control program, the theater malaria rate in American troops fell from an average of 970 admissions per 1,000 men per year to 148.[15] The 85 percent reduction was impressive, though not stable. As soon as heavy combat began again, the rate would climb once more, but overall the trend was downward. Malaria could not be beaten, but with the means at hand it could be controlled well enough to ensure that no epidemic ever again threatened the military effectiveness of the troops in the theater.

That became all-important as the epic struggle to drive the Japanese from New Guinea resumed. But it was not the only medical advance that the theater recorded. In the bitter fighting that began in mid-1943, the theme of increasing allied competence in evacuating and saving the wounded showed up in a variety of ways—in new units, new ships, and an astonishing advance by British and American researchers in the treatment of disease and infection.

Tactically, the campaign required the combined Australian and American forces to move west from Buna along the coast, with occasional forays to offshore islands. Their advance had to be amphibious, because the jungled, mountainous, disease-ridden interior was no place to march and fight. The result was a series of envelopments from the sea. Amphibious warfare, an amateurish business during the invasion of North Africa, had become a sophisticated process aided by special units that did nothing else. Engineer special brigades destroyed underwater obstacles and organized beachheads; the brigades' medical units became specialists in setting up the earliest aid stations ashore and transferring casualties to navy beach parties for movement to the ships. Preventive medicine began early, as antimalaria units landed with the combat forces and set to work within the beachhead. No two landings were precisely alike, for each had to be precisely tailored to the tactical situation, the geography, and the distance from home base. Every amphibious operation was a complicated minuet danced along an alien shoreline under enemy fire.[16]

In the Southwest Pacific Area, the fleet of landing craft that took the troops ashore and evacuated casualties belonged to the navy's webfooted Seventh Amphibious Force. Army hospital ships were beginning to show up, for the theater had converted a couple of civilian vessels and was building more in the United States. The navy's Central Pacific command assisted with its own elaborately equipped hospital ships when distances became too great for landing craft to do the whole job of evacuation. Often the hospital ships continued to serve as floating ambulances, at least until airfields could be built or repaired.[17] And air evacuation continued to grow in importance and sophistication as the front advanced and distances grew.

Since the Seventh Amphibious Force had no transports permanently assigned, most of the sick and wounded had to travel in the big LSTs and the smaller LCIs and LCTs. Many of those impromptu floating ambulances were ordinary amphibious craft, with a doctor and a corpsman or two aboard. A few, however, were converted specifically to handle the wounded. Crewmen cut hatches into the cavernous tank deck, usually devoted to hauling vehicles, and converted part of the space that normally held troops into a receiving room, a sterilizer and scrub room, and an operating room. The idea was to bring the wounded aboard over the LST's ramp into the tank deck, pass the litters through the hatch into the receiving room, and start treatment. Troop spaces became holding wards, with one-way movement from forward to aft. The accommodations that resulted were not comparable to the navy hospital ships, or even to the more spartan army hospital transports, but the surgical LST became a regular part of invasion fleets, carrying troops and vehicles forward, providing quick treatment for the wounded on beachheads, and returning them—slowly, and with much rolling about, for that was in the nature of LSTs—to rear area hospitals. Poor in standard hospital ships, the Southwest Pacific depended on the ungainly craft more than any other theater.[18]

One LST—with the bow number 464-H—was dedicated to medical purposes only. Beaverboard and wire screen partitioned the tank deck into offices, an operating room, a laboratory, an X-ray room, and an isolation ward. LST 464 became a true floating hospital, serving casualties from the beaches, crewmen of small craft that lacked sick bays, and workers constructing advanced bases with no hospitals of their own. Its medical staff provided a kind of clinic, with seven specialists, about forty corpsmen, and 175 beds for patients. During invasions, LST 464 acted as a sort of floating evacuation hospital in miniature, receiving the wounded from the amphibious craft; later she became a small station hospital, standing offshore to support a single base. Her medical officers set up a blood bank, drawing and storing whole blood for their own patients and those on other craft. Her stellar day was to come during the liberation of the Philippines, but it was off New Guinea that she began the honorable service that later won her staff a presidential unit citation.[19]

Soon medical officers treating the wounded had in their hands the most remarkable therapeutic agent produced by the war. Military use of penicillin began experimentally in the spring of 1943, when pilot studies on military casualties with chronic infections persuaded the army to buy 150 million units a week for its hospitals.[20] By the autumn the antibiotic was beginning to penetrate the combat theaters. In the Southwest Pacific, the first notice that the drug would soon be available arrived from the surgeon general's office on September 16, and the first shipment came in October—1,000 ampoules containing 100,000 units each. At first the use of penicillin was limited to American and allied military, and to patients with infections that were either life-threatening or chronic and severe. (Restrictions were needed, because a single serious case might require 2 million units.) The first to be treated in the theater was a soldier at the 118th General Hospital, who was cured of sulfa-resistant gonorrhea. But so cautious was the policy and so unfamiliar the drug that by the following April fewer than five hundred men had received penicillin.[21]

Then soaring production caused the restrictions to be abandoned. Utilizing newly discovered mass-production techniques, the United States turned out 21 billion units of penicillin in 1943, 1,633 billion units in 1944, and 7,052 billion units in 1945, and by 1944 the armed forces were receiving 85 percent of the nation's entire production. In March 1944 Washington authorities began urging overseas theaters to use the antibiotic "without hesitation whenever indicated." By midsummer the last restrictions on military use had been abandoned. Increasing numbers of doctors tried penicillin, and few had to see more than one demonstration to be converted. In May doctors at the 362d Station Hospital successfully treated T/4 Randolph W. Hughey for subacute bacterial endocarditis, a deadly infection of the heart valves; in June, T/5 George Hickey was treated at the 17th Station Hospital and began an uneventful recovery from multiple afflictions that included bronchial pneumonia, septicemia, and two kinds of skin disease.[22]

Penicillin quickly became a byword not only among medical personnel but in American popular culture. By the end of the war it would be routinely used against an extraordinary range of infections—wound contaminants, tuberculosis, some types of pneumonia, and serious venereal diseases. "No other nontoxic agent," one expert wrote, "has done so much for so many infectious diseases. It is a truly remarkable agent."[23] With the war's definitive wonder drug available to treat wounds and disease and a well-staffed and well-organized program of preventive medicine, American fighting men had a greatly increased chance of maintaining health and surviving injury, even in New Guinea.

For the footsoldier, Aussie or Yank, the fighting remained savage. Yet the jungle and diseases that made their lives miserable were now proving to be allies as well. The failure of Japan's logistical system had even worse effects on its troops in New Guinea than on Bougainville. In stark contrast to the Allies' growing sophistication and strength, disease and starvation virtually annihilated an entire Japanese field army in one of the darkest and least-known chapters of the Pacific war.

In March 1943 American and Australian aircraft devastated a Japanese convoy bringing reinforcements to New Guinea, leaving the enemy forces there more vulnerable to attack. The campaign ashore opened late in June with a series of brilliant strokes against Japanese bases at Lae, Salamaua, and the Huon Peninsula. In assaults by land, sea, and air, Americans and Australians stormed ashore. Australian forces advanced from the inland town of Wau, and American paratroopers jumped into the strategic Markham River valley.

The Japanese fought back with all their accustomed ferocity. Every medic went armed. Malaria, dysentery, and scrub typhus— New Guinea's unholy trinity—broke out. Jeeps and high-axle Australian ambulances trundled casualties down to the beaches under cover of darkness, over roads so deep in mire that time and again the natives of the region had to be called to the rescue. Fearsome in appearance, but strong and gentle in their handling of the wounded, the tribesmen littered casualties down to the beaches of

Nassau Bay, where portable surgical hospitals received them into tented operating rooms dug into the sand and revetted with logs. The Engineer Special Brigade managed evacuation from the beaches; the Seventh Amphibious Force provided LSTs with a naval medical officer and equipment for emergency surgery, and a medical corpsman rode every LCI. By the year's end the allies had the region under control, and the new airbases extended their power over the sealanes for hundreds of miles to the west.[24]

As amphibious warfare matured, much fine-tuning of details went on. A naval medical officer regulated coordination at the water's edge, where control passed from one service to another. The lack of a theater chief surgeon continued to cause problems. When the allies were caught with too few hospital beds in the forward areas, no one seemed able to make the necessary adjustments on the scene. Having a chief surgeon turned out to be less important in the planning phases of an operation, when everybody was in communication, than later on, when the fighting was under way. Then a single leader with access to the Supreme Commander was needed, to make quick adjustments to meet the unexpected.[25] Soon inspectors sent by the surgeon general were making note of the situation and pressing the theater to make changes, which were, however, slow in coming. But those were the problems associated with a victorious campaign. The Japanese situation was incomparably worse.

Japanese survivors escaping from Lae were able to bring out some of their wounded by barge. The rest were shot by their officers or supplied with hand grenades to blow themselves up when the Allies came. Japanese troops who were still healthy climbed into the towering mountains that blocked their escape route. "Officers expected the march to take sixteen days. It took twenty-six. Discipline collapsed as the strongest pushed ahead, picking the land clean of food. The weak were left to die. Two thousand of the marchers never came out. Most of them simply starved to death."[26]

So began the destruction of the enemy's Eighteenth Army. The Japanese forces were like victims of some progressive disease, in which circulation fails first at the extremities and then closer and closer to the heart. Supplies and reinforcements from overseas bases fell victim to submarine and air attacks. Although some transports got through as late as 1944, the Japanese fighting at forward locations on New Guinea increasingly came to depend for resupply upon a Dunkirk-line armada of fishing boats, sampans, and motor barges, on which American planes and P-T boats preyed without mercy.

Soon the Japanese command was receiving only about half the supplies it needed from the home islands, while forward bases got only about one-fifth of what was shipped to them from the rear. The soldier's ration fell to two-thirds, then to a half, and later was reduced "even more drastically." The attempt to move supplies forward in itself put an increasing drain on the men's energy. The Japanese tried to build roads without the aid of heavy equipment in tangled jungle, over knife-edged ridges, and through narrow ravines that were "pitch dark even at noonday."[27]

Immobilized in the jungle, unable to move quickly by either land or sea, their forces were isolated further by allied landings that fell upon their line of communications like a machete on a snake. Individual pieces were left to writhe, sometimes to bite, but the end result was a catastrophe, not only total but astonishingly quick. In January 1944 a sudden thrust at the coastal New Guinea town of Saidor put allied forces behind part of the Japanese Eighteenth Army. The enemy escaped the trap, but only by making another devastating jungle march on which half the remaining men may have died of hunger and disease. "Lonely gunshots punctuated the falling rain as the Japanese again marked their line of retreat with corpses."[28]

Then MacArthur aimed a carom shot at the Admiralty Islands, lying north of Saidor, which possessed airfields and the superb Seeadler Harbor. Here the fighting was exceptionally bitter; medical support of the 1st Cavalry Division was ample and much needed. On the main island of Los Negros, surgeons worked underground in captured Japanese bunkers, scrubbing their hands in steel helmets filled with antiseptic solution. Under blackout, the bloody work went on all night under glaring lanterns or the tremulous beams of flashlights.

Preventive medicine began early. Both army and navy antimalaria units were on hand, working with native laborers to oil, drain, and fill mosquito-breeding areas while the fighting went on. Malaria discipline was sternly maintained in the fighting units. But the environment took its toll in other ways. The inevitable "jungle rot" or "New Guinea crud" broke out. Franklin Boggs, a combat artist sent by the surgeon general's office to record the campaign, portrayed naked soldiers who were being painted by corpsmen with gentian violet. Medics with a sense of humor and a bit of creativity painted designs on their patients, and Boggs named a picture he made of such a case on New Guinea "Easter Egg."[29]

The sick and wounded rode to treatment in landing craft, Navy destroyers, LSTs, cargo planes, and bombers. Bombers did not make very good ambulances; litters had to be manhandled aboard through the gun turrets and laid on a catwalk that ran down the center of the fuselage. While hardened crewmen gazed in horror at the more appalling cases, a medic kept busy, moving from one litter to the next, wrapping his patients in blankets that winds whistling through opened turrets tried to whip away. But soon transport planes took over the burden of air evacuation, which outstripped the sea by six to one. And in short order the Admiralties justified their name—and the cost of their conquest—by becoming one of the largest allied bases in the Pacific.[30]

The conquest of western New Guinea now took a sudden leap 600 miles behind enemy lines. Allied forces assaulted Hollandia, a main enemy base with deep-water harbors and four airfields. A massive armada provided lift, protection, and air cover; complete surprise made the decisive victory remarkably cheap in casualties of all types. Combat patrols hunted down those Japanese who remained in the area, while several thousand who tried to escape by making their way through the jungle paid a heavy price to starvation and disease. Only about a thousand—roughly one in seven—survived this latest death march.[31]

The victory was substantial, and the cost—as such things were counted in the Southwest Pacific—comparatively small. But a simultaneous thrust at Aitape, 125 miles to the east, initiated a hard-fought battle. The 32d Infantry Division landed quietly on a hot, flat, wet coastal plain between the sea and the towering Torricelli Mountains. The men of Persecution Task Force were well supported by medical units, whose jobs at first were easy. On the beach, surgeons worked over a few patients under tarpaulins stretched between palm trees. Ambulances brought in new cases, most caused by accidents or illness. Of the enemy there was no sign, and the infantry expanded the beachhead west to Aitape town and eastward into the bush, crossing the leaf-stained water of small, shadowed jungle rivers—the Nigia, the Ex, Koronal Creek, and the Driniumor.

Antimalaria units were working to control the mosquitoes in what was evidently an unhealthy region when the first signs of the coming crisis appeared. Infantry patrols began to clash with small groups of Japanese in the jungle, and the medics began to set up advanced aid stations to give the wounded first aid.[32] Only gradually did it become clear that a remnant of the Eighteenth Army, isolated by the Allies and abandoned by Imperial General Headquarters, was determined to attack the beachhead in hopes of winning food and victory, or at least an honorable death.

Skirmishes came more frequently; the veteran 112th Cavalry arrived to reinforce the 32d Division, and a covering force along the Driniumor River was strengthened. On the night of July 10, 1944, the Japanese crossed the Driniumor in force and pierced the American line. Three days later the Americans counterattacked, and bitter fighting spread through the dense jungle west of the river and south to the grassy foothills of the Torricellis. Slowly the enemy was pushed back to the river's west bank. Hungry and lacking everything, the Japanese had nothing to lose and launched desperate attacks. Death came suddenly, in surprising forms: in one bizarre incident, a sword-waving Japanese officer burst suddenly from the brush, attacked a litter party searching for wounded, and slashed an enlisted medic to death.

Despite the danger, stretcher-bearers continued to carry the wounded to portable hospitals that worked close to the fighting. Hospital staffs dug foxholes, arming their patients against infiltrators; surgeons operated at night in blacked-out pyramidal tents. Native carriers under infantry guard carried patients to the little rivers to be floated to the rear, but some never reached safety, dying en route because the process of extracting them from the jungle was so slow. Disease increased as well; Atabrine discipline was neglected in combat; draining and oiling marshes became impossible. The number of malaria cases grew steadily, and scrub typhus broke out wherever the troops had to enter the fields of man-high, knife-edged kunai grass.

The commonest problems were stress, parasites, and the ubiquitous "jungle rot." About 90 percent of the combat troops at Aitape were afflicted with skin diseases, living in misery and unable to find relief until the fighting was over. Their intestines became infested with worms, especially hookworm. The rate of psychiatric casualties rose, especially among men newly arrived from the United States, who were meeting for the first time the fear and unremitting exhaustion of jungle fighting. Persecution Task Force was aptly named.[33]

The same diseases stalked the Japanese with deadlier effect, for they were starving and without medical supplies. Outnumbered and outfought as well, their corpses choked the little jungle rivers, and by mid-August their resistance had been broken. The shattered Eighteenth Army retreated, having lost about 9,000 dead to the Americans' 440 killed, 2,550 wounded and ten missing. The lesson was clear enough: The enemy could be defeated, and the environment on balance was an ally. But during combat disease could only be held at bay, and victorious Americans would continue to pay it their own tribute in lives and suffering.[34]

By now other thrusts had been made, one against a flat and swampy coastline that lay west of Hollandia and against Wakde Island, which lay offshore. It was here that the forces of the Southwest Pacific had a taste of the kind of combat—and the casualties—that would be more typical of the Central Pacific.

The island, fortified and strongly defended, was too small for maneuver and could be taken only by frontal assault. Machine gun and rifle fire hit the approaching landing craft from well-camouflaged caves and bunkers. While the defenders were being exterminated, the American wounded flooded an Army hospital ashore, momentarily stunning its commander. "The picture of so many wet, dirty, bloody, terribly wounded soldiers lying in all manner of attitudes is impossible to describe," Major William L. Garlick wrote. "For a moment it seemed there were more things to be done here in a moment than could be done in a week." His staff worked without rest for two days, while engineers cleared the airfield that had given the bloody little island its military value.[35]

Fighting ashore on New Guinea's mainland was likewise harsh and pitiless, the familiar exhausting, sweaty grind in dense rain forest and tangled undergrowth. Every unit had to provide for its own security. Medics and patients manned foxholes, learning fire discipline in the face of enemies who neither asked nor gave quarter. In night attacks the Japanese repeatedly penetrated the defenses until beaten off; ambulances moved in convoy, and their guards were savagely attacked again and again. Some hospital patients asked to be allowed to rejoin their own outfits, in the belief that line units might be safer!

The climax of the epic campaign came on the island of Biak, a mass of blazing coral in the waters of Geelvink Bay, which separates the body of New Guinea from its birdlike head, the Vogelkop Peninsula. As ever, the allies wanted airfields. The defenders, well-armed, holed up in coral caves, where they found water dripping through the porous rock. With no prospect of relief, they prepared to resist to the death as Hurricane Task Force poured ashore on the morning of May 27, 1944.

At first resistance was light. The amphibious medical system worked. Aid stations were set up by the naval beach party to care for the wounded, and medics with the amphibious engineers evacuated to a collecting station on Japanese-built coral jetties. Offshore, on the LSTs, navy surgical teams awaited patients to be returned by the landing craft. But as the American forces moved toward the airfields, Japanese soldiers, dug into the ridges above the coast road, opened up with mortar and machine gun fire. Then an enemy roadblock cut off the forward units. American casualties increased, supplies dwindled, and Biak's surface water turned out to be poor and scanty. Soon medics with the beleaguered units were depending on amphibians (the DUKW and the Buffalo) to bring supplies and water forward to the combat units and to bring back the wounded.

A flanking attack inland ran into conditions just as bad. The men marched for four days in sweltering heat, drinking only the water they carried with them, through thickets of towering evergreens swathed in vines "like thick cobwebs in a dream."[36] Human pack trains brought up supplies, while weary litter squads bore casualties to the rear. When the infantry ran into devastating mortar and artillery fire, evacuation became painful and slow; the airfield, still commanded by enemy guns, was useless.

At length, fresh forces arrived under General Eichelberger. The last act of a wearing and brutal campaign was played out in the Japanese redoubts. The Ibdi Pocket, a fortress of pillboxes, bunkers, and caves, fell to bazookas and flamethrowers. On June 21 the infantry reached another formidable complex called the West Caves. Some defenders staged a banzai charge and were slaughtered; their commander committed suicide. The Americans burned out some caves with gasoline and blasted others with massive charges of TNT. Then infantrymen plunged into the dark recesses, finding an "unimaginable purgatory" that outdid Dante. The stench of the dead was intolerable. Torn corpses lay among the excrement they had produced in life; the rotting bodies were so dismembered and mutilated by blast and fire that their numbers could only be guessed.[37]

Almost 10,000 American casualties marked the battle. Medical personnel suffered heavily from mortar and artillery fire and snipers, and won more combat decorations, proportionate to their numbers, than the infantry.[38] Yet courage was not enough. Biak was a throwback to Buna in more than its horror. Reinforcements crowded onto the island with no commensurate increase in medical strength. The number of hospital beds declined relative to the need, and epidemics broke out—dysentery, spread by flies breeding in the countless unburied dead, and scrub typhus, which devastated army hospitals on the offshore islet of Owi. Experts from the U.S.A. Typhus Commission arrived, but they could only show how to control the disease by killing rodents and burning out the rotting vegetation of ferns and rank grass. No one knew how to cure it. The 1,000-odd sick endured a long period of convalescence, and the medics who remained healthy were wearied by a long course of tending and treating them at a time when battle losses needed their undivided attention.

After their tenacious and hard-fought defense of Papua, the Japanese had lost the western part of New Guinea to a series of well-coordinated hammer blows. What remained was a grisly anticlimax. On the small island of Noemfoor new evidence turned up of the collapse of the enemy's supply system as cannibalism appeared once again. Early in August American patrols began to discover bodies that looked as if they had been butchered. According to prisoners, Formosan laborers had served the Japanese for food as well as beasts of burden. A Captain Sugahara, wearing two hats as the medical officer and the mess officer of a Japanese detachment, had skillfully dissected the dead, whose flesh, cubed and boiled, was said to look like pork and taste like any other meat.[39]

On July 30, 1944, Allied forces landed unopposed on the Vogelkop near Cape Sansapor. The defenders, who had had enough, fled. But a scrub typhus epidemic broke out with a fatality rate that was higher than Biak's. The helplessness and long convalescence of the sick drained the forces, which lost 60,000 man-days. Again strict control measures were imposed. Soldiers burned out the vegetation that harbored rodents whose mites transmitted the disease. Men wore clothing made hotter, rougher, and stiffer by dipping in a poison supposed to kill the vector.

For all that, attitudes had changed, and the change had helped to make the victory possible. Prevention—the medical theme of the war on the jungle islands—permeated American units. The need for health discipline, about which the supreme commander had had his doubts at the beginning of the campaign, was evident to noncoms at the end. "Now," the first sergeant of one outfit told his men, "I don't make these rules but I sure as hell enforce them—and I enjoy doing it. Are there any questions? Then—move out."[40]

World War II was fought in the full light of modern medical science, with means of prevention and cure undreamed of in any earlier conflict. The war between Japan and the allies was also fought in some of the most forbidding terrain to be found on the planet. Beginning in mid-1943, the Allies were able to establish the essential minimum of environmental control to save their own forces and to turn the power of disease against the enemy. But repeated outbreaks among Allied troops served to underline the fact that even for such mature and well-supplied forces the green hells remained unconquered. The best news to come from New Guinea was that the Japanese had been defeated and the front could move on.

10

The Bloody Islands

By early 1943 the war had touched every inhabited continent except North and South America. Americans had fought in desert sands, deep jungles, and oceans ranging from the storm-beaten North Atlantic to the tropical Coral Sea. Each campaign had created its own special problems for the medics, growing out of its terrain, diseases, style of warfare, and difficulties in reaching and evacuating the sick and wounded.

But they had seen nothing quite like the campaigns that began later in the year in the north and central Pacific—literally an ocean world, with tens of thousands of islands strewn in long looping chains across millions of square miles of deep blue water. Across this ocean invasion forces had to be carried in convoys, along with everything that a floating city of sailors, marines, and soldiers would need to live. At the end of the journey, some of the men had to go ashore and capture one or more fortresses, which were defended to the death, while those who remained in the ships had to fight off hostile planes and sometimes fleets. Then the

casualties resulting from all the actions, land and sea, had to be retrieved, treated, and carried back across the ocean to remote hospitals.

Compared with the South and Southwest Pacific, this would be a
better environment, without jungles and mostly free of malaria. But
the fighting would be even bloodier—a series of battles of extermi-
nation branded with all the pitiless hallmarks of the Pacific war.

Though the tropics would see most of the fighting, the struggle
really began far to the north, in the only battle of World War II to
take place on American soil. Alaska in the early days of World War
II was a strange, cold, empty place for the young soldiers who
were sent to defend it, however magnificent its dark forests,
snowy mountains, and sparkling bays. Although the men stationed there were healthy—in most respects, healthier than those
in the forty-eight states—they were apt to tell their medical officers that the country was bad for them. Part of the problem was
the boredom of dreary cantonments and the dark of endless win-
ters. But much of the depression and hypochondria reflected the
fact that Alaska's remoteness from the war made the troops feel
useless.

The enemy cured them of that. As part of their complex plan
for the Midway campaign, the Japanese in mid-1942 bombed
Dutch Harbor and seized Attu and Kiska, two islands of the Aleut-
ian chain. The Japanese naval disaster left their Alaskan outposts
hanging, useless to them and an irritant to the Americans, who
began to plan their recapture. The winter of 1942–43 saw the
forces begin to build up. Reconnaissance planes photographed the
fog-shrouded islands, the air force dropped bombs, and the navy
drove off a relief convoy. On April 1, 1943, Admiral Nimitz and
the army's Alaska Command jointly issued orders for the invasion
of Attu.[1]

A sharp fight impended, but everyone, including the medics,
approached it with little sense of what lay ahead. Marine officers
instructed the army's 7th Infantry Division in the techniques of
amphibious attack, but they did it in Monterey, California, and
they concentrated on the problems of getting ashore, which, as

matters turned out, would be the easiest part of the battle. The troops were not taught how to protect themselves against the cold, and their personal gear—leather combat boots, hoodless field jackets, and unlined woolen trousers—was better adapted to northern California than Alaska.[2]

On May 11, eleven thousand men began to go ashore on "the loneliest spot this side of hell," the fog-shrouded, treeless cairn of stone and snowmelt called Attu.[3] At first they were protected from enemy fire by the fog. With no wounded to treat, the medics went through the landing dance by the numbers, shore party medical sections relieving the collecting platoons, platoons following the combat teams inland. But on the following day the fog played the invaders false, lifting from the valleys while continuing to veil the enemy on the heights. Pushing up the appropriately named Massacre Valley without even a tree to shield them, the Americans began to take heavy rifle and mortar fire. Units landing elsewhere ran into opposition, too, and as casualties mounted the campaign ground to a halt.[4]

Vehicles bogged down in the tundra. Chaos reigned in the supply dumps on the beaches, where medical personnel were "forced to search along the beach for necessary equipment, stand guard over it afterward, and then carry it over almost impassable ground." Supplies had to be hauled forward, and the wounded endured endless carries by exhausted litter-bearers, sometimes bleeding to death "only a few miles—but many hours—from treatment." Navy corpsmen joined in the struggle, and bearers worked in relays, harassed by snipers and alternately shielded and exposed by the mist and the fickle wind. The enemy killed without discrimination; army medics and navy corpsmen died beside their patients.[5]

Green troops, poor leadership, lack of reliable intelligence—the litany was long, sad, and all too familiar at this period of the war. The 7th Division commander had to be replaced; the men, under abler leadership, pushed the outnumbered Japanese slowly to their last defensive positions. Engineers built roads to make the battlefront more accessible, and the divided American forces linked up, encircling the enemy. Needing to shorten the stretcher carries, the medics moved their aid stations close to the fighting line. And there they were caught by the last convulsion of the battle. At 3:30 A.M. on May 29, a thousand Japanese rushed the line, "screaming, killing, and being killed."

Wielding rifles and spears made from poles and bayonets, the enemy swarmed over hospital tents where medics and wounded alike lay helpless in sleeping bags. Many died as cold steel punched through the canvas of their falling tents. One doctor woke just as a Japanese bayonet sliced through his nose, tongue and neck; the weapon was pulled out and he escaped, bleeding but alive. Engineer troops at last contained the attack, and by the end of the following day the struggle was over, with only a few surviving Japanese still to be tracked down and killed.[6]

Attu was a classic Pacific fight, merciless and brief. A superficial glance at the statistics made the accounting seem overwhelmingly one-sided: 549 Americans and 2,350 Japanese had been killed. Yet more than 1,100 Americans had been wounded, and total American battle casualties equaled more than 70 percent of the Japanese losses—a figure surpassed only on Iwo Jima. Worse, poor preparations for the cold had helped to produce more than 2,100 nonbattle injuries, most of them caused by trenchfoot.[7] Some 1,400 cases were evacuated to the hospitals or the ships, more than 9 percent of the whole invasion force.

All in all, three Americans had become casualties for every two Japanese who were on Attu at the time of the invasion, and five of every hundred medics had been killed in treating or moving them. The medics had a cause for complaint: their humiliating helplessness when they were attacked. It was time to admit that the custom of denying medical personnel the right to bear arms needed revision for the conditions of the Pacific war.[8]

———————

Meanwhile, other forces gathering in Hawaii were being trained by the navy's Central Pacific command to attack the outposts of the Japanese Empire. In every possible respect, good and bad, their targets—the Gilbert Islands—were unlike Attu. Tropical Edens to a stranger's glance, they were flat, hot atolls garlanded with coral reefs, encircled by beaches of fine sand, and green with coconut palms, mangroves, and breadfruit.

But they were far away—2,000 miles—and like many paradises, they looked best from a distance. Medical intelligence officers knew that dysentery, venereal disease, and yaws harassed the native peoples, that hookworm was common, and that water was scarce and unsafe to drink. But malaria and scrub typhus were absent, and no jungle awaited the soldiers and marines. The army's target was the triangular atoll of Makin, while the marines aimed at the reversed L of Tarawa, a little over 100 miles to the south.[9]

The northern attack force—the 27th Infantry Division plus artillery and a garrison force—endured a nine-day voyage from Pearl Harbor, with the heat and tedium interrupted only briefly by gross festivities at the Equator. But the mood was tense among troops who sensed what lay ahead. Medical support was generous, roughly one enlisted medic for every ten fighters, one doctor for every 250 men, and the first portable surgical hospital to appear in the Central Pacific.[10]

Everyone prepared for action at dawn on November 20, 1943, as Butaritari Island, the chief component of Makin atoll, rose out of the sea. From the low-lying mass topped by flourishing palm and pandanus trees emerged, as darkness faded, white sand beaches, dark boulders, clumps of brush, and small grass-roofed huts undergoing a thunderous bombardment.[11]

At 8:30 A.M. amphibian tractors firing rockets and .50-caliber machine guns led the first wave ashore. Coral knobs grounded many of the landing craft that followed, forcing the men to swim or wade, stumbling on rocks and coral. Company aidmen landed with their units; medics with the second and third waves set up aid stations. The battalion medical sections, the collecting company platoons, the portable surgical hospital, and the clearing company came ashore in turn. At once, despite massive shelling that had left the island a shambles of wrecked buildings and burning supply dumps, casualties began to mount.

The flat, open terrain gave little shelter, and a sniper in the crown of a palm tree shot a surgeon as he worked. The medics dug in, like everyone else, scooping pits in the sand and coral and roofing their bunkers with coconut logs and earth. Here they worked over the wounded, combating shock, controlling hemorrhage, and splinting fractures.[12] But not all the casualties could reach them; some men arrived back on the transports with wounds filled with sand, bleeding uncontrollably, or in profound shock. Prolonging their suffering, the amphibians could evacuate only by day, for the transports put to sea at nightfall and did not return until sunrise.[13]

The small Japanese garrison did not survive long. The fight for Makin Atoll was won—like bloody Attu—by inexperienced troops overwhelming an entrenched enemy by weight of numbers. Overall, the cost was low (only 66 Americans died, with 185 other casualties) and gave no indication of what might happen in a battle against strong enemy forces. The marines found that out at Tarawa Atoll, where more than three thousand casualties provided an unforgettable lesson in the real problems of war in the Central Pacific.[14]

Tarawa is a coral reef that rises above the surface of the sea in some places, forming islands, and lies just below it in others. Around Betio, at its southwest corner, the reef prevented craft drawing more than 3 feet of water from approaching the beach. Yet this, the largest island of the atoll, held the Japanese headquarters, heavily defended and ringed with barricades and buried gun emplacements.[15]

The opening bombardment was so intense that American sailors suffered temporary deafness from the blast concussion of their own guns. A naval officer declared, "It is inconceivable that anyone could live through such a storm of shells." Yet he admitted, "Immediately afterward . . . the Japs could be seen emerging from their holes."[16] In fact, the bombardment by later standards had been too brief. Though most of the defenders' heavy guns had been destroyed, their soldiers survived in bunkers of steel, concrete, and coconut logs, and marines approaching the beaches ran into a furious concentration of fire.

Twenty amphibious tractors were knocked out crossing the reef, the men spilling out into the water, to wade shoreward and often to perish on the way. Landing craft, unable to negotiate the reef at all, lingered helplessly beyond the line of white surf, waiting for amtracks to shuttle their marines to shore. Tractors and tanks that reached the sand beaches rolled over barbed wire entanglements, but log barricades and pillboxes had to be blown up before the beachhead could expand. Supply barges could not cross the reef, denying food, ammunition, and medicine to the men pinned down on the sand. Shortly before noon a landing team radioed, "We need help. Situation bad."[17]

Navy corpsmen and doctors coped as well as they could with an almost calamitous situation. Company aidmen who had landed with the assault waves began to retrieve the wounded, and doctors to give treatment; medical officers and men died in the same proportion as the fighters. Collecting units that tried to land with the second wave were driven off and did not get ashore until the next day. Supplies of the "five basics"—morphine, dressings, sulfa drugs, plasma, and splints—were ample, but some elementary equipment was not; for lack of litters, many wounded men were piled into amtracks to lie on the deck, or on one another. The jobs of triage and medical regulation (sending wounded to the proper place for treatment) were difficult in every amphibious operation, but on Tarawa in the early hours moving the wounded was nearly impossible.

The dead washed out to sea or lingered, sunk in the sand, with hairless heads and jelly eyes. On the morning of the second day, Robert Sherrod, a correspondent, saw the wounded walking along the beach against the backdrop of tidal flats that were scattered with the dead. "Some have bloodless faces, some bloody faces, others only pieces of faces." Some were aided by corpsmen, others limped alone; two litter-bearers passed, carrying a marine with great wounds in his side and shoulder. "This scene . . . is horrible. It is war."[18]

As opportunity permitted, amphibians evacuated to the transports, some of which kept four operating rooms busy, day and night. Wounded men who were lucky reached the ships within two hours of the time they were hit, but others, isolated by enemy fire, waited for treatment as long as twelve hours.[19] Not until two days after the battle began could surgery be performed on Tarawa itself. Two hospital ships arrived three days later, and some ships ran a continuous shuttle to Pearl Harbor, ferrying the wounded to the big hospitals there. Four days of bitter fighting were needed to secure Betio, and sharp but limited engagements were necessary to destroy the enemy on the rest of Tarawa Atoll.

Overall, 1,027 Marines were killed and 2,292 wounded. Identifying the dead was a grisly business. "Many bodies," the division surgeon reported, "were found with the head, face, or entire upper portion of the body destroyed." Tropical heat added to the horror, for bodies decomposed so rapidly that even fingerprints could not always be taken. Bodies swelled with gas and burst. The Japanese dead lay abandoned in defeat, which appalled Sherrod: "The ruptured and twisted bodies which expose their rotting internal organs are inexpressibly repelling."[20]

Those were sobering experiences. There was simply no way to assault tiny plots of sand and coral except frontally; no way to deceive or feint; no way to destroy the enemy by even the most devastating preinvasion bombardment. Boats and amphibians stranded on the reefs made perfect targets, and the medics faced the problem of dealing with mass casualties who could be neither treated where they lay nor taken back to the ships. Nimitz's forces apparently faced a long series of savage episodes as they fought their way across the Pacific, with rates of loss that might ultimately prove unacceptable to a nation whose limited manpower was engaged on many fronts.[21]

Despite the absence of malaria, disease also found victims. Both Betio and Makin after the battle provided good images of hell— cratered landscapes littered with swollen corpses, feces, and rotting food, and shattered trees standing sentinel. Water stank of organic decay, and the islands droned under a blizzard of flies. Sherrod, returning to Tarawa from the freshness of the sea, was hit by the "overwhelming smell of the dead" and vomited. The troops had to camp on this wasteland, for they had nowhere else to go, and they were casual about relieving themselves, adding to the filth. As a result, both Makin and Betio marked the American victory with dysentery epidemics; on Makin, mosquitoes breeding in pools in the rubble also set off an epidemic of dengue.[22]

Pooling their experiences after the battle, army and navy medical officers urged the use of medically equipped amphibians, LSTs, and at least three hospital transports for each fighting division. They wanted more jeep ambulances, because of their low profile and go-anywhere capability. They wanted medics trained in civil affairs to care for battered natives caught in the storm. And they wanted better-disciplined troops, both soldiers and marines.

The Gilberts were the Central Pacific's baptism of fire, Tarawa its first bloodbath, and the national criticism of Tarawa's casualties a sharp warning that the theater could ill afford another such adventure. At hard-fought Biak, 2.63 Americans out of every thousand engaged had been killed or wounded in action every day. But in the Gilberts, the rates had been 12.77 for the army and 39.65 for the marines. If the lessons were bitter, to the theater's credit they were quickly learned and applied with a far surer hand in a battle that carried Nimitz's forces into islands that had been Japanese-mandated territories before the war.

The Marshalls form a huge archipelago, with thousands of low-lying coral islands flung across 700 miles of the tropical Pacific, midway between Hawaii and New Guinea. Among the thirty-odd atolls are Kwajalein, Eniwetok, and Majuro, and in 1943 the first was an enemy bastion with 14,000 defenders. Marine Major General Holland Smith commanded the attack, using the newly formed 4th Marine Division and the army's veteran 7th Infantry Division.

The medics trained for the campaign as rigorously as the line, marching, swimming, and becoming proficient with their weapons. Reflecting the experience of Tarawa, the navy designated amphibious tanks (LVTs) to act as ambulances. Each had a doctor or qualified technician aboard and three corpsmen to retrieve the wounded from the water within the reef, where boats might not be able to reach them. After giving first aid, the LVTs would carry their patients across the reef and transfer them to landing craft, to be ferried to the transports waiting in deep water.[23] In turn, the transports expanded their sick bays and collected small blood banks from their crews and passengers.

At the end of January 1944 the convoys arrived at Kwajalein—the largest atoll in the world, a ring of islands encircling an immense lagoon. Tarawa had taught the navy that the initial bombardment could not be too heavy, and carrier aircraft plus a massive fleet of battleships, cruisers, and destroyers battered the targets with methodical thoroughness. "The rolling barrage," a

young navy doctor later recalled, "would just walk back and forth
. . . so that the island was just shattered." While the marines hit
the islands of Roi and Namur, the soldiers crossed Kwajalein's
great reef in armored amphibians and invaded the main island.[24]

Yet defenders survived to fight. Shells had mangled palm trees,
flattened buildings, and gouged craters into the sandy soil, creating
an enormous rubbish heap. For the Japanese, the wreckage provided endless opportunities for defense. As S. L. A. Marshall later observed, the battle for Kwajalein resembled the conquest of a ruined
city rather than a remote island: It was "a fight against concrete, a
fight in which small skirmishes eddied around churches and out-
houses, a fight in which Jap snipers sometimes waited shoulder
high in the water of a concrete cistern on the chance that an American would pass the 8-inch space that was their field of vision."[25]

Bitter as the action was, improvements based on the lessons of
the Gilberts helped make the medical task easier. Even when the
fighting was most intense, evacuation was so quick that an infantryman said the medics "almost have a litter waiting for you to
fall on when you get hit."[26] Jeep ambulances hurried the wounded
away from the line. At low tide, amphibians collected the wounded, and an army field hospital received them on a nearby islet.
During high tide, when water was fairly deep over the reef, landing craft bore patients directly from the beaches to the ships. Hospital ships were on hand, and some casualties returned to Hawaiian Islands by sea. Air evacuation was less successful; clearing the
airfields of rubble and filling craters delayed mercy flights until
after the battle. The army counted fewer than a thousand casualties at Kwajalein, including 142 dead, as the cost of destroying a
Japanese garrison of about 5,000.[27]

The marines' fight for Roi and Namur was similarly desperate
and brief. Battalion aid stations were set up in shell craters or captured Japanese dugouts near the beaches. Enemy small-arms fire
rattled around the stations, but hospital corpsmen continued to
bring in the wounded. Offshore evacuation was smooth, with the
average time from initial wounding to arrival at the ships only
three to six hours. Like most soldiers, the marines ended in the
transport sick bays, hoisted aboard in wire basket litters from
DUKWs rocking on the gentle swells. And like the soldiers, their

seriously wounded passed from the transports (usually on LCVP landing craft) to the hospital ships *Solace* and *Relief*, to be returned to Hawaii. The 206 Japanese prisoners and the hapless locals over whom the storm had passed also received treatment. Army and navy surgeons operated on POWs, and a station hospital had arrived with the invasion fleet specifically to care for the Marshallese.[28]

In the aftermath, killing flies and hastily burying enemy corpses with bulldozers kept sickness to a minimum. "My job was to dispose of all those bodies," a future surgeon general of the navy, George Monroe Davis, recounted. "Our contempt for the Japanese was such that we thought they were animals. . . . And so the marines, once they had that opportunity, they went through all the pockets they could, they pulled out gold teeth." Davis recalled too that "we left [Roi and Namur] feeling that we were unconquerable, that the marines were indestructible."[29]

The next step saw both marines and soldiers assault Eniwetok Atoll. The infantrymen fought on the namesake island, but the heaviest fighting of the five-day battle came on the island of Parry, costing the marines, as Betio had, about 25 percent casualties. There were many reasons, but one was greater Japanese discipline in refusing to reveal their positions by premature firing. Deceptively passive, they endured a searing bombardment, then gave the marines landing on February 22, 1944, a furious reception.

Masked artillery smashed and set afire many landing craft, leaving some derelicts where boarding parties found charred bodies, dazed survivors, and loose ammunition rolling about the canted decks. Ashore, minefields sent seriously wounded men, many with traumatic amputations, back to the ships. A deck of the transport *USS Wharton* became a hospital where army and navy surgeons worked side by side, some putting in thirty-six hours without rest. With defeat facing them, the Japanese staged a final counterattack that destroyed the remnants of their garrison and sent the last wave of marine wounded to the transports and the waiting *Solace*.[30] Despite the heavy losses, the conquest of the Marshalls was a classic exposition of amphibious warfare, in whose honors a matured medical service shared fully.

With a growing preponderance of strength over the Japanese,

Nimitz's forces were now ready for an even greater challenge. Not all the islands of the Central Pacific were coral dots. A thousand miles from the new American base on Eniwetok lay an arc of large, complex islands, crowned with mountains, checkered with broad fields of sugar cane, and heavily garrisoned by troops who knew that they could not afford to be defeated.

Only 1,300 miles from Tokyo, the Marianas were a keystone of the Japanese defensive perimeter, and a large population of enemy civilians lived on the island of Saipan. The veteran planners on Nimitz's joint staff had no doubt the Japanese would fight desperately to retain the Marianas, and the attack force they put together was huge, about 128,000 soldiers, sailors, and marines. In the late spring of 1944, immense fleets set out from Pearl Harbor, the Solomons, and the West Coast of the United States: a splendid sight when they converged.

Aboard, things were not so grand. The ships were jammed; the men could not exercise in units larger than a platoon; they slept in stifling quarters, stacked atop one another like newly shuffled cards, or out on deck, drenched by recurrent tropical rains. Some ships were infested with bedbugs, and fungus infections like athlete's foot thrived in the steamy 100° heat of the holds. The men showered in brine, ate from greasy metal trays, and used foul and overcrowded latrines. The first medical problem of the campaign was an epidemic of diarrhea that afflicted 90 percent of the marines and many of the soldiers, the cases ranging from mild to severe. Understandably, "most of the Marines sleep in folding cots topside," one sailor noted. "Their compartment is full of sick men, it is being used as a sick bay."[31]

At Saipan, scenes familiar to veterans played out once again. Carrier planes devastated the enemy airfields and naval guns thundered for five days. Then a wave of gray amphibious tractors crossed the reef, to be caught almost at once by fire from Japanese artillery, mortars, and automatic weapons. Corpsmen splashing ashore with seabags of medical supplies found the beach "covered with Marines many of whom were wounded." By mid-morning calls were going out for LVTs to bring more ammunition and evacuate casualties, and for a time confusion reigned under heavy shelling from invisible enemy guns.

More medical units landed in the melée. Again navy beach party medical sections, marked by their blue-painted helmets with red crosses, set up aid stations in the open under fire; one worked in a Japanese tank trap. Again enemy fire was so heavy that a corpsman was reported as saying, "Hell, I'm going back up front; it's safer." And again in the tropical darkness lit by random flashes of light, doctors struggled to diagnose and treat the wounded by flashlight under the shelter of ponchos.[32] Enemy tactics showed the familiar mix of skilled infiltration, night assaults, and suicidal fury. By the evening of D-Day only half the planned beachhead had been secured, but one-tenth of the 20,000 assault troops had been killed or wounded, and the medics suffered like everyone else. A single evacuation station treated and evacuated more than a thousand casualties in the first three days. General Smith ordered his reserves, the Army's 27th Infantry Division, to come ashore.[33]

Saipan was crucial to the enemy as well, so crucial as to bring out the Japanese fleet. Reports of ship sightings from submarines and aircraft patrolling off the Philippines brought the campaign to its crisis. As the warships steamed away to confront the threat, the unprotected transports withdrew from the inshore waters. Their backup gone, army and navy medical units ashore were burdened with wounded men, who increased by five hundred a day, at a time when other hundreds were falling sick from dysentery and dengue. Two army portables treated almost three thousand patients; the 1,000-bed 2d Marine Division hospital admitted more than 5,000. Inevitably, blood ran short, the wounded got plasma instead, and patients accumulated for lack of evacuation.[34]

There was no deliverance from the situation except victory, and this the navy provided. The battle of the Philippine Sea ended in a crushing American triumph that permanently impaired the fighting ability of the Japanese naval air forces. The ships returned to Saipan, and a general exodus of the seriously injured relieved the pressure on the hospitals ashore.[35] Under unrelenting attack, the Japanese defenders ceased to exist as an organized force, and the medical crisis ended on the fifteenth day of the campaign.

The enormous scale of the battle and the need to fight simultaneously on land and sea made the cost of the victory high. Of

71,034 American officers and men committed to the battle, 14,111, or about 20 percent, were listed as killed, wounded, or missing—almost the equivalent of a whole division. Among the casualties were 3,674 soldiers and 10,437 marines. The defenders were virtually exterminated, and hundreds of Japanese civilians who had made the island their home wrote a grim epilogue to the struggle by leaping to their deaths from the island's northern cliffs. "The water is full of them," a sailor remarked, "the fish will eat good."[36]

The triumph was also great. Breaching the enemy's defense perimeter and savaging his naval air capacity in the "great Marianas turkey shoot" made the victory one of the most crucial in the war. The swift conquests of Tinian and Guam that followed completed the conquest of the islands at a cost in dead and wounded of about one-fifth of the total American force—24,518 soldiers, sailors, and marines. In every respect the campaign formed a fitting introduction to the bloody final phase of the Pacific war.

Now Nimitz was ordered by the Joint Chiefs to commit his forces to the conquest of two small islands—battles that remain among the most controversial of the whole conflict. In terms of suffering, the second lingers in the American consciousness beside Valley Forge.

The archipelago of the Caroline Islands spreads south of the Marianas, its jewel the Japanese base at Truk. Nimitz wisely bypassed that fortress, as MacArthur had bypassed the enemy's other bastion at Rabaul. The question of whether the group of islands called the Palaus, some 1,200 miles to the west, had to be taken either to complete Truk's isolation or to support the invasion of the Philippines remains unsettled, a source of bitterness still to survivors of the fighting for the islands of Angaur and Peleliu.

Anticipating a hard fight, the Marines strengthened their medical companies and almost doubled the number of corpsmen. The main reason was morale: To a civilian, the gathering of medics and hospital supplies had a grim look to it, but to the fighting men it signaled a greater possibility of living through the battle. Since sickness would certainly follow, a sanitary organization like the one in the Marshalls and a malaria control unit also went in with the troops. On September 15, 1944, assault troops of the 1st Marine Division crossed the reef of Peleliu, passed through mined waters, and landed on its narrow beaches.

The airfield that was their main objective fell quickly, and part of the marines' backup—two regiments of the army's 81st Infantry Division—were released from their supporting role to take the nearby island of Angaur. There the soldiers swept away resistance in a brisk, bloody campaign fought in smothering heat amid a maze of coral outcroppings. Army medics were as competent as the combat units; hospitals went up on the second day of the attack, and the two thousand-plus wounded and sick were handled with dispatch. Most of the Palaus' surviving natives were on Angaur, and foresight by navy and army planners provided them with food, water, clothing, and medical treatment.[37]

So far so good. But the Japanese garrison on Peleliu was nine times the size of the one on Angaur, and its commander, Colonel Kunio Nakagawa, had a plan. Beyond the airfield that was Peleliu's chief attraction rose a system of coral ridges, a bizarre, otherworldly landscape of jumbled rocks, ravines, and brush. The Japanese abandoned the open, where ships and planes could blast them, to build a system of tunnels and pillboxes that neither bombs nor shells could penetrate. Their defenses featured no single citadel, but rather a maze of strongpoints. Dispensing with the romantic absurdity of the banzai charge, the defenders held every position to the death.

The marines had to work their way uphill in intense heat to blast or sear each position, and at night Japanese infiltrators moved down to kill the Americans in their foxholes. The island was Biak all over again, only this time marines instead of soldiers did the dying, and there was much of it to be done: The 1st Marine Division took almost 50 percent casualties—more than 6,500 dead, wounded, and missing. When the remaining regiment of the 81st Infantry Division joined the fight on Peleliu, hundreds more were added to the army's earlier losses on Angaur.

Moving the wounded down the ridges was an excruciating business. Four bearers were needed for every stretcher, and the riflemen who did much of the work found it hard and perilous. "My heart pounded from fear and fatigue each time we lifted a wounded man onto a stretcher," wrote one, recalling agonizing trips over steep and rocky slopes while "bullets snapped through the air and ricochets whined and pinged off the rocks." Through such harrowing trips the wounded—from shock or morphine, out of confidence in their comrades or relief that their own war was over—seemed the calmest of all. The lightly wounded pitied the men who were still whole.[38]

On the transports and hospital ships, doctors gave more penicillin than ever before, and more whole blood. Comfort remained in short supply, for the sick bays were, as ever, hot, stinking places, where men who were in pain, exhausted, and dehydrated endured temperatures of 100° or more. Hospital ships, arriving late, served mainly as floating ambulances, evacuating men who had already been treated on the transports.[39] Other casualties left Peleliu by air, arriving at rear-area hospitals in their torn, filthy, and bloodstained uniforms and bringing with them the look and smell of war.

Peleliu had its own smells. Marines and soldiers found it impossible to dig cat-holes in the hard coral, and the simplest act of field sanitation—burying one's own waste—proved impossible. Fat black flies multiplied wildly during the fighting, exploiting the feasts of dead bodies, rotting food, and feces. The plague did not stop at the shoreline; flies swarmed on the ships offshore, studding the rigging of the hospital ship *Solace* as if "someone . . . drove hobnails into the wire."[40]

Chemistry had supplied a new weapon in DDT, and army and marine sanitation squads, landing on D-Day, followed the combat teams inland and sprayed pools, latrines, corpses and Japanese food dumps. But DDT was not a success in its first major trial in the Pacific. The stuff that had helped to break a typhus epidemic in conquered Naples worked poorly on a tropical island during a battle that made enemy-held areas unreachable. As soon as the fighting died down, however, DDT sprayed from planes helped to prevent a post-battle epidemic.[41]

Whether Peleliu was worth the cost remained doubtful. In earlier Pacific battles it had not been uncommon for more than twenty Japanese to die for every American, and about the same proportion would fall in the battles for the Philippines. But on Peleliu roughly six Japanese died for every American, and only 1.2 Japanese for every American who was killed or wounded. At Iwo Jima, the number would be lower still.

In October 1944 General MacArthur invaded the Philippines, a massive operation to which Admiral Nimitz contributed much of his fleet. By February 1945 large areas of the Philippines had been liberated, and Nimitz retrieved his forces for an attack upon a mere cinder lying in the ocean 750 miles south of Tokyo that was wanted as an airbase for the growing bomber assault on Japan.

Iwo Jima is a 5-mile-long heap of volcanic ashes and stony rubble cast out by a rounded cone that rises from its southern end. The rugged islet was perfect for defense and heavily fortified, for the Japanese had mined its recesses, leaving at least 13 meters of rock above every bunker to intercept shells and bombs. Reinforced concrete strengthened key points. There was no continuous enemy line, but rather an ingenious system of interlocking positions with mutually supporting fields of fire.

The whole island had been transformed into a castle rising from the sea. Since the heights of Mount Suribachi and the Motoyama plateau overlooked the prospective landing beaches on the southeast shore, tactical surprise was impossible. Even at Monte Cassino, Americans had not been forced to attack so nakedly under the enemy's eye.[42]

Navy medics rightly expected that they would have much work to do, estimating 30 percent casualties in the anticipated two weeks of fighting. Since three Marine divisions were to go ashore, and the fleet would be large, beds were provided in plenty—5,000 in medical units on or near Iwo, four hospital LSTs, two hospital ships and a converted hospital assault transport offshore, and 5,000 more in fixed hospitals on Saipan and Guam.[43] No one considered those preparations optimistic.

By now the navy had established a reshipment point at Guam and had made arrangements to deliver ample supplies of whole blood. One hospital LST served as a floating blood bank, and every ship designated to receive casualties sailed with flasks of refrigerated blood aboard. Medical battalions laid in additional blankets, gas gangrene antitoxin, and penicillin. The V Amphibious Corps added its own medical battalion to the landing force, the marines provided their Evacuation Hospital No. 1, and the army contributed the 38th Field Hospital. Everyone went through strenuous training and learned or relearned the art of climbing down a cargo net. Transports were combat-loaded (that is, by the principle of last in, first out), and corpsmen packed their seabags with battle dressings, plasma, and serum albumin—another blood substitute like plasma—to be used in first aid. The preparations looked, and were, entirely professional, the fruit of more than four years of bitter experience.[44]

Among its other charms, Iwo was believed (erroneously) to be a hotbed of disease, and as a result the marines were obliged to nurse sore arms from typhus, cholera, and plague shots as well as the usual battery of immunizations, including the inevitable tetanus booster. Carrier aircraft were to spray the island with DDT; troops wore uniforms impregnated with mite- and louse-killing chemicals. Malaria and epidemic control teams would land along with the fighters. From killing enemies to killing bugs, the Central Pacific and its veteran fighters knew their business, having learned it the hard way. But conquering Iwo proved to be harder still.

The 4th and 5th Marine Divisions began to go ashore on the island's southwest coast on the morning of February 19, 1945. The day was clear and mild, and the sea was calm. Aidmen went in with their platoons, aid station personnel with their battalion or regimental command posts. Medical shore party evacuation teams landed a half-hour after the first assault wave, beginning work just above the line where the sea beat on steeply sloping beaches of black volcanic ash. ("One hell of a hike upgrade," the 4th Division surgeon noted.)[45]

Or at any rate tried to. From the first moment of the battle Iwo's beaches were under heavy and continuous fire from the caves and tunnels of Suribachi to the left and Motoyama to the right. The fleet and planes battered back: "The attack is so frightful," wrote a Japanese in his diary, "that it seems as if it must change the shape of the island." Medical losses began early and mounted steadily. Boats with medical supplies were sunk, and corpsmen were hit as they waded ashore and tried to reach the wounded. A navy medical shore party received a direct hit from a shell and lost fifteen of its seventeen men. On the beach corpsmen scooped out foxholes for the wounded and buried casualties in the sand merely to lower their profiles. One surgeon closed four chest wounds under fire.[46]

Evacuation was perilous. Wheeled vehicles were stranded on the beach, sinking in the loose volcanic ash as they tried to move inland. Only tracked vehicles—Weasels, a sort of jeep on treads—could reach the wounded, who otherwise had to be carried. Hideously injured marines crept or staggered back to aid stations hidden in shell holes. Dragging on ponchos those who could not move themselves, trying to exploit such cover as they could find, and trying to site their aid stations to intercept the drift of the wounded, who flowed like water into channels of natural shelter, the medics took a higher rate of casualties than the assault troops they served. Many died alongside their patients.

Any concentration of men invited enemy fire. The 5th Marine Division surgeon was a casualty. Foxholes could not be dug among Iwo's few trees, because mortar rounds striking the trunks scattered fragments downward like airbursts. To protect themselves and their patients, corpsmen covered foxholes with canvas litters heaped with dirt. At night, some aid stations helped to man the perimeters, keeping all-night watch. Medical work outside the blacked-out dugouts depended on the fitful green illumination of naval star-shells and the flares cast up by mortars. Finding a man who was going into shock, Pharmacist's Mate 1/C Ray Crowder "knew that there was only one thing to do and that was to give him some serum albumin."

> I opened a can and finally rigged it without the aid of light. With a tourniquet tied on the upper portion of his arm I tried to hit his vein with the needle as I crouched under a poncho and used the light of a match. Finally, after several attempts, I felt the needle enter the vein and could feel the blood stroking the needle point. I loosened the tourniquet and let the albumin run into the blood stream. I waited a couple of minutes and checked his arm to see if a bulge had formed. It was perfect. Shortly afterward he began to revive. . . .[47]

In the darkness so many litter-bearers got lost that a policy was adopted of evacuating only the most desperate cases at night. To stumble through ankle-deep volcanic ash with a laden stretcher in total darkness under sniper fire was too much for morale. But the wounded had a better chance of making their way alive to aid stations after sunset, and as a result the hours between sundown and about 8 o'clock were busy ones at the blacked-out stations.

On the line corpsmen died so fast that the aid stations and the medical battalion headquarters had to be depleted to send more forward, knowing that their men were inadequately trained in the arts of front-line survival and that many would be cut down before they learned. By the end of the battle some aid stations had no enlisted personnel at all, except those suffering from combat fatigue or physically unfit for duty as company aidmen. Combat fatigue was common, not only because of the danger the aidman faced but because he bore a great responsibility. Knowing many of the men he treated, he practiced a most intense and personal kind of medicine, and especially when exhausted he suffered waves of guilt over the deaths of those he could not save.[48]

The 4th Marine Division hospital was a collection of dark green tents, stuffy inside with cigarette smoke and the smells of dirt, blood, and sweat. Here the division surgeon, "rawboned, red-faced" Commander Richard Silvis, was in charge. The two operating rooms were Japanese cisterns, canvas-roofed, with concrete walls and floors. On the operating tables, patients received whole blood flown in from San Francisco—"Wonderful stuff," Silvis told Robert Sherrod, "much better than plasma when they have severe hemorrhages." Walking through the wards, Sherrod noted that the wounded all found something to be thankful about. "Blinded men are thankful they didn't lose their arms; armless men are grateful to have their eyes." Most were quiet, but one severely wounded corpsman breathed with a "heavy, rasping breath" that could be heard through the whole tent. As Sherrod and Silvis stood by his cot, he died, and the ward became quiet. "We gave him everything," the doctor said, "oxygen, a lot of whole blood. . . . But he was licked from the start."[49]

The ships offshore were also taking casualties. Fighting ships were seldom able to transfer their wounded, who accumulated in sick bays and dressing stations scattered through the decks. When such refuges took random hits, the wounded had to be moved from damaged areas to relatively secure ones. In all of this there was little distinction between corpsmen and other members of the crew; seamen well trained in first aid provided initial care and served as stretcher-bearers. Smaller vessels gave first aid and then transferred their casualties as soon as possible to larger ones. Unavoidably, all the movement meant much handling, which did the injured men no good. Supply boats ran a gauntlet of fire, beached in heavy surf, hastily discharged their cargoes, took on a load of wounded, and backed into the water again. Some vanished in fountains thrown up by shell bursts or broached in the rough seas and sank offshore.[50]

The four hospital LSTs took stations, one to each landing beach. Here the wounded, brought by landing craft and DUKWs, received treatment for shock, had broken bones splinted and wounds dressed, received whole blood if they needed it, and were assigned and moved to larger ships beyond. On one LST a barge was moored alongside as a kind of reception ward; a doctor boarded each boat as it came alongside, and casualties in need of immediate care were offloaded at once. Some received treatment on the barge; others were put in metal-frame stretchers and lifted aboard the LST by a crane that swung them over the deck and lowered them through the cargo hatch.

The whole tank deck was a hospital, and the crew's quarters provided additional wards. Six medical officers, thirty-six corpsmen, an operating room with two tables, and abundant whole blood and penicillin all made a strange contrast with the filth, dirt, and grease left behind by the tanks, for these ships were converted to hospital use only after their original cargo had been unloaded. The cavernous dim-lit spaces with their rows of folding cots and sprawling naked or partly clothed bodies were hard to give care in; the unwieldy craft rolled in rough seas and from time to time had to move when enemy shells began to bracket them. The LST's saved many lives, but they were also makeshifts that provided everything necessary to healing except comfort, safety, and repose.[51]

Something of the same comment could be made about the transports. Some captains, according to reports, refused to take casualties beyond their normal capacity, leaving the coxswains of the craft that had brought the wounded from the beach to search, sometimes for hours, for a place to unload them. Most accepted the wounded and did the best they could for them. Some transports carried hospital ship platoons. On one such ship, medical officers and corpsmen worked day and night, sorting, operating, and caring for their patients. At night the ship withdrew into deep water, only to approach the shore again in daylight, sometimes concealing itself in smoke. Red alerts announced enemy air attacks every night but one, until the transport, filled at last with the two hundred or so wounded that represented its capacity, joined a convoy and departed to Saipan.

Still the fight raged on. On March 14 a medical officer noted with some irony, "Corps says Island secure. Japs not informed to Date." Combat fatigue claimed many; a correspondent saw a psychotic marine twisting and screaming on his stretcher and reflected, "There is war at its worst." The toll of American dead still mounted. The corpses were wrapped in ponchos and left by the roadside for Division teams to gather up and bury. So bitter was the fighting that some lay unattended for a week. As for the Japanese dead, many had been burned by flamethrowers, and a naval medical officer later remembered that "it was an awesome sight to see the bodies after they'd been 'flamed.'"[52]

By sundown on March 24, 1945, the invasion force counted more than 24,000 killed, wounded, and missing, of whom almost 21,000 were battle casualties. Nearly five thousand Americans lay buried ashore, and nearly eighteen thousand wounded had been evacuated. By general agreement, the medical service worked exceptionally well at Iwo Jima—better than in any conflict of the Pacific war to that time. That judgment rested on the great number of wounded treated and moved out under conditions of extraordinary difficulty and stress. It rested on the deployment of advanced techniques and discoveries, from penicillin to the hospital LST. It rested on the display of raw courage by corpsmen who took high losses themselves and doctors who operated in shell holes while mortar rounds fell around them. Yet on Iwo Jima their skill and devotion could not prevent the spiralling losses.

From Attu to Iwo Jima, the battles fought in the North and Central Pacific had been marked not only by continuing ferocity but also by improving tactics on both sides. The combination was deadly. The Japanese, their defenses failing, had been reduced to a strategy that amounted to little more than dying in place. But their tactics improved as their strategy became bankrupt. The enemy knew how to defend, embraced death with seeming eagerness, and took more Americans with them than ever before. In all of history, it seems unlikely that any plot of land the size of Iwo Jima was ever bid for at such cost by winner and loser alike. Disease was insignificant; almost every victim died by the hand of another man, and for almost every Japanese corpse there was a dead or wounded American. That was the new totality of war in the Pacific, and the work of those who tried to save life could do no more than palliate the rising cost.

11

Buildup in Britain

The progress made during 1943 in other theaters of war provided a treasury of ideas for medical officers preparing to handle the massive casualties that would inevitably result from the planned invasion of Germany's heavily defended Fortress Europe. But the London-based command called the European Theater of Operations had a priceless asset of its own—the army's most capable chief surgeon. Because the theater spent almost two and a half years preparing for the invasion, he had the time he needed to construct the most elaborate system of evacuation and treatment seen in any army during World War II.

In September 1941 Colonel Paul R. Hawley, a fifty-year-old regular medical officer, joined the Special Observers Group, senior officers working out of the American Embassy in London to plan the eventual integration of the British and American war efforts. Since the United States was still officially neutral, the members of the group wore civilian clothes and carried British papers. But on the morning of December 8, 1941, as Hawley entered the

Baker Street tube station, he was greeted by huge black headlines announcing Pearl Harbor. He returned to his apartment, put on his uniform, and set out again. The morning's business was a meeting at the office of the director general of Britain's army medical service, and when Hawley walked into the conference room in uniform "they got up and yelled and cheered."[1]

A six-footer, heavy about the midsection, Hawley was a man of force, presence, and abounding energy. An able surgeon and sanitarian and a surprisingly tactful diplomat, he embodied many of the best elements of the prewar medical service. Joining the army just four days before the United States entered World War I, he had served in France as a regimental medical officer and after the war had gone through the paces of a regular's life—serving in the United States and overseas; teaching military medicine and commanding the Medical Field Service School; winning a doctorate in public health from Johns Hopkins; and managing the day-to-day life of Walter Reed Army Hospital as its executive officer. A surgeon and an executive, equally attuned to prevention and healing, he was the complete medical officer.[2]

As a man of promise, he was selected against tough competition to attend both the Army War College and the Command and General Staff School, where he met the officers of combat arms, acquired their language, and learned to understand their outlook.[3] (Seemingly his amusements were also those dear to the officer corps, for he acquired a permanently wry neck by getting his head caught between two ponies during a game of polo.) In Great Britain, Hawley found what was, for him, the right job in the right war at the right time. Had he been capable of grand phrases, he might have said like Churchill that his whole life had prepared him for the task he now faced as chief surgeon of the ETO.

An aggressive leader, Hawley had great dreams for his own theater and small regard for the needs of others. Distressed that the American forces depended upon the British for medical care, he launched a program to build a complete system of new hospitals, where American doctors and nurses could care for American casualties using American equipment and methods. He pressed the British bureaucracy to meet his needs, wringing land, construction materials, and labor from a crowded wartime country where everything was in short supply. His primary and most characteristic method was a "note of polite blackmail," a warning that the American people demanded the best of medical care for their soldiers and that British officials who failed to grant what the medical service needed would run a serious risk of alienating their allies.[4]

But for all his energy and cunning, Hawley could not influence the grand strategy of the war. For a time in late 1942 and early 1943, the demands of the North African invasion forced the chief surgeon to scale back his plans for an ample, independent medical service and a huge hospital system. As far as the American government was concerned, Great Britain faded into a backwater. The date for the invasion of France was delayed, from 1942 to 1943, and then to 1944, while the British did all they could to divert the allies' main thrust to the Mediterranean. Even as Hawley prodded British bureaucrats and badgered Washington to send more medical troops, he was dispatching some of the best men, women, and hospitals that he already had to the North African battlefronts.

The ETO medical staff was seriously unbalanced. Talented doctors arrived who were new to the uniform, while the Regular Medical Corps officers who understood how to organize a theater medical service were few. Equipment came in erratically from the United States and had to be stored, put under some sort of inventory control, and issued as needed. But doctors who understood supply were the rarest experts of all; as Hawley once complained, his supply chief "seems to understand how supplies get *out* of a depot, but hasn't the faintest idea of how they get *in*." As a result, Americans, supposedly the citizens of democracy's arsenal, continued to depend on the British if they were wounded in the air war, injured in accidents, or taken ill. Many lay in British hospital beds, and on the operating table were carved by British scalpels, even if their surgeon was an American. In rare cases they died unnecessarily because of the trifling fact that their own nation painted oxygen bottles green, while the British used that color for carbon dioxide.[5]

Even Hawley's own place in the headquarters was uncertain. When the surgeon general was shunted off to the Services of Supply in Washington, the same thing happened to theater surgeons. Hawley found himself not only a member of a subordinate organization, but physically separated as well from the ETO headquarters, working in Cheltenham while the top dogs stayed in London. The fixed hospitals under the Services of Supply were clearly within his bailiwick, but he could give direction to the theater as a whole only by working his recommendations first upward through the SOS bureaucracy, then downward through the ETO command system to the units in the field.

Hawley's immediate superior was the SOS commander, Brigadier General J. C. H. Lee. Lee was not widely liked; his nickname, Jesus Christ Himself, suggested a robust sense of self-importance. Hawley once remarked of his commander that "he's nobody I'd ever want to go fishing with for a week," but he worked with and through Lee to get his own position strengthened and defined. Fortunately for the chief surgeon, Lee was a formidable bureaucratic infighter. He secured from ETO headquarters the right to issue orders in the theater commander's name, and he got the technical service chiefs, including Hawley, moved back to London. Lee had himself named G-4 of ETO, meaning that in addition to commanding SOS he also headed the headquarters staff section that advised the commander on supply. Hawley made the most of the improving situation. By applying his mixture of urgency and charm to a man he fundamentally disliked, not only could he set theater policy on the practice of medicine, but he could also shift the theater's medical personnel, both ground and air, by writing directives for Lee to sign on behalf of the theater commander.[6]

The final move came when General Eisenhower returned from Africa to take over the multinational Supreme Headquarters, Allied Expeditionary Forces (SHAEF). In January 1944 Eisenhower merged the ETO and SOS staffs. Through ETO, Eisenhower commanded the American forces; Lee became his deputy theater commander for supply and administration, and Hawley was, in every sense, the chief surgeon of the American forces. As he reported to the surgeon general, "our organization here seems to have completely cooked and has now jelled." If anything more was needed to clarify his position, Hawley received his second star in February 1944, giving him the same rank as the Army Surgeon General.[7]

In its final form, the chief surgeon's office had fourteen divisions and controlled all significant aspects of medical policy. Especially notable were Hawley's consultants—leading physicians and surgeons, many drawn from civilian life, whose chief business was to ensure that the ETO medical service maintained the highest possible professional standards. Colonel James C. Kimbrough, the regular who headed the division, had worn the uniform since World War I and came to the London from a top post at Walter Reed. His chief consultant in surgery was Colonel Elliott C. Cutler, a lean, wiry man with piercing blue eyes, who had succeeded Harvey Cushing as professor of surgery at Harvard. A battalion surgeon in the last war, Cutler was a gifted teacher as well as a citizen soldier who knew wartime surgery and how to convey its nature and techniques to others. Colonel William S. Middleton, chief consultant in medicine, also had served during World War I, returning to the army from his civilian post as Dean of the University of Wisconsin Medical School. The three rode herd on a staff of senior physicians and surgeons, most of whom had won distinction in civilian life but had little army experience. Middleton spoke of the problems Kimbrough faced in handling his prima donnas: "He would first cajole them. Then he would quote Shakespeare and then the Scripture. Finally he'd burst out into the vilest profanity you have ever heard."

The consultants did more than exemplify the mixed civilian and military backgrounds that typified wartime medicine. They were Hawley's brain trust. Despite his manipulative ways, the chief surgeon wanted to hear the truth from his advisers, and he demanded from them candor equal to his own. "I expect advice from this group," he said, "not only when I ask for it, but when any member of this group thinks that I need it."[8]

The last possible problem for Hawley was the arrival of another two-star, Major General Albert Kenner, the man Marshall had originally wanted to be wartime surgeon general, as the surgeon of Eisenhower's Supreme Headquarters. But the confusions of the Southwest Pacific were not replicated in the ETO, for just as Hawley was no Carroll, Kenner was no Rice. The two developed a mutually satisfactory arrangement, working together in planning the medical side of the cross-channel attack. They shared responsibilities "in an exemplary manner, often with little organizational structure or protocol to guide them." Among the American forces, Hawley's position remained unchallenged; the European Theater of Operations had only one chief surgeon, and everybody knew who he was.[9]

Everybody, that is, but the Army Air Forces. Another strong personality was at work among the airmen in England, as well as a mystique, an energy and a bumptious self-confidence born of a new organization that was fighting a new kind of war.

Enthusiasts for airpower saw it as the key to victory in World War II. It proved to be less than that. The air arm never defeated a land force and, until the advent of nuclear weapons, failed to break any nation's will to fight. Yet airpower became an indispensable part of the military equation, decisive in naval battles and a key element in defeating Germany's submarine fleet. Tactical air supremacy gave decisive advantages to any army. The role of airplanes in World War I as flying cavalry, geared to reconnaissance and intercepting enemy aircraft, survived and grew. Their role as flying artillery, able to pound the enemy with high explosives and incendiaries, expanded enormously, and the new long-range bombers emerged as clumsy but devastating weapons against industry and the populations of cities.

Air medicine developed accordingly, separating itself gradually from army medicine on two fronts, bureaucratic and clinical. The basic justification for a new medical service was scientific. The sky was a new environment for humans to live and fight in, and it became stranger and more hostile as planes flew higher and faster. American aviation medicine, which began during World War I as a way of choosing potential pilots from the hordes of airstruck volunteers, was transformed by the technical evolution of the airplane. Short of discovering Superman, there was no way to select human beings who could endure the cold of open cockpits, fly in fog and darkness with unaided vision, and inhale unlimited amounts of carbon monoxide blown back from sputtering engines. The plane had to be adapted to its occupants if it was to fly ever higher and faster in all sorts of weather. But the engineer alone lacked the knowledge of physiology and psychology needed to shape a closed environment with adequate life-support systems. Physician, psychologist, and engineer had to cooperate, and in this endeavor a new kind of medicine was born.[10]

Leading the way were some charismatic figures. One, later well known to Hawley, was a colorful, astute, short-tempered regular, Malcolm C. Grow. As a young physician in 1915, Grow had volunteered to serve in the Russian Army, which was desperately short of doctors.[11] When the United States declared war, he shifted to the Army Medical Corps and remained in the army afterward, following the slow track of field medicine rather than the fast track of service in the general hospitals. In 1928 Grow passed through the school of aviation medicine, then a three-month course intended simply to focus medical interest on the physical problems of pilots. He became post surgeon at an airfield and was soon drawn into solving the problems of the test pilots (cold and monoxide among them). Through his experimental work, he sought to incorporate the human factor into the increasingly elaborate blueprints of aeronautical design.[12]

Strange things happened when the human body entered the upper air. While air pressure dropped and the supply of oxygen diminished, gases inside the body expanded with complicated and potentially disastrous effects. The inner ear could be damaged. The escape of nitrogen from solution in the blood could produce agonizing or fatal cases of the bends. "Aero-embolisms" could be fatal to the wounded on evacuation flights in unpressurized planes. Gravitational forces were another problem, especially for men who flew fighters and dive bombers. Swirling dogfights subjected them to the potentially lethal effects that acceleration, gravity, and centrifugal force could exert on their cardiovascular systems. Men passed out from hypoxia (oxygen deprivation) when inertial forces drove the blood from their brains. The dive bomber, in particular, seemed to have been designed to produce "red-outs," "gray-outs," and blackouts.[13]

Choosing men, adapting machines, forestalling human breakdowns, managing air evacuation, and treating the injured might have been enough to keep the air force medical service busy. However, there was another fight that sometimes seemed to absorb its leaders almost as much as the war did: the fight to break free from the army and control by its surgeon general. The basic war of bureaucratic liberation was waged by the enthusiastic generals who lifted the army's air arm from an office in the signal corps to the status of a supercommand. In turn they rode the evolution of flight from an attraction at county fairs to a major means of transport. But the evolution of flying did not in itself guarantee success. After all, naval air remained an extension of the fighting fleet, even though World War II showed that tactical airpower was a more decisive weapon at sea than on land. Yet it was the Army Air Forces that became autonomous and ultimately independent.

The doctors of the evolving air service waged their own war against medical traditionalists to whom "the name 'flight surgeon' was anathema."[14] Earthbound army doctors could see no scientific reason for a separate specialty of air medicine (and in the early days of flight the rationale had been dubious at best). They also reacted with automatic resentment against upstarts who talked secession. By 1939, when war broke out in Europe, the growth of a separate medical service had become alarming to the surgeon general. He tried to stop it by bringing the air surgeons under a division of air medicine in his own office. But before the squabble could be resolved, the growing importance of airpower to the national defense put an end to it. In 1941 the Army Air Forces was created to meet the national emergency, and the new command took control of all air installations and personnel, including doctors, nurses, patients, and medical facilities on the airbases. The top medical officer, Major General David N. W. Grant, was designated the Air Surgeon, in capitals—a new surgeon general in all but name, even though he remained in the Army Medical Department and continued to report to General Kirk.[15]

In early 1942 the Army Air Forces became one of the new supercommands. As the theaters of operations took form, each acquired a chief surgeon who expected to make medical policy there, and as a result tensions developed between the local air surgeons and some theater surgeons. Who controlled hospitals where airmen were treated, who controlled their evacuation, and how was air evacuation to be integrated with the traditional chains of land and sea evacuation? Sometimes the quarrels became sharp (as in the ETO). In retrospect they seem minor incidents within the larger problem presented by the rise of airpower: how to integrate the air arm into military doctrine and practice.

In 1942 Grow, now a handsome, silver-haired senior officer, set up the medical service of the newly created Eighth Air Force in England. His importance was increased by the fact that for two and a half years almost the only fighting done by American forces stationed in Great Britain was in the air. Airmen dominated the first increment of the proposed million-man force the United States intended to concentrate in Great Britain for the coming invasion. The Eighth Air Force joined in the British air assault on Germany and became a testing ground for the theory and practice of strategic bombing, a combat mission separate and distinct from the support of ground armies. Grow planned medical air support for the North African landings and served during the bomber campaign against Germany as surgeon of the Eighth Air Force and later of the Strategic Air Forces in Europe.[16]

Being a member of a bomber crew was a strange way to fight a war, almost limitlessly demanding. Combat missions in Europe might last as long as ten hours, most at altitudes of 25,000 feet— almost 5 miles—in temperatures that often reached 50 below zero. Trying to make clear what was involved, General Grant once invited other medical officers to consider whether they could manage the 130 controls, switches, levers, dials, and gauges of a Flying Fortress cockpit from the comfort and security of their office swivel chairs. Then, he continued,

> . . . cut the size of your office to a five-foot cube—engulf it in the roar of four 1,000-horsepower engines—increase your height above ground to four or five miles—reduce the atmospheric pressure by one-half to two-thirds—lower the outside temperature to 40 or 50 below zero. . . . That will give you an idea of the *normal* conditions under which the pilots, navigators, and bombardiers must work out the higher mathematical relationships of engine revolutions, manifold and fuel pressure, aerodynamics, barometric pressure, wind drift, air speed, ground speed, position, direction, and plane altitude.

And, he suggested: "As the final touch to this bizarre picture of intense concentration amid intense distraction, add the *fear of death.*"[17]

The flight crews took heavy losses, as people trying out a new and ill-understood kind of war usually do. (Marines and soldiers learning amphibious warfare were another example.) American theories of precision daylight bombing staked far too much on the armament of the Flying Fortress and the supposed accuracy of the Norden bombsight. Flyers' equipment was poor for high-altitude flying, and many crews returned to base frostbitten and exhausted, in planes riddled by flak. Ambulances assembled at the airfields a half-hour before returning planes were due; pilots with wounded crewmen aboard fired flares, dropped out of formation, and left the flaps down after the plane had landed. Medics hurried the less serious cases to the local air force dispensary, the badly hit to one of the large SOS hospitals.[18]

Medicine and engineering came to the aid of the hard-pressed air crewmen. Both civilian and military researchers worked on their problems, with the Office of Scientific Research and Development and the National Research Council providing assistance.[19] The most critical needs of fliers were oxygen, armor, warmth, and rest. The air surgeon in Washington and Grow's office in the Eighth Air Force headquarters both made careful studies of oxygen deprivation, an insidious condition that could cause men to lapse into unconsciousness without warning. Men in isolated positions—tail and turret gunners, for example—were in particular danger, and other crew members could watch them for symptoms only through constant checks on the intercom. A man who passed out had to be reached by another crew member working his way in heavy clothing through the plane's narrow interior passages.

Rigorous training in standard and emergency procedures was a great help, preferably with the use of a low-pressure chamber to give air crewmen a preview of what they would face on actual flights. But an improved oxygen mask was needed also. The so-called continuous flow oxygen system, despite its name, required constant monitoring; the whole system seemed to have been designed for a time of peace, when intercoms were unlikely to be shot out and fliers could pay attention to dials and adjustments rather than to bombing runs, flak, and Messerschmitts. A great improvement, if not a final answer, was the demand oxygen system, introduced in late 1943, which automatically adjusted oxygen flow to the level required by the altitude. Involved in the work of development were the air force's Aero Medical Laboratory, a subgroup of the National Defense Research Committee working on aviation medicine, the staff of Harvard's School of Public Health, and private manufacturers in Massachusetts and Ohio. The introduction of improved equipment, superior training, and careful attention by surgeons reduced the accident rate from hypoxia by about four-fifths in the first year of combat, and the fatality rate fell by two-thirds.[20]

The cold of high altitudes caused half of all casualties among returning airmen during the first two years of the American bomber campaign against Germany. During most of World War II warplanes were not the tightly sealed capsules the modern flier knows; on the B-17, gunners threw open hatches to fire, and sub-zero winds whistled through the interiors. Unlike the ground troops, who suffered most from trenchfoot, fliers endured frostbite—rapid chilling by intense dry cold. Hands, feet, and faces were the most susceptible parts of the body, though ball-turret gunners curled up in their hemispheres beneath the fuselage also suffered frostbitten groins and buttocks. The injured parts became pale and waxen, ice formed in the tissues, hemorrhage or gangrene might result, and fingers and toes sometimes required amputation.[21]

Again, studies in the Aero Medical Laboratory and private industry (this time General Electric led the way) produced an answer in the electrically heated flying suit. The garment had to fit, could not be unbearably heavy, had to distribute heat more or less evenly, and had to have its various parts wired in parallel, so that—like the dependable sort of Christmas tree lights—a single broken wire would not turn off the whole suit. ("How did I freeze my right hand? Why, my goddamn left boot burned out!" one airman complained of an early model.)[22] In final form, the personal protective gear successfully reduced all causes of cold injury except those caused by wind blast. The exception underlined the importance of sealing the gaps in the bombers themselves. After all, even in wartime it was pretty absurd to have men firing machine guns through waist windows, hatches, and gunports 4 or 5 miles up, where the wind chill lowered the effective temperature on uncovered skin to 80 or 90 below zero! And in fact improved hatches that intercepted the wind while permitting the guns to be fired were installed on most bombers by the spring of 1944. Frostbite cases fell off by about half in the ETO, and by four-fifths in the Mediterranean Theater to the south. From that point improvement was steady until the end of the war.[23]

Enemy fire demanded other improvements to protect airmen. German antiaircraft crews threw up barrages of shells that seldom hit planes squarely but filled the air with flying fragments. In the Eighth Air Force, 65–70 percent of all wounds suffered in action during the first two years of combat were from flak.[24] Armor for airmen was an idea that intrigued General Grow, but his efforts to introduce it were highly unpopular. Americans had not worn armor into battle since early colonial days, and tentative efforts to provide armored vests for infantrymen, who valued their mobility more than the protection of a bulky garment, met solid rejection from officers and men. Yet plane crews, who had to sit still and be shot at, seemed perfect candidates for armor, and Grow pushed ahead with his usual tenacity, buoyed by the support of his commander, Lieutenant General Carl Spaatz.

Experiments began late in 1942, and in time the flak suit came into being. At first it was simply a bulletproof vest developed by the Wilkinson Sword Company as a twentieth-century coat of mail, with overlapping squares of manganese steel sewn onto strong fabric. Then an apron or "sporran" was added to protect the lower body as well. By New Year's Day, 1944, more than 13,000 suits had been provided for the Eighth Air Force and its progeny, the Ninth. Armor returned to modern battlefields in the air, a tribute to Grow's pioneering spirit and the technological bent of the organization he had helped to create. Nobody doubted that it was a lifesaver. Although some airmen continued to object to the flak suit, enough wore it to decrease low-velocity missile wounds by three-fifths, and the proportion of wounds to the protected parts of the body sharply decreased also.[25]

Besides the environment and the enemy, Grow's men, like all

others in combat, faced the consequences of exhaustion and stress, which were nowhere greater than in the air. Although fliers suffered from different pressures from those faced by troops on the ground, the grind of combat and the failure of nerve afflicted men in the sky as well as in the mud. In some ways, their situation was uniquely stressful. Once over enemy territory, an aircrew was cut off, facing combat with no support but what they could lend one another. A wounded man might have to survive six hours or more with only the first aid he could give himself or his comrades could give him. It was pointless to shout, "Medic!" in an airplane; the quick medical aid that men fighting on the sea or ground considered their right was impossible. Other planes in a formation might do what they could to beat off attacking fighters, but in no way could the wounded be moved from a damaged plane as they were from ship to ship at sea. Any wounded man who could not free himself from a fatally injured plane had to ride it down to earth and the final fireball. Only on a submarine were crew members so dependent on one another.

A great responsibility fell upon them. The earth was far beneath and belonged to the enemy. Locked into their expensive machines, crew members performed their complex tasks knowing that failure by any one of them could be fatal to all. Every mission left gaps in the ranks; the airman saw his friends vanish in smoke and sometimes helped the medics and ground crews remove bodies from his own plane. Inevitably, he began to think of the war as a kind of Russian roulette and believe that his own death was only a question of time. More than half of all air force casualties for the war took place in the ETO, and about 60 percent of the bomber crewmen were listed as killed or missing before they completed the standard twenty-five missions.[26]

The first year of air combat—July 1942 to July 1943—was the worst for Americans. Their doctrine committed them to precision daylight bombing unsupported by fighters. The Flying Fortresses were supposed to be exactly what their name implied, able to repel fighters with their combination of armor and firepower. The famed Norden bombsight was intended to hit military targets, enabling the air force to prove the pretensions of strategic bombing theorists while remaining morally above the kind of indiscriminate massacres produced by area bombing. In practice, no part of this program worked very well. The bombsight was a disappointment. The Fortresses (and the small number of B-24 Liberators that also flew with the Eighth Air Force) proved to be more vulnerable to German antiaircraft shells and Focke-Wulf fighters than anyone had imagined. Losses mounted steadily as the short raids typical of 1942 gave way to deeper penetrations of enemy airspace.

The airmen had to adapt to a life that featured physical comfort on the ground and acute peril aloft. According to a psychiatric study, most followed a fairly well-defined road from greenhorn to veteran. New arrivals tended to be noisy young men, heavy drinkers, scornful of the idea that they might ever be afraid. A few raids aged them quickly, making them painfully aware of their vulnerability and mortality. By the tenth raid those who survived had met fear and knew they could handle it; the crewmen knew one another and had developed confidence in themselves and their plane and pride in their squadron. They became "effective, careful fighting men, quiet and cool on the ground and in the air."[27]

By that time their whole existence revolved around combat, becoming intense and simple beyond the imagination of those who lived safe, multivalued lives. Fear was not a taboo subject among them; being scared was the norm. The crewmen talked about being flak-happy, or having the "Focke-Wulf Jitters," and denatured even those terms by applying them randomly to the anxieties of ordinary life. In combat they suffered the symptoms of stress—butterflies in the stomach, mild tremors, cold sweat on the hands and feet, rapid heartbeat, need to urinate. Sometimes they lost track of what they were doing, passed out, or suffered from diarrhea or uncontrollable tremor. In the aftermath of combat, they were overwhelmed by memory, obsessively reliving the awful things that had happened and the more awful things that might have. Some, converting fear into hostility, engaged in therapeutic fistfights; some set out methodically to get drunk.[28]

Yet they endured for a greater or lesser time. Some made it to the end of their tour of duty without incident. Others suffered the preliminary stages of a breakdown caused by interminable fatigue and fear. They became irritable and unsteady, suffered from depression, lost interest in sex and food, and slept poorly. Some who staggered through to the end found in the long-desired finale of their tour only an exaggerated sense of depression, as the thing that had been so long the center of their lives—the all-consuming fact of combat—vanished, leaving them at a loss.[29]

The experience of combat changed the doctors as well as their patients. General Grow made it a rule that every medical officer who was qualified to fly must accompany each crew in his command on at least one combat mission. One flight resulted in a classic account of group bonding and survival by the air force psychiatrist who accompanied and shared the dangers of the bomber's veteran crew.

As so often in wartime, Murphy's Law was in ceaseless operation through that mission. The Flying Fortress, its controls damaged early, had to drop out of formation. When the pilot persisted in making the bombing run, German fighters closed in like sharks around a bleeding whale. Most crewmen were wounded, and one passed out when a shellburst destroyed his oxygen system. Control cables were cut, the hydraulic and electrical systems were knocked out, and the intercom and radio destroyed. Fire started in the bomb bay, and flak punched holes in the wings, propellers, fuselage, and nose. As the battered craft headed for the English Channel and home, the enemy fighters broke off their attack, but no conceivable scenario promised a safe return.

Facing death or capture was a mixed bag of airmen. The pilot was big and easygoing; the copilot a "tightly-wound, aggressive" man with a manic-depressive history; the bombardier an irritable extravert. The top turret gunner was "uninhibited to the point of eccentricity," while the ball-turret gunner was a marked introvert, "cool, impersonal and emotionally tough." The right and left waist gunners were diametrically opposite types. Yet in the crisis the reactions of the men became "remarkably *alike*," their voices quietly precise and their actions "split-second decisive." Those who were wounded kept at their stations until their guns were destroyed. Those who stayed functional worked the remaining controls, treated the wounded, and repaired damage as far as they could, moving about their tasks rapidly, effectively, and without lost motion. The pilot consulted the copilot and bombardier and reached correct decisions quickly. There was no panic and no self-seeking; the aim of all was to save the whole crew. And in fact the battered Flying Fortress proved worthy of its name and brought them home, as the wartime song had it, on a wing and a prayer.

For the psychiatrist who had shared the hours of acute and seemingly hopeless peril the experience was source of wonder. Instead of each man falling back on his own reaction patterns, all had tended toward a common pattern. Extravert and introvert, eccentric and stable, manic-depressive and easygoing—in the face of death, all became "outwardly calm, precise in thought, and rapid in action." It was, the doctor suggested, "a matter deserving contemplation" by his professional colleagues.[30] The danger, the group spirit, and the leadership of the pilot had been decisive, while supposedly crucial individual bents and weaknesses had vanished for the time.

Yet some men broke, before, during, or after combat. If sheer physical exhaustion was often the precipitating factor in breakdowns among ground troops, the nervous tension of air warfare produced more cerebral symptoms among men who were often better able to understand their reactions than the average GI. Early practitioners of air medicine had noted pilot breakdowns but had treated the phenomenon as a unique consequence of flying, bestowing names like "flying fatigue" and "aeroneurosis." Supposedly the condition was unique because fliers, as a select group, were not subject to the same fears and anxieties as other men. Wartime made the group less select, radically increased the stress, and revealed that the symptoms of air crew members were well-known reactions to prolonged combat. Among the commonest were conversion states, marked by the transformation of inadmissible fears into respectable physical symptoms. As men of unusual intelligence, pilots in particular showed impressive subtlety in elaborating some minor organic problem into "a compelling disability that interfered with flying on a purely 'physical' basis, much to the individual's ostensible regret."[31]

As they strove to help airmen meet the stresses they faced, air force psychiatrists recognized inherent limitations both in their science and in their patients. For a variety of minor disturbances they could offer their patients only sympathy and a measure of insight into their conditions. If a man simply decided that he could not fly any longer, then—whether he declared his fear openly or whether he denied it while developing incapacitating physical symptoms—there was little to be done but remove him from flying. But the grinding-down process that psychiatrists called operational fatigue often proved to be treatable, the main reliance being the therapy developed in North Africa: put the victim to sleep for as much as four days and nights with sodium amytal, rousing him only for food and excretion.

It was also important, doctors believed, to embed a program of rest and recreation in the flier's everyday life. Rest was preventive medicine as well as therapy. Medical officers took the lead in urging a fixed tour of duty, originally set at twenty-five missions for bomber crews. (In August 1944 it was extended to thirty-five because the liberation of France and Belgium and the decay of German air power made missions less hazardous.) Men whose tour was over either returned to the United States or stayed in overseas theaters as instructors. Doctors also recommended a liberal leave policy for fliers, which was granted by the Eighth Air Force in mid-1943, when abundant replacements began to arrive. Grow urged and secured the establishment of a network of seventeen rest homes, which ultimately provided accommodations for about 6,600 officers and 6,800 enlisted men at a time.

Here combat crews got a week's leave, during which they showed in miniature some of the same psychological processes that appeared at the end of a tour of duty. Weary and anxious the first few days, they talked obsessively about combat. Then the real world insinuated itself into their lives; they began to sleep well and to talk about a variety of things, sports and politics, women and home. Hot baths, ample food, Red Cross girls, and the absence of formations and uniforms helped to revive, one combat officer said, "something warm and carefree; something which was almost forgotten."[32]

With self-prescribed outbreaks, prophylactic R&R, and sometimes sleep therapy to aid them, many men carried on despite presumably crippling personal problems. Indeed, a study of 150 successful combat pilots showed that half of them had histories of emotional instability that would have caused any psychiatrist of the

time to label them neurotic. The men, wishing to fly, had successfully concealed their backgrounds from the examiners. Such studies led some psychiatrists to conclude that the effort to exclude
from flying all men with emotional disorders was simply an "old
fallacy." With the humility and realism born of their own wartime
experience, many air force psychiatrists were ready to admit that
combat was combat. It was not like anything else, and the customary rules regarding who could function and who could not did not
seem to apply. "The *only valid test for endurance in combat*," a
classic wartime psychiatric study stated, "*is combat itself.*"[33]

The work of the air surgeons and air force researchers tended to
emphasize the distinctive aspects of aviation medicine. Yet medical
organization told another story. The integration of the air force
and Services of Supply medical systems meant that there was still
only one army medical system, and the airmen held a rather lowly
place in it. Perhaps conflict was inevitable, or perhaps the combative personalities of Grow and Hawley—men who liked and respected each other personally—made it impossible for them to co-
exist without a test of strength.

Back in Washington, the Air Surgeon gradually built himself independent personnel and supply services and pursued the ideal of
an independent hospital system as well. In the ETO, the bomber
offensive against Germany drew increasing numbers of airmen
into Hawley's domain. General Grow headed a medical service
that numbered almost 13,000, and he certainly did not lack for
dynamism or a sense of the importance of air medicine. He objected to the arrangement that made flight surgeons responsible
only for short-term care in dispensaries, while keeping the hospitals in the hands of the Services of Supply.[34]

The bureaucratic struggle between Grow and Hawley matched
able antagonists. Grow obtained convalescent centers for his airmen and built a medical school to teach air medicine to newcom-
ers. Hawley's weak spot was his supply service, and the air force
planes crossing and recrossing the Atlantic gave Grow the opportunity to establish his own pipeline, using the argument that he
could obtain what he needed in no other way. Hawley tried un-

successfully to turn off the pipeline, which kept flight surgeons ir-ritatingly well supplied while the ground and service forces went without. While the two fenced over supplies, Grow's longing for a separate air force hospital system brought him into direct con-flict with the theater chief surgeon over clinical questions as well. Grow proclaimed the uniqueness of air force medical needs, but Hawley growled that "there is not the slightest technical differ-ence between an air soldier wounded by fragments of a 20mm cannon shell and an infantryman wounded by fragments of an 88mm artillery shell." A hospital that treated one, he argued, could just as easily treat the other.[35]

Fortunately, both men were more than medical bureaucrats. Hawley's contention that separate air force hospitals would divert scarce resources was hard to dispute. On the other hand, if the Services of Supply was to go on caring for injured airmen, it had better do a good job. Hawley built hospitals close to major airbas-es and brought air force medical officers into them. He main-tained his warm personal relationship with Grow, with whom he had so many things in common—the medical profession, their service in World War I, their membership in the club of prewar regulars, and the liveliness and color of two very different person-alities. Both avoided the worst consequence of infighting, the poi-soned relationships and inability to cooperate that too often de-velop when professional and bureaucratic wrangles turn personal.

Some people in Washington were not so wise. Stories that in-jured airmen were receiving inferior care caused President Roo-sevelt to dispatch an investigating team, which included both Sur-geon General Kirk and Air Surgeon Grant. In the early months of 1944, amid all the problems of the buildup to an invasion that now lay only months ahead, Hawley had to entertain his distin-guished visitors, and in particular had to do his best to win over General Grant. He held strong cards: He had never lacked the diplomatic touch, and he had a fundamentally sound medical sys-tem to show off. The team's unanimous report vindicated him completely. Men of the air force were receiving superior care, bet-ter than British airmen got in their own RAF hospitals. That part of the argument was over for the remainder of the war, and it was notable that Hawley won his point not by bureaucratic maneuvers but by making sure that airmen received the kind of treatment they needed and deserved.[36]

By that time there was a new aspect to his and Grow's relationship. In early 1944 the focus of the war against Germany again moved north. History was veering Hawley's way. The Western Allies committed themselves to Operation OVERLORD, and the cross-channel invasion was set tentatively for May 1. No longer would the forces of the European Theater fight only in the air. And the approach of D-Day tended to bury minor feuds in the greater task of winning the war in Europe.

The greatest amphibious assault in the whole of human history was in preparation. Americans alone would contribute 1.4 million troops. When Eisenhower arrived in Britain, 100,000 new arrivals a month were disembarking. By D-Day, about 133,000 officers and men of the medical department would serve in the medical units and staff the SOS facilities.

The way the influx happened gave Hawley some new headaches. In any buildup, the fighting men have priority over support troops, and as a result medics arrived in Britain more slowly than the men they were supposed to serve. Despite such problems, the changing focus of the war tended to vindicate Hawley. His construction plans, which once had seemed exaggerated, were becoming reality as large parts of southern England turned into American bases. Among the complex of camps, depots, airfields, and firing ranges were more than a hundred major American hospitals, built of the materials that Hawley and his staff had almost literally squeezed out of Britain by methods that one of his officers called "dubious—and often devious." Linked by road and railroad to the channel ports and inland airfields, the 100,000-plus beds they provided were to be the final destination of the men wounded in the theater.[37]

By 1944 superfluity had replaced poverty. A medical system scaled for all-out war was far too big for any possible immediate need during the months that preceded D-Day. Many people were left idle, and the army's answer was the customary one of more rigorous training. On the military side, everyone had much to learn. Medical personnel had to learn to protect themselves and their patients under battlefield conditions, how to set up and tear down their tented hospitals, how to maintain their vehicles and defend against poison gas (which most knowledgeable people, especially veterans like Hawley who remembered European battlefields during World War I, expected to be used again). Amphibious medicine was added to the other subjects for study, as the time for the invasion drew closer. Field exercises at the ETO's medical field service school were hard. They left exhausted officers—including nurses, who shared in the work—and enlisted people with a clearer idea of "what Medical Department soldiers undergo to bring sick and wounded to the rear . . . for treatment."[38]

However, professionals found other activities that were a great deal more interesting than the road marches, firing ranges, and close-order drill that absorbed the average soldier's time. Medical and nursing societies and meetings multiplied, for it was hard to find any desirable purpose that they did not serve. Conferences and seminars meant improved morale and a chance for Americans to learn about war medicine and surgery from the experienced Britons. Cocktails and dinners warmed allied relations and encouraged give-and-take in a mostly common language (English) and a universal tongue (science). British medical societies enrolled American members and opened their libraries to them. Hawley himself gave dinners where the British hosts became guests. Doctors, dentists, and nurses studied at medical schools and trained in civilian and military hospitals.

Some serious science was done. The ETO was a lucky theater in many ways, including the fact that its troops went into battle after penicillin had already become part of the medical arsenal. American doctors from the 2d General Hospital collaborated with Professor Howard Florey in studies of the miracle drug at Oxford. When mass-produced penicillin began to arrive from the United States in mid-1943, American hospitals carried out their own clinical research, and the first U.S. battle casualties to benefit directly were men of the Eighth Air Force flight crews. The drug met a certain amount of initial skepticism, but no real resistance; surgeons accepted the antibiotic, understanding that it could not replace surgical cleaning of wounds as the main standby for preventing battlefield infections. Physicians followed the familiar pattern of early caution and later generosity in prescribing the drug. Hawley added his own touch, demanding close control of penicillin, since "otherwise, some damn fools are going to waste it trying it on ingrown toenails so that they can write a paper on it."[39]

The principal remaining problem in medical organization—the supply mess—now urgently demanded solution. Depots were crammed with equipment ranging from tongue-depressors to whole hospital assemblies, but inventories were confused, and many of the officers in charge seemed to have little idea of how to organize and control their vast domain, how to store materials properly or meet requisitions in a timely manner. Ahead lay the daunting task of moving mountains of equipment to an embattled beachhead and "marrying" it to the units who would use it. By the early months of 1944 both Hawley and the surgeon general were ready to admit that the job could not be done, and that unless medical supply were drastically improved, it would "fail . . . to support the coming offensive."[40]

Hawley had done what he could, making appointments and firing unsatisfactory supply chiefs in manner that recalled Abraham Lincoln's way with unsatisfactory generals. But the quantities of matériel stored in England had passed beyond the ability of people trained in the relative simplicities of peacetime to comprehend, much less control. In the civilian world a managerial revolution had produced new methods of managing warehouses and controlling inventories, but those secrets remained unknown to the medics. The supply chiefs seemed unable to take hold, not only because of their own lack of specialized knowledge but because the enlisted people below them in the system were poorly trained and too few in number for the complicated and laborious tasks they had to do.

At that point Surgeon General Kirk came to the rescue. In spite of his lack of formal authority in the ETO, he sent a committee of experts to England, and Hawley, though he was under no obligation to do so, received them warmly and adopted their proposals. The group was a good image of the mixed expertise that a modern medical system required in total war. A lawyer headed the delegation—Tracy S. Voorhees, once assigned to the surgeon general's office as General Marshall's agent to keep an eye on a suspect medical service. By 1944 he had become Kirk's favorite troubleshooter, and he brought to the ETO with him a physician, a Medical Administrative Corps officer, and a civilian consultant who, in peacetime, had run the J. C. Penney warehouses. Fresh from shaping up the once chaotic medical supply system in the United States, the team in early 1944 effectively took over Hawley's supply division, reorganized it, moved some functions to the United States, where plenty of manpower was available, and brought new people to England. Kirk sent Colonel Silas B. Hays, one of the few medical officers who had become an acknowledged expert in supply, to head up the reformed service in the ETO.[41]

There was a political side to the reforms: Hawley, by improving medical supply, ended the air force's last and most legitimate complaint against his medical system, and—at least in his own view—won his dispute with General Grow. But the process of reform also showed the chief surgeon at his best, admitting his failure and asking and accepting expert help, even from civilians, in order to solve problems that otherwise might have cost uncounted lives.

———

Despite every sign of progress, much about the coming invasion remained dark. Nothing in American experience to date exactly paralleled the situation that would exist on the French coast, especially during the first hours after the landing.[42]

ETO planners assumed that about 12 percent of the assault forces would become casualties on D-Day. But they were painfully aware that the figure was at best informed guesswork. The German Army, which many still considered the world's best, had had almost four years to entrench itself in Fortress Europe, and nobody really knew what it might do when attacked. And there was the weather—the region's notorious weather that once had scattered the Spanish Armada. General Kenner warned that the ETO could handle a combination of good weather and heavy casualties, or light casualties and bad weather. But if the weather was bad and casualties were heavy, then the wounded would accumulate on the beaches, impossible to treat where they lay and impossible to move.[43]

The fog of war enshrouded coming events more deeply than the channel mist. Everywhere, despite years of planning, loomed factors over which the allies had either little control or none at all. On the other hand, the mechanics of the landing seemed relatively clear, with the example of other landings from around the world, especially the one in Sicily, to provide a guide. Preparations were made for the sequential landing of medical units with the combat forces, the creation of an army medical system ashore, and, as the troops advanced, the establishment of a zone of communications behind the combat zone to handle major problems of medical care, evacuation, and supply.

As usual in such attacks, the most perilous time would follow the first landings, and the army, as it did elsewhere in the world, relied on the engineer special brigades and their medical sections to bring order to a fundamentally chaotic situation. The navy would have its usual important medical role to play while the invasion was in progress, on the beaches once it had arrived, and during all evacuation by sea. Navy beachmasters would decide which casualties were to be sent to which ships. The obvious answer to moving the wounded off the beaches was to use the empty landing craft, with the great wallowing LSTs, as usual, bearing the brunt. Everyone recognized the shortcomings of the Large Slow Targets, especially in the rough waters of the Channel. The theater's surgical consultant called them "rotten ships for care of wounded American boys."[44] But in the Channel as elsewhere, necessity ruled, and the LSTs would play again the role they had pioneered in the Mediterranean and the Pacific.

Supplementing them were attack transports and small British ships called hospital carriers; hospital ships, some belonging to the army and some to the navy, would serve mainly by transporting the seriously wounded back to the United States.[45] The navy would have the job of loading the landing craft and caring for the patients en route. A similar division of responsibility would hold for casualties returned by air: The army would gather and care for them at the airstrips, and the air force would take responsibility while they were in flight. Air evacuation was not neglected, but it was planned as a kind of bonus, returning the wounded to the British Isles when, as, and if possible. The reason was the same as in all other theaters of war: There were no planes dedicated entirely to medical needs. The patients would have to ride returning transports, and for that reason the availability of aircraft would depend on tactical and supply demands, not on the needs of the wounded.

As the time of battle drew closer, medics bound for France packed their supplies into waterproof cases that had originally been used to ship mortar shells. Maintenance supplies to provide backup were lashed to wooden sleds for easier dragging across beaches. Real casualties began to arrive in medical units; during a landing exercise on the English coast, German torpedo boats slipped in and attacked the landing craft at a cost of seven hundred American lives. In late May 1944, the theater's blood service began to collect and deliver its product to the LSTs—a broad hint of things to come, since whole blood could be stored for only fourteen days. "We are all ready for the kick-off," Hawley wrote the Surgeon General, after a final tour of inspection, "and I, personally, feel as nervous as players usually feel just prior to the whistle."[46]

By then the embarkation of the troops was already under way. While some echelons still waited for the signal, a droning overflight of planes on the night of June 5 announced the invasion. Air force bombers pounded the enemy's fortifications, bases, and transport system; transports set parachutes blossoming over Normandy. Five thousand ships strong, the fleet was plowing through the turbulent channel.

12

From D-Day to Bastogne

For the medics the invasion began as airborne surgeons and aid-men jumped in the darkness over Normandy. They carried all the supplies they could, for they expected to be cut off from the main allied forces for many days. But their own losses were heavy in the blind landing; the 101st Airborne lost 20 percent of its medics, along with 70 percent of the air-dropped medical supplies.

Some were captured by the Germans, along with their patients, but most survived to gather and treat the wounded. Surgeons, sometimes painfully hurt themselves, worked in makeshift quarters—a garden, a hut, a French chateau—over battered survivors of the scattered firefights that marked the opening of the battle. Often lost and confused in the predawn darkness, airborne units that had scattered over the fields and marshes began "the tense, deadly hide-and-seek game of finding comrades, assembling units, and getting on with their missions."[1]

Meanwhile the Allied fleet had reached the coast, with many of the fighting men aboard seasick from the choppy seas. Under a gray and gusty sky they began to pile ashore along 40 miles of Norman beach and headland east of the Cotentin Peninsula, an arm thrusting into the cold channel waters. Under artillery fire, American forces landed on two zones code-named Omaha and Utah. The first to treat the wounded were the navy medics and engineer special brigades that organized the beaches. The landing proceeded in disregard of the casualties; none were taken to the ships (except those who had been hit in the landing craft themselves) until all the assault forces were ashore.

Americans landing at Omaha Beach pushed up a slope of sand and round gray stones under heavy fire from the bluffs that overlooked the shore. Some took shelter behind a wooden seawall, while intrepid parties worked their way up the slopes and naval gunfire battered at enemy pillboxes. "Face downward, as far as eyes could see in either direction," an Army doctor recorded, "were the huddled bodies of men living, wounded, and dead, as tightly packed together as layers of cigars in a box."[2]

Again confusion enveloped much of the carefully choreographed landing. Medical supplies and stores of whole blood went down in the cold Channel water with mine-struck ships or shell-blasted landing craft. Ashore, units became mixed. Navy medical officers and corpsmen of the 6th and 7th Beach Battalions—some of whom had come ashore within an hour of the first landing—worked beside their army counterparts from the 16th and 116th Regimental Combat Teams. But a decision by First Army to send in medical supplies with the first waves proved to be a lifesaver. Even medics who came ashore with nothing but their own wet clothes were able to scavenge necessities from the stores piled helter-skelter on the beach.

The dead weltered like flotsam among the incoming waves, the water around them a muddy pink. Aidmen splashed into the shallows to retrieve the living before they drowned. Men who had been hit in deep water depended on Coast Guard cutters, which performed sea rescue work, often under heavy fire. In the shelter of the seawall, hasty first aid went on. Patients were dragged or carried from the beach, the water, and increasingly from the base of the bluffs, where the infantry labored to infiltrate the German positions through a few heavily mined draws. A little before 11 A.M. regimental medics set up the first aid station, digging into the face of the bluff in the lee of the storm of missiles passing overhead.

Walking wounded made their way toward the water; men on stretchers were carried by bearers who turned their backs to the continuing enemy fire. Patients were bundled into any available craft to be carried to the LSTs and APAs waiting offshore. (LSTs had been able to beach at Utah but not at Omaha, because of obstacles in the water and heavy enemy fire.) Not all could hitch a ride. Some of the wounded spent the night on the chill shore, in foxholes dug in the damp sand—graves for a few, who did not leave them alive.

The infantry broke the tactical logjam by seizing the German positions on the bluffs. Reinforcements began to come ashore, and the landing craft retrieved the wounded from the sand. Similarly busy traffic already marked the other beaches, where the Allies had triumphed with relative ease. On June 7, medical units of the 1st and 29th Divisions moved the casualties that had accumulated inland to the water's edge, and the landing craft cleared the wounded from the sand. A chain of evacuation took form, running by three main routes from the army's aid stations half a mile or so inland down to the beach, where the navy now had three of its own stations operating.

Despite continuing heavy surf, supplies began to come ashore in more orderly fashion. Whole blood began to reach the forward units. The medical system was still living, salamander-like, half on the water and half ashore; doctors and corpsmen continued to work on the ships, but auxiliary surgical teams came ashore to perform emergency surgery. The flow of the wounded, the V Corps surgeon recounted, went "in dribbles" but with "no stagnation." During the first five days of the campaign, more than three thousand men passed through the chain.[3]

As usual, the LSTs were deplored almost as much as they were used. Some, but not all, had been converted for handling casualties, and complaints were heard about the cold and wet of the tank decks and the lack of sanitary facilities. Despite the discomfort, the ships were indispensable; most LSTs carried from seventy to one hundred wounded on their return voyages, but some took many more, and one plowed homeward with 331 more or less severely injured patients aboard.[4] Air evacuation came quickly to Normandy, and—beginning on June 10—increasing numbers hopped the channel by plane, a quicker and more comfortable way to go than the ships, despite stormy and rainy weather that frequently interrupted the flights. After June 23 sea evacuation was used primarily for the walking wounded, who could better stand the rough crossing.

In the transport planes, men lay on stretchers that were locked into a system of heavy canvas straps to hold them steady. An hour or so aloft brought the wounded into British air bases, where ambulances and trains waited to move them to the Services of Supply hospitals. By July, air evacuation had settled into the condition of a standard and indispensable means of moving the wounded, not because other means were not available but because of the inherent advantages of moving them with maximum speed and minimum handling. As one officer said, the flights were routine "except that these people are sick and wounded and are accompanied by a good looking army nurse."[5]

The mood of the Allies was upbeat. Their armies had breached Fortress Europe, justifying the long years of preparation. Casualties were fewer than had been feared. The nightmare of the wounded piling up on beaches, impossible either to treat or to evacuate, had not become real except on the first day at Omaha. The evacuation system took shape more or less as anticipated. Perhaps some officers dreamed that the confusion of the first day had been no more than an aberrant episode in a war that would now proceed on schedule. If so, they would be sorely disappointed.

The first surprise came when the Germans halted the Allied advance just beyond the beaches and held them, almost immobilized, for two long months. The First Army, after capturing the Cotentin's shattered harbor of Cherbourg in June, pushed southward into a region of swamps and checkerboard farms at the base of the peninsula—an ideal region for defense. To the east, the British drive stalled at the town of Caen. As the Germans rushed in troops and armor, the Battle of Normandy took form, wrecking allied timetables and sending more than 95,000 casualties back to the medical units crowding into the narrow fringe of liberated France.

Field hospitals came ashore a day or two after D-Day, bringing nurses with them, and evacuation hospitals followed as the field hospitals were opening. The number of units was ample, almost extravagant by comparison with the Pacific. For example, the field army that invaded Okinawa six months later did not have a single army evacuation hospital, but fourteen came ashore in France within three weeks of D-Day to support the American field army fighting there. Other medical elements were equally abundant.[6] In time, of course, all would be needed, for beyond Normandy—in itself one of the bloodiest battlefields of the war—lay a whole continent and the enemy heartland.

Fighting consumed most of rain-drenched July, a bitter, slow-motion struggle that resolved itself into "thousands and thousands of little skirmishes." The country was a honeycomb of muddy fields enclosed by "ancient earthen banks, waist high, all matted with roots . . . out of which grew weeds, bushes, and trees up to twenty feet high."[7] In peacetime the little fields had held growing wheat, apple trees, or lush grass and browsing blackfaced cattle. Now every one formed a potential battleground. Snipers and machine-gunners dug into the banks; roads became defiles inviting ambushes. In the marshes that dappled the landscape with spots of vivid green, man-high thickets produced jungle-like combat that a Pacific veteran compared to Guadalcanal. Yet, unforgiving as it was, the fighting differed from that in the Pacific in important ways. Even though clouds of mosquitoes infested the hedgerows, rising in columns like smoke and tormenting the fighters, they carried no malaria, and the thousands of soldiers who fell out with the disease were all Mediterranean veterans victimized by old infections.

Another difference was the way the enemy treated the medics. The nature of the country and the intensity of fire inflicted heavy casualties on aidmen, but careful studies led to the conclusion that the Germans by and large were following the Geneva Conventions, which prescribed the rules of land warfare. Although men died wearing the white medical brassard with the red cross, the reason was that it was so hard to see in the thickets that enclosed the fields. The response of combat medics was to make themselves more visible, not less. In the Pacific, medics took off their crosses and even dyed their bandages jungle green, but in France they began to wear brassards on both sleeves and to paint crosses in white squares on their helmets, secure in the belief that most Germans would respect the symbol if only it could be seen.

Even in the heat of the fighting, both sides sometimes held their fire while German and American medics went to the aid of the wounded. Mined trails made evacuation hazardous, but a network of twisted little roads behind the front was good for jeep ambulances, each with four litter racks welded to its stubby body; most of the wounded rode to the hospitals, and quick treatment meant improved chances of survival. Thousands of German casualties who had fallen into American hands went to the rear in the bumper-to-bumper ambulance traffic, to receive hospital treatment equal to the Allied soldiers'. The first evacuation flight from the Continent took thirteen patients, seven of whom were wounded POWs.[8]

Such touches of humanity did not mitigate the ferocity of the fighting. Men quickly learned or ceased to need the arts of survival. The number of dead and wounded rose steadily. In the course of a few days, one American regiment lost more than seven hundred men. A rifle company was left with only five "veteran" noncoms, defined as men who had been unit members for more than two weeks, and four of them were combat exhaustion cases. With aidmen falling fast, extra litter-bearers had to be drafted from rifle companies that were already depleted by wounds and death.

Robert Bradley was an aidman with the 120th Infantry, 30th Infantry Division. He had a scientific bent, for he had been a medical student before the war and became a physicist afterward. Like many aidmen, he was also religious by nature, having volunteered for the duty because he preferred to save rather than to kill. He found the arrival in Normandy a sobering business; his unit, headed for the front, crossed Omaha Beach only a few days after the landing, hiking past unburied German dead and piles of gashed and punctured American helmets. Passing by the swollen bodies of dead cows, Bradley noticed that someone, out of whatever emotion, had put straw over their staring eyes. The trees were stripped and shattered by the same weapons that had killed and wounded the animals and men.[9]

Bradley and his comrades slept along a hedgerow and at dawn woke to the hammering noise of war. He soon found that the safest place for a medic was among his own combat troops, who would look out for him if they could. Yet sometimes he had to remain behind with the wounded when the fight moved on, feeling lonely and abandoned. Sometimes the wounded lay ahead of the front, remnants of a failed attack or a local retreat. Then Bradley had to go between the lines, sometimes waving at the Germans to stop firing and let him work. In basic training he had detested learning to turn somersaults, but he found that the best way to go over a hedgerow was in a dive, head first. The consolation of his work was "the unspeakable light of hope in the eyes of the wounded as we popped over a hedgerow," for they also had been abandoned and depended on no one else.[10]

Bradley's doctoring was basic in the extreme. He seldom needed to apply tourniquets, because most of the wounds he saw were neat bullet punctures or shrapnel bites sealed shut by the hot steel that had caused them. Once he saw an officer lose both legs to a "large, hot, sword-like" fragment, yet live because the heat of the metal seared shut the stumps. He tied scissors to one of his wrists with a shoestring in order to have them handy to cut away bloody clothing, and he threw away his gas mask so as to carry extra compresses in the container. His raincoat had many patches cut out of the tail, because he had learned to slap a piece of raincoat on a sucking chest wound, then cover it with a compress. This was patching in the most literal sense, and it could mean the difference between life and death.

Yet, despite all efforts, the dead were everywhere. Some were visible, old and stinking, and Bradley had to oversee retrieving and hauling them back to a graves registration crew, whose members stayed drunk to endure the smell. Some casualties simply vanished, as people do in war, like two GIs who were caught in an open field by a direct shell hit, of whom no trace was ever found, or a tank with crew that another shell reduced to a "badly bent bottom plate" and nothing else.[11]

Close shaves were the order of Bradley's day, for he had to be out and moving when others huddled in their foxholes. He became good at hitting the dirt, and as he survived longer and longer he won a reputation for being lucky (it was said that no man had ever been killed who was standing near him). Others watched him and let their knees buckle when he did. The art of survival was full of surprises. Who would have thought that it was bad to be near a tank? But tanks drew artillery fire, and he learned to stay away from them. He learned to dig a kind of side chamber to his foxhole so that he could huddle out of the line of airbursts. He learned to trust his hunches, and they must have been good ones, for he wore out "several sets of replacements."[12]

He even survived being bombed by his own air force. When the American commanders were ready to break through the German lines, they opened the assault with a massive air strike. Bradley, at the front, heard the planes and the "peculiar rustling in the sky" that announced the release of many bombs. Then the earth erupted all around him, for the first bombs fell short. Some men were entombed alive, apparently killed by concussion, for when they were dug up their corpses seemed asleep, with pink faces. The aftermath of the bombing had its own awfulness. Shocked men walked into trees like somnambulists; men walked into walls and fell down unconscious. "I recall the terrible beauty of the sunset that night," Bradley said, "and the fact that I kept repeatedly humming the 'Going Home' theme from Dvorak's 'New World Symphony' in an effort to retain my sanity."[13]

Behind the front, Hawley's medical system swiftly absorbed and treated the wounded. The worst cases to reach the forward hospitals were classed as nontransportables—too badly injured to go farther without emergency surgery. The auxiliary surgical teams with the field hospital platoons labored over men who had been disemboweled, almost drained of blood, and left in deep shock. Death rates for such patients ran two to three times the average for the war as a whole: 11 to 14 percent. Sometimes a man with multiple injuries needed as many as four major operations. Some surgeons thrived on the professional interest of such cases, and a report of the 3d Auxiliary Surgical Group called the unit a "surgeon's paradise."[14]

Yet evacuation hospital reports also suggest endless, wearying hours in the surgical equivalent of mass production. The doctors, nurses, and enlisted medics worked in twelve-hour shifts, processing about a hundred patients a day in each installation. Backlogs of patients piled up when the fighting was heavy, awaiting their turns on the operating tables and sometimes developing wound infections during the hours of unavoidable delay. Careful debridement, the sulfa drugs, and penicillin prevented or controlled most infections, a crucial fact in a battle that raged over farms and pastures where the soil was saturated with animal manure, and shell blasts buried tainted earth deep in many victims' bodies. Of the men evacuated from Normandy, less than 1 percent died after reaching England.[15]

Joseph A. Gosman was an orthopedic surgeon with the 109th Evacuation Hospital, an outfit that reached France in time to treat the survivors of the St. Lo offensive and the allied bombing. On the opening day of the attack, ambulances began to arrive at dusk. Soon the operating tent was in uproarious confusion. Casualties lay on tables or litters on the ground. Medical personnel rushed about. "I was floored by the turmoil," Gosman recalled. Then a battery of antiaircraft guns opened nearby, and the tent began to shake with the concussion, while falling metal fragments perforated the canvas.

The days that followed were filled with bad fracture cases, many the work of the bombers. Gosman cleaned wounds thoroughly, leaving them unsutured; he used blood flown in from England and drew more from the lightly wounded and the combat fatigue cases whose red and white cells were fresh, in perfect condition, and the clotting elements "at their peak." This was good practice, according to the manuals, but no rules could take account of the accidents of war. Once a nurse asked Gosman to carry out the formality of pronouncing dead a soldier who had been run over by a tank. As Gosman was about to do so, the man opened his eyes. Doctor and nurse started plasma running into the patient, and next day Gosman put a hip cast on the broken but living man, "packaged the sprung pelvis," and sent him on his way for definitive surgery in England.

Crises filled his days. On a hot midafternoon when the canvas of the tent felt like "the side of a stove," Gosman confronted a young man who had been lying in the preoperative tent, quietly receiving his penicillin and quietly going downhill. With fever blazing at 104°, pulse "sky-high," and blood pressure at 60 over zero, the patient seemed a poor bet to survive; his pulse felt "like a speedy light tap . . . uneven and hard to count." While refrigerated blood ran into the patient's veins, bringing his pulse and temperature down and his pressure up, Gosman examined a wound in the patient's badly swollen left thigh. The surgeon began to cut, and an acrid rotting odor spread as the surgical knife sliced away muscle that was a strange grayish pink.

Gosman removed more and more flesh until the wound was huge, and he was working up near the buttock and down near the knee. "In a sense," he later recalled, "it was like starting to peel a potato and finding a rotten spot, cutting this out and finding more and more to remove, and then ending up with a small piece of good potato." This was gas gangrene, the work of anerobic bacteria growing in a deep muscle wound. As the bacteria flourished on the dying tissue, they produced not only lethal toxins but also the gas that swelled and tightened the airless compartments of the wound. When the dead muscle had been cleaned away, the wound dressed, and the leg immobilized in an open cast, the soldier began to revive. Penicillin now could prevent reinfection; only the surgeon's knife could have reached its original site and saved the man's life.[16]

Like wound surgery, the handling of combat exhaustion cases on Normandy reflected the hard experience of earlier fights in other theaters. The rule of holding mild cases near the front was obeyed by battalion and regimental surgeons, administering the now traditional trinity of rest, food, and sleep. More severe cases went to the division clearing stations, where division psychiatrists—now the rule rather than the exception—gave them three days and nights of therapy. The most severe cases were taken to one of the First Army's two exhaustion centers for more extended treatment combined with physical exercise and drill.

As the fighting intensified, the number of patients predictably increased, crowding the centers and compelling some divisions to open mini-centers of their own. In all, the centers treated more than eleven thousand men, returning 75 percent to either combat or noncombat duty. Ernie Pyle interviewed one of them, a soldier who, after landing at Omaha and spending thirty-seven days in combat, had wound up in an "Exhaustion Camp." By then he was "pretty well done up," but in time he recovered and returned to his unit, like many others who felt "a duty they could not define."[17]

In fact, the combination of sound information derived from other theaters and Hawley's realistic approach to his own problems were paying off in a medical system that was ample, functional, and sound. The reformed supply system effectively delivered everything from penicillin to pajamas. Refrigerator trucks hauled blood forward as far as the clearing stations; planes were beginning to fly blood from the United States to Britain and from there, still fresh, to Normandy. For a time in June penicillin began to run low, not only because there were many wounded who needed it but because doctors had learned its value and were using the drug more freely. Fresh supplies were rushed from America, and by the end of June the depots in Britain were delivering 500 million units a day to the battle zone.[18]

The medics had no small accomplishment to look back upon. From a standing start they had supported the American forces in history's greatest amphibious invasion and then in one of the decisive battles of World War II. Normandy dwarfed the conquest of Tunisia and even surpassed Stalingrad in the number of German soldiers and tanks it knocked out of the war. And the Western Allies won their victory with a smaller investment of forces and incomparably lower losses than the Russians suffered in winning their smashing victories on the eastern front in that summer of 1944.[19]

German units had formed a tough, hard crust behind the invasion beaches, but behind them was a near-vacuum. For a variety of reasons, the western anchor of the enemy line broke up, and behind it was no mobile reserve. As the Allies pushed forward all along the line, out of the cratered moonscape of demolished villages and dismembered enemy dead, the breakthrough developed into an offensive that destroyed the German army in Normandy and opened the way to Paris. Abruptly the long, bloody weeks spent in the hedgerows gave way to a different kind of war. For two months the Allies had been behind the schedule they had set themselves; suddenly they surged ahead. The theater that had spent so long in planning every step jettisoned its carefully prepared schedules and launched a blitzkrieg.

The breakthrough rapidly gathered momentum after the activation of General Patton's Third Army. Still a cavalryman at heart, Patton loosed his forces to drive deep and exploit to the limit the increasing disintegration of the German forces. Some enemy units were penned up in fortified towns on the Breton Peninsula—the long spout of teakettle-shaped France. Meanwhile, the First Army, two of Patton's corps, and the British and Canadians all swept to the east. By early September, Allied forces occupied positions on the German border that the planners had not expected them to reach until May 1945.

The main medical problem suddenly became keeping up with a wild advance that, for a time, seemed likely to end the war before winter. During the bitter months in the Cotentin, American medics had evacuated heavy casualties over short lines. Suddenly they had to evacuate light casualties over lines that lengthened daily in giant strides. The Third Army was even more lavishly endowed with medical units than the First, and the style of organization and command followed Patton's preference for informality and decentralization. Medical groups—a new kind of unit designed to evacuate the wounded from the divisions rearward—split up the burden. Fast-moving armored columns needed medics on wheels, and medical halftracks and jeep ambulances retrieved the injured.[20]

In both armies, field hospitals exploited their mobility by following the advance, receiving all kinds of casualties, doing emergency surgery on the nontransportables, and dispatching those who could be moved to the rear. In order to be able to move while they gave treatment, the hospitals borrowed trucks to leapfrog their platoons, keeping emergency care within reach of a front that advanced nearly 200 miles in fifteen days. For all concerned it was a wild ride, through rejoicing towns little touched by the war, where the French showered their liberators with flowers and gifts (and caused a few injuries by throwing wine bottles into speeding jeeps).

But hard fighting developed at several spots—Mortain, Falaise, the siege of Brest, the crossing of the Moselle River—and three hundred to six hundred casualties a day still flowed back through medical channels from First Army alone, their initial care often at the mercy of such nonmedical considerations as distance and available transport. Medical supplies remained adequate, because they were relatively light and easy to carry; besides, casualties were so few that supplies intended for ten days lasted twenty or thirty instead.[21]

Millions of troops now operated in a continental arena. In August, allied forces leaped the Seine and liberated Paris, while to the south, armies of the Mediterranean Theater invaded the Côte d'Azur and chased the Germans up the Rhône Valley. Little by little the English Channel ports were cleared of wreckage, and a zone of communications began to develop behind the armies. General hospitals arrived from Britain, and along the coast huge logistical complexes grew up that included hospital centers—clusters of the general hospitals under a single headquarters. Geographical commands called base sections were established behind both the southern and the northern armies to manage rear areas that suddenly were vastly larger than the front.

Moving the wounded now meant transporting thousands of men for hundreds of miles. General Hawley, shifting his office to the Continent to oversee the developing medical system, found transport a baffling problem: "How in hell," he demanded, "[do] you keep up with the evacuation of three fast-moving armies with *absolutely no* communications, railroads that operate at two miles per hour, and airplanes that are never to be had when they are needed?"[22]

Distance was taking its toll on the allied armies, and the problem of maintaining the flow of supplies led to a command decision that would later haunt the armies and especially the medics. Short of fuel, General Omar Bradley—now commander of the 12th Army Group and hence of all the American field armies in northern Europe—made a deliberate decision to bring forward only fuel, ammunition and food, omitting winter clothing, which, he thought, would not be needed for a war that seemed likely to end before Christmas.

But in mid-September, lack of gasoline and stiffening German resistance combined to slow the advance in eastern France and the fringes of the Rhineland, where American forces had begun to encircle their first big German city, Aachen. The slowdown made paradoxical good news for the medical service, whose scattered units now closed some gaps that had begun to yawn too wide. Hospitals, depots, and medical group headquarters began to assemble in concentration areas near the front. The pause promised something of a return to the pattern of the early days in Normandy: a more stable front and shorter lines of evacuation. But heavier casualties impended, too. Hedgerows were absent from the new battlefields, but forests and rivers, the rough high country of the Ardennes and the Eiffel, and the dragon's teeth and pillboxes of the German West Wall made formidable obstacles, especially when defended by troops fighting to prevent an invasion of their homeland.

Robert P. Phillips, an aidman serving with a rifle company of the 28th Division, found that heavy enemy artillery fire made him dread the cry of "Medic!" which forced him into the open. Every wounded man had to be carried, dragged, or helped to shelter, and that meant moving slowly under fire. Shell fragments whittled down the trees, and casualties increased; he remembered for the rest of his life the job of examining a wounded man at night, cutting away clothes in the darkness, feeling for and discovering the wound. ("It's like putting your hand in a bucket of wet liver.") Phillips himself was hit on September 25; he was bandaging a casualty when a shell fragment tore a hole in his own chest, mangling a dogtag and sending him into the chain of evacuation along with his patients.[23]

September brought a short-lived evacuation crisis in the First and Third Armies. The cause was Operation Market-Garden, General Montgomery's unsuccessful airborne and armored thrust against German defenses in the Netherlands. Aircraft that had been carrying the wounded were diverted to the new battle, leaving casualties to pile up in forward units. The interruption was brief; Market-Garden failed, the planes came back, and a spell of bad weather that had complicated matters came to an end. Short as the hiatus was, at least five thousand casualties accumulated while it lasted, reflecting the shattered state of land transport—the ruined bridges, the bombed railways, the damaged and crowded roads. And in the south, the Seventh Army ran into similar problems because of transport problems in the Rhône Valley.

The episode underlined a gap between fact and theory. The theater still had no real commitment to air evacuation, viewing it as a kind of incidental advantage rather than a distinct mission. In fact, however, air evacuation had become a logical complement to the fast-moving, aggressive, disorderly sort of war that had developed without regard to the theater's elaborate plans and timetables. Doctrine and operations had gotten out of synch—bad news for fighting men, whose leaders had to agree on doctrine if they were to act in concert with one another and the flow of events.

Soon the march of the seasons added to the stiffening enemy resistance and the growing allied logistical problems. Moving from north to south and from highland to lowland, the old-gold hues of the European autumn began to invest the battlegrounds. In mid-October torrential rains began. Yet there were still grounds for optimism. Railroads were repaired and fuel supplies increased; allied domination of the air remained almost absolute, and hope lingered among generals and GIs alike that the war might be over by Christmas.

The autumn fighting did nothing to encourage that cheery prospect. Under lowering skies, lashed by wind, rain, and showers of snow, Allied forces advanced into bitter and costly battles of attrition. With aircraft only intermittently able to fly, they met a tenacious and skillful defense that relied on minefields, artillery, and prepared positions. First Army infantrymen fought in the grim tangles of the Huertgen Forest, where a week's combat cost some rifle companies every member of their original strength, plus all their replacements.[24]

They cleared the forest and, together with the Ninth Army, almost reached the Roer River. Meanwhile Patton crossed the Moselle and reached the Saar, and the Americans and French reached the upper Rhine. The British and Canadians opened the port of Antwerp for the movement of supplies. But progress was slow and bloody across the whole front. A surgeon gloomily surveyed his evacuation hospital:

> The pre-op tent is full to overflowing. I have seen life and death and am thoroughly distressed by the futility of it all. It is hard for me to draw a picture in words of the dingily lit tent, the grassy-mud floor, the rows of litters filled with their uncomplaining bundles of humanity. Some lie quietly; some groan softly; some lean up on one elbow and talk—almost whisper. There is no sterile white which some might expect to see here. It is all brown, a dirty brown from the doctors to the nurses to the soldiers and wounded. The poor lighting accentuates the brownness of everything. The shadows deepen into blocks of darkness. The standards supporting the plasma and blood throw sharp brown shadows. The sudden opening of a stove top momentarily transforms the brownness to red umber. The litter bearers keep bringing in more wounded.[25]

Dr. Gosman, working in a Third Army hospital, listed some of the injuries he personally saw and treated. A mine explosion under a jeep left a soldier's legs mangled, "with x-rays showing undamaged bolts, washers, bushings in the muscle as on a workbench." Another man had been shot in the flank, probably by a spent bullet. The bullet entered a big vein, the tear in the vein wall was pressed shut by the blood leak in the confined space, and the bullet "'floated' in the current of the vein into the right ventricle of the heart and then into the left auricle. The x-ray showed it bobbing in the heart chamber." A third soldier was carrying a Swiss Army knife in his pants pocket. A shell fragment hit it, and bits of knife and shell entered his thigh together. "X-ray picture looked like a table setting with knife, fork and spoon and other stuff." A fourth was crouched beside a manure pile when a shell landed on it, "filling his thigh from knee to buttocks with manure, all tightly packed . . . as into a sausage."

Gosman saw a miraculous escape as well. An infantryman was shot in the neck. The bullet entered on the left, missed the nerves, carotid artery, and jugular vein, drilled a neat hole in the spinal column without touching the spinal cord, and exited. The man needed no surgery; his chief symptom was a sore neck. Even miracles leave their mark, however. The man lay on his bunk, silent, looking "like somebody rescued from the ledge of a skyscraper." Gosman had seen the look before among survivors, an "appearance of naked bankruptcy," a stunned emptiness as if they were prisoners of war instead of men whom death had breathed on and passed by.[26]

These were a few of the almost 300,000 casualties, including 140,000 battle wounded, suffered by Americans in the autumn fighting. Injured men, if able, dusted their own wounds with sulfa powder, swallowed sulfa tablets, put on a field dressing, and waited. Medics recovering them continued to take losses of their own; one of them, T/5 Alfred L. Wilson, a company aidman with the 328th Infantry, won the Medal of Honor posthumously.[27] Carrying litters remained exhausting and dangerous work, made worse by mud and mountain slopes. Litter jeeps worked as close as possible to the actual fighting line, piling on casualties as if for a fraternity prank—sitting, lying on litters, and sprawled across the hoods. When the mud grew too deep or the fire too hot, tanks and other tracked vehicles took up the burden. Meanwhile the weather became colder by the day, surgical tents sagged under accumulations of snow, and the bellies of the wounded steamed when surgeons cut them open.[28]

Yet there were pluses. The slowing of the advance permitted a classic chain of evacuation to be established. Repaired railroads shouldered the burden that increasingly poor weather prevented the planes from carrying. The system worked well, treating and moving the heavy load of patients and delivering most into the hands of surgeons within an hour or two after they were wounded. Only about 1.5 percent of those who reached clearing stations and hospitals died. After the tangles of the hedgerows and the frenzy of the breakout and pursuit, the system had become orderly and reassuringly regular. The Allies had lost their summer impetus, but they held the initiative. They dictated the terms of the battle, and they expected to continue doing so. But Hitler had other plans.

On the cold and misty morning of December 16, three German field armies attacked the American First Army in the forested hills of the Ardennes, killing, capturing, and wounding some 40,000 men. The enemy drove a salient 60 miles deep into the line before the First, Third and Ninth Armies halted and contained them. No man was more astonished by the German attack than chief surgeon Hawley, as he later admitted with his customary blunt honesty: "All I can remember is the chaos. . . . Nobody knew anything. We were pretty much in the dark."[29]

Fortunately the least mobile hospitals and depots lay to the north of the enemy attack. Most of those in its path had wheels and were able to escape, taking their patients with them. But divisional medics were caught with the units they supported and had to survive and work as best they could under fire. Aid stations often were in the thick of the fighting, with aidmen giving plasma to the wounded behind the walls of shattered villages while the armies disputed the streets. A new danger was posed by German SS units, which showed little of the chivalry that Americans had come to expect from their foes in Europe. Tanks fired at ambulances, and once at Malmédy prisoners were massacred and left in the snow.[30]

Surgeons piled the wounded into every available vehicle. Bearing their burdens of pain, the trucks and ambulances inched through the darkness of winding lanes among the retreating columns. When a unit had too many wounded for the available wheels, medical volunteers stayed with their patients to care for them in captivity. The last men to pull out saw one such group, a battalion surgeon and his section and their patients, flying the red cross flag and the white flag of surrender while they awaited the Germans. Surrounded units sometimes had to abandon aid stations filled with their wounded as they struggled to break through the enemy lines. Concern for their wounded probably led some isolated units to surrender, especially when loss of medics and supplies left them with too many injured comrades they could neither move nor treat.

Most medics, however, got away and quickly reestablished a functioning medical service for their units, as the American lines stabilized and the German attack slowed. Some became isolated in the pocket at Bastogne, a road junction for which the 101st Airborne Division and elements of infantry and armored units waged an epic defensive battle. Fighting began on December 19 and continued for a week, while panzers and *Luftwaffe* bombers hammered at the American perimeter and the shattered town within it. Even after Third Army units broke the siege, savage fighting went on for weeks. Casualties during the days of the siege approximated 2,500, and few escaped Bastogne until the enemy circle of steel was broken.[31]

The trapped Americans should have been uncommonly lucky in their medical system. Airborne units had been formed specifically to jump ahead of the armies and to land behind enemy lines, carrying their gear with them. Their medics expected to hold their wounded until relieved by the advancing ground forces, caring for them like pioneers in a circle of wagons surrounded by hostile Indians. Since they would be cut off from the chain of evacuation, their endowment of personnel and equipment was uncommonly ample. Besides collecting and clearing elements, the 326th Airborne Medical Company had an auxiliary surgical team and carried extra reserves of blankets and stretchers. In a sense the unit had been formed to be besieged.

But much of the advantage was lost to the accidents of war. On the first day of the battle, a German armored unit captured the clearing station, surgical team, and division surgeon. A whole new medical system had to be improvised on the spot, with little to build on. A regimental aid station sheltering in a convent became the collecting point. A few hundred casualties were gotten out before the Germans cut the last road. The aid station became a mini-hospital, accumulating wounded. Doctors and aidmen from a variety of trapped units gathered under the leadership of Major Martin S. Wisely, surgeon of the 327th Glider Infantry, and moved the wounded to a basement garage for better shelter. As more and more came in, the hospital sprouted annexes in cellars throughout the town, and medics working twenty-four-hour shifts cared for lengthening rows of patients who lay on heaps of sawdust. Cognac, and Bing Crosby's voice emerging from a salvaged civilian radio, gave Christmas cheer.[32]

Medical care was summary. Surgeons tried no major operations, concentrating instead on keeping their patients alive until relief came. Two days before Christmas, a successful large-scale airdrop provided penicillin, morphine, litters, and blankets, all of which had begun to run low, and the parachute silk provided additional covering for the wounded. Yet the worst cases were in grave danger for lack of surgical attention; infection spread, and the main ward stank of gas gangrene. A call for help was answered by volunteers, experienced surgeons who flew into Bastogne by glider and light plane and set up their operating theater in a tool-room next to the garage.[33] A German bomb blew in the door, but the surgeons and their enlisted assistants worked on, part of the time by flashlight, completing fifty major operations with only three deaths.

Major Wisely was negotiating with the Germans to secure safe passage through their lines for his wounded when the Third Army arrived, breaking the siege. Soon caravans of trucks prepared by corps, division, and medical group leaders were rolling out of Bastogne. The day was brilliant with winter sunshine, but the wounded, a reporter who was there said, had gray hair from the dust of the road, which "did not look strange, because their faces were old with suffering and fatigue."[34]

From a hundred units the casualties of the Ardennes offensive came pouring back upon the medical system. Not all were wounded men or combat exhaustion cases. Tens of thousands had been knocked out of action by the cold weather as surely as by German weapons. A crisis resulted in the medical system, caused by a mix of command decisions, the exhuberant summer mood when victory seemed near, and failures in equipment and supply.

The wave of cold injury cases fell upon the chain of evacuation at exactly the moment when casualties from the winter battles were highest, and winter storms made movement by sea or air sporadic and dangerous. Thousands of riflemen were crippled by trenchfoot, caused by the wet cold of the saturated woods and muddy fields. American field shoes and combat boots were not waterproof, soldiers tended to lace them too tightly, and circulation failed. A winterized boot called the shoepac caused problems of its own, and in any case was not available in sufficient quantity. Troops were not supplied with enough overshoes and tended to throw away the ones they had, because it was impossible to walk quietly in them. Hawley was blunt, as ever: "The plain truth is that the footwear furnished U.S. troops is, in general, lousy."[35]

"Imagine the tremendous loss in experienced combat troops

with tens of thousands out of commission because of trench foot!" a surgeon exclaimed. Even relatively mild cases could be exquisitely painful. Treatment involved lengthy nursing and antibiotics to prevent gangrene; bad cases could end in charcoal-black toes, and sometimes in amputation. Replacements were green troops, who were thrown into battle among strangers to learn painfully and with high losses of their own how to fight as individuals and members of their new units.[36]

The situation first became bad in November, when losses of 10 to 15 percent of unit strength became common in infantry units. During the last two months of the year, the American forces lost 23,000 men to cold injury—almost all of them combat infantrymen. The selective nature of cold injury, aiming directly at the most crucial fighters, "sapped assault strength, and thus weakened the offensive," General Bradley said. General Patton's assessment was more vivid. "The most serious menace confronting us today is not the German Army, which we have practically destroyed, but the weather which, if we do not exert ourselves, may well destroy us through the incidence of trenchfoot."[37]

Once alerted to the danger, the leaders from General Eisenhower down responded well. Hawley, like the commanders, assumed his share of the responsibility, admitting that the medics had not been aggressive enough in alerting the theater to the danger. Vast quantities of equipment were ordered; what a later generation would have called a media blitz was opened to instruct, persuade, and command the soldiers about the importance of dry socks, foot massage, and loose laces. But most of the damage had already been done, and most of the newly ordered shoepacs and galoshes arrived after the battle and the worst of the winter weather were over. During the most critical period of the European fighting the American forces lost the services of 45,000 fighting men—three divisions—to a largely avoidable physical injury. And the growing losses burdened the evacuation system and the hospitals, which were already filling with the sick and wounded.

The marvel is that the medical system continued to operate under the burdens imposed simultaneously by weather and war. Fortunately, the chain of evacuation that stretched back from the fighting front was deep, complex, and richly developed, as General Hawley, its chief architect, had planned it to be. When casualties left the zone of the armies, they were gathered by air and rail holding units and forwarded through two advanced clusters of general hospitals at the battered Belgian city of Liège—now under attack by German V-1 "buzz bombs"—and the French fortress town of Verdun. Rail and air linked those hospitals to the hub of the system at Paris, with its seven general hospitals and convalescent camp, its airfields and train stations and complex railroad yards. Still farther to the rear, the old battlegrounds of Normandy and Brittany had been filled with more hospitals by the base sections of the communications zone. American wounded who were marked for evacuation to Great Britain by water went through the port of Cherbourg and sailed by British hospital carrier to Southampton. After journeys by air, sea, road, and rail they reached their ultimate destinations, the general hospitals that dotted the towns and countryside of southern England.

The array was worthy of the armies it supported, but when the fighting opened in the Ardennes it was already under strain and saturated with patients. Besides the casualties of Normandy and the West Wall fighting, hundreds of thousands of German prisoners had fallen into American hands, and at least 14,000 of them were hospital cases. The Germans could not be sent to the United States, like the hundreds of thousands taken earlier in Africa, because the War Department expected an early victory and stopped the overseas shipment of POWs from the fall of 1944 until February 1945. American casualties could not be returned home quickly enough to relieve the ETO hospitals, because the only shipping available to move them in adequate numbers was returning troopships, which lacked Geneva protection from submarines.

The architect of the system was immovable on both counts: Hawley objected to setting up German-run hospitals for the POWs; he objected to having badly injured Americans transported on unmarked ships. He wanted to keep as many potential replacements as possible in the ETO, and he used a high evacuation policy to accomplish his goal, holding anybody who was expected to recover in six months in the theater. Ignoring the needs of other theaters and the home front, he demanded instead 100,000 more beds for his theater, and the doctors and nurses needed to staff

them. He was astute as well as obstinate, argued his case forceful-
ly, and finally compelled the Chief of Staff to intervene. Orders
from Washington immediately before and after the Ardennes attack instructed Hawley to hold captured German medical personnel and let them treat their comrades; to fill every returning
troopship with wounded; and to cut the evacuation policy from
six months to four. Hawley got the medical equipment he wanted,
but not the medical personnel. Those were essential decisions,
and Hawley carried them out faithfully, but the changes had only
begun to be made when the wave of battle injuries and trenchfoot
victims hit.

In a dark moment, encouraging signs began to mount as the old
year played out and the new began. Best of all, the enemy failed to
break through. The heroic tenacity of the First Army and the swift
change of front and spirited counterattack of the Third halted the
Germans well short of their goals.

Most of the forward medical system survived the attack and
kept working. Despite bomb and shell damage, the general hospitals at Liège continued to function, receiving wounded direct
from the fighting like field hospitals (including one pilot who
crash-landed on the grounds). The sophisticated talents of their
staffs were mostly wasted in giving emergency treatment to patients who were then shipped hastily to the rear. But the big hospitals were neither displaced nor captured.

Unfortunately, this meant throwing an additional burden on
hospitals to the rear. The impact of the offensive spread far and
wide. The medics needed above all to clear casualties from the
fighting units, and on December 17 thousands of patients began
flowing to the rear. Because the trains still ran, while air and sea
evacuation were slowed by the weather, empty beds in the communications zone hospitals began to fill rapidly. Relieving them
was a matter of seizing the intervals of good flying weather to
move as many as possible to England. Perversely, the weather
failed to synchronize with the census of patients, either in Europe
or across the Channel. The hospitals in Great Britain also filled
and overfilled, twice forcing Hawley to stop the evacuation from
the Continent. Bright days passed when men could be moved, but
the hospitals lacked beds to receive them, and then, when troop-

ships returning to America had emptied enough beds, dark skies and rough seas closed in again. On the other hand, hospitals in the United States—thanks partly to Hawley's own earlier policies—still had beds available, and transatlantic air evacuation was growing to supplement the ships.

On both sides of the Channel, overwork for medical personnel became the norm, as it did for fliers and train crews fighting the cold to keep the system moving. Hospitals broke out expansion beds, and some wounded slept in the grand hotels of Paris, while others who were less lucky lay for days in trains parked on sidings, waiting for ships or planes. The unluckiest of all the waiting men were aboard a hospital train parked in Paris's Gare St.Lazare on the day after Christmas 1944, when a German bomb demolished both train and station. There was danger in the skies as well; an evacuation flight, lost in the fog, crash-landed, and only the heroic work of a flight nurse, Lieutenant Ann M. Krueger, enabled twenty-seven patients to be pulled out before the wreck burst into flame.[38]

Frenzied activity continued into the new year, with the oversupply of patients increased by the casualties from a subsidiary attack the Germans had launched to the south. American and French wounded from the fighting overwhelmed the southern line of communications that ran to the French Mediterranean ports, and many injured men had to be diverted north for treatment. Despite everything, they were accommodated, too.

In retrospect, the winter of 1944–45 was a time not so much of a single crisis as of an irregular barrage of crises, among which the medics dodged like people caught in a hailstorm. The converging portents never quite met to create the anticipated disaster. The weather was never bad enough for long enough to paralyze movement completely. The men lying on stretchers, in cots, on expansion beds, in hotel rooms, in Red Cross shelters, in holding units, in hallways, in offices, and on trains were always cared for somehow. The hospital trains kept running, planes flew at any break in the clouds, and the doctors, nurses, enlisted medics, pilots, and trainmen upon whom the system depended found the reserves of strength they needed to keep going.

The crisis was also a time of success and vindication for the chief surgeon of the ETO. Drawing upon massive accumulations of equipment, the medics added beds until they had 118,000 in the fixed hospitals on the Continent alone. World War II was a conflict of great masses of people and matériel, and in that respect General Hawley had caught its spirit perfectly. By his endless demands for more and yet more people and supplies of every kind, he had so overbuilt his medical system that it continued to function even when almost everything went wrong at once. In a war where nothing succeeded like excess, Hawley's great lifesaving machine worked, and the outcome of the winter crisis proclaimed his triumph.[39]

13

From War to Peace

The winter fighting marked the last great effort of the Germans to contain and drive back their enemies in the West. By the time the snows melted, the Allies in both Germany and Italy were engaged in the final battles of the war, while their medical units were facing up both to the demands of combat and the needs of conquered and liberated peoples.

Overshadowed by the events in Normandy and the Ardennes, the forces on the Italian front had won their own triumphs during the epic battles of 1944. In the spring, the VI Corps had at last ended the siege of the Anzio beachhead, while Frenchmen, Poles, and Americans were breaking through the German lines before Monte Cassino. The struggle had been desperate at first, rugged mountain fighting with litter-bearers, jeeps, and mules carrying the wounded down from the roadless heights. As the Germans gave way, allied units had pressed after them, and for a time the advancing front fled like a mirage before the medical units. A final drive launched on June 1, 1944, had carried the Allies over the Tiber bridges into Rome.[1]

Two events then had worked together to determine the future course of the war in Italy. The German forces escaped encirclement, and—two days after Rome fell—D-Day forever relegated the Mediterranean to the status of a secondary theater. Even as the Fifth Army began a combative pursuit that drove the enemy to the Arno, it lost eight divisions to a new force that was gathering to invade France from the south. The German escape and the weakening of the allied forces ensured that there would be no quick victory in Italy. The fighting would grind on, as in the past, with its customary toll of dead and wounded.

The Arno is Florence's river, and Dante's. By the late summer of 1944 it divided German from Allied forces on the western side of the Italian peninsula. Eastward, the front snaked through the harsh northern Apennines to the Adriatic Sea. German forces occupied the Gothic Line, 170 miles of trench, bunker, and strongpoint. The British reopened the assault, piercing the enemy lines near the Adriatic, and American forces crossed the Arno when German reserves were drawn away by the fighting to the east. In desperate combat Americans seized strategic passes through the mountains, and by the end of September the Fifth Army stood on the northern slopes of the Apennines, overlooking the floodplain of the river Po.[2]

Combat losses were higher than at any time since Salerno. Yet nonbattle causes drained the ranks more than wounds did, for the fighters were exhausted and racked by respiratory ailments, trenchfoot, and psychiatric breakdowns. By mid-October, almost a whole division—more than 12,000 men—had become casualties in the Fifth Army's II Corps, with heavy losses among the junior officers, and few experienced replacements were to be had. The countryside was foggy, and cold autumn rains had begun; the streams were topping their banks, and the mud seemed fathomless.[3]

Less spectacularly than in France, the forces in Italy had undergone a similar experience of assault on constricting lines, breakout and pursuit, slowdown and renewed paralysis. But in Italy there could be no equivalent of the enemy's winter counteroffensive, for the Germans had no reserves to spend. As snow whitened the peaks and blocked the mountain passes, the armies spent the last winter of the war, like the one before it, immobilized and miserable. The final campaign opened before the snow melted, with a slow and grinding allied advance marked by heavy losses. Severe opening fights on the western coastal plain and in the mountains bloodied the American forces. In the first half of April almost two thousand men were wounded in action; in the second half the total almost doubled, as two spearhead units—the all-black 92d Infantry Division and the 10th Mountain Division—fought their way across the Po, and many more units became heavily engaged.[4]

The mountain division was an unusual new unit that had only recently brought important skills as well as fresh troops to the Fifth Army. An experiment that had seemed to fail, the unit was made up in large part of skiers and mountain climbers, some of Olympic caliber; after training in Colorado, it had spent years being rejected by theater commanders who could find nothing for it to do. Then General Mark Clark, short of troops, decided—as the division surgeon, Colonel Harry L. Berman, later recalled—"that anything was better than nothing." The mountaineers were sent to Italy, and in early 1945 they plunged into the kind of combat they had been trained for, conquering enemy fortifications on Mount Belvedere that had defeated seven earlier attacks by other outfits.

Inevitably, the price was heavy. With wounded arriving in darkness and piling up in the collecting station, Berman admitted that for a time "we were in total confusion and disarray." Then the division clearing station moved up and opened, and the wounded were hastily evacuated. But problems lingered as the fighting moved north: The division surgeon—the staff officer who set medical policy—and the commander of the medical battalion had sharply different viewpoints, and friction between them was common. Berman tried to push the clearing and collecting stations closer to the moving front, while the surgeons who worked in them instead opted for stability and a chance to complete their work.

As the division approached Bologna, tortuous mountain roads meant that the actual distance from the fighting line to the clearing station was nearer 30 miles than the 5 or 6 miles shown on the map. Casualties had to be tied into litters by the three-man teams who carried them, and tramways had to be built to swing them down the steepest slopes. But the ubiquitous litter jeeps conquered the hills, serving as the mules of the medical service during its last struggle against the Italian mountains.[5]

When the breakthrough began, the number of American wounded fell drastically, while the number of wounded prisoners increased. Medical units borrowed, stole, or liberated wheels wherever they could find them, including German vehicles. Divisional units raced ahead, on average 30 miles a day, falling out of contact with their headquarters. Some medical units outran the combat outfits, and armed Germans, glad that the war was over, surrendered to their unarmed foes. Possibly the champion in the great race was a collecting company of the 34th Infantry Division that made 170 miles in one day and began to treat patients in the suburbs of Milan.[6]

Surgery, of course, could not be done on the run, and as a result American field hospitals, with their continuing burden of the severely wounded, fell far behind. Still farther to the rear, evacuation hospitals left behind holding units to care for nontransportables, while the main units moved up as rapidly as possible. A growing number of captive enemy hospitals eased the burden of caring for wounded prisoners. Captured German patients rode in captured ambulances to captured hospitals, to be cared for by captured doctors, nurses, and technicians.

In some hospitals, a remarkable mix of patients resulted. One civilian establishment in Mantova, a town a few miles north of the Po, had been used by the Germans to treat both their own wounded and Allied prisoners. A platoon of the American 32d Field Hospital arrived to find the place being run by five British enlisted men who were former POWs. The patients included about fifty Allied soldiers and 140 Germans; the staff included German medical officers, Italian doctors and nurses, a dozen or so nuns, a mixture of German and Italian medical corpsmen, and a German Army chaplain. Anti-Fascist Italian partisans stood guard, weapons in hand, to protect friend and foe alike.[7]

Once into the valley of the Po, nothing could hold the Allies back or prevent them from driving northward toward Lake Garda, Verona, and Venice. The Germans, with Italian partisans nipping at their heels and powerful Allied air support adding to their woes, fought with their backs to the Alps, in a geographical trap. On April 21, 1945, Bologna fell to the British Eighth Army. Rose- and ocher-hued Verona, the gateway to the Brenner Pass, followed only four days later, surrendering to the American 88th Infantry Division. Soon the American First Armored Division reached the Swiss frontier at Lake Como. Fighting degenerated into sharp actions around pockets of trapped units; mass surrenders began on April 29, and within four days all the German forces in Italy had surrendered unconditionally.[8]

North of the Alps the last campaign opened as bloodily and ended as gloriously, but the scale was hugely greater, and the conditions the invaders found in conquered Germany imposed new burdens on the medical service that overlapped the demands of combat.

With the Battle of the Bulge behind it, the First Army advanced in February over snow-clogged roads, heavily mined, and fought in wintry forests of fir and pine. Soldiers found the enemy's West Wall "a mass of dragon's teeth, pill boxes, barbed wire, and mine fields." Wounded men had to be pulled out of danger on sleds or carried on Weasels, little tracked vehicles that also brought in bottled blood and medical supplies. Disheartened by the failure of their winter offensive and facing disaster in both east and west, many Germans surrendered or withdrew, glad to be out of the battle. But others fought to the death. In the fantastic snow-clad ruins of Cologne the ancient cathedral alone survived, and by the time the Americans arrived the last Rhine bridge had collapsed into the river, blasted by German engineers.[9]

At the town of Remagen, however, First Army units seized a bridge intact on March 7. The 51st Field Hospital was among the units that crossed into the inner Reich. For a time the forces built up rapidly, under daily pounding by enemy artillery and planes; mobile hospitals received the wounded. Then, in the first days of April, a powerful attack shattered the Germans trying to contain the bridgehead. Two corps pushed east to meet the Russians, while two more swung north to aid the Ninth Army—by now also across the Rhine—and encircle the German units that were caught in the

Ruhr basin. With the Rhine barring evacuation to the east, the medics relied on the air as never before, for the usable bridges remained few and the traffic that choked them was all headed east.

To the north, the Ninth Army's advance was spearheaded by the last airborne assault of the war. The thunder of the air armada and the sudden blossoming of parachutes over enemy soil were bravura warfare, a spectacular gesture that had to be paid for with many wounded and far too many dead. But the invasion soon gathered speed; once across the Rhine, the Ninth's armored units made 225 miles in nineteen days, sweeping through an itinerary of famous German towns. As winter struggles turned to spring triumph, the number of patients in army hospitals fell sharply; in March, Ninth Army medics dealt with nearly eleven thousand casualties from wounds, injuries and stress, and about the same number in April. But in May the total fell to less than two thousand, and of those fewer than three hundred had been wounded in combat.[10]

The Third Army's campaign told a similar story of a hard-fought opening and a sudden end. The travail of Patton's men in early 1945 came in the snowy Eiffel, the German part of the Ardennes, a country of "steep broken hills and ravines," of shattered villages and swollen, turbulent streams. Here Americans forced their way into the defenses of the West Wall, suffering many casualties, especially to mines. Nearly sixteen thousand men had to be evacuated over deep snow, and then—after a sudden February thaw—over roads that were little but "channels of mud and slush." Third Army medics ordered thirteen dog teams from Labrador in an attempt to move the wounded, but by the time dogs and handlers arrived the thaw had come, too, and the snow had turned to muck.[11]

All the frustration, weariness, and danger of retrieving the wounded and moving them in mountainous country in winter were repeated in the Eiffel—the Italian story told over again in abbreviated form. In fighting around the small, turbulent Sauer River "evacuation was entirely by litter, an exhausting hand-carry that ultimately stretched out to four miles," and at its end the wounded were loaded into assault boats while shells crashed into the woods and the water.[12] In some places the wounded could be moved only after dark, and medics held them in captured pillboxes until night-fall, when the stretcher-bearers could resume their work.

But in March the sorely tried fighters broke through to the banks of the Rhine. Mass surrenders began among German troops, who had had enough. On the night of March 22, under a brilliant spring moon, the Third Army launched an assault cross-ing, which it followed up with a remarkable advance through Bavaria that took it across Austria and deep into Czechoslovakia. The speed and depth of the penetration transformed the evacua-tion of the wounded. In March most of its 23,000 casualties had returned to the west by road, ferried back—after the crossing of the Rhine—by landing craft or amphibians. But in April four-fifths of the 15,000 new losses were carried out by air.

Meanwhile the wild advance continued, with medical units rac-ing after the tanks and infantry. "It was France all over again," a hospital commander recalled, "save that this time the end was in sight, once and for all."[13] At the same time, a fourth American army was marching across southern Germany. The Seventh Army, formed in the Mediterranean, had invaded the Riviera and with the French First Army had fought its way north through the Rhône Valley. Like other allied forces, the Seventh Army reached the bank of the Rhine in March. Crossing the river near Worms, its forces headed for the Danube and the Tyrolean Alps.

As the Americans advanced, crushing pockets of resistance and conquering famous cities, they liberated many concentration camps, including Dachau, Buchenwald, and Mauthausen. The British uncovered a huge complex at Bergen-Belsen. Every invad-ing army found seemingly endless numbers of smaller camps and Gestapo prisons. Prisoner-of-war camps filled with Allied captives were liberated, even while others were filling with men of the de-feated Wehrmacht. Colonel Tom Whayne of the 12th Army Group medical service watched "the spectacle of a few U.S. enlist-ed men herding and directing literally hordes of German prison-ers to prison camps," while he waited in his jeep for the parade to pass. Unguarded and uncontrolled were the Reich's slave laborers, who had taken to the roads, looting and sometimes murdering their former masters as they went.[14]

As the number of battle casualties fell, unprecedented new responsibilities loomed. The liberated peoples, the captive German forces, and the enemy's civilian population, now helpless in the hands of the victors, all needed care. Epidemics were sweeping the concentration camps, and escaping prisoners took their diseases with them as they mingled with the drifting population on the roads. The situation, one of General Hawley's officers said, "could scarcely be believed by those who saw it—it cannot be appreciated by those who did not. It was [the] Wild West, [the] hordes of Genghis Khan, the Klondike Gold Rush and Napoleon's retreat from Moscow all rolled up into one."[15]

To medical personnel the problems of victory were not entirely new. Allied successes during 1944 and early 1945 had thrown increasing masses of noncombatants upon the military medical system. The distinction between war and peace began to blur, as liberation and combat overlapped, and much of the work of aiding civilians fell to a parallel and much smaller medical system that had been set up specifically to care for such people in the war zone. Civil affairs personnel were trained by the army for a variety of tasks, and many were top professionals in their fields, which included medicine. In the European Theater they formed staff sections at the various levels of command, starting at the top with G-5 in Eisenhower's headquarters. Civil affairs medical officers gave advice and assistance to the European allies about public health problems, relying on the local medical community to provide hands-on care. Civil affairs helped to obtain captured German supplies for civilian use and passed out American and British resources where necessary.

The combat forces also provided first aid and emergency care for civilians, on the grounds that the demands of humanity required it. But their surgeons had no specific mission to aid civilians; they did not control the civil affairs medical officers, though they did consult with them. The two efforts were separate, parallel, and necessarily very unequal in resources. The system worked well in France and Belgium, drawing on enemy supply dumps and the liberated nations' own rich resources of medical skill.[16] But in Germany the situation changed.

By early spring increasing areas of the German heartland were falling to Allied forces. Civil affairs began to change into military

Major General Paul Hawley (top left) was the chief surgeon of the European Theater and the builder of the war's most elaborate and successful overseas medical system, including the quonset-hut wards of the 1st General Hospital, shown below. Major General Malcolm C. Grow (top right), Hawley's friend and occasional rival for supplies and authority, built the system that supported the bomber crews of the Eighth Air Force. After D-Day much of the theater's evacuation depended on the air force transport planes that flew in cargoes of wounded on their return flights, dropping flares to alert medics waiting by the runways. *(Portraits from National Library of Medicine; Signal Corps Photo)*

In every theater of the war, hospitals were set up wherever they could find shelter: under canvas or in a barn, a church, a school, or a chateau. Seen here through the windows of a shattered building in Germany are the tents of the 48th General Hospital. On the other side of the world, San Salvador Cathedral offers its protection to the 36th Evacuation Hospital during the liberation of the Philippines. *(Signal Corps Photos)*

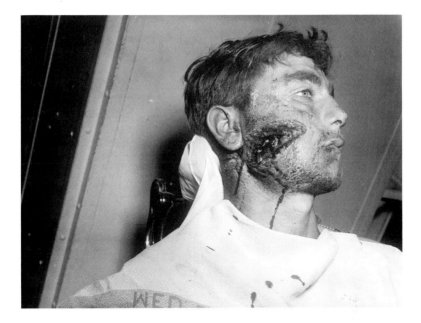

The war at sea had its own places of healing, often better equipped and staffed than most of the hospitals ashore. For this marine, wounded on Iwo Jima, and this sailor, burned by a kamikaze attack, ships like the *Solace* provided sophisticated treatment and many of the comforts of home. *(Marine Photo; Navy Photo)*

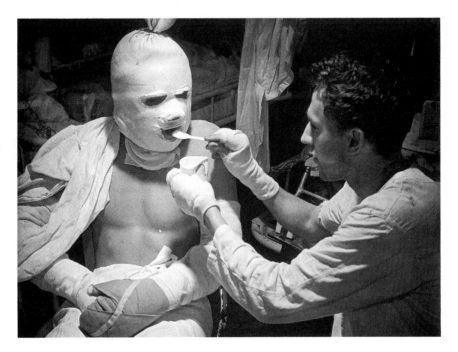

Women played a big role in combat zone hospitals and wanted to play a bigger one; beliefs that they could not endure field conditions or face danger were repeatedly proved wrong, but lingered in some theaters until the end of the war. Here, one army nurse rolls bandages during the Battle of Normandy, while another administers penicillin to a wincing patient on a hospital carrier crossing the English Channel. *(Signal Corps Photos)*

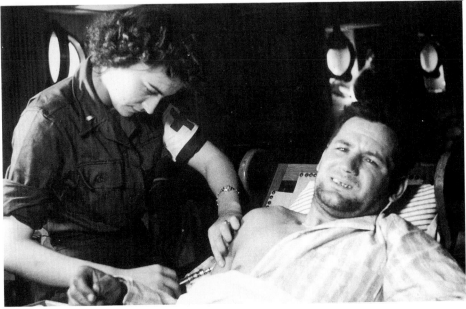

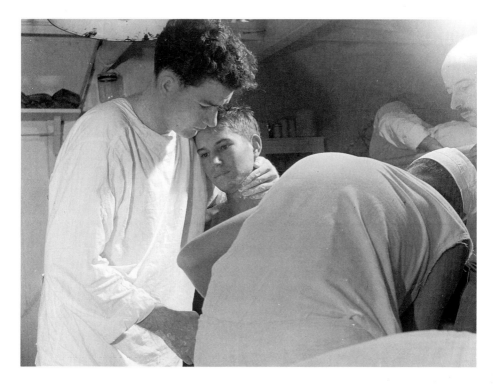

Compassion and care were essential adjuncts to healing. Here, a navy corpsman steadies a boyish veteran of Okinawa while the surgeons work; a liberated American POW flashes a grin that may owe something to the nurse and something to the ample supper tray she has laid before him. *(Navy Photos)*

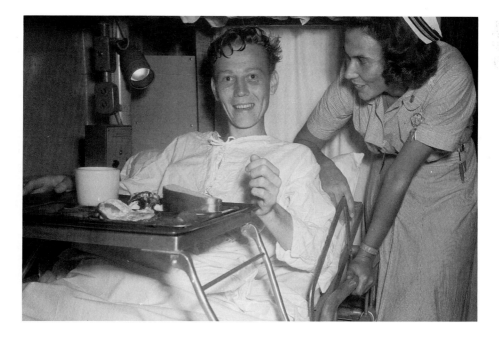

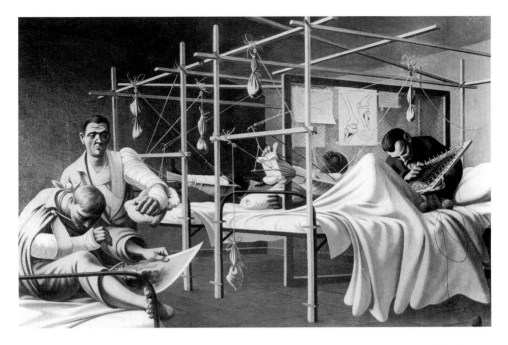

Still, getting well was long and arduous work. Here, soldiers hang in cat's-cradles in a fracture ward, waiting for their bones to knit, while others work at handicrafts to relearn deftness and manual skills. *(Painting by Peter Blume, Army Art Collection; Signal Corps Photo)*

From the field hospital to the Zone of Interior, the luckiest casualties of World War II were those who rode the airways. Here, soldiers wounded in the Philippines ride an early helicopter flying a medevac mission, while men of all services enjoy the ministrations of a navy nurse during a long flight home to America. *(Signal Corps Photo; Navy Photo)*

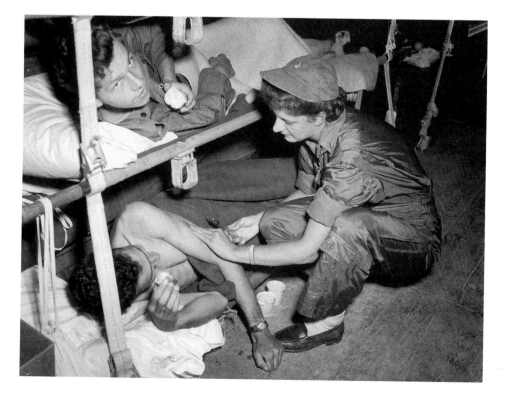

Reaching the United States
was the greatest thrill of all, as
these patients proved by leaving their beds to catch a
glimpse of home. Many
reached their final destination
by hospital train. Here, some
rest, some gamble, while others are content to watch the
familiar scenery go by.
*(Signal Corps Photo; painting
by Robert Benney, Army Art
Collection)*

government, the mission of aiding impoverished Allies into the more difficult duty of managing conquered enemies. The medical workers found themselves in danger of being overwhelmed. Western Germany was spotted with the physical ruins of cities and with even more forbidding political and social ruins left by the dreadful regime that had started the war. The life of the beaten country looked hopelessly disordered, its future dark. Western Germany was a food-deficit area even in normal times; heavily industrialized and densely populated, it possessed a complex and partially wrecked infrastructure of power, water, and sewage disposal lines, few of which were in working order. Transport was shattered; from farmers to physicians, many of the men on whom the reconstruction of the nation would have to depend were in the Wehrmacht, in prison camps, or dead. The Nazi-run central government was no more; most of its domestic opponents had been murdered, and no government-in-exile existed to take its place. Critical positions of every sort were filled with Nazis, and the medical profession was one of the most compromised. Many doctors had joined the party simply to protect their practices, but a few had been guilty of astonishing crimes, including government-ordered euthanasia and experimentation on human beings.

Germany's large nomadic population completed the picture. The foreign laborers that the Third Reich had lured or dragooned into Germany as war workers had become displaced persons (DPs). The newly conquered regions teemed with wandering bands, moving mostly on foot, pulling carts loaded with their belongings and with goods looted from their former masters. Most of the wanderers drifted in the direction of their homes, camping out or sharing makeshift lodgings with one another and the Germans. Most were louse-infested, and many carried typhus, spreading the often fatal illness as they moved. Typhus entered industrial Düsseldorf on the east bank of the Rhine with Russian laborers, had crossed the river at Neuss, and had spread to München Gladbach and perhaps to Aachen, where infected Italian DPs fell into the hands of the Ninth Army in early March. Homeless Germans caught the infection by sleeping in bomb shelters with DPs; German doctors and nurses working in civilian hospitals caught the disease from their patients. Responsible medical officers found themselves confronting a nascent epidemic among a newly conquered people in a ruined land.[17]

At General Hawley's direction, special officers were attached to the Ninth Army to guide typhus control, while the U.S.A. Typhus Commission provided experts and supplies. Outbreaks occurred throughout the Moselle region and the Palatinate, but by summer all had been stamped out; about two-thirds of the seven hundred-odd cases were among the DPs, a group only one-tenth the size of the German population. With the outbreak halted west of the river, the armies established a *cordon sanitaire* along the Rhine, compelling all who crossed from east to west, except Allied military personnel, to be dusted with DDT. Hundreds of thousands of refugees and DPs were deloused at the ports of entry under the eyes of quartermaster officers.[18]

The scale of the public health problems in Germany compelled a new approach to the medical side of military government. As matters stood, G-5 officers had the responsibility for civilian health but not the means, while the surgeons of the combat forces had the means but not the mission. Urged on by the surgeon of the 12th Army Group, SHAEF in mid-April issued orders that made civilian health a command responsibility, at least until the fighting was over. The surgeons of the field forces integrated the civil affairs medical units into their own organizations "so that all available medical resources could be mobilized to meet the tremendous task."[19]

Tremendous it was. In an attempt at control, the crowds of DPs were held in camps of their own. Americans found their new wards neither tractable nor gentle, and medics spoke of a "liberation complex" of hunger, exultation, and vengefulness. Most of the DPs wished only to go home or, if that was impossible, to escape abroad. But others who had developed a taste for loot armed themselves and skirmished with American forces trying to restrain them. Systematic attention to cleanliness wrought lasting improvement in some DP camps, but others, especially those used for transients, continued to be foul places despite the efforts of American commanders and medics. Inevitably, though unfairly, many carried away a general impression of camp inmates as an indistinguishable mass of "sleeping, eating and scratching people," whose care they were only too glad to turn over to the United Nations Relief and Rehabilitation Administration (UNRRA) in the fall of 1945.[20]

Meanwhile the number of prisoners of war mounted into the millions, filling great enclosures along the banks of the Rhine. The concentration camps were opened. Millions of German refugees surged into western Germany ahead of the advancing Red Army, which was repaying the brutality of Hitler's invasion in kind. The possibility seemed very real that the Second World War, like the First, might end in famine and epidemics.

Understandably, their own liberated soldiers and airmen were of greatest interest to the Allies and received by far the best treatment. Americans' prisoner-of-war experiences in German camps had been widely varied. Through most of the war, the majority, including American Jews, had been treated reasonably well, with medical care in camp dispensaries and German hospitals, and Red Cross packages from home to supplement the generally poor prison diet. But the soldiers of conquered nations—especially those from Eastern Europe—had fared miserably, with especially "horrible conditions" among the Russians.[21]

In late 1944 rations for Western prisoners had also begun to fail as the collapse of the German transport system blocked the delivery of Red Cross packages. When invaders surged into Germany in the spring of 1945, many prisoners were sent on exhausting forced marches to evade recapture, with little to eat but black bread and nowhere to sleep but makeshift shelters by the road. Western POWs began to suffer as Slavic captives had for many years. Freed at last, many Americans were "nothing more than wraiths of skin and bone, too weary to rise from their cots, and too emaciated to be able to eat a solid meal." Medical treatment entailed careful checkups for tuberculosis and controlled diets for those who had lost the ability to digest solid food. Reaching buffer camps set up in Belgium, France, and England to receive them, about one-fifth needed hospital care. Most responded well; the comparatively brief period of ill-treatment and starvation, as well as the youth and vigor of the captives, probably explained the very low death rates of Americans in German captivity—below 1 percent.[22]

But exaggerated reports of mistreatment, spreading in the press and by word of mouth, helped to harden American attitudes toward the German prisoners who were now in their power. German POWs had first appeared in large numbers in North Africa, after the Tunisian campaign. Initial American treatment of the captives had been inept and rough, but it had improved greatly by the time the prisoners reached the United States. Most Germans spent the rest of the war in conditions that were always satisfactory and sometimes excellent.[23]

A second wave of captured Germans followed the battle of Normandy. In the autumn of 1944 a hospital system for POWs was set up, staffed by German medics under loose supervision by American medical battalions. In effect, enemy prisoners, like friendly civilians, had been turned over to their own medical people for care, subject to American oversight and under the eye of armed guards. The remainder of the system for the medical care of POWs also took rapid form. Optimistic over the retreat of German forces in the summer and early autumn of 1944, the War Department ended its earlier practice of shipping prisoners to the United States. Prison camps were established in France, American medical units were attached to them, and serious cases were sent to the German-staffed POW hospitals. Many of the early POW enclosures—located, often, in camps where the Germans had previously held Allied prisoners—were poor and rough, with minimal shelter and rations that were ample but cold for lack of kitchens. Yet conditions improved with the new year 1945, and the medical system assured the sick and wounded adequate care.[24]

The disintegration of German armies during April and May 1945 delivered an immense number of new captives into the hands of the provost marshals of the European Theater, the army groups, and the field armies. By early June more than 4 million POWs were in American camps. The system of prison camps established on the Continent following D-Day lay far to the rear and in any case could not hold such numbers. Many prisoners surrendered in unorganized masses, and field units stripped them of tents and even mess gear in order to crowd as many as possible into trucks and cattle cars. In meadows along the Rhine the prisoners were interned in shelterless transient camps where respiratory disease, dysentery, and isolated cases of typhus quickly alarmed American medical officers.[25]

Once again the medics culled out German medical personnel, established dispensaries in the camps, and set up POW hospitals and hospital centers outside the wire. Elements of six American field hospitals supported the transient enclosures. But the prisoners had already endured years of war, defeat, and privation. In the camps, exposure to the cold European spring, unheated rations, and abominable sanitation did nothing to restore their health. During the period May 1–June 15 medical officers reported a death rate among the prisoners of 3.6 percent a year, with diarrhea and dysentery as the primary causes of mortality. By now there was a routine for handling typhus—identifying suspect cases for hospitalization, isolating those with the disease, teaching some prisoners to wield dustguns and delouse the remainder with DDT. Typhus was stamped out, but the living conditions in the camps remained miserable.[26]

With the end of the fighting, running the transient enclosures became the duty of several infantry divisions, and later exclusively that of the 106th Infantry Division. None of these units had been trained in prison management, and men of the 106th, which had suffered severely in the Ardennes fighting, had little reason to love Germans. The primary burden of managing medical care fell to the division surgeon, who wrote feelingly of his task. "PWTEs [prisoner of war transient enclosures] containing up to 160,000 louse infested people, a high percentage of whom were either sick or wounded, crammed into spaces originally meant for 20 to 50 thousand was not a pleasant picture," he wrote. Hand to mouth existence was the rule, and heavy rains continued to soak the unsheltered masses. Medical progress was halting—rich in personnel, poor in supplies. Higher headquarters were deaf to complaints, though the vehicles controlled by the surgeon and his medical battalion "were on a constant 24-hour medical supply hunt."[27]

By June 1945 the division controlled all seventeen transient facilities, two of which contained not Germans but Russian and Czech displaced persons. The surgeon counted 10,000 beds in fifteen attached hospitals, staffed largely by German personnel, where shelter and a more adequate diet probably did as much as medical treatment for the survival of the large numbers of sick men. The system seemed ingeniously designed to make as many prisoners ill as possible, and then to make them well again. When they recovered, patients were turned back into the camps, many to become sick once more—a baffling situation for the medics charged with their care, whether German or American.[28]

Complicating the poor conditions was the designation of prisoners captured after the surrender as disarmed enemy forces (or surrendered enemy personnel in the British Zone). The Allies, faced by a continuing war in the Pacific that absorbed ocean transport and resulted in worldwide food shortages, understandably saw no need to feed the prisoners at the same level as their own forces, who led far more active lives. The diets prescribed for the prison camps sensibly distinguished between working and nonworking prisoners, and were not unreasonable in themselves. But different camp commanders were allowed to go their own ways without supervision. The results were deplorable.

A medical survey ordered in August 1945 by the theater's new chief surgeon, Major General Albert Kenner (Hawley, his job completed, had returned to the United States in June), showed that nonworkers received anything from 1,250 to 2,040 calories a day, workers from 1,450 to 2,882. The report suggested that some were fed adequately, some poorly. But worse conditions existed in some of the camps that were not surveyed. In late May prisoners at one transient enclosure were receiving only 950 calories a day—a concentration camp diet—and Kenner received a report that a dozen adolescents had starved to death in a camp in Austria. In the words of one inmate, who later became the German prisoners' eloquent historian, "hunger ruled the hours" in many of the pens, and it seems to have done so needlessly.[29]

Kenner's sharp report on the conditions brought orders in September from General Eisenhower for more adequate diets, this time enforced by frequent medical inspections. But by then most prisoners had been transferred either to the British, to the French, to other allies, or to American-directed labor companies used for the work of reconstruction. Apparently the labor units and such special categories as former SS men and suspected war criminals, who remained incarcerated, became the chief beneficiaries of the more humane regime.[30]

On the whole, the record of American commanders in regard to German prisoners taken in the spring of 1945 was poor. Though unavoidable during April, when the war went on, wretched conditions lingered in the transient camps for several months afterward in violation of treaty commitments and army regulations. By taking emergency measures against typhus and providing shelter and treatment for the sick, the medical system around the Rhine camps, modeled on the larger system, with its prisoner-run hospital centers, may well have prevented mass deaths.[31]

Though hungry, cold, and miserable, German prisoners were not the worst-treated people in their homeland. The liberation of the concentration camps had uncovered conditions that went beyond the experience of American medics, even though that experience included medicine, nursing, and war. Hints of the task to come had appeared as early as 1944. The advancing armies had begun to liberate East European slave laborers whose bodies had been reduced by severe malnutrition and rampant tuberculosis to skin-covered skeletons with devastated lungs. At the mines of Sarreguemines in eastern France, shocked and astonished army doctors worked for a time in a museum of pathology. But the small number of such cases made them no more than a brief wonder until the Allies entered Germany in force.[32]

Now bewildered soldiers found themselves in a true police state that was speckled like a typhus patient with some five thousand camps and prisons. The major *Konzentrationslager* were elaborate establishments, with many satellite camps, factories where slave labor was employed, and comfortable quarters for the SS guards and their families. Hunger, overwork, and beatings constituted the norm of life for many prisoners. Yet the charnel houses found by liberating forces reflected also the breakdown of the Nazi state and the effects of Allied bombing on water, gas, and sewer lines. Lack of fuel prevented cremation of the dead and produced the heaps of corpses whose images Allied newsmen later flashed to an unbelieving world. The camps were terribly crowded with people of all nations (though comparatively few Jews, most of whom had already been murdered). Like prisoners of war, many camp inmates had been moved about on forced marches to escape the Allied invaders, or shipped to the west, unfed, in heatless boxcars. The western camps had become vast holding pens, where epidemics spread in crowded barracks and hospitals devoid of medicine. "Many people talk about Auschwitz," a survivor said, "it was a horrible camp, but Belsen, no words can describe it. There was no need to work as we were just put there with no food, no water, no anything, eaten by lice."[33]

The first American medical units thrown into the camps were usually evacuation and field hospitals. The work of stripping, scouring, bedding down, and dusting patients was grim, and medics worked in a fog of DDT to kill the omnipresent lice. The physical condition of many survivors beggared description, rail-thin but with bellies swollen by nutritional edema. They had ulcerated gums and swollen feet; their skin, thin and fragile, had been worn by the rough wooden slabs they slept upon; infected abrasions had produced boils, abscesses, and ulcers. Under camp conditions, small infections resulted in massive local swelling with "sloughing and gangrene." Some prisoners, shot or beaten, bore injured limbs in makeshift slings. At Dachau, a visiting journalist heard the leader of a penicillin squad complain, "I can't find enough muscle to get a hypodermic in."[34]

Typhus and tuberculosis were widespread. Almost everyone had diarrhea. A woman who endured both typhus and dysentery at Belsen later recalled that "everything around me became nightmarish. I existed merely as a bursting head, an intestine, a perpetually active anus." In typhus-ridden Dachau, morbidity ran about 25 percent of the 32,000-odd men and 300 women in the main camp. The 127th Evacuation Hospital admitted about 1,900 patients during May, 900 of whom had multiple diseases, and 260 more in June. Deaths continued after the liberation; by mid-month the hospital had lost 246 of its patients. The 116th Evacuation Hospital admitted more than 2,000 patients from the same camp, of whom nearly 1,500 either had typhus or were suspected of having it. The chief nurse was heard to remark, in a soft South Carolina drawl, "There is no disposition except death."[35]

Autopsies provided the clearest medical record of what passed for natural death in the camps. Doctors realized that they were viewing people who had survived long exposure to typhus, and that in consequence the cases they saw were relatively mild, but the disease had been superimposed upon tuberculosis, malnutrition, and severe diarrhea. No part of the body escaped the consequences. The dead exhibited local hemorrhages, liver and kidney damage, tuberculosis of the lungs, and pneumonia. The mucosa of the colon and rectum was commonly eroded or deeply ulcerated. "The heart," the 116th Evacuation Hospital's commander reported, "was generally pale and very soft so that a finger could easily be thrust through it." The wonder was not that so many had died but that so many survived to tell their stories.[36]

The greatest medical problem in all of Germany was, paradoxically, its healthiest people—the war-battered civilian population. The reason lay in its sheer numbers. During the spring and summer of 1945, military government detachments fanned out over the American zone, "the harbingers of a new order and the only stable influence in a world turned upside down.[37] The 19 million Germans who now depended on the military government for survival were generally well-fed in country districts and small towns, but in the bomb-shattered cities the population went hungry, lived in crowded, makeshift dwellings, and drank polluted water. Devastated Berlin was beset by a plague of flies, in part because so many buildings still contained unburied corpses. Living Berliners subsisted on a starvation diet of about 800 calories a day, and children were dying fast of typhoid and dysentery. With so many German doctors behind barbed wire, there were places where American aidmen, like Robert Phillips of the 28th Division, developed their own "practices" among civilians who had no other source of emergency treatment.[38]

General Kenner obtained an order making the military government's medics autonomous once more and authorizing them to borrow personnel from the army of occupation. Another order aimed to revive the once-excellent German public health system, for unless occupiers and occupied worked together there seemed to be little hope for the German people. But conflict quickly developed between two different aspects of American policy. While military government medics tried to revive local health offices, fill vacancies, and reopen hospitals, purges of former Nazis denied many German doctors the right to practice. In Pforzheim a tuberculosis center had to be closed; in Karlsruhe, the directors of both hospitals were dismissed; and in Stuttgart, twenty-two out of twenty-five members of the public health staff, as well as most hospital chiefs, were ousted. In the end, the military government was obliged to issue supposedly temporary work permits to doctors and public health professionals whose services were needed, and never revoked them.[39]

Providing help through the military government, reviving local civilian health offices, enrolling workers, and releasing doctors who were POWs all helped to suppress the typhoid, typhus, and diphtheria that broke out during the chaotic spring months. Typhus, the most serious threat, was successfully stamped out after some 16,000 cases had come to light. But some diseases showed greater staying power. Venereal diseases—in those pre-AIDS days, a roster that included syphilis, gonorrhea, and some lesser infections—were a kind of occupational complaint of soldiers, and they spread rapidly as both long-continent Americans and hungry German women sought sex among the ruins. With combat veterans leaving—for home if they were lucky, for the Pacific if they were not—and ill-disciplined recruits arriving to fill the ranks in Europe, a general decline in army discipline contributed to the epidemic. The main mitigating factor was treatment with penicillin. Men were sick more often, but lost fewer days of duty than ever before.[40]

Nevertheless, the complications of the VD epidemic sometimes bordered on the absurd. Until October 1945 American soldiers were forbidden to fraternize with Germans, and yet soldiers were under orders to seek prophylaxis and treatment for venereal infections, most of which were acquired from civilians. The result was an order formally forbidding any commander to use a soldier's infection as evidence of fraternization! Even after nonfraternization had been abandoned as unworkable, the epidemic continued, with further unexpected results. Penicillin treatment was authorized for Germans, in order to interrupt transmission back to Americans. One result was to shorten the time prostitutes spent in hospitals, and therefore to put them more quickly back on the street. Another, and more tragic, was to make the Allies' wonder drug available to Germans for venereal but not for more serious infections, for which they could obtain the antibiotic only through the black market.[41]

Other medical work had complex and intriguing dimensions. Army doctors gathered a variety of technical evidence later used in the war crime trials, especially those of Nazi doctors held at Nuernberg in 1946–47. Some of the worst atrocities of the war had been committed by concentration camp doctors, and Allied military surgeons were called upon to review the protocols of ghastly experiments that had been carried out at Dachau, Buchenwald, and many other camps, and to assess the value—usually negligible—of information gained at terrible cost. Medical intelligence also provided information on German wartime medicine. Most of the research held few surprises, but studies of high-speed flight excited the interest of the air force. Military doctors also looked into the rudimentary and unproductive germ warfare program and studied the physical effects of a genuinely new and alarming weapon—the nerve gases, discovered and developed by I.G. Farben scientists but never used on the battlefield.[42]

All such work aside, the medics' most important contribution to the transition from war to peace in Germany was to adapt military preventive medicine to civilian needs and to provide medical assistance to friends and former enemies alike. The nature of preventive medicine is unspectacular: if it succeeds, by definition, nothing happens. No one can prove that a great typhus epidemic, mass deaths of prisoners of war, or widespread outbreaks of disease among the German population would have taken place without the efforts of army doctors of the field forces and the military government. But conditions were ripe for such tragedies to occur, and army medics brought both professional knowledge and military discipline to forestalling what might have been the last calamities of the war in Europe.

American policy in postwar Germany had a punitive side, for it was intended to make the German people feel the full consequences of defeat and deprive them of the ability to make war again. It also had a more humane side, summed up in the injunction to the military government to prevent disease and unrest. From the perspective of the present, it was this aspect of policy that was wise and enlightened and that has been confirmed by time. And it was this side of American policy that the medics served, demonstrating under sometimes appalling conditions that their skills had never been more necessary than in the critical period at the war's end, when nations as well as individuals cried out for healing.

14

Pacific Climax

While the war swept to its conclusion in Europe, the fight in the Pacific theaters raged on. The last battles were fought by large units, on the order of the war in the Mediterranean. The fighting continued to be ferocious, and the medical service to be less than adequate in size. Disease could still ravage the troops. Fighting disease and making do with not quite enough remained hallmarks of the medics' war in the Pacific until the end.

Yet great advances had been made. When forces of the Southwest Pacific set out at last to liberate the Philippines, General MacArthur devoted to the conquest of the central island of Leyte more than 200,000 men and 700 ships, including his own Sixth Army and strong army and navy forces that Admiral Nimitz had loaned him for the fight. Surgically equipped LSTs plowed along with the huge fleet; assault transports had been equipped and staffed to receive serious cases; and cargo ships carried doctors and beds to help evacuate after the battle. The army contributed all its hospital ships that were in the theater, and the navy held three of its own ready to send to Leyte if needed.[1]

The assault forces had their own medical units, including mobile hospitals and antimalaria outfits. The Sixth Army headquarters had others, including an army service command with fourteen fixed hospitals. More than 17,000 hospital beds would be available to hold the less serious cases in the combat zone. Wounded men who had to be evacuated would go either to the Southwest Pacific or to the Central Pacific rear area hospitals, depending on whether they belonged to MacArthur's or Nimitz's forces.

There were some weaknesses in this carefully planned array. Nimitz's troops had originally been organized and equipped to attack a small Central Pacific island, and they lacked the medical resources they would need for a long fight ashore. Although the invasion force had civil affairs units, no medical units were earmarked to care for civilians, even though 900,000 friendly people lived on Leyte directly in the path of the battle. There were other problems looming that no allied planner could have foreseen. Leyte, like Saipan before it, was to be a campaign ruled by the unexpected—a huge, bloody, ultimately decisive imbroglio of jungle warfare, naval battles, and desperate fights in the air. Nature and the enemy would shape the action, and neither would be kind.[2]

On the morning of October 20, 1944, the invaders approached the eastern shore of Leyte over a calm, bright sea. While the last shells of the bombardment still thundered, assault waves raced for the beaches, accompanied by rocket ships and destroyers. To one observer the swarming craft looked like "myriad ants drawn irresistibly toward a pile of sugar."[3] Under a brilliant tropical sun, the Sixth Army's veteran troops began to go ashore.

At first the campaign moved swiftly, as the island's capital, Tacloban, fell the next day, and the tide of battle moved westward despite the almost continuous air raids that battered the invaders for their first twelve days ashore. Some problems developed with evacuation. Mixed army–navy medical teams worked well with the beach parties, collecting and moving casualties off the beaches, but shallow water prevented most of the hospital LSTs from beaching, so the wounded had to be taken offshore by small boats or amphibians, undergoing more handling and the inevitable delays that developed when transfers had to be made from one craft to another. The regulating system that was to have sorted out serious cases and sent each type of injury to teams of specialists broke down in the conditions of combat. Perhaps the plans had been too elaborate. Perhaps the intelligence about the Leyte beaches had been faulty.[4]

Yet none of the problems looked insoluble. By the end of the first week, hospitals were being established; female nurses arrived shortly afterward and set to work. Nowhere in the Pacific had penicillin been used in such abundance or so close to the fighting line; whole blood was plentiful, and during the campaign new supplies began to arrive, packed in ice, from San Francisco. But soon serious and even threatening events began to unfold, caused partly by the terrain, partly by the weather, and partly by the enemy.

To the south, Nimitz's forces of the Third Amphibious Force made slow progress against strong Japanese resistance. Men of the 7th Infantry Division slogged through the lowland swamps and mud, climbed the rugged mountain spine of Leyte, and began to descend upon the island's west coast. As distances increased, evacuation began to bog down, partly for lack of vehicles, partly because of the jungle and the poor roads, and partly because of a series of tropical deluges. The invasion came at the beginning of Leyte's wet season, which that year was very wet indeed. On rain-lashed battlefields, some wounded men drowned where they fell. Others had to be tied to litters, which in turn were bound to bamboo poles and pulled by water buffaloes to ground that was firm enough to take the weight of tracked vehicles.

Such conditions meant that a patient might wait up to thirty hours for surgical care. As a result, proportionately more of the wounded died on Leyte than in the European Theater; the ratio of killed to wounded was higher than in any prior SWPA operation; gas gangrene appeared in more of the wounded than ever before. Trench-foot became a serious problem for the first time in the Pacific fighting since Attu.[5]

But the most serious problem was the fact that the Japanese refused to play the role that allied planners had assigned them. Instead of fighting and falling back as expected, they resolved to win the battle for the Philippines on Leyte and in the broad waters and channels offshore. While enemy reinforcements landed, ominous intelligence arrived that a large Japanese fleet was approaching Leyte Gulf. On October 23–24, 1944, in one of the great naval battles of the war, the Seventh Fleet and elements of the Third narrowly defeated the enemy attack and wrecked much of the remaining strength of the Japanese Navy in the process. But it was a close thing, and American shipping took heavy losses before, during, and after the main engagements.

The clash of the surface fleets was only the most spectacular phase of the battle. Over Leyte Gulf the kamikaze entered the war. Suicide planes hurled themselves at the invaders, favoring the big ships but on occasion striking at the LSTs. The kamikazes were often downed, but sometimes they scored devastating hits. "It is a tough job to hold back this tidal wave of suicide planes," a sailor wrote. "They come at you from all directions and also straight down." The speed and impact made supposedly safe areas on a warship vulnerable, and the guiding hand of the human pilot meant that any part of the ship could be hit. Though the men joked, "This is mass suicide at its best," the result was a nightmare for everybody, including the ship's surgeon and his corpsmen.[6]

One of the worst hits was on the carrier *Princeton*. A kamikaze's bomb destroyed or engulfed in flames both the forward and amidships battle dressing stations. As fires spread, injured men from the surviving main and after stations were carried topside, and destroyers maneuvered alongside to evacuate. Uninjured crew members scrambled down lines, ladders, and nets, while motor whaleboats gathered alongside the big ship and pulled in the seriously wounded. The destroyer *Birmingham* had just arrived to aid the work when a tremendous explosion blew off the *Princeton*'s stern, raking the *Birmingham* with burning debris and killing or wounding more than half its crew. Butchered bodies littered the destroyer's deck, while "blood ran freely down the waterways, and continued to run for some time." The executive officer heard a horribly wounded man say, "Don't waste morphine on me, Commander, just hit me over the head."[7]

In such attacks the navy learned the hard way that its ships would need to carry more blood plasma and more penicillin, and that medical supplies must be distributed more widely about the ship to meet a deadly new kind of warfare. The battering of the fleet continued for the rest of the year. A kamikaze carrying a 500-pound bomb smashed through to the armored second deck of the *Maryland*, "maiming and burning all in its vicinity"; four attacks were made on the *Ticonderoga* but missed; the *Mahan* was so badly damaged that after evacuating its crew the Americans sank it with gunfire. As the toll rose, a rivulet of burned and wounded men trickled to the hospital LSTs and the hospital ships to meet the torrent running from the shore.[8]

Evacuations from Leyte were so heavy not only because of the desperate fighting but also because many of the army hospitals found that they could not work ashore. By now furious tropical rains unleashed by a series of typhoons had submerged much of lowland Leyte. Mobile hospitals had difficulty following the combat units, and headquarters politics consigned the fixed hospitals to morasses. Under kamikaze attack, service troops had trouble unloading even a third of the cargo they had hoped to bring ashore; hospital equipment remained aboard the cargo ships, leaving skilled staffs on Leyte with no shelter or gear.

Thirty-four days after the landing, fewer than one-third of the eight thousand or so hospital beds that were on Leyte were actually ready to receive the sick and wounded, for a bed meant little without shelter, equipment, and staff to care for the man lying in it. As a result, the army depended on the ships to take its casualties far longer than anyone had anticipated—notably on LST 464-H, which arrived on the scene before the conventional hospital ships. Lacking Geneva markings, 464 was under attack much of the time, handling a casualty load that forced her staff to work to the point of exhaustion. As the Sixth Army surgeon admitted, without the navy's help "the level of medical and surgical care on Leyte would certainly have been sub-standard."[9]

Men wounded in the fighting in the wild north and on the west coast endured especially difficult times. Long, tortuous lines of evacuation over jungle-clad mountains and sodden valleys lay between them and the fleet and the hospitals. Not until early December did hospitalization become available on the west coast, and the long treks over the mountains finally come to an end.[10] Meanwhile, in the north the veteran 32d Division found itself struggling in tropical forests against stubborn enemy resistance that awoke memories of Buna–Gona and Aitape. Portable hospitals working closely to the fighting were often hit by enemy fire. Heavy casualties burdened the medical units, and the wounded suffered during evacuations that sometimes took forty-eight hours—by jeep or litter to the coast, by water to Tacloban or, for the lucky ones, by small plane from crude airstrips laid out on roads or in jungle clearings to the east coast.

Filipino porters carried supplies forward, and then turned litter-bearers, taking the wounded back. The 24th Division, fighting around Carigara, suffered many casualties in an enemy ambush. The roads were blocked, and boat evacuation was impossible because of an enemy machine gun mounted on a ridge that dominated the beach. In that emergency, courageous drivers used an amphibian to extract the wounded:

> Together they maneuvered the amphibious truck off the road, across the beach and into the water. They swung offshore in a wide circle. Then they churned head on into the trouble spot. The machinegun on the ridge fired angrily. The amphibious truck hit the beach. Its driver's guns were blazing. Some of the wounded were loaded into the truck. Still firing, the amphibious Samaritans headed out to sea. The remaining wounded were brought to cover by two other volunteers, who drove a weapons carrier straight into the firing zone.[11]

Small planes brought medicine and food to isolated units, while helping to remove the wounded from the battlegrounds. As the rains eased and more airfields were put into operation, cargo planes played the same role on a larger scale for all the forces on Leyte. Patients piled up in air holding stations until the first week of November, but after that a regular system developed, with the wounded routed through evacuation hospitals to airfields, where

C-54s loaded XXIV Corps casualties for the Marianas and C-47s carried X Corps patients to bases in the Southwest Pacific.

At last the long battle neared its end. In the wild, remote Ormoc Valley the Japanese made a desperate last stand before being driven into the northwestern mountains. For practical purposes Leyte was in American hands, though bitter mopping-up campaigns remained to be fought. On the day after Christmas, control passed from the sixth to the Eight Army. Mopping up was always a dangerous, rough, inglorious task, but little by little most of the remaining Japanese soldiers were killed. The fate of the Philippines had been settled in the opening struggles on land and sea, but a hopeless situation had never prevented the Japanese from fighting tenaciously and well. Severe new tests awaited the Sixth Army on the main Philippine island of Luzon.

The invasion on the beaches of Lingayen Gulf was set for January 9, 1945. Ten thousand army medical personnel of all sorts were in the fleet of 850 vessels—more than the whole invasion force in some earlier campaigns. The navy provided eighteen medically equipped LSTs, including six with surgical teams on board, one to each invasion beach. A service command stood ready to go ashore once the region was secure, with an array of backup forces. MacArthur's theater, here as on Leyte, was displaying the kind of abundance that had come earlier to the war against Germany. But the Pacific war remained the same, to be fought on tropical terrain against an enemy who expected to resist to the death.[12]

Nevertheless, there were marked changes. On Luzon, Americans would be fighting in a more developed countryside than at any time since their ouster from the Philippines three years before. As a result, something of the look of the European war came into medical preparations, which included many ambulance companies to exploit the good roads of Luzon's Central Valley and three squadrons of radio-equipped L-5 artillery liaison aircraft for evacuation flights. A few aircraft of a totally new kind were also on hand—helicopters, which would carry out some of history's early medevac missions during the course of the campaign.[13]

Jammed with atabrine-yellowed veterans and anxious tyros, troop ships moved toward the northwest through the first days of 1945. Larger and larger groups of vessels joined at rendezvous points until the Lingayen-bound convoy was more than 40 miles long, a floating city whose appearance left both friend and foe awestruck at the demonstration of seemingly boundless power and wealth. But as the ships entered Philippine waters, kamikazes dove out of the clouds, sinking seventeen vessels and damaging fifty others. Aboard ship, the sick bays were already overflowing, mostly with burn cases. Individual first-aid kits were issued to every officer and chief petty officer, along with instructions for their use; extra medical supplies were packed in cases and dispersed throughout the ships. Physicians formed teams to triage the wounded and deal with fractures, burns, and surgery.

A four-day battle of ships against planes followed—the most severe fighting that accompanied the Lingayen landing. It featured dreadful episodes, strung together in no special order. A suicide plane hit the carrier *Manila Bay* on the flight deck directly above the sick bay, shutting off lights and ventilation and flooding it with "oil, water, gasoline and foamite from above." A kamikaze smashed into the superstructure of the battleship *New Mexico*, isolating many wounded and burned men in pockets of wreckage. The crew were almost continuously at battle stations for four days afterward; new casualties preempted the attentions of the dressing stations; the shock and noise of repeated salvos of gunfire tormented the wounded. Sailors who were still unhit had to go about their duties, not only with the wounded to remind them of what might happen to themselves, but with the realization that if they were wounded in turn, they might receive little care.

Complicating everything were the mass casualties sustained by some ships—the *California* took more than two hundred in a few seconds, the *Lexington* more than 360—and the severity and complexity of their injuries. The same man might have severe burns, blast concussion, fractures, and shrapnel wounds, enough to tax a general hospital, to say nothing of a dressing station overflowing with others as badly hit. Under the petrolatum and sulfanilamide dressings, burns began to stink after a few days, a situation not helped by the breakdown of ventilating systems and the intense heat. The erratic nature of the kamikaze attacks, the suddenness, and the devastating results caused "irritability, depression, anxiety and fatigue," which brought breakdowns among well-tried veterans.[14]

As yet there was no completely satisfactory answer to the kamikazes, "smart weapons" in all but name, and guided by that most agile of computers, the human brain. Unique to the Pacific war, deliberate mass suicide attacks were still another burden to be borne by much-tried men. The ships could maneuver and fill the air with ack-ack, and their crews could send up prayers and curses, and that was all.

Meanwhile the invasion had begun. "The hold [of the troopship] had a strong odor," battalion surgeon Captain George Sharpe wrote, "but there we sat. I wasn't scared yet and we kept up a running banter of wise-cracks. I was nervous and my pulse was quite rapid. The latrines were jammed with men lining up to vomit, defecate, and/or urinate. . . . At 0700, we got the signal to board our boats and I can tell you my knees were weak as I went up the companionway to the deck." There the smell of burnt gunpowder and the thunder of the big guns assailed him; a kamikaze appeared, burst into flames amid a storm of ack-ack, and fell into the sea.[15]

Landing craft churned through the calm waters toward a long, low shore. Despite a partial overcast, men could feel the gathering heat of the tropical day. Resistance was light; soon the invaders met cheering, wildly waving Filipinos. As the Americans advanced into the grassy plain, the enemy withdrew into hills that lay beyond, lobbing artillery and mortar shells, and wounding men who were quickly evacuated to the surgical LSTs offshore. But casualties were so few that medical units concentrated on civilian victims of the preinvasion naval bombardment and airstrikes, caring for hundreds of patients from their first hours ashore.[16]

While I Corps pushed into the mountains, pursuing the enemy, XIV Corps moved down the central plain toward Clark Field and Manila beyond. Here the enemy was absent, except as small forces meant to annoy; his signature was in the smoking ruins of towns like Tarlac. Otherwise the countryside featured broad flatlands, good roads, and fields of rice dotted with small towns and hamlets. The cultivated landscape spoke of long human residence, and a medical soldier told his surgeon that he would have "liked to wade barefooted in horse dung he was so happy to be back in civilization.[17]

For a time, blisters were the main complaint, and the increasing distance from Lingayen was the chief evacuation problem. Then sharp fighting began around Clark Field, and two divisions moved against Manila as new forces came ashore at Subic Bay and south of the capital city, encircling it. One of the world's great ports and a major city of the Far East, Manila's million-plus population sprawled over 100 square miles around the muddy Pasig River. As XIV Corps approached, the Japanese blew up bridges and set whole sections of the city ablaze.

On February 4, 1945, American forces entered Manila, and a house-to-house battle began. A medical administrative officer driving into the burning city in a blacked-out jeep noted that thousands of Filipinos were dead, massacred by the Japanese. Yet he found others celebrating their deliverance in the streets. The sky over the burning city flared orange behind the houses, and yet balconies were draped with flags as for a carnival. South of the Pasig, the Japanese fought for every building, asking no quarter and giving none. Artillery pounded the old walled city of Intramuros into rubble; in a month of bitter fighting in Manila, 20,000 Japanese defenders died, along with 100,000 civilians.[18]

Amid this holocaust, battalion surgeons set up aid stations in the ruins, one working "in the dark of a shattered building, with only an oil lamp to guide his emergency treatment." Litter-bearers braved flame-engulfed streets, enemy fire, and concealed mines to bring in the wounded. The 71st Evacuation Hospital worked in an old slaughterhouse and tannery just north of Manila, converting its sheds into wards and an operating room. The room where animals were butchered became a ward for gas gangrene cases; meat chopping blocks became beds for patients in shock. On its busiest day—February 9, 1945—it admitted 293 patients, the cost to the infantry and cavalrymen of crossing the Pasig River.

The 29th Evacuation Hospital entered Manila proper, worked in the Philippine Constabulary Academy, and admitted close to five thousand casualties. Two surgical consultants from the 6th

Army Surgeon's office arrived to inspect the hospital; finding a long line of casualties awaiting a place at the busy operating tables, they shed their battle dress, scrubbed, and joined in the work, finally falling asleep at the end of a long night on litters in a corner of the operating room. The 54th Evacuation Hospital took enemy artillery rounds during its first week working in the Santolan Tuberculosis Colony—one, fortunately a dud, passed through three floors before burying itself in the basement—where hospital personnel were treating survivors of the Santo Tomas, Bilibid, and Cabanatuan prisons.[19]

Around such islands of compassion and relative order, the demolition of the city continued. Planes approaching Manila saw first a tall column of brown smoke, and new arrivals on the ground discovered shattered buildings, huddled people, and still-burning fires. Not until March, when the enemy garrison had been virtually exterminated, could serious efforts begin to care for the health of the survivors and transform the city into a major base for the invasion of Japan.

Even after central Luzon and Manila had fallen and Manila Bay had been thrown open to allied shipping by a bloody reconquest of Corregidor, the long and formidably complex campaign for the Philippines raged on. The main Japanese Army forces on Luzon had withdrawn to mountain fastnesses, which they defended with all their usual tenacity.

East of Manila were the dams that supplied a substantial part of the city's water, plus tens of thousands of Japanese defenders who waited in caves with bunkered entrances, armed with rifles, mortars, and artillery. American forces and their guerrilla allies dug out the defenders, pocket by pocket, in myriad bloody fights. Portable surgical hospitals, working close to the front and moving often, were again in demand. Torrential rains washed out the trails, stretcher-bearers were soon exhausted, and some patients took twenty hours to reach surgical care. Helicopters and hedge-hopping single-engine L-5s helped to move the wounded out. Meanwhile the Japanese succumbed to starvation and disease, victims of the jungle as well as the allied forces.[20]

The biggest group of holdouts fought on in northern Luzon. The fighting here was the whole Pacific war in miniature, with the enemy resisting to the death in a wild landscape of towering mountains, deep gorges, and tangled forest. As usual in mountainous country, the stretcher-bearers had an exhausting job, especially when downpours washed out trails. Local tribesmen, headhunters in times gone by, carried many a wounded man to safety despite the harassing fire of enemy snipers. Even when the allies broke into Cagayan Valley, the main Japanese larder, heavy rains turned roads into miry channels and lowland bogs succeeded mountain watercourses as obstacles to speedy movement.[21]

Yet the enemy was in collapse, short on supplies and harassed by vengeful guerrillas. Medical officers began to assess what they had done right or wrong in the biggest campaign of the war to date. In surgery they had done very well indeed; gas gangrene had infected only one-half of 1 percent of their patients on Luzon, as against 1 percent on Leyte. That suggested both careful surgery and quicker evacuation, aided by the Philippine road net and air evacuation. The new chief surgeon of the Southwest Pacific, Brigadier General Guy Denit, deserved much credit also. With the support of his commander he had ended the divided leadership of the past and provided ably for the wounded, pulling specialist surgical teams from general hospitals and sending them up front to improve the quality of forward surgery. The blood supply system had provided some 25,000 pints for the men who needed it. Surgical consultants had done their work effectively as teachers and overseers. Like the lines of attack in the Pacific, the many lines of treatment developed by wartime medicine were converging in the last battles, and military surgery was the showcase of the Luzon campaign.[22]

Sickness was another matter, with the army's health record forming almost a mirror image of its accomplishments in surgery. The conditions of Luzon meant roads and cities, knowledgeable civilians and friendly hands to assist the movement of the wounded. Yet those same thronging, friendly people were in poor shape after years of occupation and formed a reservoir of disease. They mingled freely with their liberators, had sex with them, and shared their food. Diseases were spread by swarming flies, poor sanitation, and contaminated food and water. Manila itself resembled nothing so much as a huge dump, with ruined buildings, polluted water, and nonexistent sewers. While human feces spread infectious hepatitis, the familiar tropical ills spread also—skin infections and breakbone fever among them.[23]

Malaria, not a significant hazard since 1943, returned in strength during the campaigns on Luzon and the big southern island of Mindanao. Making the troops take Atabrine was as hard as ever, and exhaustion speeded relapses among men who already carried the infection. As a medical officer remarked, "It is not unlikely that a good many troops deliberately evaded the taking of atabrine in the hope that an attack of malaria would take them to the comparative luxury of a hospital." The breakdown of malaria discipline was progressive, growing worse as combat was prolonged, and the troops grew more exhausted amid the oppressive heat, the plaguing skin diseases, and the constant danger of death.[24]

Here was great medical paradox of the Philippine campaign: Never in the Pacific war had the medics been more capable, better supplied, or more amply supported. But there were limits to what they could accomplish. The Sixth Army in the Philippine campaigns had the worst disease record since the Seventh Army on Sicily, and the second worst of the entire war. Despite their best efforts, the medics were not able to overcome the double burden of European-style warfare in a tropical disease environment. If military medicine must be judged by three measures—evacuation, surgery, and preventive medicine—then the biggest of all the Southwest Pacific campaigns had been marked by two steps forward, one step back.[25]

No threats of disease awaited Admiral Nimitz's forces as they prepared to invade the large island of Okinawa in the Ryukyu chain. But the fighting was expected to be desperate, for Okinawa was a prefecture of metropolitan Japan. Considering what the troops of the Central Pacific had already undergone on the 4,000-mile trek that had begun at Tarawa, the prospect was grim.

The invasion fleet was correspondingly huge, and the medical system elaborate. The Tenth Army was half soldiers and half marines, the assault forces numbering almost 183,000. Navy personnel manned the 1,600 ships. Army units alone included almost 11,000 medics. Brigadier General John M. Willis, the army's ranking medical officer in the theater, had promised the troops "all they need, when and where required," and he deliberately sought to incorporate all the lessons his service had learned so far.[26]

Each army division had a field hospital and two portables. The marines, with two evacuation hospitals, had more ample support than the soldiers did. Four types of medically equipped ships supported the invasion: army and navy hospital ships, hospital LSTs, and converted attack transports.[27] It seemed everything possible was provided. The Tenth Army received for the assault 25,000 litters, 50,000 blankets, 7 billion units of penicillin, 30 million vitamin tablets, 100,000 cans of footpowder, and 100,000 iodine swabs. Blood banks were to be established ashore, and whole blood would be made available as far forward as the collecting stations. The men carried improved first-aid kits; hospitals would have ice cream machines and freezers. American wartime production had reached its zenith, and the casualties of the coming battle would share in its benefits. Abundant as the medical support was, however, the wounded might be more abundant still.[28]

On the ships, dread of the kamikazes drove the preparations. Entire crews were trained in first aid and handling casualties. Dressing stations and supplies were dispersed as widely as possible. Supplies of whole fresh blood were abundant. Beyond the main fleet an "outer orbit" of destroyers took up picket duty and swiftly came under almost continuous attack, "hit again and again until they were sunk or the enemy was driven off."[29]

Medical personnel could not function as units, and "each individual was reduced to rendering primitive first aid when and where he could, while praying that no additional planes would crash the ship." Planes carrying 500-pound bombs zoomed in at high speed and at any possible angle, like raindrops in a hurricane. On the destroyer *Morrison*, serving as a radar picket ship, no safe area existed; medical resources were spread as widely as possible while the ship fought off one attack after another. Wounded got what hasty care was possible. Within ten minutes four kamikazes struck the *Morrison* in turn with devastating effects. Only one wounded man reached a dressing station, where he was trapped as the ship sank like a stone. For two hours the ninety survivors floated in the oily sea awaiting rescue. One corpsman had been killed, another had suffered a compound fracture, and the medical officer and one corpsmen were left to swim from one group to another, giving aid where possible. For many the only "treatment" was the coat of oil, which "in retrospect, seemed to serve as a palliative application to the burns."

A landing craft pulled the survivors aboard at last, as well as twenty-five men from another ship that had gone down. Wildly overcrowded, lacking plasma, bandages, and almost everything else for so many injured, the little craft was a scene of "complete disorder." Only morphine was available in plenty, and this had to suffice. Wounds and burns could not be treated, and fractures could only be immobilized. Six and a half hours after the *Morrison* sank, her seriously wounded at last were transferred to the hospital ship *Mercy*. Half a dozen more were dead by that time. Cleaned of the coating of oil, the burns turned out to be serious, flash burns from high-explosive blasts at close range that had seared through shirts, undershirts, and dungarees.[30]

Unfortunately, their travail was only one example of what many others underwent during six weeks of air attack that cost the fleet more than four thousand dead. During the onslaught the navy would lose more men than the marines, despite the fact that some of the most bitter fighting of World War II took place ashore. And more of the Navy's casualties would be dead than wounded—a situation apparently unique in its annals.

By contrast, everything was easy at first ashore on Okinawa. The invasion began on April 1, 1945, a bright, cool Easter morning, as an offshore breeze dispersed the smoke of the bombardment. The island featured mountains rising from the seabed that had been encrusted over the ages with masses of coral. This was the temperate zone, a world away from the tropical atolls and jungle-covered islands where the war had been fought to that point. "The land was dry and green with conifers and the air bracing," a soldier historian wrote, and so it remained for the first six weeks of the campaign. To add to the joy of the invaders, artillery fire was light, mines few, and the enemy invisible.[31]

The amazement of the troops mounted as they moved inland

from the Hagushi beaches. As army and navy medical units deployed on schedule, with few wounded to treat, the marines moved north into a region of rugged, pine-clad mountains. The soldiers turned toward the south, where the towns of Naha and Shuri stood on an old limestone plateau, pitted with sinkholes, guarded by harsh ridges, and dotted with ancient stone tombs. Here, in a topographical maze where a sniper could be invisible at a dozen feet, the enemy lay in wait. With a force numbering more than 100,000, or almost twice the allied intelligence estimates, the Japanese commander had ordered intricate defense positions to be dug into the rough terrain. Protected from American planes and naval guns, the defenders were armed with infantry weapons, some tanks, and plenty of artillery.

Army divisions spent the first week of April capturing fortified outposts. Then they encountered the enemy's main redoubts—a system of east-west ridges honeycombed with caves, tunnels, and pillboxes. It was Biak all over again, and Peleliu, and Iwo Jima, only on a larger scale. The whole Japanese 32nd Army had gone underground, taking with it tens of thousands of conscripted Okinawans. Even middle-school children had been rounded up, the boys to be fighters or porters, the girls to be nurses. For Americans, the battle would consist in slowly killing almost all of them, and absorbing whatever losses had to be endured in the process.[32]

The assault began with heavy casualties and slow progress. Armor was obstructed by the terrain, and enemy guns and mortars zeroed in. Every attack took place under murderous fire and often ended in hand-to-hand fighting. The battle resolved itself into a form that was bloody yet featureless, with an endless number of "desperate adventure[s] in close combat." American units were lured into prepared fields of fire and decimated; on Kakazu Ridge a battalion surgeon, viewing what was left of three companies, "considered none of the survivors fit for further duty." The 383d Infantry lost 326 men in one day; one battalion lost half its complement. The American response was the artillery-supported tank and infantry team, which drove the Japanese into their caves, position by position, and then sought to blast or bury them.[33]

In late April and early May the marines of III Amphibious Corps and the army's 77th Infantry Division, fresh from a victory on the offshore island of Ie Shima, joined the attack. Fortunately for the Americans, the Japanese second-in-command was a hot-head, blindly committed to the Imperial Army's tradition of at-tack. His counterattacks were beaten off with heavy losses, and the enemy's underground lairs increasingly came to resemble the caves of Biak—filthy places, jammed with wounded men for whom there was no adequate treatment.

On May 11 the marines and soldiers opened a grinding and bloody assault on the inner Shuri line. For twenty days the two armies fought hand to hand. Japanese tactics of infiltration at night, counterattacks, and incessant sniping took their toll, while the Americans blasted, burned, or buried the defenders in their caves and tunnels. Then, in the last week of May, torrential rains added a logistical battle of the roads to the tactical battle of the heights. For days on end, Americans lived dug into sodden slopes that were part garbage dumps, part potter's fields, littered with decaying corpses that could not be buried, the air saturated with the stench of death. Those who slipped in the greasy mud went tobogganing down the slopes and found maggots in their pockets at the bottom. In the septic environment, small knocks and bruis-es became infected; in the unrelenting wet, trenchfoot began to appear.[34]

Trucks and then tracked vehicles bogged down. The wounded had to be hand-carried from the line, eight men struggling with a single litter. Tank crews came to the aid of casualties pinned down by enemy fire, straddling the victim with the treads and pulling him to safety through the escape hatch. Tanks moving at low speed also ran interference for litter teams, who otherwise could not reach the wounded. By the end of the month the Japanese had lost at least 50,000 dead, and the American ground forces more than 26,000 killed, wounded, and missing.

Then the army's 7th Infantry Division, attacking through dark-ness and rain, achieved a partial breakthrough. The Japanese, with losses mounting, chose to withdraw to the south in hopes of prolonging resistance. Bearing their wounded, they skillfully ex-tracted most of their forces, taking advantage of the awful weath-er. On May 27 the capital of Naha fell almost without bloodshed to the marines, a moonscape in all but the pervading stink of rotting flesh. Fighting began again in the hills beyond, and marine wounded had to be littered out, twelve men to a stretcher party, through waist-deep water. Enemy resistance resumed amid fortified hill masses in extreme southern Okinawa. For three more weeks American soldiers and marines fought on, until the enemy's last positions fell.

Okinawa does not yield easy comparisons with other battles or other theaters of war. Perhaps, in the size of the forces and the difficulty of the fighting, it most resembled the First Army's struggles in the Normandy hedgerows. But the suicidal fury of the defense and the assault of the kamikazes gave it the unique stamp of the Pacific war, of which it was the climax and very nearly the end.

As usual in that unforgiving struggle, those who aided the wounded were not spared. Company and battalion medics and litter-bearers from the collecting companies worked in harsh broken terrain under fire, sometimes protected by chemical smoke. Carrying weapons to protect themselves and their patients, they dragged the wounded from ravines in makeshift litters fashioned from ponchos or lowered them from ridges by ropes. Shooting at stretcher-bearers was a habit of the Japanese. In the hills before Shuri during the May rains a marine was watching a four-man stretcher team slog across the company front when enemy riflemen opened up on them.

> Each held a handle of the stretcher in one hand and stretched out the other arm for balance. . . . Four helmeted heads hung low like four beasts of burden being flogged. Soaked with rain and spattered with mud, the dark green dungarees hung forlornly on the men. The casualty lay inert on the narrow canvas stretcher, his life in the hands of the struggling four.

Suddenly two carriers were hit and dropped the litter. The other two seized the first casualty in their arms. The wounded bearers were able to hobble, and caught their other arms. All five stumbled and limped out of the line of fire, while the Marines cheered, filled with elation and a "deepened hatred of the Japanese."[35]

The medics' casualty rate on Okinawa was the higher than that of any other branch except the infantry. The 1st Marine Division alone counted almost five hundred casualties among its hospital corpsmen. The ranks were not easy to fill. Killing and wounding left a continuing deficit of trained medical enlisted personnel in the line units, partly because of the inevitable time lag in obtaining replacements, but also because the Central Pacific command did not have enough such men. As a result, those who remained bore an added burden, while bearers had to be pulled from combat support units—on one occasion, forty field artillerymen were sent forward as litter-bearers—to move accumulations of wounded who otherwise could not have been evacuated at all.

Incidents of heroism were common. The official army history relates:

> It was in such conditions that PFC Desmond T. Doss of the medical detachment, 307th Infantry, 77th Division won the Medal of Honor. A conscientious objector who refused to carry a weapon and kept the Seventh Day Adventist sabbath every Saturday, Doss at the end of April was a company aidman during his unit's assault on a 400-foot escarpment. They seized the crest, only to be hit as usual by furious fire from the reverse slope. The infantry scattered, but Doss remained alone on the crest, where he carried the wounded one by one to the edge, tied each to a litter in turn, and lowered him to friendly hands. On another occasion he treated injured men lying in the very mouth of an enemy-held cave, and on a third, wounded himself, gave up his place on a litter to a more severely injured man. Doss then splinted his own fractured arm with a rifle stock, and crawled to safety.[36]

Such were the desperate circumstances on the line. But there was another side to evacuating the wounded on Okinawa. Once out of reach of the enemy, the chain of evacuation was more normal, or at any rate more in line with tradition and regulations, than in any previous Central Pacific battle. The roads were rough and winding, sometimes a nightmare of ruts and boulders, but they were usable. Ambulances ran on regular shuttles, and patients reached the surgeons quickly and in good condition.

There were other pluses. The blood supply system had been perfected, and the Naval Air Transport Service delivered regularly from Guam. Specialist surgical teams waited in the army and navy hospitals, and Tenth Army set up an evacuation center to move the wounded efficiently to ships, airfields, hospitals, or prisoner of war stockades. Not all the wounded were Americans; more Japanese surrendered on Okinawa than in any previous battle, partly because the navy ran an effective psychological warfare program to persuade them to give up, partly because increasing numbers of Japanese and Okinawans realized that the war was almost over. As a result, the Tenth Army set up a 500-bed POW hospital, staffed by army doctors and enlisted medics, where captives received able professional care.[37]

The problems that marked the medical side of the battle developed simply because the number of wounded was so great. Marines, with their field hospitals supported by the 2d Corps Evacuation Hospital, found their backup treatment "entirely adequate."[38] Soldiers, not so lucky, had only portables and field hospitals until late May, when station hospitals began to arrive. Until then the army's problem was not so much lack of beds—Okinawa turned out to be healthier than expected, so that beds allotted to the sick were standing empty when the wounded needed them—but in the number of surgeons. Surgical teams, each of two surgeons, an anesthetist, a surgical nurse, and three surgical technicians, worked steadily, thirty-six to forty hours at a stretch, when the heavy influx of wounded began. Surgeons slept in foxholes a few feet from the operating tables; sometimes they split up to handle more cases, the individual surgeon working with little assistance but that of his technician.

The teams were excellent, but there were not enough of them, and the field hospitals were overworked and understaffed. Field hospitals by their nature were small forward units, and even with strengthened staffs could not meet the needs of a huge and desperate battle—especially minus their women nurses, who were not allowed on Okinawa during the first month. Consultants rated at least four field hospitals as weak in surgery, and the portables were hindered by their meager staffs and the heavy pressure under which they worked.

A basic reason why the surgeons had so many injuries to repair—and such complicated injuries at that—was the Japanese artillery. The same patient might have a compound fracture, a perforating wound of the abdomen, and multiple soft tissue wounds. Astonishing injuries turned up, often ending happily in equally astonishing recoveries. At the 31st Field Hospital a soldier was admitted on April 20 with an unexploded 50 mm mortar shell embedded in his back; at another hospital, amazed surgeons removed a 20 mm shell from a man's bladder. Both survived.[39]

Disease was not much of a problem on Okinawa. Except for diarrhea, which was probably inevitable given the battlefield stew of flooding rain, feces, and rotting bodies, the troops remained physically healthy. Rates of illness were high, yet individual cases were not severe. Amazingly, for the Pacific war, preventive medicine on Okinawa was quite successful but not very important. Daily casualties from sickness did not outnumber battle casualties until May 28, fifty-eight days after the invasion. Disease rates remained low, and total nonbattle casualties, both sick and injured, numbered only two-thirds of those killed, wounded, and missing in battle. In fact, the main disease scare of the campaign came after it was over, when Okinawans began falling sick of a serious neurological disorder, Japanese B encephalitis. Experts rushed to the scene— the invasion of Japan was being staged partly from Okinawa, and the island was thronged with troops—and Lieutenant Colonel Albert B. Sabin, later to be a conqueror of infantile paralysis, hastily prepared a vaccine.[40] Only two Americans died in the outbreak, however.

Combat fatigue was another story. Like surgery, its rates recorded the effects of the intense and unrelieved combat. Men had to attack an entrenched foe; they had to endure ceaseless pounding from artillery and mortars; they lived under atrocious conditions, soaked by the rain and forced to be their own pack animals when downpours immobilized jeeps, trucks, and even tractors. In battle they measured their gains in yards and fought long, bloody struggles for a ridge that led only to another battle for another ridge indistinguishable from the first. It was the worst sort of war, as bad as Peleliu, only wetter and longer.

Most depressing of all was the fact that many veterans had come to believe that they faced battle after battle without relief. They did not precisely expect their own death, but they anticipated the death of friends and their own wounding, and they felt what a marine veteran called "the sickening dread of fear itself and the revulsion at the ghastly scenes of pain and suffering among comrades that a survivor must witness." As a result, about one in every seven casualties who reached a hospital was a victim of combat exhaustion and psychological breakdown.[41]

It was the job of Colonel Moses Kaufman, the theater psychiatric consultant, to deal with them by "active therapy at the earliest possible time and at the most forward possible echelon." Those who suffered only from exhaustion and anxiety received sedation and rest at aid stations, and most returned to duty after twenty-four hours. There were now division psychiatrists on hand to check more serious cases in the clearing stations and to see that they got reassurance, rest, hot meals, sleep, and a change of clothes. Field hospitals had psychiatric wards, staff psychiatrists, and trained enlisted men to manage the more difficult cases that reached them.

Late in April the command devoted the 82d Field Hospital entirely to the care of psychiatric patients, both soldiers and marines. The hospital became the best staffed of its kind in the Pacific war. Kaufman deliberately placed it closer to the front lines than the other field hospitals, for he was convinced that if patients were to recover they must remain in the danger zone, "hearing the shells whiz overhead." Rest camps for recuperating patients were set up even closer to the line. This was tough treatment, rooted in what was now a long tradition of combat psychiatry and its recognition of the active, purposeful character of the disorder. On the one hand, the victim of combat stress could not simply will himself back to being an effective soldier or marine; on the other, he could not be allowed to perceive his illness as a means of escaping his duty.

The prescription worked on Okinawa, as it had elsewhere. In some units, the results were as good as any in World War II. In the 77th Infantry Division, for example, 76 percent of all neuropsychiatric cases returned to full duty. Less than 10 percent of those who returned to combat broke down again under stress. The failures of the program resulted from the fact that more than half of the 3,118 Army and Marine psychiatric patients had to be evacuated, simply because the wounded filled the beds on Okinawa. Once off the island, they had every reason to stay sick or become sicker, and many did.[42]

By the summer of 1945 both the Central and the Southwest Pacific had fought and won major campaigns. The Japanese were still fighting in the mountains of northern Luzon when the Joint Chiefs of Staff began to reorganize for the planned Armageddon that was to be the invasion of Japan. The end of the war in Europe meant that almost unlimited supplies of men and matériel could be counted upon. But to many veterans of earlier campaigns, the prospect was for a victory that they might not be able to enjoy.

With the reconquest of the Philippines, American forces in the Pacific left the tropical islands for good. The long contest with the jungle was over, and the medical services could rightly claim a practical sort of victory: Disease had been held at bay, and victories at sea and in the air had turned it against the Japanese by denying them supplies, reinforcements, and escape. To the other aspect of the Pacific war, its sheer bloodthirstiness, no equivalent answer had been found, though combat surgery and evacuation had advanced to impressive maturity. The invasion of Japan could be supported, and the wounded could be extricated and given every chance of life, but by medical estimates something on the order of half a million casualties impended.

MacArthur's and Nimitz's men would fight the new battle, but they would do so in the shadow of Iwo Jima and Okinawa, knowing beyond doubt that the war in the Central Pacific would end as it had begun so many thousands of miles to the west, *mano a mano*, with man's only enemy war and his only slayers other members of his own species.

15

The War's Long Shadow

The greater the storm, the greater the wreckage. While a few fortunate medics headed for home from Europe, most remained in uniform to aid the victims of the war.[1] A worldwide army of damaged human beings that included both countrymen and former enemies had survived the holocaust only to face new hardships in its aftermath.

American casualties needing treatment and rehabilitation thronged general hospitals and convalescent centers in the United States. While the seriously hurt had been filtering home throughout the war, the big transoceanic "lift" came in May–June, 1945, when almost 100,000 arrived in the Zone of Interior to face the ordeal and hope provided by reconstructive surgery and definitive care. Some came by troop transport, some by hospital ship. Planes of the Army Air Transport Command and the Naval Air Transport Service brought some of the worst cases produced by the last, most savage battles of the war—among them a regular army master sergeant, who arrived in California minus parts of four limbs, lost to a Japanese land mine on Okinawa.[2]

Most arrived in good shape, considering what they had undergone. Patients who came by air were usually in better condition than those who had spent a long time at sea, and veterans of the European fighting were healthier than men from the Pacific theaters. Even if a man had dreadful injuries, like the basket case from Okinawa, he was likely to be in amazingly good spirits. Getting home gave him a great emotional lift; at least for a short time, he could believe that things might work out after all.[3]

Whether he came by air or sea, the patient went through a fairly standardized process. He was carried onto American terra firma wearing a tag with his diagnosis. There was always a receiving or debarkation hospital near the port or airport to accommodate him, check his condition, and do triage. Of course, the casualty had been through this sorting process several times since being hit, but triage now had a particular meaning. The receiving hospital had to keep shipping its patients out in order to make room for new arrivals (by 1945, 30,000 soldiers were coming home on stretchers or as walking wounded every month). But any given man might not be able to travel; he might be bleeding, exhausted, or have an infection signaled by a foul smell rising from his wound. In that case, he had to stay where he was until he was better.

Physicians' accounts make the whole process of receiving patients from overseas sound like controlled frenzy. Sometimes the hospital had plenty of notification that ships or planes were on the way, but sometimes the news arrived along with the patients. Clerks had to process paperwork quickly, and the men had to be carried to the wards to be fed and bathed. Specialists of every sort had to check out injuries and make instant judgments. Eventually some doctors became so skilled in the art of triage that they could stroll through a ward, making decisions on the basis of the patients' paperwork and general appearance.[4]

Sometimes there was an immediate crisis. Halloran General Hospital on Staten island was one of the biggest in the nation, with 3,000 beds and 3,500 more for use in emergencies. A major receiving hospital, it also specialized in neurosurgery and in orthopedic (bone and joint) injuries. One of its patients, a soldier, arrived with a bloody cast on one leg and documents indicating that he had already had one hemorrhage overseas. Apparently he was close to another. Blood was given to him, he was prepared for surgery, and a tourniquet was slipped around the injured leg, ready for tightening if need be. He began to bleed before he reached the operating room, but the whole surgical team was waiting for him, the hemorrhage was stopped, and the leg was saved.

The collaborative work of doctors and nurses who worked thousands of miles apart, never seeing one another in the flesh, was one of the wonders of the time. The staffs of overseas and stateside hospitals were tied together by their science, common calling, and membership in a matured system of integrated care. Still, with so many returning wounded, there were inevitably some horror stories to be told.

A surgeon at Letterman General Hospital in San Francisco recounted how two men wounded at Peleliu had arrived after losing a leg each to gas gangrene. The tragedy resulted from poor emergency treatment, Pacific distances, and, surprisingly, air transport. On Peleliu no one had debrided the wounds; they had been simply dusted with sulfanilamide and bandaged. The soldiers were evacuated to the Admiralty Islands, arriving feverish and in discomfort but not in great pain. After staying overnight, they were flown on to the Solomon Islands, where they complained of increasing pain. At last somebody took them seriously and looked under the dressings—or perhaps by then the smell was impossible to ignore. Gangrene had set into both wounds, in one so severely that the leg had to be amputated at the hip. Apparently some medical personnel along the way imagined that air evacuation, in and of itself, meant a quick arrival at definitive treatment. The result was two men crippled for life.

"It was too late in the war for such surgical catastrophes to be occurring," the Letterman surgeon concluded. The patient "must receive the necessary care at the first stop, as if it were to be the last stop."[5]

Most of the men who showed up in the receiving hospitals were ready to move on by train or plane within seventy-two hours. Transport was arranged by a medical regulating unit set up by the surgeon general in the headquarters of the transportation corps. When the patients learned where they were to be sent for final treatment, however, a rather nasty fly sometimes embedded himself in the ointment of their bliss. Many had been told overseas that they would be sent to a hospital near their homes, but of course it was more important to get them into empty beds in hospitals that specialized in handling their types of cases. Many men learned that they would, in fact, be a long way from the place they had been fantasizing about.

If they were stretcher patients, they could do little about it, but if they were ambulatory they could take action. In some instances as many as 15 percent turned up missing when the trains they had been assigned to pulled out. The men simply hid among the thousands of other patients in the receiving hospital. Some commanders responded by trying to conceal where they were going until the men were safely aboard the trains. But the inspector general ruled that the truth had to be told to patients, and the game of hide-and-seek continued.[6]

Even the most resistant wounded man eventually ended up at the general hospital that had been chosen to treat him. Here specialists undertook to restore him as far as possible to his former self. That might involve combating some intransigent disease or performing complex reconstructive surgery to repair the effects of serious wounds—or both. Rehabilitation might involve getting a prosthesis, and it always entailed a period of therapy to help the patient either to live a normal life again or else to adjust to a not so normal life with a permanent handicap.

The commonest of all wartime injuries were fractures, some caused by accidents, many by missiles or high explosives. Orthopedic wards at big hospitals contained cases in which every possible bone was broken in every possible way, and often many were broken at once. Most fractures were compound—that is, they involved a surface wound as well as a broken bone. Fortunately, fractures were also among the easiest injuries to treat successfully. Surgeons in the zone of the interior praised their colleagues overseas for many things, but for nothing more than the good care given to fractures. Plasma and blood, tetanus boosters, and (after 1943) penicillin shots, careful debridement, and fixation in plaster casts made for many a happy outcome. Despite the filth of battle-fields, gangrene was rare, and the worst of wound infections—tetanus—was almost never seen in Americans.

Other cases were more difficult. Multiple injuries, which were common, demanded the skills of an array of specialists. Sometimes the patient was riddled with foreign objects that for one reason or another had proved impossible to remove overseas. Fragments of metal and other rubbish were found embedded in the "brain, eye, sinuses, lung. . . . heart, liver, scrotum, spinal canal, bone, joint, muscles." In fact, just about anywhere. Missiles found their way even into protected sites like the rectum; one foreign object was discovered only when the patient passed wind that exited through a wound in his thigh with "a high musical note."[7]

Some missiles could safely be left in the body, and some could not be taken out with the surgical techniques of the time. A fragment in a knee joint had to come out, a surgeon at Halloran reported, while in another case a bullet causing no symptoms was left in the liver. Wounds of the bowels could be repaired if small, but on occasion sections of the gut had to be cut out and the ends anastomosed (joined end to end). Colostomies—artificial outlets for the bowel—formed a standard part of surgery for handling wounds of the colon. But infection dogged some cases, and the same surgeon spoke of "the seriously sick and emaciated patient with colostomy, abscesses, fistulas, and profound sepsis" sometimes to be seen on the wards.

Amputations had always been a grim aspect of wartime, and despite greatly improved techniques for saving damaged limbs they remained so. A single army general hospital (Percy Jones, in Battle Creek, Michigan) treated 2,783 major amputations, more than the whole army had suffered during World War I. Some were traumatic (caused by weapons), with land mines a leading culprit. Infection and blood clots were common problems. A nurse in a debarkation ward described a "brown-eyed, curly-haired boy," in appearance about sixteen, although he claimed to be twenty, who arrived at Mitchel Field missing a left arm. He had been hit in Germany near the Dutch border, his lower arm crushed, and an artery cut near his clavicle. Under mortar fire, two aidmen took turns holding the artery shut for six or seven hours. Gangrene set in, and surgeons amputated at the elbow, then at the shoulder. Cheerful like most new returnees, he rejoiced that he had lost only an arm and "patted his sound pair of legs."[8]

A bizarre aspect of amputation was the phantom limb. A patient's eyes might show him that an arm or leg was gone, but his mind remained unconvinced. A surgeon at Percy Jones said flatly, "Every individual with an amputation has a phantom limb." The patient felt it, sometimes suffered with it. In some ways the phantom was helpful; when a man donned an artificial limb he needed something to tell him where it was and what it was doing. The prosthesis had no feeling, but the absent limb did, and gave him at least an inkling of its location.

Doctors tended to explain the phenomenon in terms of their own specialties—surgeons thought of nerve damage suffered during the amputation, while psychiatrists treated some painful cases as neuroses. But it was a surgeon who told a curious story of a wiry little paratrooper, energetic and valorous, who had lost an arm to a German .88. Fitted with a prosthesis, he seemed to be doing well; the only odd thing about him was his relentless determination to get back overseas with a paratroop unit. When he was rejected for overseas duty he reacted with fury, and at the same moment felt the fingers of his absent hand dig into the palm with excruciating pain. He was readmitted to the hospital and more surgery was done without relieving his suffering. He could not sleep because of the pain of "the nails cutting the flesh and burning like fire." Then suddenly he announced that he had no more pain and was completely cured. He had received a telegram ordering him to duty back overseas.[9]

Other injuries lengthened the catalogue of the awful accidents of war. Damage to the genitourinary system was fairly common, including the loss of one or both testicles, sometimes—especially in the case of mine victims—accompanied by traumatic amputation of one or both legs. Bomber crewmen suffered severe frostbite. Many men had deep burns that required grafting, and others arrived home with empty eye sockets or eyeballs that still had a bit of metal in them. Eardrums were ruptured by concussion, and infections invaded the middle ear. Faces were partly shot away, jawbones smashed. The heavy scarring left by wounds and burns interfered with movement, and plastic and orthopedic surgeons had to work together to restore functional limbs in many cases.

In fact, plastic surgeons found endless work to do in their unique specialty, a mingling of science, technique, and art. They rebuilt acceptable or at least believable faces from hideous masks, sometimes sculpting new organs from living tissue. "A replaced new ear seems like a miracle," a general surgeon said in some awe, "but to the plastic surgeon its creation is considered a minor reconstructive job."[10] Some plastic surgeons were quick to discount the miracle stories. Scar formation was a complicated physical process, and large scars were difficult to reduce. Some human bodies for unknown reasons showed a baffling tendency to overrepair injuries, building up unsightly masses called keloids. Skin grafts could not be transplanted from one person to another; transplanted skin, except when applied to an identical twin, liquified after a few days. "Why? We in plastic surgery do not know why!"[11]

Yet there were cases that seemed to deserve the well-worn journalistic phrase "medical miracle." During the Battle of the Bulge a young infantry lieutenant was slogging with his platoon down a road deep in mud and slush when a German tank appeared, churning forward with its .88-mm turret gun trained directly on him. A "deafening concussion" knocked him into the mire, and one tread of the tank rolled over his head.

The man remembered nothing more until a stretcher-bearer awakened him. At a mobile hospital, Major Francis A. Carmichael, Jr., unwrapped a turban of bandages that swathed the patient's head. Though an experienced neurosurgeon, he was "utterly and completely horrified at the underlying mess, which was a conglomeration of mud and blood . . . there was virtually no skull in this mass of debris." The man had lost the top of his head and the covering of the brain. He was paralysed on the left side of the body, and his memory was clouded, but against all logic he was alive, conscious, and talking.

What to do? The surgeon cleaned the wound but could not get enough of a flap from the scalp to cover the opening. He consulted the plastic surgeons, and at last "in utter despair and panic" sliced skin from the man's abdomen and grafted it directly over the brain. To his amazement, the graft took. With more grafts, he was able to enclose the brain beneath a flimsy but all-important wall of protection. With antibiotics, abscesses that had formed on the brain cleared up. The man's memory cleared, and there were signs of partial recovery from his paralysis. He was promptly evacuated to the zone of interior.

Here Colonel Malvin F. White took over. He removed the grafts, carried out some "very brilliant reconstructive work," and the amazing lieutenant, his left side near normal, returned home with a promotion to captain and an honorable retirement on full disability. (Presumably the missing portion of his skull was replaced by a tantalum plate, the most commonly used material at the time.) He remembered the surgeons who had rebuilt his head, writing them warm letters at Christmas and dropping in to see them. He apparently suffered no psychiatric or other long-term problems from what Carmichael described as "this mutilating and somewhat horrifying wound, the most spectacular I encountered during my military career."[12]

Others were not so fortunate. It is not easy to conceive of a higher calling than the application of superb knowledge, nerve, and skill to a humane purpose—which is what able surgeons did day after day. But miracles were as rare for them as for the rest of humanity. In many men with head wounds, personalities changed, the brain waves showed persistent abnormalities, and patients had difficulty thinking clearly and expressing themselves in speech. Some suffered from posttraumatic epilepsy; they became dizzy, fell into dreamlike states, and had hallucinations. Anticonvulsive drugs controlled the condition in some patients but not in others.[13]

There were worse fates than epilepsy. Spinal cord injuries often left the victim partly paralyzed, no easy fate for anybody, especially a young and vigorous man. Paraplegics went through well-marked phases. First came the shock, fear, and hysteria of discovering their condition and realizing that they would never recover from it. More or less immobilized, many sank into a grim and bitter mood. Their injuries interacted with their inability to move to afflict them with painful and humiliating problems. They had to relearn how to control bladder and bowels; they suffered from bladder stones, urinary infections, and decubitus ulcers (bedsores). Surgeons excised the ulcers, and therapists worked with

the patients to get them moving as much as possible and as quickly as possible. But not all could achieve the ultimate goal of walking with leg braces and canes—as President Roosevelt, the nation's model of a paralytic who had triumphed over his affliction,
was able to do for short distances.[14]

Rehabilitation—physical and occupational therapy and retrain-
ing—formed a big part of the program in the stateside hospitals.
Officially sanctioned and sponsored by army, navy, and air force,
the medical logic behind rehabilitation began with the observation
that "absolute bed rest kills more patients than anesthesia and all
the drugs in the pharmacopoeia added together." An inert patient
lost muscle tone, developed blood clots, suffered reduced lung
volume, and developed kidney and bladder stones. He resented
his helplessness yet clung to it, bitter at his childish condition,
querulous and discontented with himself and others.[15]

Therapy began early, while the patient was still in bed with his
injury. When he was still hurting and obsessed with his own problems, activities might simply be intended to distract him. Then he
might be ordered into a regular program geared to exercise particular parts of his body or to improve his coordination. The amputee got his prosthesis and learned to move himself around the
world again, or to master such arts as tying his shoelaces with the
hooks that replaced his lost hands. Finally, therapy might extend
to reeducation in useful trades or skills, at which point it became
less the rebuilding of a body and more the reconstruction of a life.

At the big general hospital in Battle Creek, Michigan, civilian
teachers ran a tutoring program on the wards. Patients earned
high school credits, and some graduated in the hospital. They
were encouraged to take part in athletics, and Purple Heart Field
Days were held where they could show off their prowess to the
public. Work was even more important than games. Amputees,
paraplegics, and psychiatric patients all got training in an array of
fields—aviation and auto mechanics, electronics and radio repair,
drafting, printing, tailoring, and many others. The local community pitched in, sponsoring courses and providing teachers in
everything from salesmanship to music. Patients published their
own newspaper and staged their own radio show.

A convalescent hospital formed part of the complex, with two

2,000-man regiments for military organization and its own reconditioning program in shops, classrooms, and gymnasiums. On occasion the patients in the convalescent hospital showed a quite remarkable venereal disease rate—possibly a sign of returning vigor,
possibly of undue haste in the choice of partners. (Most of the
cases resulted from convalescent furloughs, which were freely
given for up to ninety days.)[16]

Other hospitals opened convalescent wards with good results.
Many medical officers received training in reconditioning at the
Mayo Clinic, but the programs were as much military as medical.
At Fitzsimons General Hospital in Denver, Colorado, the program
was all-male and decidedly vigorous. There were no female nurses
on the convalescent wards, and drill, calisthenics, and sports occupied much of the time. Patients were back under full military discipline, and strangely enough seemed to like it; at least their time
of helplessness was over, and they were being treated like adults
again.

At a nearby resort, a large navy convalescent hospital boasted
the "world's largest mineral water swimming pool," fed by a hot
spring and usable year round, though the hospital stood at an ele-
vation of 2,400 feet. By manipulating the inflow of hot springs
and chill mountain creeks, baths of all temperatures were created,
and the patient's therapy, though appropriately wetter than at the
army hospital, was no less vigorous. Other navy convalescent hospitals stood in Yosemite National Park; in Palm Beach, Florida;
and on the grounds of the Averell Harriman estate in upstate New
York; many other navy hospitals had convalescent wings. The aim
of therapy, according to a naval medical officer, was not only to
strengthen bodies but to foster "diligence and self-respect" by
converting "indolent and often discontented patients into happy
men who soon begin to feel that they are becoming useful members of society." Sports were found to be shrewdly adapted to
both purposes, for they awoke the combative spirit that is so
much a part of the will to recover.[17]

Even in conditions from which physical recovery was impossible, rehabilitation had an important role to play. Facing blindness
required great courage, especially from a young patient with his
life still to live. The rehabilitation of the blind veteran became the

focus of national attention, the personal interest of President Roosevelt, and the subject of a complex program at military and Veterans Administration hospitals. The military hospitals where blind men got medical treatment were Valley Forge and San Francisco for the army, Philadelphia for the navy.[18]

At the end of his medical treatment, the blind patient began a course in independent living. The aim was not only to give him basic skills but to convince him that he still had a life, in some measure like the one he had known in the past. He learned how to shave and dress himself, find his way about, use tools, and travel. He learned Braille and typing, to fit him for the vocational training that was the business of the VA center in Connecticut. (Some men almost immediately found jobs in local factories and offices.) For exercise he bowled, swam, and even played golf, though he needed a sighted companion for teeing up and keeping track of the ball.

Most men faced their fate courageously; those who had been wounded in combat and those who were totally blind were the strongest of all. A man blinded by accident or illness sometimes blamed himself for his condition, rationally or not (if only he had done so-and-so instead of such-and-such, this wouldn't have happened). A man with a limited disability sometimes deluded himself that his vision would return completely in time. It was better to feel no guilt and to cling to no illusions, and the people who worked with the blind were taught never to raise false hopes.

Enlisted men, WACs, and civilians, including blind instructors, played a big role in this basic training for a life to be spent in dusk or darkness. The enlisted men were called orientors. As one physician said, they formed "the backbone of the rehabilitation program for the blind." They taught their patients where everything in the hospital was, from the latrines to the PX; they helped them to dress, handle money, and travel. Orientors were a varied lot. At Valley Forge General Hospital, where almost three hundred blind men entered the rehabilitation program in 1944 and almost six hundred in 1945, one of the best orientors had been a truck driver in civilian life, and others included a former salesman, a musician, a farmer, and a golf pro.

There was no way to predict how a particular patient would

react, or how rapport could best be established with him. Orientors needed a feel for the human situation, and they developed their own ways of relating to the blind; some were always serious and sober in dealing with their patients, some never so. The best let the patient teach himself, while remaining alert to lend a hand with those things that only a sighted person could do. Grieving for the blind man was bad, and so was taking a proprietary attitude toward him. Neither sentimentality nor egotism was wanted. The compassion and common sense of ordinary, decent people took up the healing task at the point where science had reached its limit.[19]

Difficult as the lives of American wounded might be, they lived in a nation that was not only victorious but virtually unscathed by the war. Overseas the need for medical knowledge was even greater, because the losses and ruin left by war were incomparably worse. In Japan as in Germany, men and women who had served in the military medical services of contending armies worked together at the tasks of lifesaving among the victims of war of all nations.

The explosion of two atomic bombs over Japanese cities in August 1945 ended not only a war but the prospect of all the calamities that would have followed the invasion of Japan.[20] Instead of fighting their way ashore, Americans landed peacefully, only to find themselves saddled with extraordinary responsibilities in the land they had conquered. Their first priority was aiding the newly liberated prisoners of war. Roughly four of every ten Americans who had been captured by the Japanese were dead. For the survivors, liberation meant a sudden transition from near-slavery to freedom, and from being remnants of a beaten army to being members of a triumphant one.

In Japan, former prisoners were taken to repatriation centers on the coasts, while those on the Asian mainland, after their liberation by the Red Army, were airlifted or brought by train or Russian military vehicles to the ports. In physical examinations, medical officers catalogued the effects of captivity: amoebic dysentery, chronic coughs, beriberi, atrophied muscles, tuberculosis. Few of the POWs, despite what they had undergone, showed mental or emotional disorders. The chief treatment for all but the dying was abundant food—on average, each man gained 20 pounds in three weeks. Observers saw them as tough survivors, closely bonded by the suffering they had shared.[21]

For American medics the second obligation was to support their own troops. That duty proved to be easy to the point of absurdity. After enduring three and a half years of bitter warfare with a minimal medical support system, American forces came ashore with a profusion of field medical units that briefly formed an embarrassment of riches. Some medical officers, nurses, and corpsmen were essentially at loose ends until summoned home.[22] For many others, however, there was ample work to be done among the Japanese people. No longer enemies but dependents, they formed the last and by far the most difficult medical problem facing the occupation government. The men who had launched the empire's great experiment in overseas conquest would soon be dead, in hiding, or in prison awaiting trial as war criminals. For their conquerors, the Japanese people remained, to be governed for a time and lived with forever.

In some respects, the plans that had been drawn up during the war for the occupation of Japan closely resembled those for Germany. Following the conquest of Kyushu and a final Armageddon on the Kanto plain outside Tokyo, a military government was to be set up on principles that were severe but not inhumane. The economy was not to be rehabilitated, but a basic civilian ration of 1,500 calories was to be assured, with supplements for workers, and medical supplies were to be provided on a minimal basis to prevent disease and unrest. The surgeon general proposed to attach to every army corps a field hospital to be dedicated to the treatment of civilians alone. Planning under Colonel Crawford F. Sams for medical support was still under way when the atomic bombs ended the war with shocking abruptness in August 1945.

Now occupation forces faced a new situation, quite different both from their previous expectations and from the European model. No equivalent of the Nazi party existed in Japan, and the nation's surrender, unlike Germany's, was conditional. The emperor remained, and with him a civil government that would continue to function under allied military control. In the field of public health, a few highly placed medical officers supervised an existing civil administration without the complications of a divided nation, power sharing with the allies, or disqualification on political grounds of the health workers they most needed to assist them.[23]

In late August a few men chosen for leading roles in the occupation were pulled abruptly from planning sessions and transported by warship to the shores of Japan to survey the situation. Among them was Colonel Sams, a man of average height with a clipped mustache, a positive demeanor, and bustling energy. His first glimpse of Yokohama was a revelation about the job to be done, for he saw "only ashes, literally miles of ashes interspersed with tall isolated chimneys and steel safes." In the first hospital he visited, he found vacant, dirty wards scattered with empty tatami mats and three doctors who were drinking tea and tensely awaiting death at the hands of the conquerors. (Sams told them to go home.)[24]

That moment of mutual incomprehension was his own introduction to the gulf that yawned between the two cultures. The days that followed underlined it in matters large and small. A Japanese officer brought the disquieting news that a cholera epidemic was raging in Tokyo; only by inspection of the sick was Sams able to determine that the Japanese called any severe dysentery cholera. The rigid Japanese class system gave them an understanding of events quite different from the Americans'. Sams in his practical way visited the Japanese health minister to obtain information he needed, only to read in the newspapers that he had gone to "pay his respects"—which had the look of a kowtow about it. Clearly, he was not dealing with a people who admired informality, and Sams began to learn aloofness from his commander, General MacArthur, who provided a superb model in this respect.[25]

Meanwhile Sams lived in Tokyo's Imperial Hotel, where top officers drew their water from lister bags, walked on straw mats, and worked by dim and flickering bulbs suspended from the ceilings. They got little sleep at night, for the ventilating ducts had become runways for thousands of rats. Outside, among the Japanese, things were much worse. The country was filled with impoverished people who moved restlessly from city to country and back again in search of food and work. Millions more, who had colonized the empire's overseas conquests, would soon return to a land that could not shelter them.

The firebombed cities were heaps of ashes; Hiroshima was a moonscape. The island nation's merchant marine lay at the bottom of the sea. The Japanese diet, always deficient in protein, had become totally inadequate with the collapse of the transport system. Newspapers carried scare reports of hundreds dying of starvation; the stories were false, but the anxiety was real. Both the Japanese and the occupation authorities feared the possibility of famine and disorder, and the first requirement for both was to cooperate in preventing it.

"So began," Colonel Sams wrote in his memoirs, "the greatest experiment in human relations in history." In setting public health policy, he possessed—and needed—ample powers. The Japanese, hustled into the modern age in the course of a few generations, had produced both distinguished medical scientists and a public health system that was poor and ill-informed. Directed by the police rather than by people of medical training, public health administration in Japan had been inadequate before the war and had languished during it. In September 1945, the supreme command launched a survey of hospital facilities, stocks of medical supplies, and food. The navy quarantined the ports, and army medical supplies intended for the invasion were diverted to civilian use. But life-threatening illnesses began to spread among a hungry and crowded people.[26]

Repatriates from the mainland of Asia introduced typhus into port cities, notably Osaka. Infected Korean laborers heading home from mines in Hokkaido spread the illness to Honshu from the north. The foci of infection were many, but the railroads were among the most dangerous. Stations sheltered shivering vagrants, and Sams recalled as "one of the more horrible sights I have seen in a lifetime" the underground passages of Tokyo's Ueno Station: "dark, damp with the air foul, with the stench of thousands of unwashed humans lying in rows on the cold concrete." Many were dying of smallpox, typhoid, and typhus. The trains were so crowded that a Japanese doctor saw the passengers clinging to the exteriors "in clusters like swarming bees or like a tree overburdened with fruit." In the cars people not only transmitted lice but inhaled the microbes that cause typhus from dry louse droppings in one another's clothes and hair.[27]

By December 1945 the disease had reached "epidemic proportions." The occupation authorities reorganized the Japanese Ministry of Welfare, and under Sams's supervision the new ministry launched a national campaign using American army medics, Japanese health workers, the assistance of the U.S.A. Typhus Commission, and supplies of vaccine and DDT imported from the United States. Cities were divided into manageable units, and a case-finding team armed with dust-guns was assigned to each. A program of public education utilized posters, pamphlets, radio, and the press. The result was a renewed demonstration of the control methods worked out during wartime. By March 1946 the epidemic had been contained, after 30,000 cases had been reported.

Other textbook attacks on major diseases also gained success. A typhoid outbreak ended after 20 million people had been inoculated and sanitation improved. Smallpox was rooted out by the systematic vaccination of the entire nation, some 75 million people. During the war Japan had experienced one kind of military control; in the aftermath, it embraced another, directed toward a quite different goal. Military medicine had no more basic mission than to prevent and control epidemic disease in large, disciplined masses. In Japan as in Germany, its skills were beautifully adapted to meeting the problems of an occupation regime.[28]

Reforms were accomplished in many fields. Life expectancy increased for both men and women. Much of the damage of the war was undone. Disease was controlled, health improved, a new constitution imposed. The industry and ingenuity of the Japanese rebuilt the ravaged cities and began to reconstruct a new and better industrial system to replace the one destroyed by the war. But the way the war had ended left another legacy that threatened the conqueror as much as the conquered—ultimate weapons that implied the possibility of irreparable destruction in the future.

Atomic weapons did not, comparatively speaking, kill many people during World War II—approximately 200,000 of the 50 million or so victims of the war. Conventional fire-bombing destroyed many more Japanese cities, probably killed many more people, and was more destructive to the empire's war effort. The A-bombs did not decide the outcome, either. They brought the war to an end only after conventional warfare had entirely deprived the Japanese of any strategy except that of dying in place.[29]

Yet almost from the day of Hiroshima thinking people realized that nuclear weapons mattered overwhelmingly as a portent. When the first American occupiers arrived in Japan, the problem was immediate—thousands of survivors of the bombs who were suffering from radiation and flash burns. One of Sams's first actions was to dispatch medical supplies and personnel to Hiroshima and Nagasaki, and one of the first orders issued by the Supreme Commander, Allied Powers, to the Japanese government was to provide security for the American medics who took the supplies in. Among them were investigators eager to study the medical effects of atomic warfare, for the field was brand-new, and its future importance was only too clear.[30]

Interviews with survivors evoked memories of a "great violet bright light"; of crushing blast and searing heat; of ordinary mornings, with rituals of waking and breakfasting, suddenly transmuted into nightmares filled with dust and smoke driven by the hot, swirling wind of the firestorm. Survivors were transformed in an instant from human beings into apparitions of suffering and horror. "You couldn't tell men from women," a Korean who had been caught in Hiroshima recalled. "If there were breasts, that was a woman. Faces hung down like icicles. Skin in strips from arms held out in front of them. 'Water! Water!'" Processions of shocked refugees tried to escape the city, trudging "in the realm of dreams" until they died along the roads.[31]

The most immediate and widespread injuries were burns—mostly severe flashburns of the kind that exploding ordnance had been producing since the war began. Attendants could do little but apply oil—almost any kind, including machine oil—in an attempt to alleviate the pain. The commonest wounds were caused by "countless glass splinters embedded in the skin and muscles." At the Red Cross Hospital, John Hersey wrote in his classic *Hiroshima*, "Dr. Sasaki, worn out, was moving aimlessly and dully up and down the stinking corridors with wads of bandage and bottles of mercurochrome . . . binding up the worst cuts as he came to them. Other doctors were putting compresses of saline on the worst burns. That was all they could do."[32]

Other symptoms quickly began to appear, baffling the doctors, who, with little equipment, tried not only to treat but to make sense of the calamity that had fallen upon them. Bleeding was difficult to stop. Within a few days bloody diarrhea was common, and culturing the stools yielded none of the usual dysentery bacteria. Lack of blood-count devices prevented doctors from discovering the leukopenia—deficiency in white blood cells—that signaled the onset of radiation sickness. Many victims lost all or part of their head, facial, and body hair. Later examination of the dead showed damage to the mucous lining of the gastrointestinal tract, lymphoid tissues, and reproductive organs.[33]

The smell of the smog that hung over Hiroshima and Nagasaki, a mixture of nitrous oxide with ozone produced by the ionizing radiation of the bombs, convinced many that the new weapon, whatever it was, had contained poison gas. But soon able investigators, led by Dr. Masao Tzuzuki of Tokyo Imperial University, began to clear away the confusion. Colonel Ashley W. Oughterson, formerly of Yale's medical faculty, was appointed to head a mixed commission of Japanese and American scientists to examine the consequences of the atomic bombs. The Manhattan District's Colonel Stafford L. Warren and the navy's Commander Shields Warren joined the group. Dr. Takeo Tamiya, a Harvard graduate who had become dean of the Imperial University Medical School, placed its facilities at the commission's disposal.[34]

One of Oughterson's first actions was to dispatch 100 million units of penicillin to aid the survivors, many of whom had spent weeks in a few shattered hospitals almost without medicines— packed "like rice in *sushi*," one of the doctors who had survived the Hiroshima blast said. Oughterson and Stafford Warren visited Nagasaki, where Western medicine had first entered Japan, and where the historic medical school had been erased with all its faculty and students. In the Omure Naval Hospital, which had survived, members of the commission studied the effects both on those who had died and on those who had lived through the war's catastrophic ending. Teams entered both cities, examining survivors; assembling records, photographs, and films; and collecting autopsy material.[35]

Scientific data gathered by the mixed commission remained classified during the occupation but were made public by the Atomic Energy Commission in 1951. By that time, surveys by the Manhattan District and the United States Strategic Bombing Survey had also been carried out.[36] The scientific study of the effects of the bomb gradually became institutionalized in the decades after the war. For a time, under the occupation and apparently for some years afterward, American scientists dominated the effort, to the resentment of the Japanese who had been first on the scene. The National Research Council played an important role through the Atomic Bomb Casualty Commission, while the Japanese worked through their own National Institute of Health. After 1974 the two nations jointly sponsored the Radiation Effects Research Foundation, which continued work on the roughly 100,000 survivors of the two blasts of August 1945.[37]

The result was a constantly growing body of accurate knowledge about precisely how the new weapons affected their victims. On the more general question of how medicine might try to organize itself in order to save the largest possible fraction of survivors in future nuclear wars, the studies yielded little that was encouraging. Of 298 doctors mobilized for civil defense in Hiroshima at the time of the attack, 274 had been killed by the bomb, along with 80 to 93 percent of pharmacists and nurses. "For all practical purposes, the well-prepared medical care system was rendered totally useless." The military took over care of the injured as well as it could, setting up relief stations, giving first aid, securing food and drinkable water, and attempting to start a cleanup of the corpses. Medical personnel from surrounding areas arrived to help out; at the same time, "streams of refugees were flowing out of Hiroshima" to the surrounding counties, some ending up in doctorless villages that quite suddenly had thousands of burned people to help.[38]

The spread of nuclear weapons in the postwar years suggested all too clearly that such scenes might be repeated, only in worse form and multiplied over wide areas of the earth. During the 1950s the American government tended to be upbeat about the chances of surviving atomic warfare, but the arrival and proliferation of thermonuclear weapons made optimism hard to maintain. Medical studies, even when officially sanctioned, tended to be less than hopeful. A Defense Department–Atomic Energy Commission essay published in 1950, when weapons were still comparatively small and the Russian bomb was less than a year old, noted that a single explosion would produce not less than 40,000–50,000 severely burned casualties and that ideal treatment for a single case would require 42 tanks of oxygen, 2.7 miles of gauze, 36 pints of plasma, 40 pints of whole blood, 100 pints of other fluids, drugs including morphine and antibiotics, and the services of three nurses. By the 1980s, both liberal professional groups (like the International Physicians for the Prevention of Nuclear War) and conservative organizations (like the American Medical Association) had simply dismissed the idea of an adequate medical response to nuclear war.[39]

Strategic nuclear weapons erased the distinction between military and civilian emergency medicine and left both at a loss. The new weapons established a limit on the power of medicine to respond to all-out war. In so doing, they pointed to one of World War II's most enduring legacies. The war was not only a time when medicine and public health saved millions who would otherwise have been lost in the conflagration. It was the time also when the technology of destruction moved decisively ahead of the science of healing. In the future, the ability of medicine to support and care for the victims of war would depend upon deterrence and treaty, and upon the refusal of warring parties—for whatever reason of mutual interest or mutual fear—ever to fight a total war again.

Yet conflicts there would be, and the achievements of American medicine in World War II provided a massive and durable model of successful lifesaving during one of the most destructive calamities in human history.

From a military viewpoint, wartime medicine made important contributions to victory. Preventive medicine accelerated the pace and reduced the cost of the jungle war; combat psychiatry made it possible for ordinary men to endure the almost unendurable; military surgery combined with antibiotic therapy and air transport to achieve unparalleled success in saving the wounded. It is hard to imagine how much longer World War II's casualty lists might have been without modern medicine aided by modern transport. Even by comparison with World War I the improvements of 1941–45 were striking. Despite the proliferation of lethal new weaponry, American battle death rates shrank by about half, disease death rates by twenty-seven times—and that despite the jungle war of 1941–45. If the army's overall death rate in first war had continued in the second, half a million more Americans would not have returned home.[40]

When the fighting stopped, medicine became an instrument of practical and humane policy, aiding the captives of all nations. That enabled war-battered populations not only to recover their health but to live longer lives than before the war. As a result, a great number of men, women, and children were saved, with all the hopes and talents they represented. In them the wartime medical services find their true memorial. Most monuments to victory age quickly and encumber the landscape; the memory of the war fades along with the generation that sacrificed to win it, and the destruction that is the chief work of war is soon repaired. But life has a claim on the future. The best work the medics did still survives in those they saved and healed, and in the lives to be lived and the work to be done by them and their descendants forever.

Notes

Introduction: War and Healing

1. Lew Giffin, "History of a Surgical Team in World War II by Lew Giffin, Former Lieutenant Colonel in the Medical Corps of the Army of the United States," ms. memoir, 1983, pp. 264–69. Copy in U.S. Army Center of Military History, Washington, D.C. (hereafter CMH). Despite the interjection of re-created conversations and other "docudrama" effects, Giffin's memoir is detailed and knowledgeable.

2. Cited in Mary C. Gillett, *The Army Medical Department, 1775–1818* (Washington, 1981), pp. 59–60.

3. Richard A. Gabriel and Karen S. Metz, *A History of Military Medicine*, 2 vols. (New York, 1992), 1:2–4; W. H. Lewis, *The Splendid Century: Life in the France of Louis XIV* (New York, 1957), p. 31.

4. Mary C. Gillett, *The Army Medical Department, 1818–1865* (Washington, 1987), p. 280.

5. Stanhope Bayne-Jones, *The Evolution of Preventive Medicine in the United States Army, 1607–1939* (Washington, 1968), p. 151.

6. On typhoid, see Harry F. Dowling, *Fighting Infection: Conquests of the Twentieth Century* (Cambridge, Mass., 1977), pp. 24–27. On typhus, see Hans Zinsser, *Rats, Lice and History* (Boston, 1935), especially pp. 229–39;

Stanhope Bayne-Jones, "Typhus Fevers," in Ebbe Curtis Hoff, ed., *Preventive Medicine in World War II: Communicable Diseases*, 9 vols. (Washington, 1964), 7:176 ff.; and Richard P. Strong, George Shattuck *et al., Typhus Fever with Particular Reference to the Serbian Epidemic* (Cambridge, Mass., 1920).

7. Harvey Cushing, *A Surgeon's Journal, 1915–1918* (Boston, 1936), p. 52. The War Department has published an exhaustive, indeed exhausting account: *The Medical Department of the United States Army in the World War*, 15 vols. (Washington, 1923–24). A new and concise account is currently in preparation: Mary C. Gillett, *The Army Medical Department, 1917–1941* (forthcoming).

1. Before the Battle

1. Crawford Sams, "Medic," unpublished memoir, undated, p. 101, copies in CMH, and Uniformed Services University of the Health Sciences, Bethesda, Md.
2. Lamont Pugh, *Navy Surgeon* (Philadelphia, [1959]), p. 126; Ernest R. Eaton, "The Medical Reserve Officer of the United States Navy Afloat," *War Medicine*, 1 (March 1941): 188–95. Eaton's article apparently is based upon his experience of active duty at sea during the 1930s.
3. Madeline M. Ullom, "The Philippines Assignment: Some Aspects of the Army Nurse Corps in the Philippine Islands, 1940–1945," unpublished memoir, n.d., in CMH.
4. *Report of the Surgeon General, U.S. Army, to the Secretary of War, 1939* (Washington, 1940), pp. 3, 172; *The History of the Medical Department of the United States Navy in World War II*, NAVMED P-5031, (2 vols. Washington, 1953), 1:1. The navy history will hereafter be cited as *Navy Medical Department in World War II*.
5. Leigh C. Fairbank, "The Dental Service in the Military Establishment," *The Military Surgeon*, 88 (January 1941): 29–31; R. A. Kelser, "Veterinary Service in the Defense Effort," *The Military Surgeon*, 90 (March 1942): 266–72; Frank E. Etter, "The United States Navy Dental Officer in Combat," *The Military Surgeon*, 96 (May 1945): 408–12; *Navy Medical Department in World War II*, 1:128–32.
6. Tom F. Whayne, Sr., M.D., in his comments on the draft of this volume, pointed out to me that life on the small, stable Regular Army posts during the 1930s formed a partial exception to this rule: "One developed a devoted and loyal coterie of patients who were upset not to see 'their doctor.' . . . For the unmarried noncommissioned officers and enlisted men [however] your thesis is for the most part valid." Review and critique, April 1993, in author's possession.

7. Sams, "Medic," p. 25; Colonel Robert B. McLean, "Leonard D. Heaton, Military Surgeon," *Military Medicine* 147 (September 1982): 717.
8. On Kirk, see his obituary in the Washington *Sunday Star*, August 14, 1960.
9. Edward D. Churchill, *Surgeon to Soldiers: Diary and Records of the Surgical Consultant, Allied Force Headquarters, World War II* (Philadelphia and Toronto, 1972), p. 29.
10. I am indebted for these insights to the medical historian Dale Smith of the Uniformed Services University of the Health Sciences.
11. Interview with Colonel Harry L. Berman, MC, USA (Ret.), Bethesda, Md., April 10, 1993.
12. On medical mobilization in the Army, see Clarence McKittrick Smith, *Hospitalization and Evacuation, Zone of Interior*, United States Army in World War II series (Washington, 1968), pp. 3–168; Blanche K. Armfield, *Organization and Administration in World War II*, Medical Department, United States Army, in World War II series (Washington, 1971), pp. 13–41; John H. McMinn and Max Levin, *Personnel in World War II* (Washington, 1963), pp. 111–66; *Annual Report of the Surgeon General* (1940), pp. 172–93, and (1941), pp. 141–42, 153–54. On training of enlisted medics, see also William E. Looby, "Medical Replacement Training Center, Camp Grant, Illinois," *The Military Surgeon*, 91 (July 1942): 157–60. Important topics in medical mobilization will be treated at greater length in later chapters.
13. Smith, *Hospitalization and Evacuation*, pp. 3–7; Armfield, *Organization and Administration*, pp. 24–25, 36–39.
14. *Navy Medical Department in World War II*, 1:1; *Report of the Surgeon General, U.S. Army, to the Secretary of War, 1941* (Washington, 1941), pp. 143, 243.
15. Eli Ginzberg, James K. Anderson, Sol W. Ginsburg, MD, and John L. Herms, *The Ineffective Soldier: The Lost Divisions*, 3 vols. (New York, 1959), 1:12.
16. William B. Foster, Ida Levin Hellman, Douglas Hesford, and Darrell G. McPherson, *Physical Standards in World War II* (Washington, 1967), pp. 1–3; *Physical Examination of Selective Service Registrants*, Special Monograph no. 15 (Washington: Selective Service System, 1947), pp. 78–79; *Selective Service in Peacetime: First Report of the Director of Selective Service, 1940–41* (Washington, 1941), p. 211. Failure by Selective Service to provide a dental examination was a serious error; dental problems accounted for the majority of rejections. See Colonel Leonard G. Rowntree, "Some Problems of Selective Service," *Military Surgeon*, 90 (March 1942): 240. Rowntree was chief of the medical division of the Selective Service System. On causes of rejection and the racial differential, see Leonard G. Rowntree, Kenneth H. McGill, and Thomas I. Edwards, "Causes of Rejection and the Incidence of Defects in 18 and 19 Year Old Selective Service Registrants,"

Journal of the American Medical Association, (hereafter *JAMA*), 123 (September 1943): p. 181–85.

17. *Selective Service in Peacetime*, pp. 209–11; Bill Mauldin, *The Brass Ring* (New York, 1971), p. 80.

18. Rowntree, "Problems of Selective Service," pp. 238–45; Lewis B. Hershey, "Medicine and Selective Service," *JAMA*, 117 (November 1941): 1894–97, and "The Selective Service and Its Medical Problems, *JAMA*, 119 (August 1942): 1205–6; "Guide to Physical Examination of Registrants (Medical Circular no. 3)," *JAMA*, 121 (March 1943): 949–50.

19. Hershey, "Medicine and Selective Service," p. 1897.

20. "Army to Train Psychologists to Sift Illiterate Selectees," *JAMA*, 120 (October 1940): 541; "The Prehabilitation of Registrants: A Plan for Rendering Registrants Fit for Examination and Service," *JAMA*, 116 (April 1941): 1777–78; Charles F. Reynolds, "Rehabilitation and Follow Up of Selective Service Men Rejected for Military Service," *The Military Surgeon*, 90 (March 1942): 232–37; "Physical Rehabilitation of Registrants," *JAMA*, 118 (January 1942): 383–85.

21. The General Classification Test administered to recruits was developed by psychologists working for the Adjutant General of the Army and the Selective Service System. Later in the war, specialized tests for a variety of special needs and duties were developed by psychologists working for, or in conjunction with, the Army and Navy Medical Corps. See Donald S. Napoli, "The Mobilization of American Psychologists, 1938–1941," *Military Affairs*, 42 (February 1978): 32–36.

22. Uno H. Helgesson, "The Scope of Psychiatry in Military Medicine with Special Reference to the Navy," *U.S. Naval Medical Bulletin*, 40 (January 1942): 80; Theodore J. C. von Storch and George O. Pratt, "Neuropsychiatric Examination for Induction or Enlistment in the Army, *The Military Surgeon*, 88 (June 1941): 630–31. See also C. L. Wittson *et al.*, "Detection of the Neuropsychiatrically Unfit," *U.S. Naval Medical Bulletin*, 40 (April 1942): 342; Crawford N. Baganz *et al.*, "So-Called 'Shell Shock': Types, Etiological Factors and Means for Its Prevention," *The Military Surgeon*, 88 (March 1941): 282–86; James A. Brussel, "Military Psychiatry," *The Military Surgeon*, 88 (May 1941): 539–41; Foster *et al.*, *Physical Standards in World War II*, pp. 195–96.

23. Eli Ginzberg, John L. Herma, and Sol W. Ginsburg, *Psychiatry and Military Manpower Policy: A Reappraisal of the Experience in World War II* (New York, 1953), pp. 10, 12–13.

24. *Ibid.*, pp. 14–17.

25. Foster *et al.*, *Physical Standards in World War II*, pp. 36–42, 106. In a study conducted by Columbia University in 1953, the vast majority of psychiatrists who responded disavowed their earlier "enthusiastic belief" in psychi-

atric screening as practiced in World War II and asserted that "only those individuals with a clear history of psychotic behavior and those with very severe neuroses which are certain to interfere with performance in a military environment should be kept out of service. This change in attitude [added the authors of the study] is as complete as it is striking." Ginzberg *et al.*, *Psychiatry and Military Manpower Policy*, pp. 20–21.

26. Colonel King to Editor of the History of the Medical Department, U.S. Army, in World War II, March 22, 1950, p. 6 (italics in original), in CMH; Mary Ellen Condon-Rall, "The U.S. Army Medical Department and the Attack on Pearl Harbor," *The Journal of Military History*, 53 (January 1989): 65–78.

27. On naval preparations, see "The United States Navy Medical Department at War, 1941–1945," prepared by the Bureau of Medicine and Surgery, Navy Department, 1946, pp. 1–2, 11. Copies in the Bureau of Medicine and Surgery, Washington, D.C. (BuMed), and CMH. Hereafter cited as "Navy Medical Department at War."

28. On sulfa drugs, see Dowling, *Fighting Infection*, pp. 107–23; Lewis Thomas, *The Youngest Science: Notes of a Medicine Watcher* (New York, 1983), p. 35; Henry K. Mohler, "The Therapeutic Use of Sulfanilamide and Related Compounds," *The Military Surgeon*, 88 (May 1941): 473–86.

29. Pugh, *Navy Surgeon*, p. 153; Obituary, "John J. Moorhead," *JAMA*, 165 (September 1957): 79; Moorhead, "Surgical Experience at Pearl Harbor," *JAMA*, 118 (February 1942): 712; *The Honolulu Advertiser*, December 2, 1941, p. 8, and December 7, 1941, p. 3.

2. Awakening to War

1. Gordon W. Prange, *At Dawn We Slept: The Untold Story of Pearl Harbor* (New York: 1981), pp. 505 ff; Hilda W. Combes, "First Year on the Solace," p. 2, ms. in Solace File, BuMed Archives. A version of this essay was later published in *Woman's Day*, June 1943, pp. 24 ff.

2. "Navy Medical Department at War," (ch. 1, note 27), pp. 1–2, 11. The *Solace* was to be a feature of many Pacific campaigns; she had been a tour ship in civilian service, the Clyde Line's *Iroquois*.

3. George A. Eckert, "The 'Solace' in Action," *U.S. Naval Medical Bulletin*, 40 (July 1942): 552–57.

4. "First Hand Lessons at Pearl Harbor: Fleet Medical Newsletter," *The Army Medical Bulletin*, no. 61 (April 1942), pp. 9–12; Newton T. Saxe, "Burns en Masse," *U.S. Naval Medical Bulletin*, 40 (July 1942): 570–76. About 15 percent of the burn cases died in the first thirty-six hours. Tannic acid formed a leathery eschar (scab) that supposedly protected the injury, but the chemical was later shown by researchers to be toxic, and its use was aban-

doned. See Oliver Cope, "The Burn Problem," in E. C. Andrus *et al.*, eds., *Advances in Military Medicine Made by Investigators Working Under the Sponsorship of the Committee on Medical Research*, 2 vols. (Boston, 1948) 1:149–58.

5. Quote in I. S. Ravdin and Perrin S. Long, "The Problems of the Hickam Station Hospital, the Tripler General Hospital, and the Schofield Station Hospital," p. 5, in CMH; see also John J. Moorhead, "Surgical Experience at Pearl Harbor," *JAMA*, 118 (February 1942): 712–14; Mary Ellen Condon-Rall, "The U.S. Army Medical Department and the Attack on Pearl Harbor," *The Journal of Military History*, 53 (January 1989): 65–78. A more detailed account of army medicine in the Pacific war will be found in a volume to be published by the Center of Military History: Mary Ellen Condon-Rall and Albert E. Cowdrey, *Medical Service in the War Against Japan*, ch. 1. The manuscript will hereafter be cited as MSWJ.

6. J. E. Strode, "Reminiscences of a Surgeon at Pearl Harbor," *Review of Surgery*, 22 (1965): 229–33; Honolulu *Advertiser*, December 7, 1941, p. 3.

7. I. S. Ravdin and Perrin S. Long, "The Treatment of Army Casualties in Hawaii," *Army Medical Bulletin*, no. 61 (April 1942), pp. 1–8; Tripler General Hospital, 1941, Annual Report, p. 19. For a wide-ranging review of injuries and treatment at Pearl Harbor, see "Symposium: Disposition of War Casualties," in *Hawaii Medical Journal*, 2 (September–October 1942): 17–46, comprising eight articles by military surgeons.

8. Wibb E. Cooper, "Medical Department Activities in the Philippines from 1941 to 6 May 1942, and Including Medical Activities in Japanese Prisoner of War Camps," pp. 5–47, in CMH; Mary Ellen Condon-Rall, "U.S. Army Medical Preparations and the Outbreak of War: The Philippines, 1941- 6 May 1942," *The Journal of Military History*, 56 (January 1992): 35–56.

9. Ullom, "Philippine Assignment" (ch. 1, note 3).

10. Quote in Alfred A. Weinstein, *Barbed Wire Surgeon* (New York, 1948), p. 2. Because of the International Date Line, the initial air attacks on the Philippines came on December 8, 1941.

11. *Ibid.*, p. 52.

12. *Ibid.*, p. 53.

13. "Navy Medical Department at War," p. 36.

14. Quote from Julien M. Goodman, *M.D.P.O.W.* (New York, 1972), p. 14; see also James O. Gillespie, "Malaria and the Defense of Bataan," in Ebbe Curtis Moff, *Preventive Medicine in World War II: Communicable Diseases (Malaria)*, 9 vols. (Washington, 1963), 6: 497–512. General Hospital Number One was moved after an Allied retreat to Mariveles on the extreme south of Bataan and was set up in a site called Little Baguio.

15. James O. Gillespie, "Recollections of the Pacific War and Japanese Prisoner

of War Camps, 1941–1945," pp. 1–13, ms. history in CMH; Gillespie, "Malaria and the Defense of Bataan," 6:500.

16. Florence MacDonald, "Nursing the Sick and Wounded at Bataan and Corregidor," *Hospitals*, 16 (December 1942): 33; Cooper, "Medical Department Activities," pp. 35, 44–45; Louis Morton, *The Fall of the Philippines*, United States Army in World War II Series (Washington, 1953), pp. 367–68.

17. Cooper, "Medical Department Activities," p. 53; MacDonald, "Nursing Sick and Wounded" pp. 31–33; Mary Ellen Condon-Rall, interview with Percy J. Carroll, September 29, 1980, in CMH.

18. See Juanita Redmond, *I Served on Bataan* (Philadelphia and New York, 1943), pp. 46–56; Cooper, "Medical Department Activities in the Philippines," p. 66.

19. Gillespie, "Malaria and the Defense of Bataan," pp. 509–10; Saburo Ienaga, *The Pacific War: World War II and the Japanese, 1931–1945* (New York, 1978), p. 140.

20. Gillespie, "Malaria and the Defense of Bataan," p. 511.

21. General Edward P. King, "Recollections of the Defense Battles in Bataan," in notebook of James Gillespie, in CMH; Morton, *Fall of the Philippines*, pp. 404, 458, 463.

22. Redmond, *I Served on Bataan*, p. 134.

23. Quoted in Morton, *Fall of the Philippines*, pp. 544–45.

24. Philip A. Towle, "Japanese Treatment of Prisoners in 1904–05: Foreign Officers' Reports," *Military Affairs*, 39 (October 1975): 115–17.

25. Edward J. Drea, "In the Army Barracks of Imperial Japan," *Armed Forces and Society*, 15 (Spring 1989): 329–48.

26. Stanley Falk, *Bataan: The March of Death* (New York, 1962); Alfred A. Weinstein, *Barbed-Wire Surgeon*, (New York, 1948), p. 72; James O. Gillespie, "Recollections of Pacific War and Japanese POW Camps," pp. 111–12; Cooper, "Medical Department Activities," p. 116; W. H. Waterous, "Reminiscences of Dr. W. H. Waterous Pertinent to World War II in the Philippines," pp. 68–70, unpublished memoir, in CMH.

27. Charles G. Roland, "Stripping Away the Veneer: P.O.W. Survival in the Far East as an Index of Cultural Atavism," *The Journal of Military History*, 53 (January 1989): 79–84; Waterous, "Reminiscences"," p. 102.

28. Condon-Rall and Cowdrey, *MSWJ*, Chapter 13; file on *Oryoku Maru–Enoura Maru–Brazil Maru*, Box 148, Record Group 407 (Philippine Archives), National Archives, Washington, D.C. (NARA).

29. Jan K. Herman, "Prison Diary," *U.S. Navy Medicine*, 70 (1979), Part 2: 6. See also Weinstein, *Barbed-Wire Surgeon*, pp. 190–99, 272–84; E. Bartlett Kerr, *Surrender and Survival: The Experience of American POWs in the Pacific, 1941–1945* (New York, 1985), p. 176.

30. *MSWJ*, ch. 11; Knox, *Death March*, p. 377; Goodman, *M.D.P.O.W.*, pp. 185–86.

31. Weinstein, *Barbed-Wire Surgeon*, pp. 189–211; "Prisoner of War Camps in Japan and Japanese Controlled Areas, as Taken from Reports of Interned American Prisoners," July 31, 1946, pp. 7, 49, 118, in Historical Ms. 4-4.5A AA, and "History of the Non-Military Activities of the Occupation of Japan: Trials of Class 'B' and 'C' War Criminals," Historical Ms. 8-5 AA2, pp. 112, 115, and 183–201, both mss. in CMH.

32. The classic study of this aspect of the war is John W. Dower, *War Without Mercy: Race and Power in the Pacific War* (New York, 1986).

3. Medics Afloat and Ashore

1. See Robert Sherrod's description in *On to Westward: War in the Central Pacific* (New York, 1945), pp. 119–24; Combes, "First Year on the Solace" (ch. 2, note 1), p. 3.

2. "Navy Medical Department at War" (ch. 1, n. 27), pp. 106–7; *Navy Medical Department in World War II*, 1: 133–45; John H. Robbins, "Experiences in a Theater of Operations," *Bulletin of the American College of Surgeons*, 29 (June 1994): 106–7.

3. Interview with William Jordan, MD, Bethesda, Md., April 9, 1993.

4. Jordan interview; James J. Fahey, *Pacific War Diary, 1942–1945* (Westport, Conn., n.d.), p. 48.

5. Fahey, *Pacific War Diary*, p. 66.

6. Gerald W. Smith, "Conversion of Cruiser into Temporary Hospital Ship," *The Military Surgeon*, 94 (March 1944): 204–12 (quote on p. 204).

7. Smith, "Conversion of Cruiser," pp. 205–6.

8. Samuel Eliot Morison, *The Struggle for Guadalcanal, August 1942–February 1943*, vol 5 in *History of United States Naval Operations in World War II*, 14 vols. (Boston, 1964), pp. 251–52; *Navy Medical Department in World War II*, p. 52.

9. Samuel Eliot Morison, *Coral Sea, Midway and Submarine Actions, May 1942–August 1942*, volume 4 in *Naval Operations in World War II*, 1:45; Charles W. Shilling, "Medical Problems of Submarine Warfare," *The Military Surgeon*, 96 (March 1945): 224. Pharmacist's mates were strongly discouraged from performing appendectomies, but three cases occurred anyway, all seemingly with successful outcomes. See, e.g., Jan Herman interview with Wheeler B. Lipes, November 1986, in Oral History File, BuMed Archives, Washington, D.C. I am indebted to Robert C. Bornmann, M.D., for his comments on submarine medicine.

10. Smith, "Conversion of Cruiser," pp. 208–9.

11. "History of U.S. Naval Research and Development in World War II," 5:1307–1309, in Naval Historical Center, Washington Navy Yard, Washington, D.C.; *Navy Medical Department in World War II*, 1:209–10.

12. *Navy Medical Department in World War II*, 1:210.
13. Condon-Rall and Cowdrey, *MSWJ*, ch. 4; John Miller, Jr., *Guadalcanal: The First Offensive*, United States Army in World War II series (Washington, 1949), pp. 1–21; Jack Coggins, *The Campaign for Guadalcanal: A Battle that Made History* (Garden City, New York, 1972), p. 28.
14. James Jones, *The Thin Red Line* (New York, 1962), p. 51; 1st Marine Division, Commander's Final Report on the Guadalcanal Operation, dated 25 June–1 July 1943, Phase V, File A7-5, Annex T, p. 2. In Marine Corps Historical Center (MCHC), Washington Navy Yard, Washington, D.C.
15. 1st Marine Division, Final Report, Phase I, in File no. A7-1, Annex M, p. 2, and Phase II, A7-2, Annex H, p. 1, in MCHC.
16. Quote in "Navy Medical Department at War," p. 27; 1st Marine Division, Final Report, Phase V, File no. A7-5, Annex T, p. 7, in MCHC.
17. Edward L. Smith, "Still Bravely Singing," *Hospital Corps Quarterly*, 17 (January 1944): 5.
18. 1st Marine Division, Final Report, Phase III, File no. A7-3, pp. 11, 13, in MCHC.
19. John Hersey, *Into the Valley: A Skirmish of the Marines* (New York, 1943), pp. 100, 112.
20. *Ibid.*, pp. 8, 18.
21. 1st Marine Division, Final Report, Phase IV, File no. A7-4, pp. 3–4, in MCHC.
22. The most recent comprehensive study of the campaign states that the Battle of the Tenaru River actually occurred on a bayou or marshy inlet the Marines called Alligator Creek. Richard B. Frank, *Guadalcanal* (New York, 1990), p. 150.
23. 1st Marine Division, Final Report, Phase V, File no. A7-5, Annex T, p. 5, in MCHC.
24. Herbert S. Gaskill and Thomas Fitz-Hugh, Jr., "Toxic Psychosis Following Atabrine," *Army Medical Bulletin*, no. 86, March 1945, pp. 63–69.
25. Albert J. Glass, ed., *Neuropsychiatry in World War II: Overseas Theaters*, 2 vols. (Washington, 1973), 2: 626–27; "Navy Medical History," pp. 70–71; Jones, *Thin Red Line*, p. 79; S. J. Merro, "Report of Two Cases of Toxicity to Atabrine," *The Military Surgeon*, 89 (October 1941): 668–70.
26. Miller, *Guadalcanal: First Offensive*, pp. 210, 227
27. Hoff, ed., *Preventive Medicine in World War II: Communicable Diseases, Malaria* (ch. 2, note 14), pp. 423, 426.
28. Richard Tregaskis, *Guadalcanal Diary* (New York, 1943), p. 169. Dengue was carried by *Aedes* rather than *Anopheles* mosquitoes, and as a result its occurrence did not necessarily coincide with that of malaria, for the different species have widely varied habitats and habits.
29. Quoted in "Navy Medical Department at War," p. 85.

30. "Jap Medical Problems in the South and Southwest Pacific, 25 December 1944," p. 9, in File Documents of Current Interest to Dr. Pincoffs, in Pincoffs Papers, Military History Institute Carlisle Barracles, Carlisle, Pa. (MHI); Frank, *Guadalcanal*, p. 260.

31. Miller *Guadalcanal: First Offensive*, pp. 155, 159; Frank, *Guadalcanal*, pp. 338, 354.

32. Frank, *Guadalcanal*, p. 407.

33. USS *Wasp*, After Action Report, Ser. 006, Report of Medical Officer B. W. Hogan, September 22, 1942, p. 1; USS *Hornet*, After Action report, Ser. 00100, Annex L, Report of Acting Ship's Medical Officer Lt. Cmdr. E. H. Osterhoh, October 30, 1942 (entire), both in Operational Archives, Naval Historical Center.

34. Frank, *Guadalcanal*, p. 298.

35. Edward C. Kenney, "Experiences in a Theater of Operations", *Bulletin of the American College of Surgeons*, 29 (June 1944): 110–16.

36. Captured Japanese Diaries, Excerpts, December 1942–January 1943, p. 3, in Box marked "World War II Service", in collection The Infantry: The Americal Division Papers, in MHI. See also Miller, *Guadalcanal: First Offensive*, p. 229.

37. Frank, *Guadalcanal*, p. 527.

38. "Jap Medical Problems in the South and Southwest Pacific", p. 7.

39. Frank, *Guadalcanal*, p. 588.

40. *Ibid.*, pp. 57–58.

41. Japanese Monograph no. 35, ms. no. 8-5.1 AC 35, Southeast Asia Operations Record, 17th Army Operations, vol. 2, pp. 49–50. Frank, *Guadalcanal*, pp. 613–14, gives the total of Japanese soldiers on Guadalcanal as 31,400 and the fatalities as 20,800, or 67 percent; he states that about 4,800 naval personnel also died ashore, for a total (on land) of 25,600.

42. Americans suffered about one quarter as many deaths as the Japanese, though they had twice as many men engaged.

4. The Green Hells

1. D. Clayton James, *The Years of MacArthur*, 3 vols. (Boston, 1970), 2:247.

2. Lida Mayo, *Bloody Buna* (New York, 1974), p. 48; Allan S. Walker, *The Island Campaigns* (Canberra, 1957), p. 16; Raymond Paull, *Retreat from Kokoda* (Melbourne, 1958), p. 174.

3. "Jap Medical Problems in the South and Southwest Pacific," (ch. 3, note 30), p. 4; H. D. Steward, *Recollections of a Regimental Medical Officer* (Melbourne, 1983), pp. 90, 161; Alison Pilger, "Courage, Endurance and Initiative: Medical Evacuation from the Kokoda Track, August–October 1942," *War and Society*, 11 (May 1993): 53–72.

4. Japanese Monograph no. 37, 18th Army Operations, vol. 1, p. 64. Micro-

film copy at Command and General Staff School, Fort Leavenworth, Kansas.

5. *Ibid.*, pp. 66–67.
6. "Jap Medical Problems in the South and Southwest Pacific," p. 22.
7. *Ibid.*, p. 21.
8. Robert L. Eichelberger, *Our Jungle Road to Tokyo* (New York, 1950), p. 23.
9. Mayo, *Bloody Buna*, pp. 145–68; Samuel V. Milner, *Victory in Papua*, United States Army in World War II series (Washington, 1957), pp. 260–321; Colonel S. A. Challman, Report of a trip through Base Sections 2 and 3 and U.S.A. Advanced Base, March 5, 1943, p. 9, in File HD 333, CMH. Among others, enlisted medics Private Hymie Y. Epstein and T/5 Edwin C. DeRosier were awarded the Distinguished Service Cross posthumously; both were killed while aiding the wounded.
10. Milner, *Victory in Papua*, pp. 323–24 (quotes); *Report of the Commanding General, Buna Forces, on the Buna Campaign, Dec. 1, 1942–Jan. 25, 1943* (n.p., n.d. [1943]), p. 105.
11. "Histories of Portable Hospitals in World War II: 3rd Portable Hospital," p. 6, May 14, 1943, in CMH.
12. *Report of Commanding General, Buna Forces*, p. 79.
13. George Wheeler, "With a Portable Hospital in New Guinea," n.d., in CMH.
14. Robert F. Futrell, "Development of Aeromedical Evacuation in the USAF, 1909–1960," USAF Historical Studies, no. 23 (Air University, May 1960), p. 6, copy in CMH.
15. *Ibid.*, p. 104.
16. Marion M. Kalez, "Observations on the Odd and Strange War in the Pacific," *Journal of Aviation Medicine*, 15 (April 1944): 85.
17. Memorandum, Lieutenant Colonel H. S. Tubbs to Chief Surgeon, United States Army Forces in the South Pacific Area, June 6, 1943, in File no. 370.5; Surgeon, XIV Corps, Medical Experience, New Georgia, pp. 15–16, File no. 370, both in CMH. See also "Navy Medical Department at War," 1:95–96. For a more detailed account of army medical care on New Georgia, see Condon-Rall and Cowdrey, *MSWJ*, ch. 6.
18. Japanese Monograph no. 35, vol. 2, p. 75, in CMH.
19. *Navy Medical Department in World War II*, 1:75.
20. Ashley W. Oughterson, "From Auckland to Tokyo," *Surgery in World War II: Activities of Surgical Consultants* (Washington, 1964), p. 786.
21. "Navy Medical Department at War," 1:108.
22. Surgeon, XIV Corps, Medical Experience, New Georgia, p. 23.
23. Buell Whitehill, "Administrative History of Medical Activities in the Middle Pacific," Office of the Surgeon, HUSAFMIDPAC, Block 18G, p. 36, in CMH. Hereafter cited as Whitehill, "Middle Pacific History." For a fuller treatment of combat fatigue, its causes, and its treatment, see Chapter 7.

24. Surgeon, XIV Corps, Medical Experience, New Georgia, Summary.
25. Quote from Whayne, review and critique (ch. 1, note 6) p. 9.
26. James H. Stone, ed., *Crisis Fleeting: Original Reports on Military Medicine in India and Burma in the Second World War* (Washington, 1969), p. 295.
27. Charlton Ogburn, Jr., *The Marauders* (New York, 1959), p. 5.
28. Charles F. Romanus and Riley Sunderland, *Stilwell's Command Problems* (Washington, 1956), p. 285; James H. Stone, "United States Army Medical Service in Combat in India and Burma," p. 163, ms. History, in CMH.
29. Stone, *Crisis Fleeting*, pp. 346–47.
30. *Ibid.*, p. 354.
31. Romanus and Sunderland, *Stilwell's Command Problems*, pp. 287–88; Stone, "United States Army Medical Service in Combat in India and China, 1942–1946," *passim*, in CMH.

5. Gearing Up

1. Forrest C. Pogue, *George C. Marshall: Ordeal and Hope* (New York, 1966), p. 289.
2. Whayne, review and critique (ch. 1, note 6), p. 10.
3. Armfield, *Organization and Administration*, (ch. 1, note 12), p. 145, 148; R. L. Parker *et al.*, *Medical Department, United States Army: Medical Supply in World War II* (Washington, 1968), pp. 11–12; *Investigation of Manpower Resources*, Hearings on Senate Resolution 291, 77th Cong., 2d Sess. (Washington, 1942–43).
4. Physical survival was another matter; he lived to the age of ninety-two. See Magee's obituary in the Washington *Star*, October 16, 1975. On discrimination, see McMinn and Levin, *Personnel in World War II* (ch. 1, note 12), 317; Robert J. Parks, "The Development of Segregation in U. S. Army Hospitals, 1940–42," *Military Affairs*, 37 (December 1973): 145.
5. Memorandum, Chief of Staff for Secretary of War [February 21, 1942], subject: Appointment of Surgeon General, quoted in Armfield, *Organization and Administration*, p. 200.
6. Memorandum, Secretary of War for the President, February 25, 1943, subject: Recommendation for Appointment of Surgeon General, quoted in *ibid.*, p. 201.
7. On Kirk, see his obituary in the Washington *Sunday Star*, August 14, 1960.
8. Secretary of War to the President, April 10, 1943, quoted in Armfield, *Organization and Administration*, p. 202.
9. "Navy Medical Department at War," p. 2:18. During the same period the strength of the Navy and Marine Corps increased from 149,000 to 349,000. McIntire's role as Roosevelt's physician has lately come in for a great deal of criticism. See Bert Edward Parks, MD, *The Impact of Illness on*

World Leaders (Philadelphia, 1986), pp. 222–85; James MacGregor Burns, *Roosevelt, 1940–1945: The Soldier of Freedom* (New York, 1970), pp. 447–50; and Jan Herman interview with Dr. Howard G. Bruenn, in BuMed Archives, Washington, D.C.

10. See McIntire's testimony in Wadhams Committee Testimony, File no. HD:322, 3:1008–43, in CMH.

11. Vannevar Bush, *Pieces of the Action* (New York, 1970) is Bush's informal but informative autobiography.

12. Andrus *et al., Advances in Military Medicine* (ch. 2, note 4), 1: xli.

13. *Ibid.*, 1: xliii.

14. See Detlev W. Bronk, "Introduction to Aviation Medicine," in *ibid.*, 1:208–9.

15. See James G. Burrow, *AMA: Voice of American Medicine* (Baltimore, 1963), p. 285; "Speeding Production of Physicians," *JAMA*, 118 (January 1942): 229. The ASTP provided the medical schools with 20,336 students between May 1943 and October 1945.

16. "Procurement and Assignment Service for Physicians, Dentists, and Veterinarians," *JAMA*, 118 (January, 1942): 231.

17. Roscoe G. Leland, "A Census of Physicians for Military Preparedness," *War Medicine*, 1 (January 1941): 97.

18. "Procurement and Assignment Service for Physicians, Dentists and Veterinarians," *JAMA*, 117 (December 1941): 1984, and *JAMA* 118 (February 1942): 625–36; McMinn and Levin, *Personnel in World War II*, pp. 73–74.

19. McMinn and Levin, *Personnel in World War II*, pp. 281–82.

20. *Ibid.*, p. 283; testimony of Frank Lahey, MD, before the Wadhams Committee, n.d., Wadhams Committee Testimony, 3:703–50; "Procurement and Assignment Service," 118: 625–37.

21. "A Call to the Medical Profession," *JAMA*, 117 (December 1941): 2254.

22. Paul V. McNutt, "The Urgent Need for Doctors," *JAMA*, 119 (June 1942): 605–7.

23. "U.S. Senate Committee on Education and Labor, Report of Hearings Held Before a Subcommittee of Which Senator Claude Pepper Is Chairman," *JAMA*, 120 (November 1942): 927–29.

24. Burrow, *AMA*, pp. 282–83; "More Doctors Needed for the Armed Forces," *JAMA*, 122 (August 1943): 1016; George Q. Flynn, "American Medicine and Selective Service in World War II," *Journal of the History of Medicine and Allied Sciences*, 42 (July 1987): 309; testimony of Paul McNutt before the Wadhams Committee, 3:675–702; George F. Lull, "Fifty Thousand Doctors," in Morris Fishbein, ed., *Doctors at War* (New York, 1945), p. 94.

25. Major General Raymond W. Bliss, in Surgeon General's Conference Notes, 19 July 1950, cited in Albert E. Cowdrey, *The Medics' War* (Washington, 1987), p. 158.

26. Lull, "Fifty Thousand Doctors," p. 95.
27. Wadhams Report, recommendation no. 95, in CMH.
28. Richard V. N. Ginn, *The History of the U.S. Army Medical Service Corps* (forthcoming), p. 225 (quote), manuscript in CMH. Cited with permission of the author. See also McMinn and Levin, *Personnel in World War II*, pp. 10–15, and 319. By this time black enlisted medics had their own training facility at Camp Breckinridge in Virginia.
29. Quote from Lieutenant General Leonard D. Heaton in MacMinn and Levin, *Personnel in World War II*, p. xi; Samuel V. Milner, interview with Colonel Frederick H. Gibbs, MSC (Ret.) Washington, October 24, 1963, in CMH.
30. Ginn, *History of MSC*, pp. 254–60.
31. In 1947 the MAC was abolished, along with the small (and ill-named) Pharmacy Corps and the Sanitary Corps. All were then reincarnated as the Medical Service Corps, an arrangement that survives today.
32. Barbara W. Northrup *et al.*, "Organization of a Physiotherapy Section at an Army Hospital," *The Military Surgeon*, 91 (July 1942): 90–93; Helen S. Willard, "Salvaging the Nation's Man Power," *The Military Surgeon*, 91 (October 1942): 416–18.
33. Pauline E. Maxwell, "History of the Army Nurse Corps, 1775–1948," ch. 8, pp. 24–26, copy in CMH.
34. *Ibid.*, p. 39.
35. "The Cadet Nurse Corps," *JAMA*, 127 (April 1945): 995; *The United States Cadet Nurse Corps and Other Federal Nurse Training Programs*, Public Health Service Publication no. 38 (Washington, 1950), pp. 1–33; Brigadier General Charles C. Hillman, keynote address at banquet of the 147th District Rotary International, Stevens Hotel, Chicago, May 16, 1944. pp. 8–9, in Hillman File, no collection indicated, Military History Institute.
36. *U.S. Cadet Nurse Corps*, p. 46.
37. "The Wac in Hospital Service," *The Military Surgeon*, 96 (May 1945): 438; "Open First Hospital Corps School for Women," *JAMA*, 124 (January 1944): 303.
38. "Three Officers of Nurse Corps Awarded Silver Star," *JAMA*, 124 (April 1944): 992; Ruth Y. White, "At Anzio Beachhead," *American Journal of Nursing*, 44 (April 1944): 370–71. For a list of medals and other citations won by nurses during the war, see "The Nurses' Contribution to American Victory," *American Journal of Nursing*, 45 (September 1945): 683–84.
39. For the basic statement of national policy, see Ulysses Lee, *The Employment of Negro Troops*, United States Army in World War II series (Washington, 1966), p. 76.
40. Phillip McGuire, "Judge William H. Hastie and Army Recruitment, 1940–1942," *Military Affairs* 42 (April 1978): 75–79.

41. "The Liaison Committee of the N.M.A.," *Journal of the National Medical Association*, 33 (1941): 86–87, 92–94; Herbert M. Morais, *The History of the Afro-American in Medicine*, International Library of Afro-American Life and History (Cornwells Heights, Pa., 1976), p. 128.
42. "Report of Officers," *Journal of the National Medical Association*, 33 (1941): 178–79.
43. Parks, "Segregation in U.S. Army Hospitals," p. 145.
44. *Ibid.*, pp. 146–49.
45. Paul B. Cornely, "Distribution of Negro Physicians in the United States in 1942," *JAMA*, 124 (March 1944): 829.
46. Parks, "Segregation in U.S. Army Hospitals," p. 149.
47. On the British conscription of doctors, see C. L. Dunn, *The Emergency Medical Services*, vol. 1 in History of the Second World War: United Kingdom Medical Series (London, 1952), pp. 410–24.
48. Quoted in McMinn and Levin, *Personnel in World War II*, p. 74.

6. School of Battle

1. Medical manuals and casualty estimates seem to have been based on the outcome of disastrous Dieppe raid, where Canadian forces suffered heavy losses. See W. R. Feasby, *Official History of the Canadian Medical Services, 1939–1945* (Ottawa, 1956), pp. 113–22.
2. Major General Albert W. Kenner, "Medical Service in the North African Campaign," *Army Medical Bulletin*, no. 76, May 1944, p. 76; George F. Howe, *Northwest Africa: Seizing the Initiative in the West*, United States Army in World War II series (Washington, 1957), pp. 106–7; Charles M. Wiltse, *Medical Service in the Mediterranean and Minor Theaters*, United States Army in World War II series (Washington, 1965), pp. 107–9 (hereafter cited as *MSMT*); Ernie Pyle, *Here Is Your War* (New York, 1948), pp. 29–30.
3. Compilation of Reports on Lessons of Operation Torch, December 16, 1942, p. 30, in Allied Force, Mediterranean, Box 903, Operational Archives, Navy Historical Center; Theresa Archard, *G.I. Nightingale: The Story of an Army Nurse* (New York, 1945), pp. 48–49.
4. Wiltse, *MSMT*, pp. 120–21.
5. "Navy Medical Department at War," pp. 661–70; Wiltse, *MSMT*, pp. 111, 119; Archard, *G.I. Nightingale*, pp. 48–49; Martin Blumenson, *Kasserine Pass* (Cambridge, Mass., 1967), p. 57.
6. See, e.g., Klaus H. Huebner, *Long Walk Through War: A Combat Doctor's Diary* (College Station, Tex., 1987), p. 16.
7. Churchill, *Surgeon to Soldiers* (ch. 1, note 9), pp. 79–83.
8. *Ibid.*, p. 85.

9. Kenner, "Medical Service in North African Campaign," p. 74; Wiltse, *MSMT*, p. 124.

10. Churchill, *Surgeon to Soldiers*, p. 120 (quote); Wiltse, *MSMT*, p. 126; Archard, *G.I. Nightingale*, pp. 86–87.

11. Howard E. Snyder, "Fifth U.S. Army," in B. Noland Carter, ed., *Surgery in World War II: Activities of Surgical Consultants*, 2 vols. (Washington, 1962), 1:335.

12. Casualty estimates for Kasserine are notoriously hard to pin down. The estimate given here is from a new study by Roger Cirillo, *The Kasserine Battles*, to be published by CMH in 1994.

13. Churchill, *Surgeon to Soldiers*, p. 89.

14. Mae Mills Link and Hubert A. Coleman, *Medical Support of the Army Air Forces in World War II* (Washington, 1955), p. 427. At a later time, some hospitals were attached to airdromes.

15. *Ibid.*, p. 428. Malaria was not a problem at the time, because of the season; as will be seen, typhus, though much feared, caused no difficulties.

16. *Ibid.*, p. 482.

17. Wiltse, *MSMT*, p. 129.

18. Kenneth Macksey, *Crucible of Power: The Fight for Tunisia, 1942–1943* (London, 1969), p. xii; Pyle, *Here Is Your War*, pp. 232, 241, 259, 265.

19. Churchill, *Surgeon to Soldiers*, p. 165.

20. On typhus, see Zinsser, *Rats, Lice and History* (Introduction, note 6), pp. 229–39; Yves M. Biraud, "The Present Menace of Typhus Fever in Europe and the Means of Combatting It," *Bulletin of the Health Organization of the League of Nations*, 10 (1942–43): 3; Gaines M. Foster, "Typhus Disaster in the Wake of War: The American Polish Relief Expedition, 1919–1920," *Bulletin of the History of Medicine*, 55 (1981): 221–32; Albert E. Cowdrey, *War and Healing: Stanhope Bayne-Jones and the Maturing of American Medicine* (Baton Rouge and London, 1992), pp. 151–59.

21. Since the war, a number of drugs have been developed that are effective against typhus, including chloramphenicol, tetracycline, and doxycycline.

22. H. R. Cox and J. E. Bell, "Epidemic and Endemic Typhus: Protective Value for Guinea Pigs of Vaccine Prepared from Infected Tissues of the Developing Chick Embryo," *Public Health Reports*, 55 (1940): 110; John P. Fox, "Immunization Against Epidemic Typhus," *American Journal of Tropical Medicine and Hygiene*, 5 (May 1956): 464–79.

23. Stanhope Bayne-Jones, "The United States of America Typhus Commission," *Army Medical Bulletin*, no. 68, July 1943, p. 8, and *idem.* "Typhus Fevers" (Introduction, note 6), 7:176–274. See also materials in File IA, Box 1, Records Related to the Organization, Administration, and Policy of the U.S.A. Typhus Commission, Record Group 112, NARA, and in Folder March–April 1945, in United States of America Typhus Commission Papers,

National Library of Medicine, Bethesda, Maryland. Hereafter abbreviated NLM.

24. Cowdrey, *War and Healing*, pp. 154–55; materials in Folder November 1942–May 1943, USATC Papers, NLM.

25. G. Grenoilleau, "L'Epidemie de typhus en Algerie (1941–1942–1943)," *Archives de l'Institut Pasteur d'Algerie*, 22 (December 1944): 353–79.

26. Soper to Fox, September 2, 1943; Office of the Surgeon, NATOUSA, Circular Letter no. 43, November 11, 1943, subject: Typhus Fever Control. Both in Folder June 1943–November 1943, USATC Papers, NLM. See also F. L. Soper *et al.*, "Louse Powder Studies in North Africa (1943)," *Archives de l'Institut Pasteur d'Algerie*, 23 (September 1945): 183–223.

27. F. L. Soper, William A. Davis, Louis A. Riehl, and Floyd Markham, "Typhus Fever in Italy, and Its Control with Louse Powder," *American Journal of Hygiene*, 45 (May 1947): 305–54; *idem*, "Notes on Experience with Louse Powders in Control of Typhus in Italy, 1943 to 1945," in *Reunion Interamericano del Tifo, Mexico D.F. 7–13 Octobre 1945, Memorias* (Mexico City, 1946), pp. 441–50; Herbert D. Chalke, "Typhus: Experiences in the Central Mediterranean Force," *British Medical Journal*, 1 (June 29, 1946): 977 and 2 (July 6, 1946): 5. For a popular account, see Allen Raymond, "Now We Can Lick Typhus," *Saturday Evening Post*, April 22, 1944, pp. 14–15, 17.

28. Wiltse, *MSMT*, p. 149; Ernie Pyle, *Brave Men* (New York, 1944), pp. 11–12; Albert J. Garland and Howard McGraw Smyth, *Sicily and the Surrender of Italy*, U.S. Army in World War II series (Washington, 1965), p. 110; Carlo D'Este, *Bitter Victory: The Battle for Sicily, 1943* (New York, 1988), p. 153.

29. Action Report, Western Naval Task Force, the Sicilian Campaign, Operation "Husky," in Operational Archives, Naval Historical Center; Report on Sicilian Operation, Force Medical Officer, NAVNAW, BuMed Archives. Cited in Dale C. Smith, "LST(H) Medical Support off the Beach," paper read at the 1992 meeting of the Society for Military History, Fredericksburg, Virginia, pp. 7–8. As Smith noted, reports on the Mediterranean innovations soon reached the Pacific, where the LST was already being remodeled as an ambulance and floating hospital.

30. Wiltse, *MSMT*, pp. 162–66.

31. Garland and Smyth, *Sicily*, pp. 117, 171.

32. Wiltse, *MSMT*, p. 157.

33. *Ibid.*, p. 162.

34. See D'Este, *Bitter Victory*, pp. 467–68; *Health*, October 31, 1943, p. 11.

35. Churchill, *Surgeon to Soldiers*, pp. 229–31.

36. *Ibid.*, p. 238; Wiltse, *MSMT*, pp. 162–65.

37. Churchill, *Surgeon to Soldiers*, pp. 217, 222–23; Archard, *G.I. Nightingale*, pp. 160–62.

38. Wiltse, *MSMT*, p. 165; Garland and Smyth, *Sicily*, p. 419.
39. Wiltse, *MSMT*, pp. 172–73.
40. See "Medical Problems in the Recent Sicilian Campaign," ASF Monthly Progress Report, October 31, 1943, Sect. 7: *Health*, pp. 10–12. This report attributes a two-division loss to malaria alone. Cf. D'Este, *Bitter Victory*, 1990 edition, p. 402n.

7. The Stress of Combat

1. Pyle, *Here Is Your War* (ch. 6, note 2), pp. 247, 173, 245.
2. Wiltse, *MSMT*, p. 145.
3. *Ibid.*, p. 172; Roger J. Spiller, "Shell Shock," *American Heritage*, May–June 1990, pp. 78–79. Combat fatigue was most common in the fighting elements of the army and the Marine Corps, followed by the Army Air Forces; rates in the navy were always low, except under kamikaze attack. See Brian H. Chermol, "Wounds Without Scars: Treatment of Battle Fatigue in the U.S. Armed Forces in the Second World War," *Military Affairs*, 49 (January 1985): 9–12.
4. Interview with Leon D. Gurjon, medical officer with the 182d Regimental Combat Team, August 20, 1943, p. 3, in CMH.
5. Chief Surgeon, SWPA, 1945 Annual Report, p. 49; Challman, Report of a trip through Base Section 2 and 3 and USA Advanced base, March 5, 1943; Albert J. Glass, ed., *Neuropsychiatry in World War II* (ch. 3, note 25), 2: 748–49.
6. The similarity of the symptoms in some afebrile malaria cases to those in combat exhaustion cases was also noted among Canadian troops in the Italian campaign. See Terry Copp and Bill McAndrew, *Battle Exhaustion: Soldiers and Psychiatrists in the Canadian Army, 1939–1945* (Montreal, 1990), p. 55. On the slapping incident, see Garland and Smyth, *Sicily*, (ch. 6, note 28), pp. 426–31; D'Este, *Bitter Victory* (ch. 6, note 28), pp. 483–96.
7. Garland and Smyth, *Sicily*, p. 427.
8. *Ibid.*, p. 431. On Patton's personality—which featured a bold, brutal warrior image masking deep feelings of inadequacy and unworthiness—see Martin Blumenson, *Patton: The Man Behind the Legend, 1895–1945* (New York, 1985); D'Este, *Bitter Victory*, pp. 127–41.
9. Glass, *Neuropsychiatry in World War II*, 2:458–63; Roy D. Halloran and Malcolm J. Farrell, "School of Military Neuropsychiatry for the Army," *Army Medical Bulletin*, no. 68, July 1943, pp. 195–98.
10. Glass, *Neuropsychiatry in World War II*, 2:1; Copp and McAndrew, *Battle Exhaustion*, pp. 16, 18, 25, 50.
11. Albert J. Glass, "Psychosomatic Medicine," in W. Paul Havens, Jr., ed., *Internal Medicine in World War II: Infectious Diseases and Internal Medicine, 3*

vols. (Washington, 1968), 3:705; Archard, *G.I. Nightingale* (ch. 6, note 3), p. 108.

12. Glass, *Neuropsychiatry in World War II*, 2: 8–9.

13. *Ibid.*, 2: 6.

14. Pearce Bailey, Frankwood E. Williams, and Paul O. Komora, *Neuropsychiatry*, vol. 10 of *Medical Department of U.S. Army in World War* (Introduction, note 7) (Washington, 1929), pp. 313–20. "The rapid cure of these patients," the rules for psychoneurotic wards stated, "depends on food, sleep, exercise, and the hopeful attitude of those who come in contact with them" (p. 313).

15. Glass, *Neuropsychiatry in World War II*, 2: 9–10; Roy R. Grinker and John P. Spiegel, *War Neuroses in North Africa: The Tunisian Campaign (January–May 1943)* (New York, September 1943), p. 152.

16. Gerald N. Grob, "World War II and American Psychiatry," *The Psychohistory Review*, 19 (Fall 1990): 41–69; Frederick B. Hanson, *Combat Psychiatry: Experiences in the North African and Mediterranean Theaters of Operations, American Ground Forces, World War II* (Washington, 1949), p. 159.

17. Hanson, *Combat Psychiatry*, pp. 153–54; Glass, *Neuropsychiatry in World War II*, 2: 16–17.

18. Hanson, *Combat Psychiatry*, pp. vii–viii. In commenting on the draft of this volume, Robert J. T. Joy, MD, remarked, "Nowadays we say 'acute situational stress' as a diagnosis. This marries cause and response." In author's possession.

19. Hanson, *Combat Psychiatry*, p. ix.

20. In putting a practical system in place, Hanson and his colleagues passed beyond the British, who had hitherto been their mentors. The British psychiatrist with the Eighth Army, Brigadier G. W. B. James, understood the problem perfectly, but "the Eighth Army went into the difficult battles in Tunisia without a system of forward psychiatry and doctors evacuated most patients to Tripoli without attempting forward treatment." Copp and McAndrew, *Battle Exhaustion*, p. 47.

21. Wiltse, *MSMT*, p. 236; Pyle, *Brave Men*, p. 142 (quote).

22. Glenn R. Infield, *Disaster at Bari* (New York, 1971, reprint 1988), esp. pp. xi, 178–227; Stewart F. Alexander, "Medical Report of the Bari Harbor Casualties," *The Military Surgeon*, 101 (1947): 1–17.

23. *Health*, September 30, 1944, p. 10.

24. Quote from Pyle, *Brave Men*, p. 235.

25. "Problems of Medical Service at Anzio," *Health*, October 31, 1944, p. 12.

26. *Ibid.*

27. Tom F. Whayne and Michael E. DeBakey, *Cold Injury, Ground Type* (Washington, 1958), pp. 108–10; *Health*, October 31, 1944, p. 13.

28. Glass, *Neuropsychiatry in World War II*, 2: 39–40.

29. Wiltse, *MSMT*, p. 285; Glass, *Neuropsychiatry in World War II*, 2: 48.
30. Glass, *Neuropsychiatry in World War II*, 2: 50.
31. *Ibid.*, 1: 403; *Health*, August 31, 1944, pp. 10–11.
32. Glass, *Neuropsychiatry in World War II*, 1: 405.
33. "Neuropsychiatric Problem in the Southwest Pacific," *Health*, February 28, 1945, p. 7.
34. "Fifth Army Experience in the Italian Campaign," *Health*, March 31, 1945, p. 7.

8. Wounded in Action

1. Richard Tregaskis, *Invasion Diary* (New York, 1944), p. 201.
2. *Ibid.*, p. 208.
3. Wiltse, *MSMT*, pp. 187, 189, 196.
4. *Ibid.*, pp. 195–96.
5. Graham A. Cosmas and Albert E. Cowdrey, *The Medical Department: Medical Service in the European Theater of Operations*, U.S. Army in World War II series (Washington, 1992), p. 377, 456, 532. Hereafter cited as *MSETO*.
6. Quoted in Cowdrey, *Medic's War* (ch. 5, note 25), p. 70.
7. Ralph W. French and George R. Callender, "Ballistic Characteristics of Wounding Agents," in James C. Beyer, ed., *Wound Ballistics* (Washington, 1962), pp. 115–33.
8. Michael E. DeBakey, ed., *Surgery in World War II: General Surgery*, (Washington, 1955), pp. 3–15.
9. Fred W. Rankin, "American Surgeons at War," in Fishbein, *Doctors at War* (ch. 5, note 24), p. 175.
10. Churchill, *Surgeon Among Soldiers* (ch. 7, note 9), p. 180.
11. Richard Hooker [pseud. of H. Richard Hornberger], *M*A*S*H* (New York, 1968), p. 160.
12. Quoted in Major General George F. Lull, "Problems Relating to Assignment of Duties of Military Surgeons," *JAMA*, 124 (January 1944): 105.
13. Rankin, "American Surgeons at War," p. 177.
14. Churchill, *Surgeon to Soldiers*, pp. 180–81.
15. Michael E. De Bakey, "Military Surgery in World War II: A Backward Glance and a Forward Look," *New England Journal of Medicine*, 236 (March, 1947), p. 347.
16. Churchill, *Surgeon to Soldiers*, p. 37.
17. *Ibid.*, pp. 5–6; The Board for the Study of the Severely Wounded, North African-Mediterranean Theater of Operations, *Surgery in World War II: The Physiologic Effects of Wounds* (Washington, 1952), pp. 1–13; Gerald Shortz, "Anesthesia in the Combat Zone," *Bulletin of the U.S. Army Medical De-*

partment, no. 79, (August 1944), pp. 60–65; Howard E. Snyder and James W. Culberson, "Study of Fifth U.S. Army Hospital Battle Casualty Deaths," in Beyer, *Wound Ballistics*, p. 488.

18. L. R. Newhauser and D. B. Kendrick, "Blood Substitutes: Their Development and Use in the Armed Services," *U.S. Naval Medical Bulletin*, 40 (January 1942): 1–13; John Elliott *et al.*, "Blood Plasma," *The Military Surgeon*, 88 (January 1941): 118–43. See also Board for the Study of the Severely Wounded, *Surgery in World War II: The Physiologic Effects of Wounds* (Washington, 1952), p. 6.

19. DeBakey, *General Surgery*, p. xiv.

20. Douglas B. Kendrick, *Blood Program in World War II* (Washington, 1964), p. 391; I. E. H. Whitby, "The British Army Blood Transfusion Service," *JAMA*, 124 (February, 1944): 421–24.

21. Whitby, "British Army Transfusion," pp. 418–19.

22. Cosmas and Cowdrey, *MSETO*, p. 174.

23. Kendrick, *Blood Program*, p.97; Churchill, *Surgeon to Soldiers*, p. 48.

24. Douglas B. Kendrick, "Prevention and Treatment of Shock in the Combat Zone," *Military Surgeon*, 88 (February 1941): 106. The earliest serious proposal for supplying whole blood to the battlefronts I have found was advanced by two physicians at the State University of Iowa. See Elmer L. De-Gowin and Robert C. Hardin, "A Plan for Collection, Transportation, and Administration of Whole Blood and of Plasma in Warfare," *War Medicine*, 1 (May 1941): 326.

25. Charles E. Wynes, *Charles Richard Drew: the Man and the Myth* (Urbana, Ill., 1988), p. 67.

26. Parks, "Segregation in U.S. Army Hospitals" (ch. 5, n. 4), p. 148; "Again, the American Red Cross Blood Bank," *Journal of the National Medical Association*, 35 (1943): 102.

27. Board for Study of Seriously Wounded, *Physiologic Effects of Wounds*, p. 8; DeBakey, *General Surgery*, 2: 21–23; Kendrick, *Blood Program*, p. 136.

28. Ray Crowder, *Iwo Jima Corpsman* (Gadsden, Ala., 1988), p. 61.

29. Kendrick, *Blood Program*, p. 394.

30. Henry Blake, "Pacific Whole Blood Program," July 27, 1988, ms. memoir, copy in author's collection.

31. Kendrick, *Blood Program*, p. 136.

32. Edward D. Churchill, "Surgical Management of Wounded in Mediterranean Theater at the Time of the Fall of Rome," *Bulletin of the U.S. Army Medical Department*, no. 84, January 1945, pp. 58–65; DeBakey, "Military Surgery in World War II," p. 345. Adoption of these ideas by the Army is reflected in the language used by the official technical bulletin, TB MED 147, March 1945, and reprinted in *Bulletin of the U.S. Army Medical Department*, 4 (September 1945): 246–47.

33. HQ Seventh Army, Circular Letter no. 2, Subject: Surgery, 18 July 1944, in Carter, *Activities of Surgical Consultants* (see ch. 6, note 11), 1:583, 587.

34. *Ibid.*, pp. 584–85.

35. *Ibid.*, p. 588.

36. Editorial, "Chest Surgery in Wartime," *Military Surgeon*, 97 (October 1945): 331; Clarence R. Straatsma, "Plastic and Reconstructive Surgery," *Military Surgeon*, 96 (March 1945): 255.

37. Tregaskis, *Invasion Diary*, pp. 208–40.

9. Jungle Victories

1. George A. Carden, "Malaria: Introduction," in Andrus *et al.*, *Advances in Military Medicine*, (ch. 2, note 4), 2:665–68

2. N. H. Fairlie, "Researches on Paludrine (M. 4888) in Malaria," *Transactions of the Royal Society of Tropical Medicine and Hygiene*, 40 (October 1946): 150–51; Hoff, *Malaria*, (ch. 2, note 14), 6:8–10.

3. Hoff, *Malaria*, 6:6.

4. *Ibid.*, 6:3.

5. *Ibid.*, 6:15; Mary Ellen Condon-Rall, "Allied Cooperation in Malaria Prevention and Control: The World War II Southwest Pacific Experience," *The Journal of the History of Medicine and Allied Sciences*, 46 (October 1991): 493–513.

6. Sanitation Branch, Annual Report (1943), pp. 33–34, in File no. 319.1-2, Box 18, RG 112, NARA. A school of malariology was established in the Panama Canal Zone under the army.

7. Japanese Monograph no. 35, vol. 2, p. 95, in CMH.

8. "Japanese Attack U.S. Naval Field Hospital During Operation," *JAMA*, 123 (December 1943): 909.

9. Hoff, *Malaria*, 6:2.

10. Hoff, *Malaria*, 6:513, 536–37; quote from Brigadier General Hugh J. Morgan, Chief of Medical Services, Office of the Surgeon General, "Comments and Recommendations to Medical Department, United States Army Forces, Far East, August 12, 1943," p. 4, in File Malaria: Historical Summary of Malaria Control in SWPA in 1942–43; MacArthur to Commanders, Allied Land Forces, Allied Air Forces, and Commanding General, United States Army Forces in the Far East, March 2, 1943, reproduced in Maurice C. Pincoffs, "History of Preventive Medicine, Southwest Pacific Area," pp. 3–4, in box labeled DAP 350-5 thru 385-5. Both in Pincoffs Papers, MHI.

11. Pincoffs, "History of Preventive Medicine, Southwest Pacific Area," p. 1.

12. *Ibid.*, p. 3.

13. Hoff, *Malaria*, 6:6 (quote).

14. Quote in Orth to Brigadier General Carroll, September 25, 1943, in File

Malaria, in Box Dr. Pincoffs Papers (B); copies of the newsletter File Malaria: Malaria Research Group—Administration (C-III-17). Both in Pincoffs Papers, MHI.

15. Draft report, Pincoffs to Chief Surgeon, USAFFE [August 1943?], in File Documents of Current Interest to Dr. Pincoffs, in MHI.

16. John Miller, Jr., *Cartwheel: The Reduction of Rabaul*, United States Army in World War II series (Washington, 1959), pp. 1–19, 26–27; Samuel Eliot Morison, *Breaking the Bismarcks Barrier: 22 July 1942—1 May 1944*, vol. 6 in *History of United States Naval Operations in World War II* (Boston, 1950), pp. 95–96; D. Clayton James, *The Years of MacArthur* 3 vols. (Boston, 1975), 2:308. On the development of landing craft, see Frank D. Hough, Merle E. Ludwig, and Henry L. Shaw, Jr., *Pearl Harbor to Guadalcanal* (Washington, 1978), pp. 23–34. On the engineer brigades, see William F. Heavey, *Down Ramp! The Story of the Army Amphibian Engineers* (Washington, 1947).

17. Command History, Seventh Amphibious Force, 10 January 1943–23 December 1945, Part II(e): Medical Services and Casualty Care, pp. II-63 and II-64. In Navy Historical Center, Washington Navy Yard (hereafter NHC).

18. *Ibid.*, p. II-66.

19. *Ibid.*, pp. II-76, 77.

20. David P. Adams, *"The Greatest Good to the Greatest Number": Penicillin Rationing on the Home Front, 1940–1945* (New York, 1991), p. 38; Champ Lyons, "Penicillin Therapy of Surgical Infections in the U.S. Army," *JAMA*, 123 (December 1943): pp. 1007–18. The studies were carried out at Bushnell General Hospital in Brigham City, Utah, and Halloran General Hospital, Staten Island, New York.

21. John A. Rogers, Executive Office, SGO, to Commanding General, SWPA, September 16, 1943; Headquarters, Army Service Forces, Office of the Chief Surgeon, Technical Memorandum no. 23, December 30, 1943, sec. 6; Major Frank Glenn, Report on Penicillin to the Chief Surgeon, USASOS, April 23, 1944. All in File SN 7618, Pincoffs Papers (Personal Papers Files), MHI. The boxes in this collection, bafflingly, have no numbers, and most have no identifying marks of any kind. On the rationing system and the civilian studies, see Adams, *"Greatest Good,"* pp. 65–130.

22. See Colonel F. W. Petters, Deputy Chief Surgeon, Army Service Forces, to Commanding Officer, 362d Station Hospital, May 9, 1944, in File SN 7618, Pincoffs Papers, MHI.

23. Chester Scott Kiefer, *The Uses of Penicillin and Streptomycin* (Lawrence, Kan., 1949), p. 201.

24. See the following quarterly reports: Surgeon, 162d RCT, 1943/3; 10th, 16th, and 24th Port Surg Hosps, 1943/3, in RG 112, File no. 319.1, National Archives. See also Alan S. Walker, *The Island Campaigns*, vol. 3 in Aus-

tralia in the War of 1939–1945, Series V: Medical (Canberra: Australian War Memorial, 1957), pp. 169–89; and "Navy Medical Department at War," pp. 188–90.

25. Command History, Seventh Amphibious Force, p. II-65.

26. Edward J. Drea, *MacArthur's ULTRA: Codebreaking and the War Against Japan, 1942–1945* (Lawrence, Kan. 1992), p. 85.

27. Quotes in Japanese Monograph no. 37, pp. 189, 171, in CMH.

28. Drea, *MacArthur's ULTRA*, p. 92; Quarterly Report, Sixth U.S. Army Surgeon, 1944/1, and similar reports of the 5th, 6th, 18th, and 22d Portable Hospitals; the Surgeon, 32d Inf Div; the 134th Med Rgt; the 23d Fld Hosp, 1944/1; 670th Clearing Co, 1944/1; and the Flight Surgeon, Adv Echelon 5th AF, 1944/1. All in RG 112, File no. 319.1-2, NARA. See also Medical Services and Casualty Care in the Seventh Amphibious Force, Pt. 2(e), p. 67, and interview, Charles Downer, 23 Jan 45, both in CMH.

29. DeWitt Mackenzie, *Men Without Guns* (Philadelphia, 1945), p. 17.

30. After Action Report, 30th Portable Hospital, April 3, 1944, with enclosures. See also the following quarterly reports: 30th Portable Surgical Hospital, 1944/1/2/3; Surgeon, 1st Cavalry Division, 1944/1/2/3; Surgeon, Sixth U.S. Army, 1944/1/2/3; 58th Evacuation Hospital, 1944/1/2/3. All in RG 112, File no. 319.1-2, NARA.

31. Quote in Report, Surgeon, 32d Infantry Division, 1944/3, p. 6, in CMH; see also Drea, *MacArthur's ULTRA*, p. 118.

32. See the following quarterly reports: Surgeon, 32d Infantry Division, 1944/2; 135th Medical Regiment, 1944/2; 3d Portable Surgical Hospital, 1944/2; Surgeon, Sixth U.S. Army, 1944/2; 54th Evacuation Hospital, 1944/2. All in RG 112, File no. 319.1-2, NARA.

33. Quote in quarterly report, Surgeon, 32d Infantry Division, 1944/3, pp. 8–9. See also Operations Report, 118th Medical Battalion, July 17–August 15, 944; Surgeon, XI Corps, Report on the Aitape Operations. All in RG 112, File no. 319.1-2, NARA.

34. Edward J. Drea, *Defending the Driniumor: Covering Force Operations in New Guinea, 1944* (Fort Leavenworth, Kan. 1984), p. 28; see also pp. 129, 132.

35. Quote from Report, 3d Portable Surgical Hospital, 1944/2, pp. 7–8.

36. Eichelberger, *Our Jungle Road to Tokyo* (ch. 4, note 8), p. 143.

37. *Ibid.*, p. 153; Harold Rigelman, *The Caves of Biak* (New York, 1955), pp. 136–55.

38. See quarterly reports for the following units, 1944/2/3: Surgeon, Sixth U.S. Army; Surgeon, I Corps; Surgeon, 41st Infantry Division; 8th, 12th, 26th Portable Surgical Hospitals. All in RG 112, File no. 319.1-2, NARA. See also Surgeon, 41st Infantry Division, Report on Hurricane Task Force, Aug.

30, 1944, in Staff Reports, 41st Infantry Division, in RG 407, File no. 341.2, NARA; and interview, William J. Shaw, September 2, 1944, in CMH.

39. See following Quarterly Reports for 1944/3: Surgeon, Sixth U.S. Army; Medical Detachment, 158th Infantry; 3d Portable Surgical Hospital; 71st Evacuation Hospital; 361st Station Hospital. All in RG 112, File no. 319.1-2, NARA.

40. Hoff, *Communicable Diseases* (Introduction, note 6), 7:287–91; Link and Coleman, *Medical Support of AAF*, (ch. 6, note 14), pp. 811–14; *The Sixth Infantry Division in World War II* (Washington, 1947), pp. 52–63. Quote in Robert Ross Smith, *Approach to the Philippines*, United States Army in World War II series (Washington, 1953), p. 446.

10. The Bloody Islands

1. Louis Morton, *Strategy and Command: The First Two Years* (Washington, 1962), pp. 421–28; Stetson Conn, Rose C. Engelman, and Byron Fairchild, *Western Hemisphere: Guarding the United States and Its Outposts* (Washington, 1964), pp. 270–76. Both volumes in United States Army in World War II series.

2. 1943 Annual Report, Surgeon, 7th Infantry Division, pp. 2–3. All army documents in CMH.

3. Gordon H. McNeil, "History of the Medical Department in Alaska in World War II," p. 548, in File HD:314.7-2 (Medical Activities, Alaska).

4. Robert J. Kamish, "Report of Medical Evacuation on Attu," pp. 1–2; 1943 Annual Report, Surgeon, 7th Infantry Division, p. 3.

5. 29th Field Hospital, 1943 Annual Report, p. 14 (quote); quote from *MSWJ*, ch. 5.

6. Conn, Engelman and Fairchild, *Western Hemisphere*, pp. 294–95.

7. Whayne and DeBakey, *Cold Injury* (ch. 7, note 27), pp. 90-2; Albert Lesser, "Report on Immersion Foot Casualties from the Battle of Attu," *Annals of Surgery*, 121 (March 1945): 259; Robert S. Anderson and Ebbe Curtis Hoff, eds., *Preventive Medicine in World War II, vol. 9, Special Fields* (Washington, 1969), pp. 242–44, and vol. 3, *Personal Health Measures and Immunization* (Washington, 1965), pp. 66–67.

8. Kamish, "Report," pp. 16, 19. Under the Geneva Accords of 1929, "sanitary formations and establishments" lost their special protections if used "to commit acts injurious to the enemy." However, such units were allowed to be armed and to use their arms for the defense of their patients, and it is not clear why, in the early days of the war, American medics were not permitted to do so. See the text of the accords, Chapter 2, Articles 7 and 8, in *Treaties, Conventions, International Acts, Protocols, and Agreements between the United States of America and Other Powers* (Washington, 1938), 4: 5215.

9. Whitehill, "Middle Pacific History" (ch. 4, note 23), Block 18a: "The Makin Operation," pp. 4–5; Philip A. Crowl and Edmund G. Love, *Seizure of the Gilberts and Marshalls*, U.S. Army in World War II Series (Washington, 1955), p. 210.

10. Samuel Eliot Morison, *Aleutians, Gilberts and Marshalls, June 1942–April 1944*, vol. 7 in *History of United States Naval Operations in World War II* (Boston, 1951), pp. 86–90, 102–7. *MSPW*, Ch. 7, provides additional details about the army units.

11. Morison, *Aleutians, Gilberts, and Marshalls*, pp. 86–90; *MSPW*, Ch. 7, p. 7.

12. Whitehill, "Middle Pacific History," Block 18a, pp. 13–17; letter, Hering to C/S, Fifth Amphibious Corps, Medical Situation, Galvanic, in Encl. F to Report, HQ, Fifth Amphibious Corps, Special Staff Officers on Galvanic, in CMH.

13. Edmund G. Love, *The 27th Infantry Division in World War II* (Washington, 1949), pp. 23–55.

14. See 2d Portable Surgical Hospital (Provisional), Report on Gilbert Campaign in Surgeon, 27th Infantry Division, 1943 Annual Report, pp. 16–21; 147th General Hospital, ETMD, Special Report on Wounds in General Hospitals, CPA, 1 Oct. 43–1 Dec. 44, dated 10 December 44, copy in CMH.

15. 2d Marine Division Narrative Account of GILBERT ISLANDS Operation, p. 3, Box 9, File A7-1, Acc. no. 65A-4556, Washington National Records Center, Suitland, Maryland (WNRC).

16. "Navy Medical Department at War," p. 163.

17. 2d Marine Division Narrative Account of GILBERT ISLANDS Operation, p. 6.

18. Robert L. Sherrod, *Tarawa: The Story of a Battle* (New York, 1944, 1983), pp. 81–82; see also pp. 279–80 for a roster of Navy Medical Department dead.

19. Preliminary Report of the Medical Department Activities at Tarawa, December 12, 1943, Division Surgeon, 2d Marine Division, p. 3, Box 10, File A7-16, Acc. no. 65A-4556, Marine Archives, Marine Corps Historical Center (MCHC); Special Action Report, 8th Marine Regiment, 2d Mar Div, December 1, 1943, p. 3, Box 9, File A7-3, Acc. no. 65A-4556, WNRC.

20. "Navy Medical Department at War," pp. 161–83; Norman A. Randolph, "Handling Casualties on Assault Transports," *Hospital Corps Quarterly*, 17 (September 44): 94–95; Preliminary Report of the Medical Department Activities at Tarawa, p. 4; Sherrod, *Tarawa*, pp. 132, 136n.

21. National shock over the losses at Tarawa also reflected naïveté at this stage of the war and information policies that had consistently downplayed American losses. The Academy Award-winning short film *Tarawa*, com-

posed exclusively of real combat footage, marked a great advance in candor
with its grisly depictions of the wounded and the dead.

22. Surgeon, U.S. Army Forces Middle Pacific, History 7 Dec 41–2 Sep 45, sec.
2, p. 74. See also Headquarters, V Amphibious Corps to Chief of Staff
[CPA], from Medical Observer [Commander E. R. Herring, MC, USN],
Forward Echelon, GALVANIC, subject: Medical Situation, Galvanic, in En-
closure F, Report to Headquarters Fifth Amphibious Corps by Special Staff
Officers on GALVANIC, p. 5; Central Pacific Area, Essential Technical Med-
ical Data Report (January 1944), Enclosure 1, Sanitary Survey with Special
Reference to Dysentery, in File no. 350.05, RG 112, NARA; Louis Shattuck
Baer and Ralph F. Allen, "Prevention of Fly Borne Diseases in Islet and Atoll
War," *The Military Surgeon* 94 (May 1944): 296–301.

23. Whitehill, "Middle Pacific History," Block 18B, pp. 10–15, and Block 3, sec.
2, pp. 77–79; Central Pacific Area, Essential Technical Medical Data Report
(March 1944), Enclosure 5, pp. 1–2, in File no. 350.05, RG 112, NARA.
See also Report, Surgeon, 7th Infantry Division, Kwajalein, 27 Mar 44, pp.
1–4, in File no. 319.1, RG 112, NARA.

24. S. L. A. Marshall, *Island Victory* (Washington, D.C., and New York, 1944),
pp. 12, 49; interview, Jan K. Herman with Vice Admiral George Monroe
Davis, May 21, 1992, in Longwood, Florida. Tape in BuMed. Davis was
later surgeon general of the navy, 1969–73.

25. Robert O. Heinl, Jr.; and John A. Crown, *The Marshalls: Increasing the
Tempo* (Washington, 1954), pp. 26–27; Marshall, *Island Victory*, p. 103.

26. Report of the Activities of the 7th Medical battalion during the FLINT-
LOCK Operation, pp. 17–18.

27. Marshall quotes from *Island Victory*, p. 103, 43–44; see also Heinl and
Crown, *Marshalls*, pp. 53–58, 100–114; statistics, p. 301. Whitehill, "Middle Pacific History," Block 18B, Append. I, gives the total wounded as
1,001.

28. "Navy Medical Department at War," pp. 210–15; Provisional Station Hospital no. 2, 1944 Annual Report, in File no. 319.1-2, RG 112, NARA.

29. Davis interview by Herman.

30. "Navy Medical Department at War," pp. 221–26.

31. Whitehill, "Middle Pacific History," Block 2, pp. 17–18, and Block 18D, pp.
20–22; "Navy Medical Department at War," p. 241; Fahey, *Pacific War
Diary* (ch. 3, note 4), p. 157. Among the Marianas, Guam, an American
possession, had been captured by the Japanese at the start of the war. The
other islands had been mandated to Japan after World War I—hence the
large enemy civilian population on Saipan.

32. John Iemp, Observer Report on the Marianas Operation (Forager), 11 July
44, p. 6, in File no. 350.09, in CMH; Historical Data—Medical Section,

Third Battalion, Sixth Marines, Second Marine Division, January 1, 1944–Dec. 31, 1944, p. 85, in Box 77, no file number, Acc. no. 65A-4556, WNRC. See also Sherrod, *On to Westward* (ch. 3, note 1), pp. 52, 57.

33. "Navy Medical Department at War," p. 246; Historical Data—Medical Section, Third Battalion, Sixth Marines, Second Marine Division, p. 88.

34. *Health*, January 31, 1945, pp. 4–5; Surgeon, 38th Field Hospital, Observer's Report, Operation Forager, 20 June–30 August 1944, pp. 1–5; "Navy Medical Department at War," p. 258.

35. On offshore support from the navy's viewpoint, see *Navy Medical Department in World War II*, pp. 171–81.

36. Statistics from Philip A. Crowl, *Campaign in the Marianas* (Washington, 1993), p. 265; see also Morison, *New Guinea and the Marianas* vol. 7 of *History of United States Naval Operations in World War II* (Boston, 1964), pp. 170–212. On civilians, see "Medical Aspects of Marianas Campaign," in ASF Monthly Progress Report, sec. 7: *Health*, 31 Jan 45, pp. 6–7; quote in Fahey, *Pacific War Diary* (ch. 3, note 4), p. 190.

37. "U.S. Navy Medical Department at War," pp. 322–23, 338; Smith, *Approach to the Philippines* (ch. 9, note 40), pp. 530–31.

38. E. B. Sledge, *With the Old Breed: At Peleliu and Okinawa* (Novato, Cal., 1981), pp. 131–32.

39. *Ibid.*, p. 332.

40. H. C. "Pat" Daly, "The USS Solace Was There," ms. memoir, in File USS SOLACE, Archives of the Bureau of Medicine and Surgery, Observatory Hill, Washington, D.C. Daly later published a lengthy collection of recollections and interviews under the same title: *The USS Solace Was There* (San Anselmo, Cal., 1991).

41. "U.S. Navy Medical Department at War," p. 341.

42. Action Report, 5th Marine Division, 19 Feb–26Mar 1945, Annex QUEEN, p. 22, in Box 20, File no. A14-29, Archives, MCHC. See also the Regimental S-2 report, 26th Marines, Annex QUEEN, Appendix 3, p. 13.

43. "Navy Medical Department at War," p. 401.

44. *Ibid.*, p. 412.

45. 4th Marine Division, Surgeon's Log (Rough) Iwo Jima, D+4 (February 23, 1945), p. 17, in Box 20, File no. A14-29, Acc. no. 65A-4556, Archives, MCHC.

46. "Navy Medical Department at War," pp. 417–18; Diary of Hanazomo Fujio, February 1, 1945, to March 1, 1945, entry for February 20, 1945, no file number, Box 77, Accession no. 65A-4556, Washington National Record Center; Action Report, 5th Marine Division, Annex QUEEN, p. 27, and Annex NAN, D+2, p. 26.

47. Ray Crowder, *Iwo Jima Corpsman* (Gadsden, Ala., 1988), p. 78.

48. Action Report, 5th Marine Division, Annex QUEEN, p. 55, and Appendix 3, pp. 10–11; Crowder, *Iwo Jima Corpsman*, pp. 25–26.

49. Sherrod, *On to Westward*, pp. 216–21. The route followed by the plasma was San Francisco–Hawaii–Guam (where it was re-iced)–Iwo Jima.
50. "Navy Medical Department at War," p. 424.
51. *Ibid.*, p. 445.
52. Sherrod, *On to Westward*, p. 173; Action Report, 5th Marine Division, Annex QUEEN, Appendix 3, pp. 10–11; quote from 4th Marine Division, Surgeon's Log, March 14, 1945, p. 30; Davis interview by Herman.

11. Buildup in Britain

1. Cosmas and Cowdrey, *MSETO* (ch. 8, note 5), p. 15.
2. Description of Hawley from Tom Whayne, Sr., telephone interview, October 18, 1993. After he retired from the army, Hawley's impressive career continued; he served as chief medical officer of the Veterans Administration, director of Blue Cross and Blue Shield, and director of the American College of Surgeons.
3. The competition continued among the students. "As family physician to many of the students I saw first hand evidence of the strain. . . . The competition was so great that the school had to stop publishing listing of class standings because of the number of suicides that occurred in the bottom listings." Whayne, review and critique (ch. 7, note 6), p. 15.
4. *MSETO*, p.43.
5. *Ibid.*, p. 50.
6. *Ibid.*, p. 31.
7. *Ibid.*, pp. 63–64.
8. *Ibid.*, p. 76.
9. Whayne, review and critique, p. 15.
10. Harry G. Armstrong, *Aerospace Medicine* (Baltimore, 1961), p. 10; Mae Mills Link and Hubert D. Coleman, *A History of the Origin of the U.S. Air Force Medical Service (1907–1949)* (n.p., n.d.), pp. 46–51, and *idem, Medical Support of AAF* (ch. 6, note 14), pp. 6–49.
11. Link and Coleman, *Origin of Air Force Medical Service*, pp. 15–19; Malcolm Grow, *Surgeon Grow* (Philadelphia, 1918).
12. Grow, *Surgeon Grow*, p. 33; Eugen G. Reinartz, "The School of Aviation Medicine—And the War," *The Military Surgeon*, 92 (March 1943): 233.
13. Reinartz, "School of Aviation Medicine," p. 240; David N. W. Grant, "The General Mission of Military Aviation Medicine," *The Military Surgeon*, 90 (March 1942): 281–90; *idem*, "The Medical Mission of the Army Air Forces," in Fishbein, *Doctors at War* (ch. 5, note 24), pp. 275–301; Walter S. Jensen, "Today and Tomorrow in Aviation Medicine," *The Military Surgeon*, 94 (February 1944): 89.
14. Link and Coleman, *Origin of Air Force Medical Service*, p. 58n.

15. *Ibid.*, pp. 58–68.
16. Link and Coleman, *Medical Support of AAF*, pp. 534–35.
17. David N. W. Grant, "Work of the Flight Surgeon," *The Military Surgeon*, 94 (March 1944): pp. 131–35.
18. Link and Coleman, *Medical Support of AAF*, p. 547.
19. Andrus *et al.*, *Advances in Military Medicine*, (ch. 2, note 4), 1: 207–21.
20. Link and Coleman, *Medical Support of AAF*, pp. 253–60, 648–55; Reinartz, "School of Aviation Medicine," p. 242. The Aero Medical Laboratory was set up in 1937 in Dayton, Ohio. See the postwar analysis in John Fulton, *Aviation Medicine in its Preventive Aspects* (London, 1948).
21. Link and Coleman, *Medical Support of AAF*, p. 636, 644–45. Between November 1942 and December 1943, frostbite was responsible for almost 60 percent of injuries that caused men to to be removed from flying duty.
22. *Ibid.*, p. 637.
23. *Ibid.*, pp. 645–47; Whayne and DeBakey, *Cold Injury* (ch. 7, note 27), pp. 130–34; "Health of the Eighth Air Force," in *Health*, August 31, 1944, pp. 6–9.
24. "Health of the Eighth Air Force," p. 9; Link and Coleman, *Medical Support of AAF*, p. 617; M. S. White, "Medical Problems of Air Warfare," *The Military Surgeon*, 96 (May 1945): 385–86.
25. Link and Coleman, *Medical Support of AAF*, pp. 617–32.
26. *Ibid.*, pp. 703–7.
27. Donald W. Hastings, David G. Wright, and Bernard C. Glueck, *Psychiatric Experiences of the Eighth Air Force, First Year of Combat (July 4, 1942–July 4, 1943* (New York, 1944), p. 23.
28. *Ibid.*, pp. 8–10.
29. *Ibid.*, p. 25.
30. *Ibid.*, p. 19.
31. D. M. Green, "Aeroneuroses in a Bomb Training Unit," *Journal of Aviation Medicine*, 14 (December 1943): 374; David B. Davis, "Phobias in Pilots," *The Military Surgeon*, 97 (August 1945): 105–11; Glass, *Neuropsychiatry in World War II* (ch. 7, note 5), 2:881–82.
32. Link and Coleman, *Medical Support of AAF*, p. 663. Ground crews were apparently the forgotten men of the Air Forces; they were punished if they did their jobs poorly and ignored if they did them well. They did not qualify for rest homes or rotation, and the psychological symptoms brought on by the monotony of their lives evoked little interest. See p. 666.
33. Glass, *Neuropsychiatry in World War II*, 2:890–91; Roy R. Grinker and John P. Spiegel, *Men Under Stress* (Philadelphia, 1945), p. 11. Emphasis in original.
34. Cosmas and Cowdrey, *MSETO*, pp. 68–69.
35. *Ibid.*, p. 70.

36. *Ibid.*, p. 71.
37. *Ibid.*, p. 85.
38. *Ibid.*, p. 133.
39. *Ibid.*, p. 126.
40. *Ibid.*, p. 178.
41. *Ibid.*, pp. 185–86.
42. The closest analogy was to Sicily, which provided planners with their working model of needs and problems on the French coast.
43. Cosmas and Cowdrey, *MSETO*, pp. 167–68.
44. *Ibid.*, p. 167.
45. "Navy Medical Department at War," p. 719; *Navy Medical Department in World War II*, 1:122.
46. Cosmas and Cowdrey, *MSETO*, p. 199.

12. From D-Day to Bastogne

1. *MSETO* Cosmas and Cowdrey, (ch. 8, note 5), p. 203.
2. Colonel Charles E. Tegtmayer, cited in *ibid.*, p. 211.
3. "Navy Medical Department at War," p. 722; Cosmas and Cowdrey, *MSETO*, p. 216.
4. "Navy Medical Department at War," p. 730. The same history, p. 742, also records that hospital ships were "unsatisfactory in general" on various grounds, including their lack of special equipment for amphibious operations.
5. Futrell, "Development of Aeromedical Evacuation" (ch. 4, note 14), p. 213.
6. The Army had four corps in France at this time, and only one on Okinawa; by the logic of numbers, roughly three evacs should have been sent to Okinawa.
7. Pyle, *Brave Men*, (ch. 6, note 28), pp. 440–41.
8. *Ibid.*, pp. 228–30. This is a useful generalization; however, see Martin Blumenson, *Breakout and Pursuit*, United States Army in World War II series (Washington, 1961), pp. 68–69; see also "Navy Medical Department at War," pp. 735–36. Many German wounded taken in captured enemy field hospitals were in poor condition, especially from infection.
9. Robert B. Bradley, *Aid Man!* (New York, 1970), p. 48.
10. *Ibid.*, pp. 58, 121.
11. *Ibid.*, pp. 60–61, 63.
12. *Ibid.*, p. 64.
13. *Ibid.*, p. 66.
14. Cosmas and Cowdrey, *MSETO*, p. 333.
15. *Ibid.*, p. 234.
16. Joseph A. Gosman, "War Without Blood," manuscript memoir, pp. 77–80, at CMH.

17. Pyle, *Brave Men*, p. 451.
18. Cosmas and Cowdrey, *MSETO*, p. 237.
19. John Keegan, *Six Armies in Normandy: From D-Day to the Liberation of Paris, June 6th–August 25th, 1944* (New York, 1982), pp. 314–17.
20. Cosmas and Cowdrey, *MSETO*, pp. 292–96.
21. *Ibid.*, p. 300.
22. *Ibid.*, p. 317.
23. Albert E. Cowdrey interview of Robert P. Phillips, Washington, D.C., October 5, 1993. Tape in author's possession.
24. Cosmas and Cowdrey, *MSETO*, p. 355.
25. Captain Sydney W. Stringer, letter of October 21, 1944, in Helen D. Stringer, *Prisms: As We Were, March 23, 1944–July 12, 1945* (Manlius, N.Y., 1989), pp. 183–84.
26. Gosman, "War Without Blood," pp. 100, 149–50.
27. Cosmas and Cowdrey, *MSETO*, p. 362.
28. *Ibid.*, pp. 387–88.
29. *Ibid.*, pp. 496.
30. *Ibid.*, pp. 383–84.
31. *Ibid.*, pp. 414–15.
32. Leonard Rapport and Arthur Norwood, Jr., *Rendezvous with Destiny: A History of the 101st Airborne Division* (Washington, n.d. [1948]), pp. 469–71; Charles S. Phalen, "Medical Service at Bastogne," *The Military Surgeon*, 100 (January 1947): 37–42.
33. Cosmas and Cowdrey, *MSETO*, p. 420.
34. *Ibid.*, p. 424.
35. *Ibid.*, p. 492.
36. Gosman, "War Without Blood," p. 145.
37. Cosmas and Cowdrey, *MSETO*, p. 495; Omar N. Bradley, *A Soldier's Story* (New York, 1951), p. 445; Whayne and DeBakey, *Cold Injury* (ch. 7, note 27), p. 169; George S. Patton, *War As I Knew It* (Boston, 1947), p. 415.
38. Cosmas and Cowdrey, *MSETO*, p. 500.
39. For this insight I am indebted to my colleague at the U.S. Army Center of Military History, Graham A. Cosmas.

13. From War to Peace

1. Wiltse, *MSMT*, pp. 291, 293.
2. *Ibid.*, p. 416.
3. *Ibid.*, p. 422.
4. *Ibid.*, p. 468.
5. Interview, of Colonel Harry L. Berman, MC, USA (Ret.), by author, Bethesda, Md., April 10, 1993.
6. Wiltse, *MSMT*, pp. 464–65.

7. *Ibid.*, p. 478.

8. *Ibid.*, p. 462.

9. See Cosmas and Cowdrey, *MSETO*, ch. 15; History of Medical Units of the 78th Infantry Division for the Year 1945, p. 2, and Combat Operations Data, First US Army, Europe, 1944–45, both in File no. 319.1-2, CMH.

10. Surgeon, Ninth US Army, Semiannual Report, January–June 1945, Section III, pp. 18, 22, 26, 33, 37.

11. Surgeon, Third US Army, Semiannual Report, January–June 1945, pp. 16–22.

12. Cosmas and Cowdrey *MSETO*, p. 524.

13. 110th Evacuation Hospital Semiannual Report, January–June 1945, p. 5.

14. Whayne, review and critique (ch. 1, note 6), p. 17.

15. Lieutenant Colonel Sanford V. Larkey, "Administrative and Logistical History of the Medical Service, ETO," ch. XIV, p. 56, in CMH.

16. Stanhope Bayne-Jones and Thomas B. Turner, "Planning and Preparations for the European Theater of Operations," in *Preventive Medicine in World War II*, vol. 8, *Civil Affairs/Military Government Public Health Activities* (Washington, 1976), pp. 404–10; Thomas B. Turner and Glen W. McDonald, "Civil Health in Theaters of Operations," *The Military Surgeon*, 96 (January 1945): 131–34; European Civil Affairs Medical Group, 1944, Annual Report secn. 3, in Historian's File (CA-ECA Med. Grp.); and John W. Bailey, "An Outline Administrative History of Civil Affairs in the ETO," p. 23, in File no. 314.7-2, CMH.

17. Bayne-Jones, "Typhus Fevers" (Introduction, note 6), 7: 164ff; Military Government Detachment El-H2, 2d European Civil Affairs Regiment, Report to Chief Surgeon, ETOUSA, May 28, 1945, Subject: Typhus Epidemic, Koln, Germany, 1945, in File No. 350.05 (ETO); Preventive Medicine Division, ETOUSA, Periodic Report, January–July 1945, pp. 5–7, in File no. HD319.1-2 (Prev. Med.), CMH.

18. Essential Technical Medical Data Report (April 1945), ETOUSA, pp. 3-4, in File no. 350.05, CMH. The development of the U.S.A. Typhus Commission is discussed in the Bayne-Jones essay on typhus, cited above. Composed of army, navy, and Public Health Service officers, the commission functioned under the War Department as an advisory body.

19. *Civil Affairs/Military Government*, pp. 4:488–89.

20. "The 108th Evacuation Hospital Travelogue" (n.p.: June 1945); Surgeon, 2d Armored Division, Semiannual Report, 1945/1, in File no. 319.1-2, both in CMH.

21. See David A. Fry, *For You the War Is Over: American Prisoners of War in Nazi Germany* (New York, 1984), esp. pp. 17–81, 114-15. Quote from Interview with Captain H. Weintraub, September 30, 1944, in File no. 383.6 (Interviews, Repatriated POWs), in CMH.

22. Quote from 110th Evacuation Hospital, Semiannual Report, 1945/1, p. 5. On the medical problems involved in treating recovered American military personnel, see Herbert Pollack, "Nutritional Disorders," in *Internal Medicine in World War II*, vol. 3, *Infectious Diseases and General Medicine* (Washington, 1968), pp. 242–63. About 94,000 American prisoners were recovered in Germany and evacuated through medical channels.

23. Stanhope Bayne-Jones, "Enemy Prisoners of War," in Anderson and Hoff, *Special Fields* (ch. 10, note 7), pp. 343–50. On army doctrine for handling prisoners of war, see *Rules of Land Warfare*, Field Manual 27-10 (Washington, 1940); *Enemy Prisoners of War*, Technical Manual 19-500, October 5, 1944, pp. 1–3; letter, Headquarters, Services of Supply, ETOUSA, to Provost Marshal, Services of Supply, and Headquarters Commandant, Services of Supply, November 26, 1942, in File no. 383.6; and, in the same file, Regulations Governing Prisoners of War, Office of Theater Provost Marshal, Office of the Chief of Staff, July 10, 1943. All documents in CMH.

24. On POW camp conditions, see 2029d Prisoner of War Overhead Detachment (Provisional) [PWOD], 1944 Annual Report, pp. 2–3, and Semiannual Report (1945/1), pp. 7–8; see also 2021st PWOD, 1944 Annual Report, p. 5; 2018th PWOD, Period Report, April–December 1944, p. 3; 6832d PWOD, Period Report, August 25, 1944 to June 30, 1945. All in Box 383, Entry 54A, Record Group 112, NARA. On POW general hospitals, see materials in File no. 319.1-2, Box 440, Entry 54A, RG 112.

25. The number of prisoners remains uncertain. Estimates of the transient camps in particular, with their rapidly fluctuating populations, were unreliable and contradictory. See James B. Mason and Charles H. Beasley, "Arrangements for Prisoners of War En Masse," *The Military Surgeon*, 107 (December 1950): 345; Bayne-Jones, "Enemy Prisoners of War," pp. 372–400; Kurt W. Boehme, *Zur Geschichte der Kriegsgefangenen im Westen* (Bonn, 1962), pp. 95–135.

26. See 7th U.S. Army, Memorandum: Consolidated List of PW, PWX & DP Installations, May 13, 1945, in Box 316, and Surgeon, Advance Section, Communications Zone, Report on PWTE, May 13, 1945, in Box 313. Both in Entry 31, Record Group 112, NARA. The death rate is reported in Essential Technical Medical Data Report, ETOUSA (July 1945), pp. 4–5 and enclosure 11, and repeated in Larkey, "Administrative and Logistical History," pp. 88–89, both in CMH.

27. Surgeon, 106th Infantry Division, 1945 Annual Report, p. 5, in File no. 319.1, Box 392, Record Group 112, NARA.

28. *Ibid.*, pp. 6, 8; ETO, Communications Zone, POW Enclosure Reports: Daily PWTE Situation Reports, in Box 17, Record Group 332, NARA.

29. Kurt W. Boehme, *Die deutschen Kriegsgefangenen in amerikanischer Hand:*

Europa (Munich, 1973), p. 316; Memorandum, Nutrition Survey Team to Chief, Preventive Medicine Division, European Theater, Subject: Report of Nutritional Survey of German Prisoners of War and Disarmed Enemy Elements, Under Control of the United States Army on the European Continent, August 31, 1945, in Box 327, Entry 31; Camp Surgeon, PWTE A-10, Weekly Sanitary Report, May 21, 19345, in Box 392. Manuscripts in Record Group 112, NARA.

30. Letter, Chief Surgeon, Theater Service Forces European Theater, to Surgeons, All Major Commands and Sectors, September 15, 1945, Subject: Multivitamin Capsules for Prisoners of War and Disarmed Enemy Elements; Letter, Headquarters, U.S. Forces European Theater to Commanding Generals, September 25, 1945, Subject: POW Menu #2, Fifth Revision. Both in Box 36, Entry 54B, Record Group 112, NARA. The prisoners who were transferred to the French suffered, in many cases, from continuing malnutrition, which formed a subject of numerous sharp exchanges among the former Allies.

31. German POW hospitals also benefited recovered Allied military personnel and displaced persons; ETOUSA reports from late June 1945 show such patients sharing bed space in captured hospitals with men of the Wehrmacht. See Information for G-4 Report, Week Ending July 13, 1945, Office of the Chief Surgeon, Headquarters ETOUSA, in ETOUSA Semi-Annual Report, 1945/1, Annex 5, in CMH. A sensational account alleging mass deaths has recently appeared: James Bacque, *Other Losses: An Investigation into the Mass Deaths of German Prisoners at the Hands of the French and Americans after World War II* (Toronto, 1989). The absence to date of any physical evidence and the author's bizarre mathematics do nothing to dispel the basic implausibility of the thesis that large numbers of deaths could have been concealed for so long. See the essays in Guenter Bischof and Stephen Ambrose, *Eisenhower and the German POWs: Facts Against Falsehood* (Baton Rouge and London, 1992).

32. The workers at Sarreguemines were Soviet prisoners of war captured in 1941–43 in the Ukraine–Black Sea region. See Carter, *Activities of Medical Consultants*, (ch. 6, note 11), 1:444–45.

33. Statement of Violette Finz, cited in Martin Gilbert, *The Holocaust: A History of the Jews of Europe during the Second World War* (New York, 1987), p. 785. It was in such conditions that Anne Frank, another refugee from Auschwitz, died of typhus in early 1945.

34. Medical Section, Third U.S. Army, Semiannual Report, 1945/1, p. 139, in File no. 319.1-2, in CMH; First Lieutenant Marcus J. Smith, Medical Corps, to Post Surgeon, Dachau Concentration Camp, May 5, 1945, Health and Sanitation Report, in File no. 383.6 (Dachau Camp), in Source Materials Collected by Colonel M. P. Rudolph, Medical Corps, in Box 312, Entry

31, Record Group 112, NARA. See also Marcus J. Smith, *The Harrowing of Hell: Dachau* (Albuquerque, 1972), p. 91.

35. See Annex to 116th Evacuation Hospital, Semiannual Report, 1945/1, pp. 7–8, RG 112, NARA.

36. Statement of Fania Fenelon, quoted in Gilbert, *The Holocaust*, p. 791; 116th Evacuation Hospital, Semiannual Report, 1945/1, p. 2, in CMH.

37. Earl F. Ziemke, *The U.S. Army in the Occupation of Germany 1944–1946* (Washington, 1975), p. 186.

38. Phillips interview (ch. 12, note 23).

39. Headquarters, U.S. Forces, European Theater (Office of the Military Government), Weekly Civil Affairs/Military Government Field Reports, November 1 and 15, 1945, in File Weekly CA/MG Rpts, in Box 541, Record Group 260, NARA; Ziemke, *U.S. Army in Occupation of Germany*, p. 387; John W. Bailey, "An Outline Administrative History of Civil Affairs in the ETO," pp. 201–210, in File no. HD 314.7-2, in CMH. Bailey, a lieutenant colonel in the Sanitary Corps, served the Military Government as a typhus control officer.

40. "Improvements in Treatment of Venereal Disease," *Health*, February 28, 1945, pp. 16–18.

41. Ziemke, *U.S. Army in Occupation of Germany*, pp. 220, 324–35, 421–22; Interview with Lieutenant Colonel Paul Padget, Venereal Disease Control Officer, August 1, 1945, in Historian's File (PH & VD in Occupied Germany and Liberated Nations), in CMH; Venereal Disease Control Branch, Preventive Medicine Division, ETOUSA, Periodic Report, January–July 1945, p. 1, also in CMH; Headquarters, ETOUSA, Letter to Commanding Generals of Major Commands, June 4, 1945, Subject: Policy on Relations between Allied Occupying Forces and Inhabitants of Germany, in *Medical Section, 12th Army Group, Report of Operations (Final After Action Report)*, January 1, 1945–July 31, 1945, pp. 225–29. Graham Greene's *The Third Man* makes a telling parable of the underground trade in penicillin in one occupied city.

42. German activities in biological warfare are treated in a comprehensive report by British and American intelligence: "A Review of German Activities in the Field of Biological Warfare," September 12, 1945, in Folder 22, Entry 295A, Record Group 112, NARA. Both technical intelligence and war crimes investigations are covered in the published reports of the Combined Intelligence Operations Subcommittee (CIOS), in Record Group 319, NARA. The published literature is, of course, extensive.

14. Pacific Climax

1. M. Hamlin Cannon, *Leyte: Return to the Philippines*, United States Army in World War II Series (Washington, 1954), p. 26; "Navy Medical Department at War," 1: 356–57; Condon-Rall and Cowdrey, *MSWJ*, ch. 10.

2. Surgeon, X Corps, Report of Medical Service, Leyte Operation, 20 Oct 44–10 Feb 45, RG 407, File No. 210, NARA; Chief Surgeon, Army Forces in the Western Pacific, 1945 Annual Report, Part I, p. 18; Surgeon, Sixth US Army, Quarterly Report, 1944/4, p. 14. Except as otherwise noted, army manuscripts are in CMH.
3. "Navy Medical Department at War," 1: 354–55.
4. Seventh Fleet, Historical Report, Amphibious Operations Invasion of the Philippines October 1944 to January 1945, p. 2.
5. Condon-Rall and Cowdrey, *MSWJ*, ch. 10; "Navy Medical Department at War," 1:357; *Health*, June 30, 1945, p. 4; Central Philippine Operation: Medical Aspects of Leyte–Samar Campaign, p. 5.
6. Fahey, *Pacific War Diary* (ch. 3, note 4), p. 230.
7. "Navy Medical Department at War," p. 364.
8. *Ibid.*, pp. 355–56.
9. Cannon, *Leyte*, p. 194; Command History, Seventh Amphibious Force, pp. II-76, II-77. See also Central Philippines Campaign: Medical Aspects of Leyte–Samar Campaign, pp. 1, 9, in File no. 370.2.
10. Edmund G. Love, *The Hourglass: A History of the 7th Infantry Division in World War II* (Washington, 1950), p. 258; Colonel Frank J. McGowan, Consultant in Surgery, Eighth U.S. Army, Leyte Campaign, 1944: Difficulties caused by terrain, climate and other purely local conditions, p. 1.
11. Surgeon, 32d Infantry Division, Quarterly Report, 1944/4; Jan Valtin [pseud. of Richard Julius Herman Krebs], *Children of Yesterday* (New York, 1946), p. 280.
12. Robert Ross Smith, *Triumph in the Philippines*, United States Army in World War II Series (Washington, 1963), p. 29. Operational narrative, except where noted, will be from this source. See also Walter Krueger, *From Down Under to Nippon: The Story of Sixth Army in World War II* (Washington, 1953), pp. 211–19.
13. Surgeon, Army Forces in the Western Pacific, 1945 Annual Report, pt. 1, pp. 17, 40; Surgeon, Sixth US Army, Quarterly Report, 1945/1, pp. 9–10; Commanding General, Sixth US army, Report of Luzon Campaign, 9 Jan 45–30 Jun 45, 3: 56, 155–56; "Navy Medical Department at War," 1:375-76.
14. "Navy Medical Department at War," pp. 370–86; Surgeon, Sixth US Army, Quarterly Report, 1945/1, p. 10.
15. George Sharpe, *Brothers Beyond Blood: A Battalion Surgeon in the South Pacific* (Austin, Tex., 1989), p. 114.
16. Surgeon, Sixth US Army, Quarterly Report, 1945/1, p. 12; Surgeon, XIV Corps, Quarterly Report, 1945/1, p. 5; "Navy Medical Department at War," pp. 374–78; Krueger, *From Down Under to Nippon*, pp. 225–27.
17. George Sharpe, "Battalion Surgeon," p. 605, ms. in CMH.
18. 29th Evacuation Hospital, Report of Activities, 6 February 1945, p. 6, in

CMH; see also Krueger, *From Down Under to Nippon*, pp. 234–70; Stanley A. Frankel, *The 37th Infantry Division in World War II* (Washington, 1948), pp. 294–96; B. C. Wright, *The 1st Cavalry Division in World War II* (Tokyo, 1947), pp. 125–40.

19. See Quarterly Reports, 1945/1, for 71st Evacuation Hospital, pp. 1–5; 29th Evacuation Hospital, pp. 1–2; 54th Evacuation Hospital, pp. 1–4. All in File no. 319.1-2, RG 112, NARA. See also Medical Department Information Service, Report of Activities, 17 February 1945, pp. 6–11, in File no. 370.05 (Manila Activities Reports), in CMH.

20. Krueger, *From Down Under to Nippon*, pp. 289–320; Surgeon, Sixth US Army, Quarterly Reports, 1945/1, pp. 24–27 and 1945/2, pp. 6–15; *The 6th Infantry Division in World War II* (Washington, 1947), pp. 108–22; Wright, *1st Cavalry Division in World War II*, pp. 144–56.

21. Surgeon, Sixth US Army, Reports of the General and Special Staff Sections, Luzon Campaign, 3: 158; Surgeons, 25th, 32nd, 33d, and 37th Infantry Division, Quarterly Reports, 1945/1 and 1945/2. See also Krueger, *From Down Under to Nippon*, pp. 321–29.

22. Lieutenant Colonel Frank Glenn, "Notes on Surgery in the Forward Area of the Southwest Pacific," pp. 10–11, in CMH; M. J. Musser and Emmett C. Townshend, "Use of Small Planes for Medical Evacuation on Luzon," *The Bulletin of the U.S. Army Medical Department*, 4 (August 1945): 196.

23. Surgeon, X Corps, Quarterly Report, 1945/2, pp. 6–7; *Health*, November 30, 1945, pp. 8–11.

24. Surgeon, X Corps, Quarterly Report, 1945/2, pp. 6–7.

25. *Health*, November 30, 1945, pp. 8–11; Surgeon, Sixth US Army, Quarterly Reports, 1945/1, pp. 21, 28–33, 1945/2, pp. 20–25.

26. Roy E. Appleman, James M. Burns, Russell A. Gugeler, and John Stevens, *Okinawa: The Last Battle*, United States Army in World War II series (Washington, 1948), p. 492; Condon-Rall and Cowdrey, *MSWJ*, ch. XII; Tenth US Army, Operations Report, Ryukyus Campaign: Historical Account of Experiences since Pearl Harbor, Plans and Operations Section, Surgeon's Office, Middle Pacific, p. 2, in File no. 052.06, in CMH.

27. *Health*, July 31, 1945, pp. 34–35.

28. Whitehill, "Middle Pacific History," (ch. 4, note 23), Block 18f, 1:50.

29. "Navy Medical Department at War," p. 562.

30. *Ibid.*, pp. 564–65.

31. Quote in Appleman *et al.*, *Okinawa*, p. 74. See also Whitehill, "Middle Pacific History," Block 18f, 1:22–23, 45–47; "Navy Medical Department at War," pp. 557–58; Samuel Eliot Morison, *Victory in the Pacific, History of United States Naval Operations in World War II* (Boston, 1964), pp. 140–55.

32. Appleman *et al.*, *Okinawa*, pp. 189–90, 210; Thomas M. Huber, *Japan's*

Battle of Okinawa, April–June 1945, Leavenworth Paper no. 18 (Leavenworth, Kan., 1990), pp. 13, 19.

33. Quote, Appleman *et al.*, *Okinawa*, p. 256.

34. The best picture of the battle from the perspective of the infantry is in Sledge, *With the Old Breed* (ch. 10, note 38), pp. 192–323.

35. *Ibid.*, pp. 221–22. As a member of a mortar crew, Sledge was often called upon to act as a litter-bearer himself, hence understood the exhaustion and danger of the duty.

36. Quote from Condon-Rall and Cowdrey *MSWJ*, ch. XII. See *America's Medal of Honor Recipients: Complete Official Citations* (Golden Valley, Minn., 1980), pp. 300–301; *Ours to Hold It High: The History of the 77th Infantry Division in World War II* (Washington, 1947), pp. 303–4.

37. Surgeon, 77th Infantry Division, Quarterly Report, 1945/2, p. 3; 96th Infantry Division, After Action Rpt, Ryukyu Campaign, 1 Apr–30 Jun 45, p. 182; Tenth US Army, Operation Report, Ryukyus Campaign, September 5, 1945; 71st Medical Battalion, After Action Report, Ryukyus Campaign, July 9, 1945, in File no. 052.06. All in CMH.

38. "Navy Medical Department at War," p. 576.

39. US Army Force, Pacific, Essential Technical Medical Data (ETMD) Report, September 18, 1945; Tenth US Army, ETMD, July 20, 1945, p. 3; Surgeon, XXIV Corps, Medical Report, Iceberg Operation, in File no. 024, p. 7; 31st Field Hospital, [After] Action Report for the Okinawa, Ryukyus Mission, n.d., p. 3. All in CMH.

40. Albert B. Sabin, "Epidemic Encephalitis in Military Personnel: Isolation of Japanese B Virus on Okinawa in 1945," *JAMA*, 133 (February 1947): 281–93.

41. Glass, *Neuropsychiatry in World War II: Overseas Theaters* (ch. 7, note 5), p. 643; Whitehill, "Middle Pacific History,???" Block 18f, 1:182–86; XXIV Corps, After Action Report, Ryukyus Campaign (1 Apr–30 Jun 1945), pp. 78–79; Sledge, *With the Old Breed*, p. 241.

42. 77th Infantry Division, After Action Report, Iceberg (Okinawa), 25 Apr–30 Jun 1945, p. 76; Glass, *Neuropsychiatry in World War II*, pp. 639–78.

15. The War's Long Shadow

1. For the transition from war to peace as it affected the Army Medical Department, see Cowdrey, *The Medics' War* (ch. 5, note 25), pp. 7–35.

2. Cosmas and Cowdrey, *MSETO*, p. 484; Colonel Howard A. Rusk, "Convalescence and Rehabilitation," in Fishbein, *Doctors at War* (ch. 5, note 24), pp. 303–18; "Redeployment and Separation of Medical Department Officers," *JAMA*, 128 (August 1945): 1104; "Nursing in a Debarkation Ward,"

American Journal of Nursing, 45 (February 1945): 134–36; Link and Coleman, *Medical Support of the AAF* (ch. 6, note 14), pp. 376, 384; History of Medical Department, ATC, pp. 81, 83–84. ATC took the patients of all services until March 1945, when the Naval Air Transport Service started its own trans-Pacific evacuation over AAF protests that it was "well prepared to accomplish all air evacuation needed by *all* the armed services" (p. 82).

3. George K. Carpenter, MD, Mather Cleveland, MD, and Alfred R. Shands, MD, "Status of Orthopedic Casualties Returned to the Zone of Interior," in *Surgery in World War II: Orthopedic Surgery in the Zone of Interior* (Washington, 1970), p. 262.

4. *Ibid.*, p. 260.

5. Leonard T. Peterson, MD, "General Clinical Considerations of Amputation," *Orthopedic Surgery in Zone of Interior*, p. 928.

6. *Ibid.*, pp. 262–63; "Hospitalization of Returning Casualties," *JAMA*, 127 (January, 1945): 163.

7. D. Carpenter [?], "Battle Casualties as Seen at Halloran General Hospital" [1943], pp. 1–7, in World War II Administrative Records, Entry 54A, File no. 319.1, RG 112, NARA; Harold Laufman, "The Initial Surgical Treatment of Penetrating Wounds of the Rectum," *Surgery, Gynecology, and Obstetrics*, 82 (February 1946): 219.

8. "Nursing in a Debarkation Ward," p. 135.

9. Francis M. McKeever, "A Discussion of Controversial Points in Amputation Surgery," *Surgery, Gynecology and Obstetrics*, 82 (May 1946): 495–511.

10. Carpenter, "Battle Casualties as Seen at Halloran" p. 8.

11. Lieutenant Commander Clarence R. Straatsma, "Plastic and Reconstructive Surgery," *The Military Surgeon*, 96 (March 1945): 255.

12. Eldridge H. Campbell, Jr., MD; Hartwig Huhlenbeck, MD; Robert L. Cavenaugh, MD; and Aage E. Nielsen, MD, "Clinicopathologic Aspects of Fatal Missile-Caused Craniocerebral Injuries," in *Surgery In World War II: Neurosurgery* (Washington, 1986), 1:397–98.

13. A. Earl Walker, M.D., "Posttraumatic Epilepsy," in *Surgery in World War II: Neurosurgery*, 1:288.

14. See "Secondary Closure of Decubitus Ulcers with the Aid of Pencillin," *JAMA*, 127 (February 1945): 396.

15. Colonel Augustus Thorndike, "The Reconditioning Program in the United States Army," *The Military Surgeon*, 96 (March 1945): 227–29; W. D. Dock, "Evil Sequelae of Complete Bed Rest," *JAMA*, 125 (August 1944): 1083–85; Major General David N. W. Grant, "The Medical Direction of Human Drives in War and Peace," *JAMA*, 126 (November 1944): 607–10; "Physical Training Routine Ordered in Naval Hospital," *JAMA*, 126 (November 1944): 841.

16. 1945 Annual Report, Percy Jones General Hospital, pp. 260–78, in Box 74, World War II Administrative Records, Entry 54A, File no. 319.1, RG 112.

17. Frank H. Krausen, "Wartime Physical Reconstruction," *The Military Surgeon*, 94 (March 1944): 147–56; Jennifer Mitchum, "BUMED's World War II 'Resorts,'" *Navy Medicine*, 82 (November–December 1991): 20–25.

18. M. Elliott Randolph, "Ophthalmology," in Carter, *Activities of Surgical Consultants* (ch. 6, note 11), pp. 95–100.

19. James N. Greear, Jr., "The Rehabilitation of Blinded Casualties," in M. Elliott Randolph and Norton Canfield, ed., *Surgery in World War II: Ophthalmology and Otolaryngology* (Washington, 1986), pp. 147–209; on orientors, see pp. 167–68.

20. On medical casualty estimates, see Condon-Rall and Cowdrey *MSWJ*, ch. XIV.

21. *POW: Study of Former Prisoners of War* (Washington, 1980), p. 10; *Effects of Malnutrition on the Mortality and Morbidity of Former United States Prisoners of War and Civilian Internees of World War II: An Appraisal of Current Information*, House Document 296, 84th Cong., 2d Sess. (Washington, 1956), p. 33; Bernard M. Cohen and Maurice Z. Cooper, *A Follow-Up Study of World War II Prisoners of War* (Washington, 1954), p. 15. The follow-up studies showed that the physical and psychological effects of imprisonment were long-lasting and condemned many former prisoners to an early death.

22. Surgeon, I Corps, 6th U.S. Army, 1946 Annual Report, p. 3, in File no. 319.1-2, Box 565, Entry 54A, Record Group 112, NARA; William Craig, *The Fall of Japan* (New York, 1979), pp. 316–21; Essential Technical Medical Data Report, U.S. Army Forces, Pacific, October 1945, pp. 19–21, in File no. 350.05, Box 72, Entry 54B, Record Group 112, NARA. On the condition of the prisoners of war, see Cohen and Cooper, *Follow-Up Study of Prisoners of War*, pp. 15–23, 65, and pp. 106–8 of the ETMD report cited above.

23. Thomas B. Turner, "Japan and Korea," in *Preventive Medicine: Civil Affairs/Military Government* (ch. 13, note 16), pp. 659–61.

24. Diary of Colonel Ashley W. Oughterson, September 4, 1945, p. 68, in CMH.

25. Sams, "Medic" (ch. 1, note 1), 2:368-69, 372–73.

26. *Ibid.*, 2:342, 349, and Crawford F. Sams, "American Public Health Administration Meets the Problems of the Orient," *American Journal of Public Health and the Nation's Health*, 42 (May 1952): 557–65. See also Oughterson Diary, September 4, 1945, p. 67; General Headquarters, Supreme Commander for the Allied Powers, Mission and Accomplishments of the Occupation in the Public Health and Welfare Fields, December 1949, p. 1, in File

no. 091.4 (Health), CMH; and, from the same headquarters, History of the Nonmilitary Activities of the Occupation of Japan, 1945 Through December 1950, Vol. 8: Public Health, September 1945 Through December 1945, Manuscript no. 8-5AA7V5, in Record Group 319, NARA.

27. Michihiko Hachiya, *Hiroshima Diary: The Journal of a Japanese Physician August 6–September 20, 1945* (Chapel Hill, N.C., 1955), p. 93; Sams, "Medic," 2:404.

28. "Mission and Accomplishments of the Occupation in the Public Health and Welfare Fields," p. 3.

29. Widely varying estimates of the number of atomic bomb victims have been put forward at various times, with the numbers growing as delayed effects take their toll. See The Committee for the Compilation of Materials on Damage Caused by the Atomic Bombs in Hiroshima and Nagasaki, *Hiroshima and Nagasaki: The Physical, Medical and Social Effects of the Atomic Bombings,* trans. Eisei Ishikawa and David L. Swain (New York, 1981), pp. 113–16. The firebomb raids are discussed in Wesley Frank Craven and James Lee Cate, eds., *The Army Air Forces in World War II: Matterhorn to Nagasaki,* 5 vols. (Chicago, 1953), 5: 614–75. The single attack on Tokyo on March 9–10, 1945, apparently killed more people than the atomic bombing of Nagasaki five months later.

30. Sams, "Medic," p. 361.

31. Hachiya, *Hiroshima Diary,* pp. 8, 55; Haruko Taya Cook and Theodore F. Cook, *Japan at War: An Oral History* (New York, 1992), p. 390.

32. John Hersey, *Hiroshima* (New York, 1946), pp. 61–62.

33. Committee for Compilation, *Hiroshima and Nagasaki,* pp. 523–33; Colonel Paul D. Keller, "A Clinical Syndrome Following Exposure to Atomic Bomb Explosions," *JAMA,* 131 (June 1946): 504–6; Samuel Glasstone, ed., *The Effects of Nuclear Weapons* (Washington, 1957), 498–502.

34. Oughterson Diary, pp. 72–73; Vincent C. Jones, *Manhattan: The Army and the Atomic Bomb* (Washington, 1985), pp. 543–50; Ashley W. Oughterson and Shields Warren, *Medical Effects of the Atomic Bomb in Japan* (New York, 1956), pp. 6–9; Committee for Compilation, *Hiroshima and Nagasaki,* pp. 508–9.

35. Hachiya, *Hiroshima Diary,* p. 13.

36. Ashley W. Oughterson, George V. LeRoy, Averill A. Liebow, E. Cuyler Hammond, Henry L. Barnett, Jack D. Rosenbaum, and B. Aubry Schneider, *Medical Effects of the Atomic Bombs: The Report of the Joint Commission for the Investigation of the Effects of the Atomic Bomb in Japan,* 6 vols., Office of the Air Surgeon NP-3040 (Oak Ridge, Tenn., 1951). The number of alleged victims has continuously increased since 1945, as people exposed to the bombs die of illnesses attributed to the aftereffects of radiation sickness.

37. Committee for Compilation, *Hiroshima and Nagasaki,* pp. 510–15.

38. *Ibid.*, pp. 516, 524.

39. *Medical Aspects of Atomic Weapons* (Washington, 1950), p. 10; George A. Gellert, "Global Health Interdependence and the International Physicians' Movement," *JAMA*, 264 (August 1990): 610–13. Two recent studies of interest are the World Health Organization's concise *Effects of Nuclear War on Health and Health Services* (Geneva, 1987), and Frederic Solomon and Robert O. Marston's comprehensive *The Medical Implications of Nuclear War* (Washington, 1986).

40. Frank A. Reister, ed., *Medical Statistics in World War II* (Washington, 1975), pp. 11–12.

Index